GEARS OF WAR 2

COG TRAINING

WELCOME BACK!

If you're a diehard Gearhead, we know you've been waiting for this game with rabid anticipation.

***Gears of War 2* improves on every aspect of the first game—the campaign is larger, longer, and filled with even more amazing encounters. Multiplayer has been massively improved, with many new game modes and tweaks to improve the multiplayer experience. The cover system has been polished, refining the core mechanic that defines Gears of War gameplay.**

We hope you use this guide to enhance your enjoyment of Gears of War 2. We've provided all the coverage you could possibly want within these pages. Our complete campaign walkthrough, which includes all the War journal collectible locations, uses a new style that we hope you find helpful and intuitive.

We've also greatly expanded the multiplayer coverage, giving it as much care and attention as the campaign. Long after you finish going through the campaign, many of you will still be playing multiplayer, and we hope the information we provide creates a strong foundation for your multiplayer beat-downs.

I'M NEW TO GEARS!

What are you doing starting with *Gears of War 2*?! Go find a copy of *Gears of War* and play through the campaign! Seriously, the storyline of *Gears of War 2* picks up a few months after the events in *Gears of War*, and you'll appreciate it that much more if you've played the first game.

Of course, if you're more of a multiplayer person, you can find plenty to keep you occupied. The many multiplayer modes and improved matchmaking make it easy to play with your friends online, either competitively or in the cooperative Horde mode.

Check out the multiplayer section of this guide for more details on the maps, how the weapons specs change, and a range of tactical advice.

MULTIPLAYER EVOLUTION

We know multiplayer coverage in any print guide is always a tricky thing. No one *really* knows how the multiplayer experience will play out in the real world until weeks or months after the game ships.

To that end, we've provided detailed maps, plenty of weapon stats, as well as information on tweaks and tidbits that aren't immediately noticeable when you first start playing.

As the community improves, the tactics and strategies used by loners, duos, and full teams will evolve, but we'll give you a solid edge over players who jump in cold.

WHAT'S NEW?

If you're looking for the highlights, here's the big new stuff in *Gears of War 2*, although there are far too many additions and changes in all aspects of the game to list here:

MEAT SHIELDS

Players can now pick up a downed foe and use the unfortunate chap as a bullet sponge! When you carry an enemy, you move at reduced speed, and you can use *only* pistol-class weapons. In exchange, your damage-soaking buddy provides a safe way to move across exposed areas with no cover.

The Submission multiplayer mode focuses heavily on this feature, as a computer-controlled target must be downed and then carried to a target area.

There is also an actual, non-flesh shield in the game. This functions similarly to carrying a body as a shield, but you can also plant the shield in the ground to use as a form of portable, stationary cover. You can also use it to perform a brutal execution... One important distinction is that a meat shield will degrade and be dropped once it takes a certain amount of damage, whereas a non-flesh shield does not degrade. Also, you can run with a non-flesh shield: you can't run with a meat shield.

These features add mobile cover to *Gears of War 2*, so they impact all aspects of the game, both in the campaign and in multiplayer.

VEHICLES

No more beat up Junker. This time around, you can pilot the mighty Centaur Tank during specific parts of the campaign. In addition, a few other *special* vehicles show up. Locust Reavers and even the awesome Brumak become living chariots for the Gears.

NEW MULTIPLAYER MODES

Old modes have returned in a refined state, but *Gears of War 2* has also added Submission, Wingman, and Horde, completely new forms of multiplayer.

Submission is similar to capture the flag...with a living flag. Wingman lets you and a buddy take on four other teams of two players each, and Horde is an awesome cooperative battle with four friends against the Locust.

Warzone is largely unchanged, while Execution, Annex, and Guardian have been modified. Check the multiplayer chapter for specifics.

SELECTABLE DIFFICULTY

Cooperative players can now choose their difficulty level individually! This is great if you're a veteran but your partner is a newer player. Higher difficulty settings cause you to receive more damage and inflict less yourself, while lower difficulties act in reverse, greatly easing combat.

THE WAR JOURNAL

A new tool for organizing and cataloguing your exploits in *Gears of War 2*, the War Journal keeps track of your progress toward campaign and multiplayer Achievements, as well as giving you bits of back story about the world of Sera as you gather the 41 collectibles scattered throughout the campaign.

Check this guide's *COG Intel Archive* chapter for a quick checklist of the collectibles, or use the main campaign walkthrough to track them all down—they're marked on the maps and noted in the text.

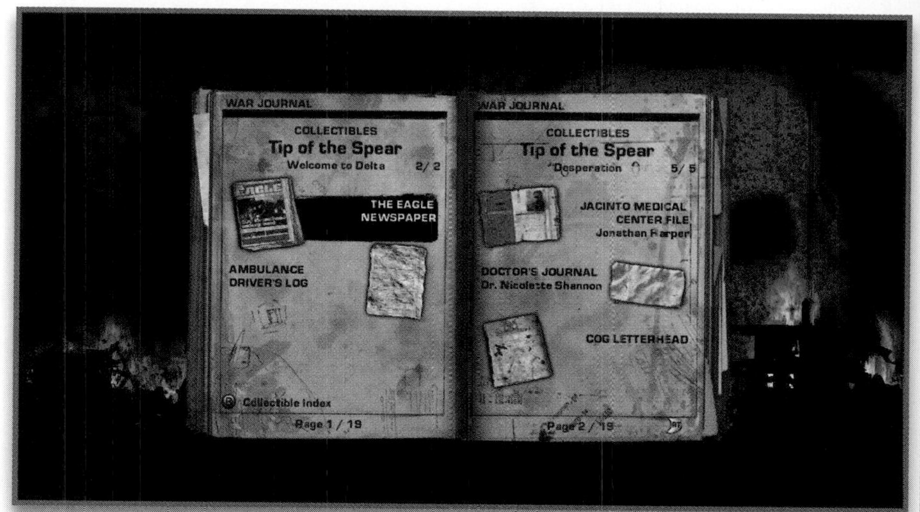

SPOILER WARNING!

We've made every effort to conceal major story points in the body of the walkthrough. We skirt around character-specific events and significant revelations as best we can. We did this so that you could enjoy the story as it unfolds, without advance knowledge of the events.

That said, there *are* spoilers in this guide. It's simply unavoidable due to some of the locations you visit and some of the enemies you face.

If you stick to the Act and Chapter you're on, you shouldn't have any serious story-spoiler problems.

CONTROLS

READ YOUR USER MANUAL!

This chapter is intended as a *supplement* to the game's user manual, not a *replacement* for it. While we touch on a few of the basics in this chapter, we avoid rehashing content that the user manual already covers. We assume that you've either read the user manual or are already comfortable with the game's control scheme. The best way to learn basic functions, such as how to move into and out of cover or how to aim and fire, is to consult the user manual, complete the in-game training, and practice.

ALTERNATE CONTROL SCHEME

In *Gears of War*, some players had a difficult time adjusting to the novel 'one button for actions' feature and desired a way to split up the character actions among multiple buttons. Epic responded by adding an option that would allow just that. In the Options menu under the XBox 360 Controller Settings, a player can choose to change the control scheme from Default to Alternate. This allows the character to continue to use the A Button for cover actions, but maps the roadie run and evade actions to the X Button. The default X Button functions are moved to the Y Button, leaving the Point of Interest function to be operated by pressing in the Right Thumbstick. If you like the idea of having finer control over cover versus evade actions, or if you ever find yourself ducking into cover when you want to evade, this might be the new control scheme for you. Otherwise, the default control, in which the A Button handles character combat maneuvers, is the bread and butter for most players.

CONTROLLER COMMAND	FUNCTION
L Trigger	Aim
R Trigger	Fire
L Bumper	Taccom (displays squad location and objectives in campaign)
R Bumper	Reload and Active Reload
Left Thumbstick	Move Player
Right Thumbstick	Look, Click to Zoom
Directional Pad	Select Weapon

CONTROLLER COMMAND	FUNCTION
A Button	Roadie Run (hold) / Roll (press with Left Analog Stick) / Enter Cover (press near cover) / Pick up Meat Shield
B Button	Melee / Stick Grenade / Rev Lancer Chainsaw (hold)
X Button	Use / Interact / Curbstomp
Y Button	Look at Point of Interest / Special Execution on Downed Enemy

SPECIAL COVER COMMANDS

ACTION	COMMAND SEQUENCE
Cover Slip	Press Forward while at the Edge of Cover, then Hold A
SWAT Turn	While in Cover, Press Sideways Toward Another Piece of Cover, and then Press A
Cover Slam	Hold A while Approaching Cover in a Roadie Run
Cover Break	Press Away from Cover
Mantle	Press Toward Low Cover, then Press A

COMBAT

The basics of combat in Gears of War 2 are quite simple. Doubly so if you're a returning veteran—there are new toys, but the fundamentals have not changed. In essence, cover is life. While this is an action-oriented shooter, the use of cover as a defense is vital to survival. This is especially true in the campaign, where Locust forces can take you down in a matter of seconds if you're caught out in the open, particularly on the higher difficulty levels.

COMBAT IN MULTIPLAYER

In multiplayer, being out of cover as you traverse the map (or up close) isn't quite the death sentence it can be in the campaign. But cover is still vitally important; see the *Multiplayer Warfare* chapter for more information about combat against other players.

While in or out of cover, you can fire your weapon from the hip (blindfiring) or sight and take aim. Aiming from behind cover exposes you to enemy fire slightly, but it greatly increases your accuracy. In addition to using and shooting from cover, you must learn to move smoothly and swiftly from one position to another as the situation changes and new threats emerge from different directions.

Fallen rubble might provide a great defense against a pack of Drones swarming you from the front, but if an Emergence Hole opens up on your flank, you might as well be standing out in the open.

LONG RANGE

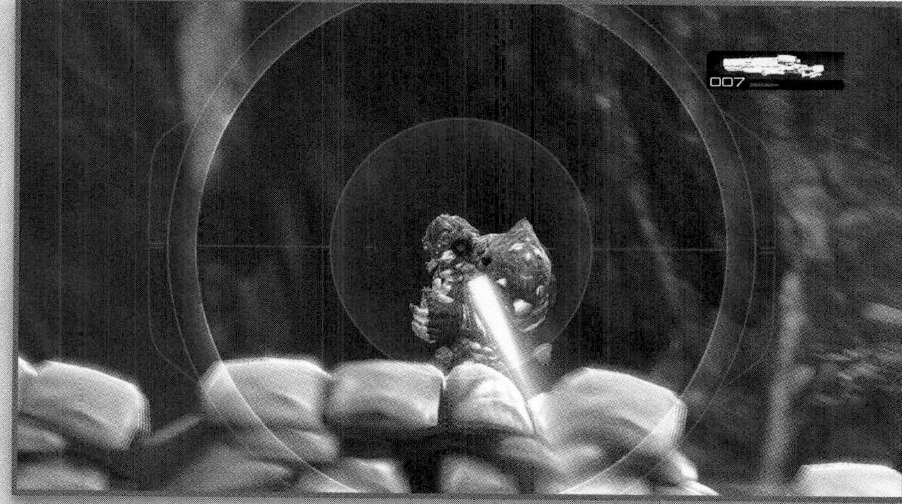

Fighting at a great distance is generally ineffective. It's difficult to score hits at a distance with most weapons, and cover becomes more effective, as you cannot easily target small bits of exposed Locust. Furthermore, a lot of weapons inflict reduced damage or are simply ineffective at long range.

Fortunately, the Longshot excels at a distance, and some other heavy weapons can be fairly potent—the Mulcher, Mortar, and turrets all work well.

Of the more 'standard' weaponry, the Locust Hammerburst is generally a better long-range weapon than the Lancer. It can scope and fire in semi-automatic mode to deliver more damage per shot than the Lancer.

However, other than those exceptions, it's usually not worth the ammo you waste firing at a distance, unless you *really* need to take down a specific target.

Instead, close to a range that's suitable for the available weapons. Or even better, let your enemies come to you while you fire at them when they break from cover.

MEDIUM RANGE

Medium range is the better zone for most weapons in *Gears of War 2*. At this distance, you can usually inflict optimal damage. But of course, the reverse is true, so you're more vulnerable to accurate enemy fire as well.

Generally in the campaign, if you're accurate, pick your weapons well, and heal up between attacks, you will do well at medium range even on the highest difficulty levels. This is good, because most combat in the game occurs at medium range!

CLOSE RANGE

Close-range combat in the Gears universe is short, messy, brutal, and lethal.

A host of weapons can inflict instant death at close range, and plenty more deal grievous damage in seconds. Furthermore, most cover is ineffective at close range, so any conflict at this range tends to be over with in a hurry, one way or another.

Close-range combat in the campaign is generally *not* a good idea. The problem is that, while *you* are much more lethal, so are your enemies. And there are a *lot* more enemies than there are of you.

Close-range combat is a lot of fun, but when you're fighting against several thousand Locust, the odds just aren't in your favor. You might score that sweet grenade tag, but then that gibbed Drone's five buddies get revenge on your exposed rear end in short order.

Of course, this varies somewhat depending on the difficulty level and whether you're playing co-op. It's also not quite so true in multiplayer, where going for a close-range kill can be a quick solution to remove an annoying target.

Close-range combat is nearly unavoidable in some situations. For these times, be sure to use appropriate weapons. The Shotgun works well, as does the Scorcher. Grenade tagging, melee hits, and the Lancer's chainsaw are all highly effective at close range.

ACTIVE RELOADING

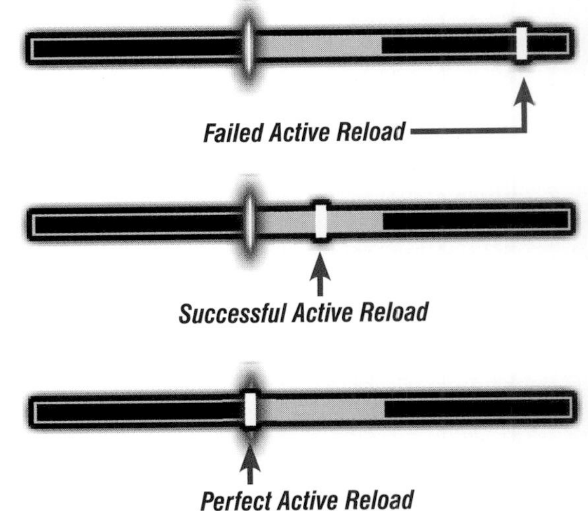

Reloading your guns in *Gears of War 2* is simple—run out of ammunition and try to fire again, and your weapon automatically reloads.

However, you can manually reload your weapon. And *while* your weapon is reloading, you can perform an *Active Reload*.

There's a timing bar on your weapon indicator at the top-right of the screen. If you press the reload button a second time while the bar's indicator is inside the narrow 'active' portion, your weapon reloads more quickly. See the following 'Timing the Reload' sidebar for greater detail on how to perform Active Reloads.

One important point: there is a certain element of risk involved in performing an Active Reload. If you attempt to Active Reload and miss the window of opportunity when you press reload a second time, you jam your gun, causing the reload to take even longer than it normally would if you had not attempted an Active Reload at all!

The timing for Active Reloading varies depending on the weapon, but performing a basic active reload is a fairly simple task for most weapons.

Beyond Active Reloading, one can perform a *Perfect Active Reload*. Do this by pressing the reload button a second time with *perfect* timing, while the indicator is on a very thin sliver at the start of the active reload bar.

A Perfect Active Reload has several benefits. First, because it counts as a 'normal' Active Reload at the earliest possible point, you get the fastest possible reload.

Second, and more importantly, every weapon in the game confers some benefit when it is perfectly reloaded. For example, the Scorcher gets a boost in range when you score a perfect active reload. Some simply give a slight damage boost, while others receive an upgrade for a short time or for a single shot.

TIMING THE RELOAD — There are four different ways to time an active reload:

Reload Bar: The most basic, and probably the best way to begin, is to simply watch the reload bar at the top-right of the screen. Press reload once to start the reload process, then simply watch the slider and press reload again when the slider enters the reload zone.

Reloading by watching the bar is a good method to start with, but it has some drawbacks. For one, you're staring up at the corner of the screen instead of at the enemies trying to kill you. For another, hitting Perfect Active Reloads using this technique is actually rather difficult.

Visual Cue: A second method is to use the *animation* of the weapon reloading as your cue. Every weapon has a distinct reload animation, which can look slightly different if you are against cover standing or crouching, or walking in the open.

You can use these visual cues as your Active Reload signal. With enough practice, you should be able to nail at *least* an Active Reload, and often a Perfect Active Reload, particularly for certain weapons with very distinct visual reloading.

Audio Cue: Another way to time your reloads is to use sound. Each weapon has a distinct reloading sound, some more obvious than others. If you have a decent sound setup, this is much easier. The distinct 'chak chak' sound of the Longshot's bolt action is a good example of an audio cue you can use to reload, but many weapons have similar sounds.

Spend some time practicing on an empty map. Listen to the weapon's complete reload cycle with your eyes closed, then try to time the reload, again with your eyes closed.

Audio cues are handy because you can use them even if you can't fully see your character to use a visual cue.

Timing: For a new player, the last and most difficult method is simply timing. Each weapon has a specific Active Reload timing. Once you learn these timings, you may find yourself automatically performing Active Reloads. This is especially useful in multiplayer, as it allows you to perform combat rolls and time a reload while you evade enemy fire.

There's a catch. For Perfect Active Reloads, the window for success grows smaller each consecutive time you perform one. If you miss one or switch weapons, the Perfect Active Reload area returns to its original size. But this makes continually nailing perfect reloads via pure timing more difficult.

VISUAL RELOADING

The following visual guide to all of the reloadable weaponry should help you identify the visual cues in various stages of movement. Some weapons have much more noticeable tells than others, but keep an eye on your character and use these images as practice aids. Static screen captures are no substitute for studying the in-game animation.

LANCER

POSITION	ANIMATION
Standing	As your hand hits the ammo pouch
Crouching	As your hand goes fully behind your knee
Walking	As your hand touches and rises from the ammo pouch

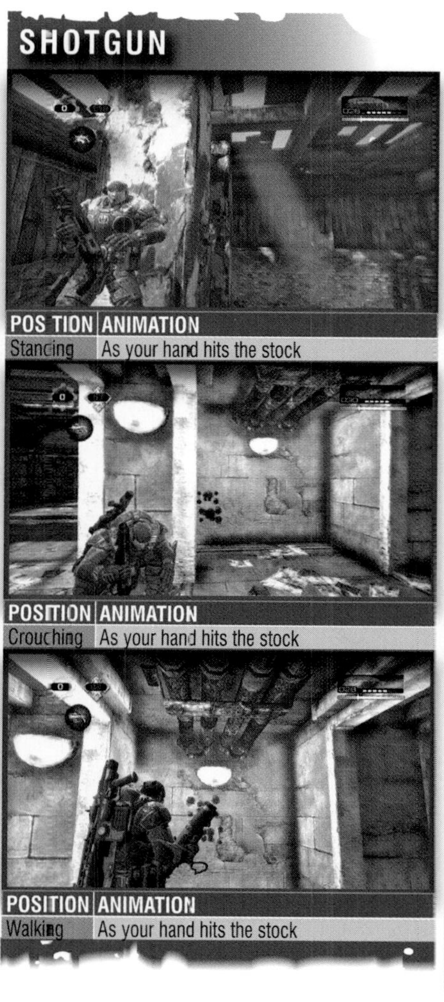

SHOTGUN

POSITION	ANIMATION
Standing	As your hand hits the stock
Crouching	As your hand hits the stock
Walking	As your hand hits the stock

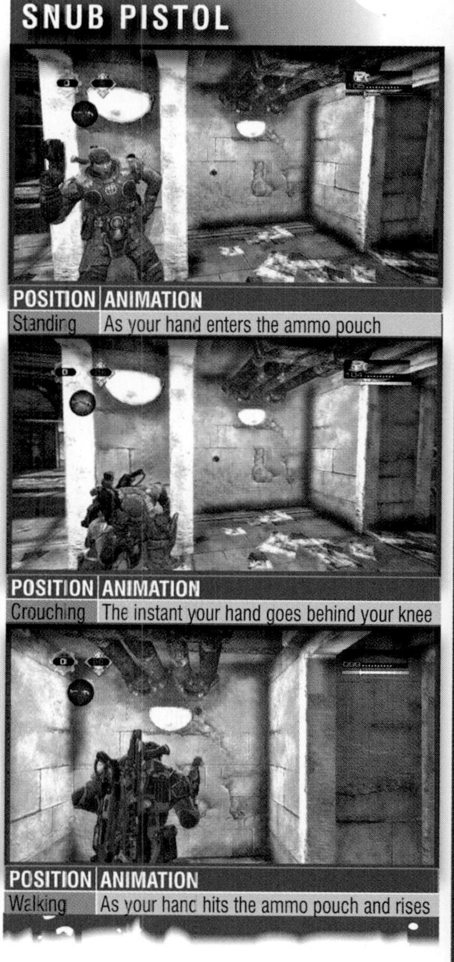

SNUB PISTOL

POSITION	ANIMATION
Standing	As your hand enters the ammo pouch
Crouching	The instant your hand goes behind your knee
Walking	As your hand hits the ammo pouch and rises

BOLTOK PISTOL

POSITION	ANIMATION
Standing	Tricky to time—as your hand comes up, just before your thumb fully reaches the cylinder

POSITION	ANIMATION
Crouching	Same animation, very fast

POSITION	ANIMATION
Walking	Your left elbow comes up, reload as soon as it moves to the right

TORQUE BOW

POSITION	ANIMATION
Standing	As the bolt is brought up behind the bow, before it moves in front of the bow

POSITION	ANIMATION
Crouching	Same as standing, but slightly farther from the front of the bow due to the position of your legs

POSITION	ANIMATION
Walking	As the bolt approaches the bow, there's a slightly longer wait as it crosses your body

BOOMSHOT

POSITION	ANIMATION
Standing	As your hand hits the ammo pouch and moves into it

POSITION	ANIMATION
Crouching	As your hand goes behind your knee and sinks slightly

POSITION	ANIMATION
Walking	As your hand hits the pouch and rises slightly

LONGSHOT

POSITION	ANIMATION
Standing	After the bolt slides back and the shell casing pops out

POSITION	ANIMATION
Crouching	Same as standing

POSITION	ANIMATION
Walking	Also the same animation, but wait for the shell to move a bit farther in the air than you might expect

GORGON PISTOL

POSITION	ANIMATION
Standing	As the clip is just about to meet the pistol

POSITION	ANIMATION
Crouching	As the clip is just about to meet the pistol

POSITION	ANIMATION
Walking	As the clip is just about to meet the pistol

SCORCHER

POSITION	ANIMATION
Standing	As soon as your hand goes up to pump, just before the first pump begins

POSITION	ANIMATION
Crouching	As your hand is about to push down to pump

POSITION	ANIMATION
Walking	As your hand looks about to move to the right of the pump

MORTAR

POSITION	ANIMATION
Standing	As your hand comes back and grips the body of the mortar

POSITION	ANIMATION
Crouching	Same as standing; just wait until you grip the body fully

POSITION	ANIMATION
Walking	After the mortar is raised into the air, as your hand touches the body

HAMMERBURST

POSITION	ANIMATION
Standing	As soon as you release the tossed ammo clip

POSITION	ANIMATION
Crouching	Same as standing, just low to the ground

POSITION	ANIMATION
Walking	Just as your left arm crosses your body to the left and your elbow becomes visible

COVER

Fighting from behind cover can take some getting used to if you're not a *Gears of War* veteran. The flow of combat in *Gears of War 2* has its own distinct feel as you move from cover to cover. Often, you fight against opponents who are just as likely to use and move between cover on the battlefield.

Cover can be just about anything: a stone wall, a low barricade, sandbags, a rocky ledge, a wrecked car, and lots of other things. It generally doesn't matter *what* the cover is, so much as what shape the cover takes.

High Cover fully conceals your body while you are behind it. You can crouch or stand while you're pressed against it, allowing you to swing out and fire from a raised or lowered position, possibly throwing off your enemy's aim. Click the Left Stick to duck down, even when you are in high cover.

On the downside, you cannot fire over high cover, only around it, so you can shoot only from its edges, mildly limiting your offensive options.

Low Cover forces you to crouch when you're behind it. It is also slightly more exposed than high cover. Your exposed extremities *can* be shot while you move behind it, or if you reload. You're fairly safe if you aren't moving at all, but you have to move or attack eventually. It is also very vulnerable to enemies on different elevations than you, one reason height is so important on the battlefield.

Low cover can be more flexible than high cover, as you can blindfire over the top easily. You can also move from left to right to pop up and shoot, mixing up your attack location. Be aware this is slightly less effective in multiplayer, where savvy opponents can track your movement behind low cover.

Note that some cover is destructible. Concentrated weapon fire or a single explosive can often destroy softer cover (i.e. furniture and other materials that aren't solid stone or metal). Whenever you enter a new battlefield, scan the area and evaluate the available cover. If much of the cover can be destroyed and only a few places provide hard cover, seize the hard cover if at all possible. You can destroy the soft cover and then mow down your hapless foes as they're left in the open.

FIGHTING FROM COVER

Fighting from cover is pretty simple—take cover, then either blindfire or aim over it or around it. You can move from side to side and stand or crouch behind high cover.

The real trick to master is positioning yourself well in relation to your enemies. Ideally you want solid cover in front of you, facing your opponents. Likewise, you want your target's cover at an angle to your own, so you can more easily hit parts of your foe's exposed body.

Throughout the campaign, staying behind cover allows you to recover from even critical damage. As long as you're motionless behind hard cover and your enemies aren't flanking you, you're somewhat safe. This gives you time to recover from damage that you've endured, and you *will* get hurt…a lot.

Certain enemies are still a threat, even when you're behind cover. Locust mounted on Reavers or Bloodmounts can fire down at you from a naturally elevated position. The Reaver can strike with its tentacles and the Bloodmount can rush around cover and bite you. Tickers and Wretches love stationary targets behind cover. And of course, grenades are always dangerous.

Other than those specific cases, most of your opponents are far less effective against you while you're behind cover. For this reason, watch out for the enemies that can render your cover unsafe and prioritize them as targets.

FIGHTING ENEMIES IN COVER

Because you often fire at targets that are behind cover, it's worth knowing what you can do to damage such targets.

First, you *can* hurt targets behind hard cover, but it isn't easy. Some weapons are better suited to it than others; check this guide's *COG Armory* section for a better idea of which. In brief, most weapons have reduced effectiveness against targets behind low cover, and next to no effectiveness against targets behind high cover.

Your chance to inflict damage on opponents behind cover comes when they expose themselves. Any time a player blindfires from cover he or she becomes exposed. From high cover, they are also exposed when they aim around their cover. From low cover, you can target opponents when they aim, when they move quickly from left to right, or when they reload.

Depending on your angle to your target, you may also be able to get some shots in from the side. You don't have to fully flank a target to get a better line of fire, so make a point of moving to positions that give you an offensive edge.

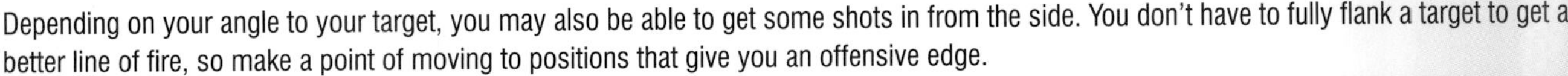

Targets behind high cover may expose themselves slightly when they reload if they're pressed up against a wall's edge. Even a slight angle on their position can give you the line of sight you need to deliver damage.

Grenades are ideal for flushing out or eliminating targets behind cover. Blind-throwing grenades at enemies behind cover usually isn't effective (though Ink grenades can be). But aiming and tossing a grenade beside or behind your target in cover can be lethal. At worst, it forces your foe to move, often in a damaged state.

MOVING BETWEEN COVER

There's an art to moving around in *Gears of War 2* combat, because exposing yourself is so very dangerous. Not only are you fully exposed to enemy fire, but you also have to deal with a new concept known as *stopping power*. In short, when you get shot, your rate of movement temporarily slows.

The degree to which your pace slows depends on the type of weapon that hits you. But quite simply, rushing targets head-on, in the open, while they are firing at you is a *very* bad idea.

Instead, it's far safer to traverse the battlefield using your cover maneuvers. You can SWAT turn between nearby pieces of cover, and cover slip forward around them to move toward your enemies. You can mantle cover to quickly get out of the line of fire, or to get behind enemy cover to assault targets at close range.

If all else fails, you can Roadie Run in the open, and then dive into a roll before slamming safely into cover.

FLANKING

Because *Gears of War 2* is so focused on using cover, it naturally follows that flanking is a major part of combat. If you can eliminate the cover that your targets use, they tend to drop very quickly indeed.

Most cover (though not all) tends to be fairly short and very straight. As a result, flanking your target often completely removes any benefit the cover would provide from the frontal arc.

In the campaign, and especially in multiplayer, targets usually move to avoid getting fired at from the flank or rear. But you can still inflict heavy damage in the few seconds they are exposed. In some cases, your target simply may not have any defensible locations to retreat from your assault.

Other factors make flanking lethal, both to you and your opponents. For one, taking aim from cover focuses your field of view on your target and tends to block your 'peripheral' vision. This makes you vulnerable to getting flanked while you myopically focus on a single target.

This is more noticeable with some weapons than others. Sniping with the Longshot or zoomed in with the Hammerburst, you're less aware of your surroundings than if you're marching around with the Shotgun or Scorcher.

Moving from cover to cover is generally easiest while you face a single direction. For example, it's tempting to cover-slip forward from one spot to the next, then SWAT turn to another adjacent piece of cover, all while facing toward the bulk of your enemies. But if you don't scan to your left and right, you won't be aware of threats creeping up on you until you see the damage indicator flashing…or hear the disconcerting rev of a chainsaw.

Generally, it's always worthwhile to try to flank your targets. There are times when flanking your target can get you in trouble, exposing you to enemy fire. But in most situations, getting into a flanking position means the rest of your squad can pin down enemies from the front while you devastate them from the side.

If you find yourself getting flanked, quickly assess the situation and fall back to the nearest defensible cover that nullifies the flanking attack. Of course, try to do this without exposing yourself to excessive enemy fire. This can be easier said and done, but the risk of getting shot on the move while you retreat is preferable to staying put and eating fire from the side—at least you're a tougher target to hit on the move.

WALLBOUNCING

Wallbouncing is simply sliding into cover from a good distance, detaching from the cover, and then sliding into a nearby piece of cover again. When you do this quickly, it's *much* quicker than simply walking around. In some cases, it's even faster than Roadie Running to a location.

To use wallbouncing effectively, practice the distances from which you can slide into cover. From the front, you get the longest slide, but you can also slam into cover that's off to your left or right at about half the distance of a forward slide.

Also, remember that you can cancel a SWAT turn into a Roadie Run in *any* direction.

Using these moves in combination lets you negotiate the battlefield in a quick and erratic manner, making you a difficult target for anyone firing at you.

ROADIE RUN

The Roadie Run allows you to travel quickly around the battlefield. This is important, as moving in the open at walking speed is dangerous unless you're doing so for a very specific reason (e.g. burning close-range foes with a Scorcher).

You can slip from cover directly into a Roadie Run by holding the A Button. This is useful for moving from cover to cover quickly. When you approach cover, if you're still holding run, you automatically slam into it. Alternately, you can tap the A Button when you're close to the cover to perform a Cover Slide.

Combining Roadie Run with wallbouncing and cover movement allows you to move extremely quickly, minimizing your exposure to enemy fire in the open.

COG ARMORY

The potent arsenal available to you in *Gears of War 2* covers everything from the explosive Boomshot to the searing flames of the Scorcher and the devastating firepower of the Mulcher.

Many weapons in *Gears of War 2* have a distinct purpose; they are very useful for a few specific combat situations and less effective outside that role.

It's certainly possible to play through much of the game using only a few weapons that you're comfortable with, but it's definitely worthwhile to master all of the weapons. Many are highly effective against certain types of Locust or during certain encounters.

Note that weapons have different statistics and behavior when you play multiplayer. Additionally, while their general role usually stays the same, some weapons become significantly more or less powerful in a multiplayer game, simply due to the way that human opponents fight. Consult this guide's *Multiplayer Warfare* chapter for information about multiplayer weapon statistics. Also, it's good to use all weapons in order to earn the "Variety is the Spice of Death" achievement.

DIFFICULTY AND DAMAGE

One interesting fact about the way weapons and health are handled in *Gears of War 2* is that each difficulty level puts a scaling value on the damage you inflict with weapons, as well as the damage enemies need to deliver in order to kill you. You can see these damage values in the weapon charts, but for the sake of completeness, we've included the scaling modifiers on the damage.

You normally have 600 health (in Hardcore difficulty), which is then modified by difficulty level, giving us the following breakdown: 900 on Casual, 720 on Normal, 600 on Hardcore, and 480 on Insane. Be careful!

AI partners have a *lot* more health, though they are not invincible. Most squad mates have 1800 health. Dom has 1200 and Hoffman is incredibly sturdy, with 7000, though he's rarely exposed to direct enemy fire.

Meat shields have 1000 'health,' just enough to sponge up a big explosion or a lot of smaller hits.

DIFFICULTY	PLAYER HEALTH MOD (SINGLE-PLAYER AND HORDE)	PLAYER DAMAGE MOD
Casual	2.35x	2x
Normal	1.5x	1.6x
Hardcore	Normal (1x)	1.1x
Insane	0.35x	1x

Because you can select your difficulty in co-op play, it is entirely possible for one player to burn through ammo more quickly and die more often. But this is usually compensated by the player that selects a higher difficulty, who, we assume, possesses greater accuracy and better tactical acumen.

VARIETY IS THE SPICE OF DEATH

Be sure to use every weapon, as doing so is the key to earning the Variety is the Spice of Death achievement.

LARGE WEAPONS

You can carry up to two large weapons in any combination. If you greatly favor one specific large weapon, feel free to carry it around and just swap out your secondary slot.

If you're comfortable with a range of weapons, don't hesitate to freely equip new weapons as you encounter them in the campaign.

In multiplayer, large weapons are typically the most powerful and most sought-after gear on the battlefield. Securing and employing the power weapons available on each map is a crucial skill to master.

LANCER

DESCRIPTION

If you're looking for a weapon that's useful in most situations, the Lancer is perhaps the best all-around weapon in the game, and it comes as standard equipment for all Gears.

At a distance, the Lancer's solid rate of fire make it effective for suppressing an area or quickly downing a target out of cover. Up close, you can blindfire effectively around cover. At extreme close range, the brutal chainsaw can be used to lethal effect.

CLOSE RANGE

Blindfire is solid at close range, though it pales in comparison to real close-range weaponry. Just be aware of what your enemy is using. Longshot? Good! Shotgun? Bad!

If an enemy is advancing into this range, you can possibly take him down by cover-firing or even just blindfiring, but stay alert. If multiple enemies are closing on your position, it's time to relocate, not stand and fight.

At extreme close range, you can use the Lancer's brutal chainsaw bayonet, instantly killing all human-sized and smaller Locust.

MEDIUM RANGE

The Lancer excels at medium range, where its solid accuracy and good rate of fire make for great damage output, even against targets behind cover. You can usually accurately target the smallest exposed limbs to deliver damage.

Against targets moving in the open, the Lancer can down them very quickly if you track them while they are exposed.

Blindfiring at this distance is mediocre at best. You can inflict a bit of damage if you're moving from cover to cover. You're usually better off getting behind cover more quickly with a cover slip and roadie run than you are risking enemy fire in the open.

If you're blindfiring at an enemy directly approaching your cover, you can usually deliver a decent amount of damage.

WEAPON STATISTICS

CLIP SIZE	MAX AMMO	RATE OF FIRE	RELOAD TIME
50	550	550/m	2.5s

DAMAGE STATISTICS (PLAYER), SHORT/MEDIUM/LONG

CASUAL DAMAGE	CASUAL MELEE
80/80/48	Special
NORMAL DAMAGE	**NORMAL MELEE**
56/56/33.6	Special
HARDCORE/INSANE DAMAGE	**HARDCORE/INSANE MELEE**
40/40/24	Special

DAMAGE STATISTICS (AI)

CASUAL DAMAGE	CASUAL MELEE
20/20/12	Special
PERFECT ACTIVE RELOAD BONUS	**SPECIAL WEAPON NOTES**
Increases damage for the reloaded shots by 18-22% per shot.	Chainsaw bayonet instantly kills human-sized or smaller enemies.

LONG RANGE

The Lancer is mediocre at great distances. You *can* deal damage, but it tends to be very expensive in terms of consumed ammo. Plus, you usually have to stay exposed longer in order to aim carefully at a distant target.

If you have no better options, don't hesitate to take some shots, but you might want to look at the terrain and see if you can move in safely.

COVER

The Lancer is *okay* against targets in cover, but not great. Against targets exposing themselves to fire, it does well, particularly at medium range. If they're mostly concealed and blindfiring or not shooting at all, you'll have a harder time dealing damage efficiently.

Try to reposition to a flanking angle. Or, at the very least, move to expose part of the target, even if you're not at a full ninety-degree angle.

HAMMERBURST

DESCRIPTION

The Hammerburst is the Locust analog to the COG Lancer. It's standard equipment for most Locust Drones you encounter throughout the game, so it's always available to you as a primary weapon if you choose to use it instead of the Lancer. One great perk of the Hammerburst is that you get head shots with it, so it prevents the Kantus from reviving downed Locust. As an enemy weapon, there is usually plenty of ammo to pick up afterward.

The Hammerburst lacks the Lancer's chainsaw bayonet, but that isn't it's only weakness at close range. Rather than the Lancer's sustained automatic fire, the Hammerburst fires a bit more slowly. But it can be fired in semi-auto mode more quickly if you squeeze the trigger rapidly.

In exchange, the Hammerburst is slightly more accurate at a distance, hits harder per shot, and can zoom in slightly, making it a better mid-long-range weapon compared to the Lancer's superiority at close-mid range.

CLOSE RANGE

The Hammerburst does not excel at close range. Your best bet is mashing semi-auto as fast as you can squeeze the trigger. The resulting lack of accuracy isn't much of a problem up close—you're nearly guaranteed to hit something. Otherwise, another option is a melee hit. You're better off disengaging and getting some distance if you're under attack by more than a single enemy.

MEDIUM RANGE

The Hammerburst is very solid at medium range, though semi-automatic fire becomes more difficult to use accurately, depending on your target. It's great against enemies with a larger profile: Reavers, Boomers, etc.

LONG RANGE

The Hammerburst isn't *great* at long range, but it is good, and it's better than the Lancer. You can zoom in and fire small bursts, or fire in semi-auto with excellent accuracy.

WEAPON STATISTICS

CLIP SIZE	MAX AMMO	RATE OF FIRE	RELOAD TIME
17	306	250/m	2.5

DAMAGE STATISTICS (PLAYER), SHORT/MEDIUM/LONG

CASUAL DAMAGE	CASUAL MELEE
160/160/96	192
NORMAL DAMAGE	**NORMAL MELEE**
112/112/67	134
HARDCORE/INSANE DAMAGE	**HARDCORE/INSANE MELEE**
80/80/48	48

DAMAGE STATISTICS (AI)

CASUAL DAMAGE	CASUAL MELEE
40/40/24	48
PERFECT ACTIVE RELOAD BONUS	**SPECIAL WEAPON NOTES**
18%-22% damage bonus.	Can zoom, can be fired semi-auto or automatic.

COVER

The Hammerburst is very similar to the Lancer against targets in cover—it's okay, but not great. You do have the advantage of zoom though. Even against targets at medium range in cover, zoom can help you fire accurately at the smallest bits of exposed Locust.

LARGE WEAPONS

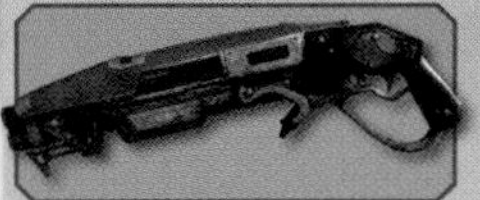

SHOTGUN

DESCRIPTION The premiere close-range weapon, the Shotgun is ideal for blasting apart Locust in your face. The Shotgun is particularly strong against smaller Locust, such as Wretches and Tickers.

It's often best to use the Shotgun while you're mobile, not up behind cover. Blindfired over cover, the shotgun is mildly useful against Locust closing on your position. But it's difficult or impossible to hit targets at a distance with any accuracy.

CLOSE RANGE The Shotgun is ideal. It can inflict grievous wounds up close. It's usually best to fire the Shotgun on the move, as you don't need precise accuracy with the Shotgun's cone-like spread.

MEDIUM RANGE At medium range, it's better than you might expect. The only real issue is that firing it from the hip exposes you to considerable danger in most fights, especially on higher difficulty levels.

You *can* blindfire over or around cover even at medium range and deal decent damage to targets in the open. This is especially true for targets moving toward you. Trying to hit enemies farther away or behind cover isn't worth your time.

LONG RANGE The Shotgun is exceedingly poor at long range; don't use the Shotgun in these situations.

WEAPON STATISTICS

CLIP SIZE	MAX AMMO	RATE OF FIRE	RELOAD TIME
8	39	50/m	3

DAMAGE STATISTICS (PLAYER), SHORT/MEDIUM/LONG

CASUAL DAMAGE	CASUAL MELEE
900/900/600	1000
NORMAL DAMAGE	NORMAL MELEE
630/630/420	700
HARDCORE/INSANE DAMAGE	HARDCORE/INSANE MELEE
450/450/300	500

DAMAGE STATISTICS (AI)

CASUAL DAMAGE	CASUAL MELEE
247/247/165	275
PERFECT ACTIVE RELOAD BONUS	SPECIAL WEAPON NOTES
20% damage bonus	Inflicts heavy melee damage.

COVER The Shotgun isn't great against targets behind cover, but it can be good if you're moving up to close range. Cover does little good against the shotgun's spread at fairly close range. Again, evaluate the situation carefully before you advance. You can get into trouble moving up on enemy positions if reinforcements arrive midway through the battle.

LONGSHOT

DESCRIPTION The Longshot is the premiere long-distance weapon in the COG arsenal. Its slow rate of fire and precise accuracy render it less effective up close, but it is very powerful through much of the campaign.

In general, keeping the Longshot and your preferred medium-to-close-range weapon on hand is very effective for nearly all campaign chapters. Many battles start with Locust that you can snipe safely from a distance before you switch to weaponry more appropriate for a brawl.

CLOSE RANGE Bad. *Very* bad. Don't use this weapon up close if you can avoid it. A last-second snapshot to the head can take down a single Locust. If you're getting swarmed by a group, this is the last weapon you want in your hand. Switch to something more appropriate or back off. However, the Longshot is strong as a melee weapon.

MEDIUM RANGE The Longshot isn't bad at medium range. The rate of fire puts a damper on how much damage you can inflict. But if you take precise shots, you can down a lot of Locust fairly quickly. Evaluate the situation before you commit to this weapon at medium range. If you're in a stalemate of a firefight and there aren't any good approach avenues for flanking the enemy (or getting flanked by them), using the Longshot is usually fairly safe and effective.

LONG RANGE Not surprisingly, the Longshot is perfect at long range. This is essentially the best weapon in the game at great distance. Really, it's one of the only effective weapons at this range. Any time you have a Longshot and Locust Snipers aren't around, you have the upper hand for as long as foes stay at a distance.

WEAPON STATISTICS

CLIP SIZE	MAX AMMO	RATE OF FIRE	RELOAD TIME
1	23	60/m	3

DAMAGE STATISTICS (PLAYER), SHORT/MEDIUM/LONG

CASUAL DAMAGE	CASUAL MELEE
840/700/700	840
NORMAL DAMAGE	NORMAL MELEE
588/490/490	588
HARDCORE/INSANE DAMAGE	HARDCORE/INSANE MELEE
420/350/350	420

DAMAGE STATISTICS (AI)

CASUAL DAMAGE	CASUAL MELEE
360/300/300	360
PERFECT ACTIVE RELOAD BONUS	SPECIAL WEAPON NOTES
10% damage bonus.	Headshots are instantly fatal to nearly all humanoid Locust.

COVER The Longshot is surprisingly good against covered foes. You can target even the smallest bit of exposed enemy. Plus, any time the target moves or reloads behind low cover, you might get a split-second shot at its melon. Watch for these opportunities to up your headshot count.

BOOMSHOT

WEAPON STATISTICS

CLIP SIZE	MAX AMMO	RATE OF FIRE	RELOAD TIME
1	11	60/m	2.5

DESCRIPTION Perhaps the most powerful 'normal' weapon besides the Torque Bow, the Boomshot fires clustered grenades that detonate on impact, inflicting lethal damage to a single target or solid radius damage to nearby enemies. The explosion also stuns neighboring enemies, temporarily disabling them. This is great for stopping an onslaught of fire.

Boomshot ammunition and availability tend to be limited. You rarely find the weapon, except from downed Boomers, who aren't particularly common. You can resupply ammo from *Locust* ammo crates, but not from COG ammo crates—Locust crates are red rather than blue.

The Boomshot can close Locust Emergence holes with its explosions.

CLOSE RANGE This weapon is dangerous at close range! You can use it effectively in these situations, but you must be very careful, or you'll end up fragging yourself along with your target.

MEDIUM RANGE The Boomshot is ideal at medium range. It's easy to hit with and easy to kill with. Targets in the open are so much meat, while you can hit those behind cover with the splash damage.

LONG RANGE It's not great at long range. The Boomshot's arcing trajectory makes long-distance shots dicey, as your targets can actually move out of the danger zone before the shots impact. Plus, landing your shots precisely is difficult. If there are a *lot* of enemies in an area, go for it—splash damage is sure to cause some pain.

DAMAGE STATISTICS (PLAYER), SHORT/MEDIUM/LONG

CASUAL DAMAGE	CASUAL MELEE
1050/1050/630	1260
(Bomblet) 300/300/180	n/a
NORMAL DAMAGE	**NORMAL MELEE**
735/735/441	882
(Bomblet) 210/210/126	n/a
HARDCORE/INSANE DAMAGE	**HARDCORE/INSANE MELEE**
525/525/315	630
(Bomblet) 150/150/90	n/a

DAMAGE STATISTICS (AI)

CASUAL DAMAGE	CASUAL MELEE
525/525/315	630
PERFECT ACTIVE RELOAD BONUS	**SPECIAL WEAPON NOTES**
23%-28% larger blast radius, 6 bomblets instead of 3.	The Boomshot's explosion causes nearby humanoid Locust to cower. Detonates three bomblets on impact.

COVER The Boomshot is decent against enemies behind cover. It can damage or kill targets by splashing off of any hard surface that's beside, behind, or above them. The best bet is nailing direct shots against grouped enemies. But if you really want to kill a particular enemy that's behind cover, the Boomshot can do the job.

TORQUE BOW

WEAPON STATISTICS

CLIP SIZE	MAX AMMO	RATE OF FIRE	RELOAD TIME
1	11	60/m	3

DESCRIPTION An unusual weapon, the Torque Bow builds up tension as you hold the trigger, gradually straightening its projectile's arc of travel.

Once it's charged enough, the explosive 'arrow' will stick to a target. This guarantees that the stuck target suffers massive damage from the impact and resulting explosion.

Like the Boomshot, the Torque Bow's availability is often limited in the campaign. When you have the weapon, you can use Locust ammo boxes to refill it. Save your shots for dangerous targets: Theron Guards, Palace Guards, etc.

Be *very* careful around enemies using this weapon. Watch for the glow of a fully-charged shot. If you see it, stay behind cover until the shot is fired. Because the Torque Bow automatically fires if it's charged for too long, you can usually avoid taking direct shots while you're exposed.

CLOSE RANGE The Torque Bow isn't good at close range. You need time to charge the weapon, and you usually need time to aim it too. The overall fire rate is slow, making this a poor choice up close. However, it does have a rather cool melee execution…

MEDIUM RANGE The Torque Bow is very good at this range. You have time to fully charge the weapon and pick your target. You can aim with enough accuracy at this distance to peg a target in low cover, which is nearly always fatal.

LONG RANGE This weapon is decent but not spectacular at long range. You can often nail targets at this distance, but you must be precise, which can be difficult if you're under fire from anything closer. If you don't have a better long-range alternative and you *really* want to kill a distant enemy, take the shot.

DAMAGE STATISTICS (PLAYER), SHORT/MEDIUM/LONG

CASUAL DAMAGE	CASUAL MELEE
1416/1416/849	1699
NORMAL DAMAGE	**NORMAL MELEE**
991/991/594	1189
HARDCORE/INSANE DAMAGE	**HARDCORE/INSANE MELEE**
708/708/424	849

DAMAGE STATISTICS (AI)

CASUAL DAMAGE	CASUAL MELEE
708/708/424	849
PERFECT ACTIVE RELOAD BONUS	**SPECIAL WEAPON NOTES**
25% larger blast radius, 25% greater damage.	Under-charged shots can be 'bounced' off hard cover to deliver the explosive warhead behind cover or around corners.

COVER The Torque Bow is surprisingly good against enemies behind cover. It's fatal to targets if you stick the shot. As long as you aim carefully, you can nail exposed regions and reliably kill the target.

HAMMER OF DAWN

WEAPON STATISTICS

SPECIAL WEAPON NOTES
Must spot target area for several seconds before the satellite fires.

DESCRIPTION Strictly speaking, the mighty Hammer of Dawn is not an actual weapon, at least not the part that you carry. It's a targeting device for the orbiting COG military satellite system. As the damage rains down, you can guide the devastating bombardment by moving the target painter along the ground.

The Hammer of Dawn's only real downsides are that you gain access to it *very* late in the campaign, and it requires open sky to use. Otherwise, fried Locust!

CLOSE RANGE This isn't a great close-range weapon. You have to paint the target for a few moments before the devastation commences. Plus, the resulting blast wave can be dangerous!

MEDIUM RANGE The Hammer of Dawn is a superb medium-range weapon. Locust at this range are easy prey.

LONG RANGE It's just as good at long range as it is at medium distance. If you can see it and sight it, then you can kill it.

COVER The Hammer of Dawn is fantastic against enemies behind cover. The roving wave of destruction can easily incinerate targets behind objects. But again, you must have open sky to use it.

SCORCHER

WEAPON STATISTICS

CLIP SIZE	MAX AMMO	RATE OF FIRE	RELOAD TIME
50	300	850/m	2.5

DAMAGE STATISTICS (PLAYER), SHORT/MEDIUM/LONG

CASUAL DAMAGE	CASUAL MELEE
1400/1400/840	1630
NORMAL DAMAGE	**NORMAL MELEE**
980/980/588	1176
HARDCORE/INSANE DAMAGE	**HARDCORE/INSANE MELEE**
700/700/420	840

DAMAGE STATISTICS (AI)

CASUAL DAMAGE	CASUAL MELEE
700/700/420	840
PERFECT ACTIVE RELOAD BONUS	**SPECIAL WEAPON NOTES**
20% distance bonus.	None.

DESCRIPTION A short-range weapon, the Scorcher is a nasty flamethrower, ideal for incinerating the Locust up close and personal. The Scorcher's jet of flame is extremely easy to aim as you walk around, but it is range-limited—past a certain distance, you simply can't hurt anything.

Perfect reloads with the Scorcher are important, as they extend the flames' range, letting you toast targets just a *bit* farther away.

CLOSE RANGE The Scorcher is superb for clumped packs of enemies. The continuous flame jet is ideal for pumping out continual damage on an entire group without pauses—unlike the Shotgun.

On the downside, you *must* get close to deliver this damage. Using it from cover is less impressive, though you can very easily blindfire it around corners or over low cover.

MEDIUM RANGE Past a certain point, the Scorcher can't even reach a target, but it is fairly effective at a close-medium distance, depending on the enemy composition and terrain. Wretches are prime flame bait, while massed Snipers and Torque Bow-wielding Locust are somewhat less so.

LONG RANGE The Scorcher is no good at long range; it simply can't reach that far!

COVER For hitting enemies behind cover, the Scorcher is decent. The weapon's flames do *not* 'flow over' the front of cover, but you *can* hit any exposed portion of an enemy in cover. This is pretty easy to do, given the giant cone of flame you can project.

Of course, this necessitates closing on a covered enemy with a relatively short-ranged weapon. Be mindful of enemies to your flanks if you advance in the open to use the Scorcher in this fashion.

HEAVY WEAPONS

Heavy weapons are a new and special weapon class in *Gears of War 2*. While you carry a heavy weapon, you move more slowly, and you cannot use your other weaponry; equipping another weapon causes you to drop the heavy weapon.

The tradeoff is that heavy weapons are *very* powerful. They tend to be sharply limited in supply. You often have to wrest them from the cold, dead hands of downed Locust who previously used them against *you*. When you get them, use them for all they're worth.

MULCHER

WEAPON STATISTICS

CLIP SIZE	MAX AMMO	RATE OF FIRE	RELOAD TIME
n/a	500	1000/m	n/a

DAMAGE STATISTICS (PLAYER), SHORT/MEDIUM/LONG

CASUAL DAMAGE	CASUAL MELEE
100/100/60	120
NORMAL DAMAGE	**NORMAL MELEE**
70/70/42	84
HARDCORE/INSANE DAMAGE	**HARDCORE/INSANE MELEE**
50/50/30	60

DAMAGE STATISTICS (AI)

CASUAL DAMAGE	CASUAL MELEE
40/40/24	48
PERFECT ACTIVE RELOAD BONUS	**SPECIAL WEAPON NOTES**
n/a	None.

DESCRIPTION The Mulcher is a devastatingly powerful chaingun. You usually find it in the hands of the Grinder or very rarely on the ground. You don't often get a chance to use it, but when you do, it shreds Locust easily.

The Mulcher has to be planted to spin up, preferably on cover, though you can also plant it in the open. You *can* fire it while you're moving, but it is almost absurdly inaccurate.

The Mulcher does not reload. Instead, you cool it down by holding the reload button, similar to turrets and Troika in the game.

Whenever you have the chance to grab the Mulcher, bring it along. There few enemies or situations that it can't handle in the campaign.

CLOSE RANGE The Mulcher isn't great at close range, but it depends on the situation. If you're at close range with your enemies lined up in front of you or out in the open, they're as good as dead.

If the action is up close and you're getting swarmed on all sides or attacked by highly mobile enemies, the speed reduction can be problematic. Don't hesitate to drop the Mulcher for a moment to clear the area if necessary; you can always pick it up again afterward.

MEDIUM RANGE Fantastic at medium range, the Mulcher can devastate any Locust presence out in the open. It's ideal for stopping a rush on your position by any number of Locust troopers. It's also great against heavier Locust forces at this distance.

LONG RANGE The Mulcher isn't ideal at long range. While its field of fire is impressive, the natural spread of the shots renders it less dangerous over great distance. Drop it and use a better long-range tool. Then carry it along to the next batch of enemies at a more suitable distance.

COVER The Mulcher isn't well suited for dealing with enemies behind hard cover. You can make an impressive show of chipping away at the rock around them, but it won't penetrate. You may be better off using grenades or picking off dug-in foes with other weaponry.

BOOMSHIELD

WEAPON STATISTICS

SPECIAL WEAPON NOTES
Blocks all damage from the front. Blocks less damage as shots approach the user's side.

DESCRIPTION Not exactly a weapon, the Boomshield is a superb defensive tool. While you hold the Boomshield, you can use only pistol-class weaponry. In return, the Boomshield makes you nearly invulnerable to frontal fire from the Locust.

You can plant the Boomshield in the ground as a piece of stationary cover, allowing you to use your other weaponry. You can also use it to perform a brutal melee execution...

Unlike a meat shield, which gradually deteriorates in a messy fashion, the Boomshield soaks up even heavy firepower without breaking.

Note that you have to 'deploy' the Boomshield by aiming to make it active. Doing so slows your rate of movement further. However, unlike a meat shield, you can Roadie Run (albeit at a slower pace) as you carry the Boomshield, so you aren't quite as speed-limited.

The Boomshield is *very* powerful. Any time you find it in the campaign, pick it up and take it with you for as long as you can. Whenever you need more firepower, you can simply plant it. The rest of the time, you can easily sponge up Locust fire from the front.

MORTAR

DESCRIPTION The powerful Mortar is a standoff weapon, perfect for dealing with clustered Locust forces at a distance. However, it is bad for dealing with quick foes or enemies up close. Its explosive power makes up for this shortcoming when you face Locust groups in many parts of the campaign.

The Mortar must be planted and aimed carefully. While it's planted, you can hold the fire button to increase the distance of the shot. After you fire, you'll see a hash mark on the rangefinder marking the last shot's distance. This helps you fix your range when you need to fire multiple shots at the same area.

The Mortar's arcing trajectory sends the projectile into the air. It then detonates, raining havoc down on your foes. Using the Mortar requires lots of open space, and you're exposed for a fair amount of time while you aim. Don't go using it when you're under heavy fire up close!

You can fire the Mortar from the hip. Doing so launches the bombshell straight ahead (Mortar bowling…), but this is a desperation move at best.

The Mortar's explosions can seal Locust Emergence Holes.

CLOSE RANGE The Mortar is exceptionally poor at close range. You can fire it from the hip up close and hope to blast your opponents quickly. In general, you're better off dropping this weapon for a moment and then picking it up when the area is clear.

MEDIUM RANGE This weapon's effectiveness varies at medium range. Sometimes it's great, and sometimes it's just okay. Evaluate the situation: if there are lots of enemies clustered at medium range and you've got good cover, go for it. You can usually take out many enemies with just a few shots.

However, if you face highly mobile foes—say, Wretches or Bloodmounts—you may not have the time to line up a shot safely. The same is true if you're under heavy fire by Drones; exposing yourself to sight the shot may be too risky.

WEAPON STATISTICS

CLIP SIZE	MAX AMMO	RATE OF FIRE	RELOAD TIME
1	100	60/m	3.5

DAMAGE STATISTICS (PLAYER), SHORT/MEDIUM/LONG

CASUAL DAMAGE	CASUAL MELEE
1600/1600/960 (direct) 2000/2000/1200	n/a
NORMAL DAMAGE	**NORMAL MELEE**
1120/1120/672 (direct) 1400/1400/840	n/a
HARDCORE/INSANE DAMAGE	**HARDCORE/INSANE MELEE**
800/800/480 (direct) 1000/1000/600	n/a

DAMAGE STATISTICS (AI)

CASUAL DAMAGE	CASUAL MELEE
800/800/480	n/a
PERFECT ACTIVE RELOAD BONUS	**SPECIAL WEAPON NOTES**
18%-22% more damage, 23%-28% larger blast radius.	Mortar shell splits into 10 bomblets, all dealing full damage. Mortar blasts cause nearby Locust to cower.

LONG RANGE The Mortar is generally quite good at long range. The only difficult part is finding the correct distance. But since you usually have more time, you can afford to take a test shot and then home in on your targets and obliterate them.

COVER The Mortar is great for dealing with cover. The shots burst in the air and rain down fury from above. There are few situations in which Locust can take cover from well-placed Mortar shells.

PISTOLS

These sidearms are typically weapons of last resort in normal engagements. However, as pistol-class guns are the only weapons you can use when you carry a meat shield (or a real shield, for that matter), it's important to pick a pistol that you're comfortable using. The new Gorgon burst pistol joins the ranks of the Snub and Boltok semi-automatic pistols from the original *Gears of War*.

SNUB PISTOL

DESCRIPTION The Snub Pistol is the default COG sidearm. You have one with you at the start of the game, and it is a solid pistol. It has a good semi-auto rate of fire, a quick reload, and delivers decent damage. Most of the time, you should use heavier weapons, but there are special cases, notably when you're using a Boomshield or meat shield.

CLOSE RANGE The Snub Pistol isn't fantastic at close range. But you can fire pretty quickly from the hip without having to worry too much about aiming. This can come in handy if you're backpedaling to get behind cover, though you may be better off Roadie Running or rolling to get away from close-range enemies.

MEDIUM RANGE It's solid at medium range. With the Snub Pistol's zoom function, you can hit targets dependably. If you're trying to down a Locust to use as a meat shield, using the Snub Pistol on a Drone's legs is a reliable way to acquire made-to-order mobile cover.

LONG RANGE The Snub Pistol isn't really effective at long range. The spread becomes noticeable at greater distances, even if you carefully aim each shot. Use a different weapon!

WEAPON STATISTICS

CLIP SIZE	MAX AMMO	RATE OF FIRE	RELOAD TIME
12	120	700/m	2

DAMAGE STATISTICS (PLAYER), SHORT/MEDIUM/LONG

CASUAL DAMAGE	CASUAL MELEE
110/110/66	132
NORMAL DAMAGE	**NORMAL MELEE**
77/77/46	92
HARDCORE/INSANE DAMAGE	**HARDCORE/INSANE MELEE**
55/55/33	66

DAMAGE STATISTICS (AI)

CASUAL DAMAGE	CASUAL MELEE
50/50/30	60
PERFECT ACTIVE RELOAD BONUS	**SPECIAL WEAPON NOTES**
18%-22% bonus damage.	Can zoom.

COVER The Snub Pistol is average against targets behind cover. At closer ranges, it's accurate enough that you can pick away at a foe's exposed bits, but generally, there are better alternatives at hand.

BOLTOK PISTOL

WEAPON STATISTICS

CLIP SIZE	MAX AMMO	RATE OF FIRE	RELOAD TIME
6	36	60/m	2

DAMAGE STATISTICS (PLAYER), SHORT/MEDIUM/LONG

CASUAL DAMAGE	CASUAL MELEE
350/350/210	420
NORMAL DAMAGE	**NORMAL MELEE**
245/245/147	294
HARDCORE/INSANE DAMAGE	**HARDCORE/INSANE MELEE**
175/175/105	210

DAMAGE STATISTICS (AI)

CASUAL DAMAGE	CASUAL MELEE
175/175/105	210
PERFECT ACTIVE RELOAD BONUS	**SPECIAL WEAPON NOTES**
Doubles rate of fire.	Inflicts triple damage on headshots.

DESCRIPTION This powerful revolver, favored by Locust forces, is a common sight. If you prefer its tradeoff of a bigger kick with a slower rate of fire, you shouldn't have any trouble finding one.

The Boltok is a good choice if you have a Boomshield, or if you use meat shields frequently.

CLOSE RANGE The Boltok Pistol isn't too good at close range. Its slow rate of fire makes it a dangerous weapon to use up close. It does hit hard, but if you face more than one enemy, you don't want to get stuck shooting them with this up close.

MEDIUM RANGE The Boltok Pistol is surprisingly effective at mid range, especially if you go for headshots. The Boltok packs a serious punch, and you can pop the heads off humanoid Locust with well-aimed shots. Go for a Perfect Active Reload if you use this weapon with any regularity.

LONG RANGE It's not as bad as you'd expect at long range. Because you usually have to line up single shots to use the Boltok effectively, it tends to train you for accuracy. If you manage to score the hits, you can deliver surprising damage at a distance. Still, this isn't an ideal distance weapon. If you really have nothing better, it can work for you.

COVER Similar to the Snub Pistol, the Boltok isn't bad against covered targets at medium distances. In some cases, it can be a lot better—if you can score headshots, you can take down Drones very efficiently.

GORGON PISTOL

WEAPON STATISTICS

CLIP SIZE	MAX AMMO	RATE OF FIRE	RELOAD TIME
32	504	1200/m	2

DAMAGE STATISTICS (PLAYER), SHORT/MEDIUM/LONG

CASUAL DAMAGE	CASUAL MELEE
110/110/66	132
NORMAL DAMAGE	**NORMAL MELEE**
77/77/46	92
HARDCORE/INSANE DAMAGE	**HARDCORE/INSANE MELEE**
55/55/33	66

DAMAGE STATISTICS (AI)

CASUAL DAMAGE	CASUAL MELEE
40/40/24	48
PERFECT ACTIVE RELOAD BONUS	**SPECIAL WEAPON NOTES**
18%-22% damage increase.	None.

DESCRIPTION The Gorgon Pistol is a seldom-encountered weapon of the Locust Kantus. It fires a burst of shots, inflicting fairly high damage if the bulk of the burst connects. Its effectiveness fades at a distance, and the time between shots can get you in trouble against multiple opponents.

CLOSE RANGE The Gorgon Pistol is somewhat effective at close range. Against small numbers, you can take down targets pretty quickly, but the long delay between shots can be a death warrant if you're dealing with a large enemy group. Very quick targets, which are difficult to hit with every shot in each burst, also present problems.

MEDIUM RANGE The Gorgon Pistol is solid at medium range. Pick your shots carefully, and you can do well against targets in the open, particularly if you have a meat shield or Boomshield.

LONG RANGE This weapon isn't good at long range. The burst's spread, plus the delay between shots, makes this pistol ineffective over long distances.

COVER The Gorgon Pistol's burst fire lacks the precision of the Snub or Boltok. Because its damage is spread over the shots in each burst, it is generally inefficient against targets in cover. You *can* take them down, but you can usually find a better weapon to do the job, wasting less ammo in the process.

GRENADES

Each grenade type is a powerful tactical weapon. Grenades are useful against crowds, great for area denial, or to flush out targets from behind hard cover.

PROXIMITY MINES!

In Multiplayer, you can stick grenades to walls to serve as makeshift proximity mines. Enemies passing within a close radius of the placed grenade trigger its detonation. Even non-lethal grenade types can provide a valuable warning of an enemy approach.

FRAG GRENADES

WEAPON STATISTICS
MAXIMUM AMMO
4

DAMAGE STATISTICS (PLAYER)	
CASUAL DAMAGE	2000
NORMAL DAMAGE	1400
HARDCORE/INSANE DAMAGE	1000

DAMAGE STATISTICS (AI)	
DAMAGE	1000
SPECIAL WEAPON NOTES	10-yard radius on blast, causes Locust to cower. Planted grenades can be detonated prematurely by shooting them.

DESCRIPTION Frag Grenades are standard-issue for COG troops. Also, Locust Grenadiers occasionally use (and drop) them.

Frag Grenades pack a powerful punch and are vital for flushing targets out of cover. They're ideal for coping with large enemy groups or more powerful Locust.

You can blindfire Frag Grenades with surprisingly good accuracy, though only at fairly close range. They also work well when blindfire-tossed over cover. If you aim, you can throw them with pinpoint accuracy, but you have to expose yourself to do so, and it takes a bit longer. Save the aiming for long-range throws.

If you tap the melee button near a wall, you can stick Frag Grenades to the surface to act as proximity mines. This is very handy if you're defending an area. Stick Frags on any approaches to your defensive position and watch the fireworks.

Frag Grenades can close Locust Emergence Holes prematurely.

CLOSE RANGE Frag Grenades aren't good at close range. However, you can stick Frag Grenades to enemies by hitting them melee-style. This works very well against Boomer-class Locust. Of course, getting that close usually is a very bad idea. Generally, this is an unsafe tactic unless you're feeling showy, or you happen to round a corner into a Locust when you have a grenade in your hand. If you land the stick, quickly roll and run to escape the blast!

MEDIUM RANGE Frag Grenades are great at medium range. A well-aimed blindfire toss at this distance usually obviates time lost to exposed aiming. You can certainly toss these grenades at emergence holes or at enemies in awkward to reach areas.

LONG RANGE At long range, Frag Grenades are better than you'd expect, as long as you aim the throw. However, choose your targets carefully. If they're mobile, you'll usually waste grenades. But if they're clustered or seem to be stationary, go ahead and make the throw.

COVER Frag Grenades are dandy against enemies behind cover! They're ideal for flushing out Locust. Even if they don't kill your targets, they often run from cover to avoid the blast, leaving them in the open, partially damaged from the explosion. Easy pickings!

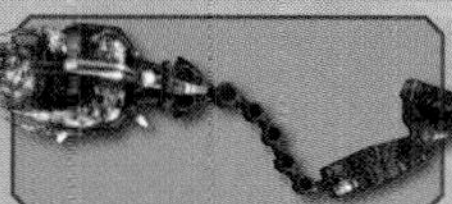

INK GRENADES

WEAPON STATISTICS
MAXIMUM AMMO
4

DAMAGE PER SECOND (PLAYER)	
CASUAL DAMAGE	600
NORMAL DAMAGE	420
HARDCORE/INSANE DAMAGE	300

DAMAGE PER SECOND (AI)	
DAMAGE	300
SPECIAL WEAPON NOTES	10-yard radius.

DESCRIPTION Locust Ink Grenades are actually immature Nemacysts mounted on a grenade body. The Locust Kantus use them as poisonous weapons. You can occasionally find these on the body of a downed Kantus, so don't expect to use them with any regularity.

Ink Grenades detonate on impact, spewing poisonous clouds of 'ink' into the air. Anything in the area suffers painful damage. Because the cloud lingers, Ink Grenades are perfect for suppressing an area or forcing Locust to move from cover.

If the ink cloud hits *you*, move fast. Not only does the poison drain your health, but the black cloud also obscures your vision, making it nearly impossible to fight effectively from within its boundaries.

CLOSE RANGE Ink Grenades aren't good at close range. You don't want to release any ink clouds at this distance!

MEDIUM RANGE At medium range, Ink Grenades are great. You can blindfire-toss or aim these grenades and easily hit your target area. Any foes near the impact zone will either end up dead, or will be forced into the open.

LONG RANGE Because you may be too far to capitalize on enemies that flee from the ink, you may want to save these scarce grenades for more certain damage at a closer range.

COVER Ink Grenades are superb against enemies behind cover. The toxic cloud saturates an entire area, so even if you drop the grenade near cover, the resulting poison bloom guarantees that any Locust nearby will be hurting.

SMOKE GRENADES

DESCRIPTION Smoke Grenades are not available in the Campaign. However, they are vital tools in Multiplayer. Use these weapons to create a vision-obscuring cloud of smoke radiating from the detonation point. These come in handy for concealing your movements, creating a diversion, and causing confusion in the enemy ranks when deployed in their midst. They can save your life when you're caught out of cover. Furthermore, the smoke grenade's concussive detonation knocks targets off their feet within a short radius of the initial blast. This effect is particularly handy in Multiplayer matches for dislodging an enemy's hold on a capture point or a Meatflag.

LOCUST DATABANK

THE LOCUST

The seemingly unending Locust Horde has brought ruin and desolation to the surface of Sera and despair into the heart of humanity.

The Gears of the Coalition of Ordered Governments are the last bastion of defense against the Locust. If the war is to be won, it will be won by the Gears.

TO DEFEAT YOUR FOE, YOU MUST KNOW YOUR FOE.

DRONE

The Locust Drone (referred to as 'Grubs' by the Gears) is the basic foot soldier of the Locust Horde. They are brutish foes, but they're cunning enough to use cover and teamwork effectively. Drones frequently attack in sizable numbers, meaning that you need to watch out for flank attacks.

It's best to deal with Drones at medium or long range, where most of their weaponry is only moderately dangerous, and you aren't at risk of getting overwhelmed by their numbers.

Drones have by far the largest variety of subtypes. Beyond normal Drones, you can expect to encounter the following variants: Grappler Drones that can swing hooks up to reach you in elevated positions; Bolter Drones armed with a Boltok that move more quickly but have less health; and occasionally, a Drone armed with a Lancer, a Mortar, or manning a Troika. All of these are more dangerous than the normal Locust soldier that uses a Hammerburst.

VITALS

WEAPONRY — Variable

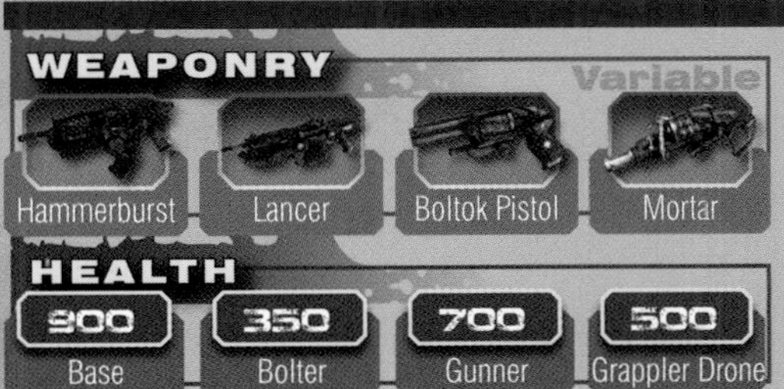

HEALTH

900	350	700	500
Base	Bolter	Gunner	Grappler Drone

COVER

Drones use cover much like Gears do, hiding out and occasionally taking aimed shots or blindfiring. They are reasonably mobile, and you can expect to see them shift their position from wherever they emerge to advance on your team's location.

Beware of getting caught out in the open if Drones are pushing on your position. You can get cut down quickly if you're targeted by several Drones at once.

GRENADIER

Grenadiers are a Drone variant, but they are dangerous enough that they warrant special attention. Grenadiers are one of only two types of Locust that use grenades with any regularity.

Grenadiers *can* drop Frag Grenades for you, but they don't *always* drop grenades. Be sure to check their bodies after you finish them off.

Despite their name, Grenadiers don't always continually fling grenades at you, but they can and will, and this is especially dangerous on higher difficulty levels.

You can usually spot Grenadiers at a distance due to their lack of chest armor—their pale flesh makes them stand out. Grenadier variants include the Flame Grenadier, which carries the Scorcher, and the Beast Rider, that usually drives Reavers and Bloodmounts.

Be sure to shoot the fuel tanks that Flame Grenadiers carry. This is one of the best tactics for dealing with this enemy type.

VITALS

WEAPONRY

HEALTH

COVER

Much like Drones, Grenadiers use cover fairly well. However, unlike most Drone types, Grenadiers are very dangerous to you when you're *in* cover.

Make them priority targets if you can't easily retreat to safer ground should they toss a grenade your way.

SNIPER

Drone Snipers are, as you might expect, Drones armed with Longshots. They are very dangerous opponents if you lack long-range weaponry of your own. Fortunately, they are fairly weak. Upon death, a Sniper provides you with a Longshot as long as you can get to its body safely.

Keep an eye and an ear out for Snipers. They aren't extremely common, but they do show up throughout the campaign, and they should always be a priority target on the battlefield.

If you can't kill them immediately, see if you can fight off the other nearby Locust from behind cover to prevent the Snipers from getting a bead on you. It's always better if you can focus on Snipers without fear of getting munched on by a Bloodmount or blasted by a Boomer.

VITALS

WEAPONRY

Longshot

HEALTH

350

COVER

Snipers tend to stick to cover, and they are dangerous to you even when you're in cover. If you're behind low cover and move or reload, you just might get shot.

Snipers are always dangerous when you aim around cover or walk in the open. To reduce the chance of taking a direct shot, try to minimize your time away from cover or aiming when Snipers are around.

KANTUS

Kantus are a very special type of Locust, almost priest-like. They are armed with a pistol and can throw potent Ink Grenades. But their special abilities make them more dangerous than the weapons they carry.

First, Kantus can raise downed Locust, restoring them to full battle effectiveness. This means that Kantus must be your primary target in any mixed engagement. If you don't prioritize them, you'll see downed Drones stand right back up and rejoin the battle.

Kantus can also scream to summon Tickers. This can transform a standard battle into a very unpleasant one. Try to take them down at a distance before they can get close and compromise your cover.

Finally, the Kantus' scream can knock you down at close range, so getting into a short-range fight is not advisable.

VITALS

WEAPONRY

Gorgon Pistol, Ink Grenades

HEALTH

2000

COVER

Kantus tend to stay out of cover, but they are also fairly mobile. They like to keep their distance from you—all the better to raise downed Drones and summon Tickers. Picking them off with distance weaponry works well.

Kantus can be a serious threat to your cover, as the Ink Grenades they toss render whole areas unusable for several seconds. You may occasionally get lucky enough to find Ink Grenades on their bodies, though they don't always drop them.

THERON GUARD

The powerful Theron Guards are elite Drone droops, often armed with the lethal Torque Bow.

Theron Guards behave much like Drones, but they are tougher and tend to have nastier weaponry. They are all around harder to deal with than regular Drones. Don't be stingy with your heavy weapon ammo when they're around.

VITALS

WEAPONRY

Variable

Hammerburst, Lancer, Torque Bow, Shotgun

COVER

Theron use cover very well, and they can be extremely dangerous if they're armed with Torque Bows. Watch for the telltale glow of a charged bow shot, and stay fully behind cover until it discharges.

HEALTH

1350

PALACE GUARD

You encounter Palace Guards in only one portion of the game, which is good, because they are easily the toughest normal Locust troops.

Other than their increased health, Palace Guards are otherwise very similar to Theron Guards… and just as dangerous. Even more menacing, some Palace Guards ride Bloodmounts.

VITALS

WEAPONRY

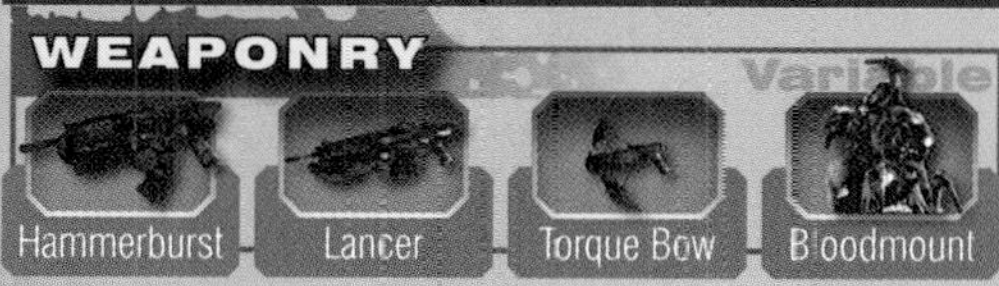

Hammerburst, Lancer, Torque Bow, Bloodmount

COVER

Nearly identical to Drones and Theron Guards, Palace Guards use cover effectively.

HEALTH

1500

MAULER

A Boomer-sized Locust, the Mauler is a large, aggressive, and comparatively fast-moving Locust shock trooper.

Maulers are armed with a flail that explodes on impact and knocks you off your feet. They also carry a Boomshield that can soak up frontal fire. Maulers can be a serious pain to exterminate.

To down a Mauler, wait for it to lower its shield, and then hit it with strong, single-shot weaponry. You can use Grenades, the Longshot, Boomshot, a Shotgun, or even a Boltok in a pinch. Rapid-fire weaponry tends to be somewhat less effective, as the Mauler can keep its shield raised, blocking much of your damage output.

If you need to slow down a Mauler, but can't deal with it immediately, fire at it to force it to raise its shield. This slows it down for a few seconds while it guards itself.

VITALS

WEAPONRY

Explosive Flail, Boomshield

HEALTH

2500

Whatever you do, *don't* let a Mauler get close to you. Its flail is short range only, but it is lethal up close. Even if the explosion doesn't kill you, getting knocked on your butt with other Locust nearby can certainly ruin your day.

On the bright side, killing a Mauler leaves a lovely reward in the form of the powerful Boomshield.

COVER

Maulers ignore cover, but they are a serious threat to you behind cover. Once they're up close, cover will not help you.

Try to take them out before they can force you to break from cover and possibly expose yourself to other nearby Locust.

BOOMER

The mighty Boomer and his ever-present Boomshot returns, and it is a serious menace.

The Boomer can take you down in a single shot if you aren't careful. Duck whenever you hear them yell "BOOM!" You have a split second to get out of sight before the Boomshot projectile impacts. You don't want to be in the open and drawing fire when Boomers are stomping around.

Boomers are disturbingly tough, so don't spare your heavy weapons or grenades whenever you spot one.

Occasionally, you encounter the rare Flame Boomer variant. These walls of meat are dangerous foes, as they possess the durability that Flame Grenadiers lack. They are relatively slow, but you have to take them down before they close with your position. An undamaged Flame Boomer at close range can put you in a very unpleasant situation if other enemies are around. Be sure to shoot the fuel tanks that Flame Boomers carry. This is one of the best tactics for dealing with this enemy type.

VITALS

WEAPONRY

Boomshot

HEALTH

2000

Killing a Boomer is usually cause for celebration, as you can put the Boomshot it drops to good use, quickly executing key enemies for the next several encounters.

COVER

Boomers scorn cover, marching toward you and cackling as they unload with their heavy weaponry. For your part, get behind nice, solid cover whenever Boomers are near—they're too dangerous to risk exposing yourself.

BUTCHER BOOMER

The singular Butcher is a very rare and unusual type of Boomer. Encountered deep in the heart of Locust territory, they provide an insight into Locust dietary habits. Unfortunately, they're not as interested in sharing culinary secrets as they are in splitting you apart with their massive cleavers.

Armed with only their close-range weapon, Butchers aren't serious threats as long as you down them before they get close. While their melee attack is brutal, you can actually survive one hit. But don't let them get that close in the first place; down them at a distance!

COVER

Like the rest of the Boomer family, Butchers have no interest in cover. Instead, they attempt to close the distance and attack with their meat cleavers.

VITALS

WEAPONRY

Butcher's Cleaver

HEALTH

2000

FLAME BOOMER

The rare Flame Boomer is a nasty pyro-enhanced type of Boomer. While they lack the long-range punch of the Boomer or Grinder, Flame Boomers compensate with the danger of their advance. When a Flame Boomer appears, taking it down at range is vital. If it gets into close range, you're guaranteed to get incinerated.

Flame Boomers are just as tough as their Boomer brethren, but you can usually take them down before they become a threat. Just make sure you don't mistake a Flame Boomer for a Flame Grenadier at a distance! Their lumbering march and larger target profile should clue you in to the greater threat.

VITALS

WEAPONRY

Scorcher

HEALTH

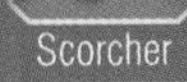

2000

COVER

Like Boomers, Flame Boomers ignore cover. They march implacably toward your position, seeking to bring their close-range flamers to bear.

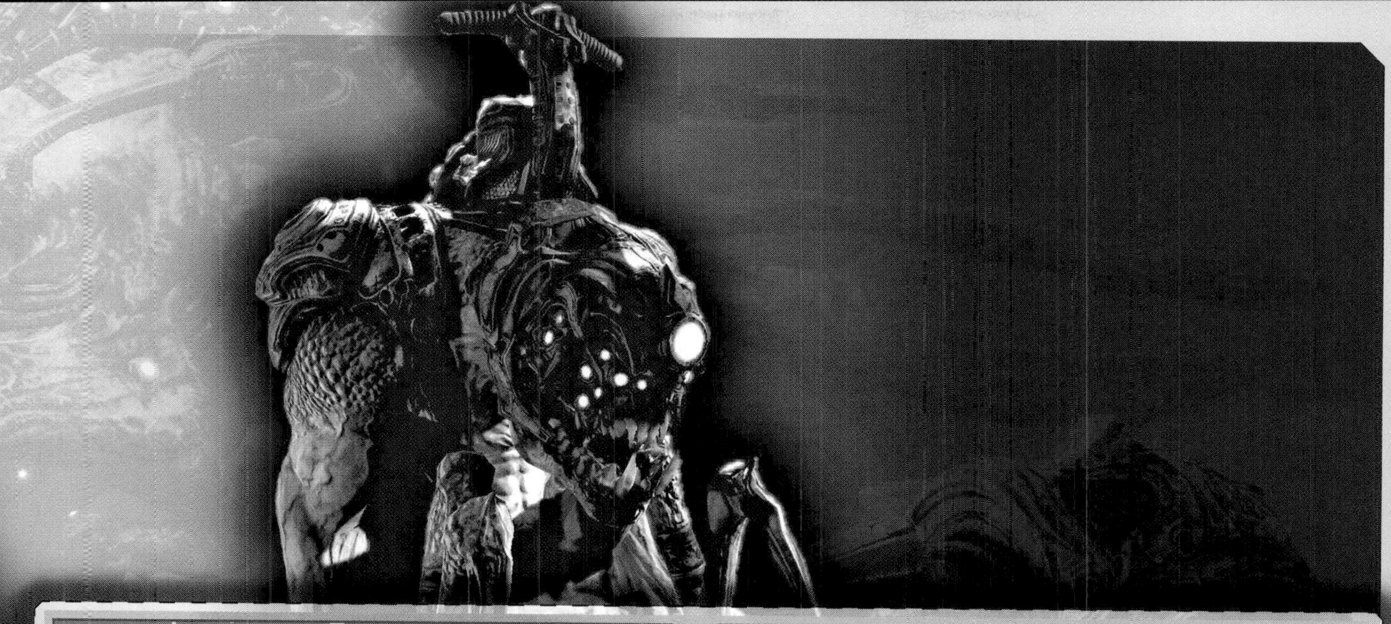

BLOODMOUNT

Thankfully, the Bloodmount is a fairly rare Locust beast. This creature is usually ridden into battle by a Beast Rider Grenadier and occasionally by stronger Locust, such as the Palace Guard.

The Bloodmount is dangerous for a few reasons. First and foremost, it can stab you with it's small legs. Also, it likes to come at you behind cover. This can put you in the same unpleasant situation that a Wretch rush does with other Locust in the area.

Second, the Bloodmount's rider has the benefit of an elevated position. This can make low cover a lot less safe when the Bloodmount closes on your position.

Try shooting the Bloodmount in the face to daze it and make it pry off its helmet. The time it and its thrown rider spend in a stunned state can give you time to finish them off.

You can shoot the rider off the Bloodmount, but doing so won't save you. The Bloodmount continues its pursuit, and you don't want its vicious maw anywhere near you.

VITALS

WEAPONRY

Teeth!

HEALTH

2500

COVER

The Bloodmount generally ignores cover, but it is fast moving and can easily force you to break cover when it gets close. Any time you spot a Bloodmount and you have some distance on it, try to take it out as quickly as possible.

NEMACITE

The Nemacite is a very rare enemy, encountered only in one very specific part of the game. These strange creatures are all fangs and spikey bits, but they are exceedingly weak.

Even hip fire from a Lancer can down them, which is good, because they tend to attack in packs. Fire on the move and deal with them much like you would a pack of Wretches.

VITALS

WEAPONRY

Claws

HEALTH

100

COVER

Nemacites ignore cover, aggressively rushing toward you and your squad mates.

GRINDER

Grinders are a special type of Boomer armed with the lethal Mulcher minigun. Like Boomers, they love to yell, "GRIND!" This is your signal to duck and stay behind cover.

Grinders unload with their Mulchers for a few seconds and then pause. Hit them hard during this gap, because it is totally unsafe to expose yourself when they're firing.

Downing a Grinder leaves a grand reward: the Mulcher it drops is a very, very powerful heavy weapon.

VITALS

WEAPONRY

Mulcher

HEALTH

2500

COVER

Much like their Boomer bretheren, Grinders are uninterested in using cover, preferring to stay out in the open and unload with their Mulchers.

WRETCH

The feral Wretches are weak and degenerate Locust, but they are still dangerous. Wretches move quickly and aggressively advance on your position, forcing you to break cover and deal with them up close.

It's best to deal with Wretches on the move, using weapons like the Shotgun, the Scorcher, or even a Lancer from the hip.

Be careful when large packs of Wretches attack. It's to avoid getting surrounded, lest you take a punishing beating at the hands of the pack.

VITALS

WEAPONRY

Claws

HEALTH

200

COVER

Unfortunately, Wretches are aware of cover, and they use it fairly well to close on your position. They also like to hop over low cover quickly and can close on your position with surprising speed.

Because they have a low target profile and move fast, dealing with them at a distance is harder than it might seem. This is particularly true when they lie in wait and ambush you already at close range.

TICKER

The Locust Ticker is an organic mine, a literal walking (or scuttling) bomb.

Tickers rush your position and then stop to begin their internal combustion. Before they explode, you have a brief second to hit them with a melee strike, knocking them back through the air. This is very useful to avoid a punishing blast.

Ticker detonations can stun their explosive brethren, and take out any other Locust forces within range. If you have the chance, knocking a Ticker back into a nearby Locust's face is a satisfying and effective tactic.

VITALS

WEAPONRY	HEALTH
Self-Detonation	50

COVER

Tickers use cover in a very irritating and dangerous manner They scuttle quickly from cover to cover like cockroaches, often staying completely out of view, thanks to their low height.

Once they get close enough, they abandon cover and rush your position to detonate. Be prepared for it. Either kill them on the move with a Shotgun or concentrated fire, or be ready to melee them back when they get too close.

SEEDER

The Locust Seeder is a very rare opponent in the campaign. They are more of a threat for friendly COG forces, acting as mobile jammers that interfere with troop communications.

Seeders aren't 'armed' in the traditional sense, but they can launch Nemacysts as living mortars, making them a threat to both infantry and vehicles.

VITALS

WEAPONRY	HEALTH
 Nemacyst	5000

NEMACYST

Nemacysts aren't an enemy in the traditional sense, but there are moments in the campaign when you must destroy these floating bombs.

Nemacysts can float or fly quickly, and their darting movements make them difficult targets. Fortunately, they are very weak, and any automatic weapon fire can down them easily.

VITALS

WEAPONRY	HEALTH
Self-Detonation	25

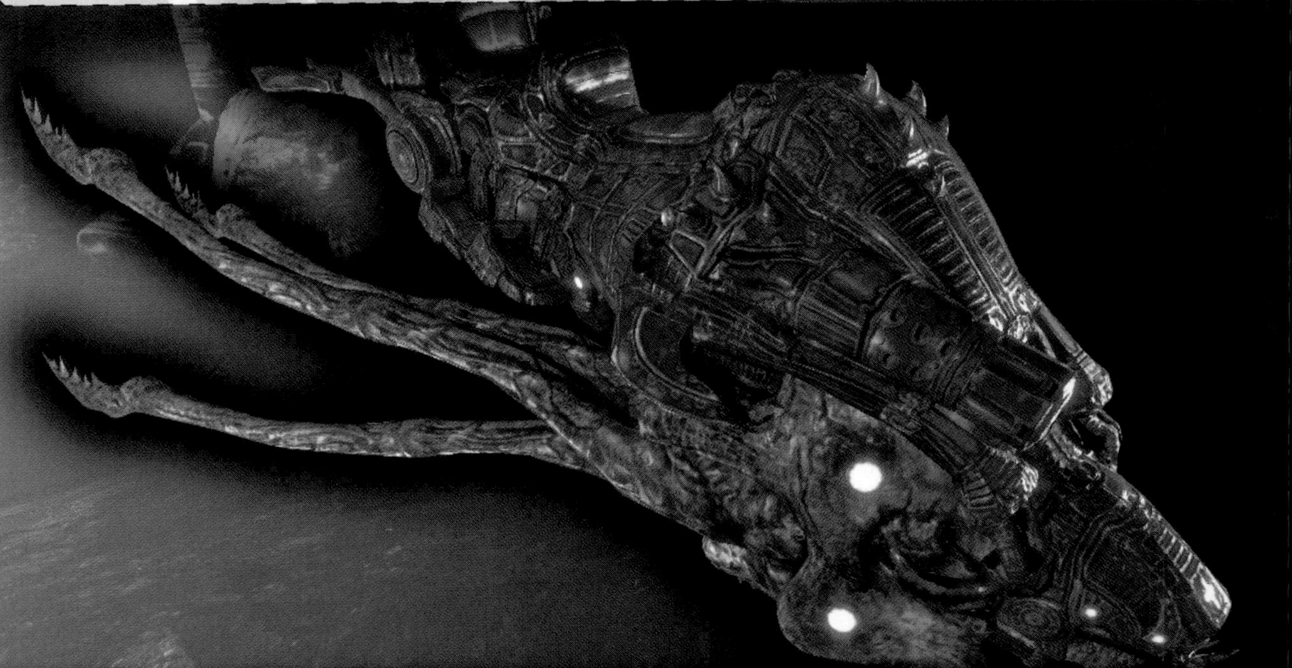

REAVER

The mighty flying Reaver is a serious threat and a distressingly common sight on the battlefield. Reavers strafe ground positions from the air, blasting them with rockets from a distance.

However, Reavers now often land on the ground and approach, firing rockets while their riders suppress you with shots from their elevated perch.

This is bad enough, but it gets worse. If a Reaver gets close enough to you, it attempts to stab you with its talons—and it can do this over low cover!

Whenever Reavers are around, give them your full attention, and unload with the strongest weaponry you have. You can use Grenades against them on the ground—don't hold back!

You can kill their riders, but it's usually not worth the time. Take down the Reaver, and the threat is removed completely.

VITALS

WEAPONRY	HEALTH		
Rockets	1200 In Air	5700 On Ground	1000 Driver

COVER

Reavers don't use cover, but they *do* nullify cover in a very dangerous way. Not only can their pilots fire at you from their greater elevation, but the Reaver itself is a dangerous weapon against you in cover. No matter where you are, if a Reaver starts getting close to you, back off!

BRUMAK

The mighty Brumak is the Locust version of a siege engine and a main battle tank all in one. These bipedal monsters are equipped with twin arm-mounted chainguns and a shoulder-mounted rocket pack.

Thankfully, direct conflict against Brumaks is fairly rare. When you must face them, it's usually with the benefit of serious heavy weapons.

You can blow off their arm or back weaponry. However, in most encounters with them, you're better off simply focusing on their bodies and taking them out as quickly as possible.

VITALS

WEAPONRY

Arm-Mounted Chainguns | Pack-Mounted Rockets

HEALTH

5000	300	500
Body	Arm Weaponry	Main Gun

COVER

Brumaks don't use cover. As for *your* cover, find some and stay out of sight if you're forced to deal with one of these monsters on foot.

CORPSER

The Corpser is as much a tunneling machine for the Locust as it is a biological weapon. The Corpser rarely engages in direct conflict with COG forces, but it can be a serious danger to vehicles.

You don't have to deal with the Corpser directly on foot, but you do have a few run-ins with unfriendly Corpsers during the campaign. Fortunately, in situations where you have to fight, you ride in a powerful vehicle.

VITALS

WEAPONRY

Claws

HEALTH

SPECIAL

HYDRA

Skorge's mutated Reaver mount, the Hydra appears a few times during the story, but you eventually must face it in direct battle.

Your encounter with the Hydra takes place over the course of an entire chapter. It is a lengthy and grueling aerial duel, as Skorge chases you on the back of the beast.

VITALS

WEAPONRY		HEALTH
Rockets	Troika Turret	SPECIAL

ROCKWORM

Rockworms are an unusual subterranean life form. You encounter them when you are forced below ground to confront the Locust on their home turf.

These crawling, armored worms are generally docile creatures, but don't get in front of them when they're moving—they can and will take a bite out of you!

Otherwise, Rockworms are not a threat. They can actually be a useful asset on the battlefield, thanks to their incredibly sturdy rock hide.

Rockworms are also apparently a Locust food source, as you encounter Locust butchering pens at one point in the campaign!

VITALS

WEAPONRY	HEALTH
Viscious Bite	N/A

COVER

Rockworms don't *use* cover, Rockworms *are* cover. The thick, rocky hide that protects the Rockworm can just as easily shield you and your squad mates!

Whenever you see a crawler nearby, you can slam into cover on its hide and move along with it as it crawls through the area. You can mantle over it too, even while it's shuffling around.

Rockworms don't move particularly fast, so they can be very helpful in situations where no 'normal' cover is present.

SKORGE

Skorge has a very special place in the Locust hierarchy, acting as hatchet man for the Locust Queen. You encounter him fairly early in the story, but you don't get a chance to (literally) lock blades with him until much later in the game.

You encounter Skorge as a boss battle at only one point in the game, though he makes other appearances during the story. He does not go down easily!

VITALS

WEAPONRY (Variable)	HEALTH
Gorgon Pistol, Ink Grenades, Chainstaff	SPECIAL

LAKE MONSTER

The massive Lake Monster is a dreadful underwater beast. When you encounter it deep beneath the ground, you are in for a dangerous struggle.

Traditional weaponry cannot harm the Lake Monster, so you must devise more innovative methods to drive it off...

VITALS

WEAPONRY	HEALTH
Tentacles and Giant Mouth	SPECIAL

ACT I

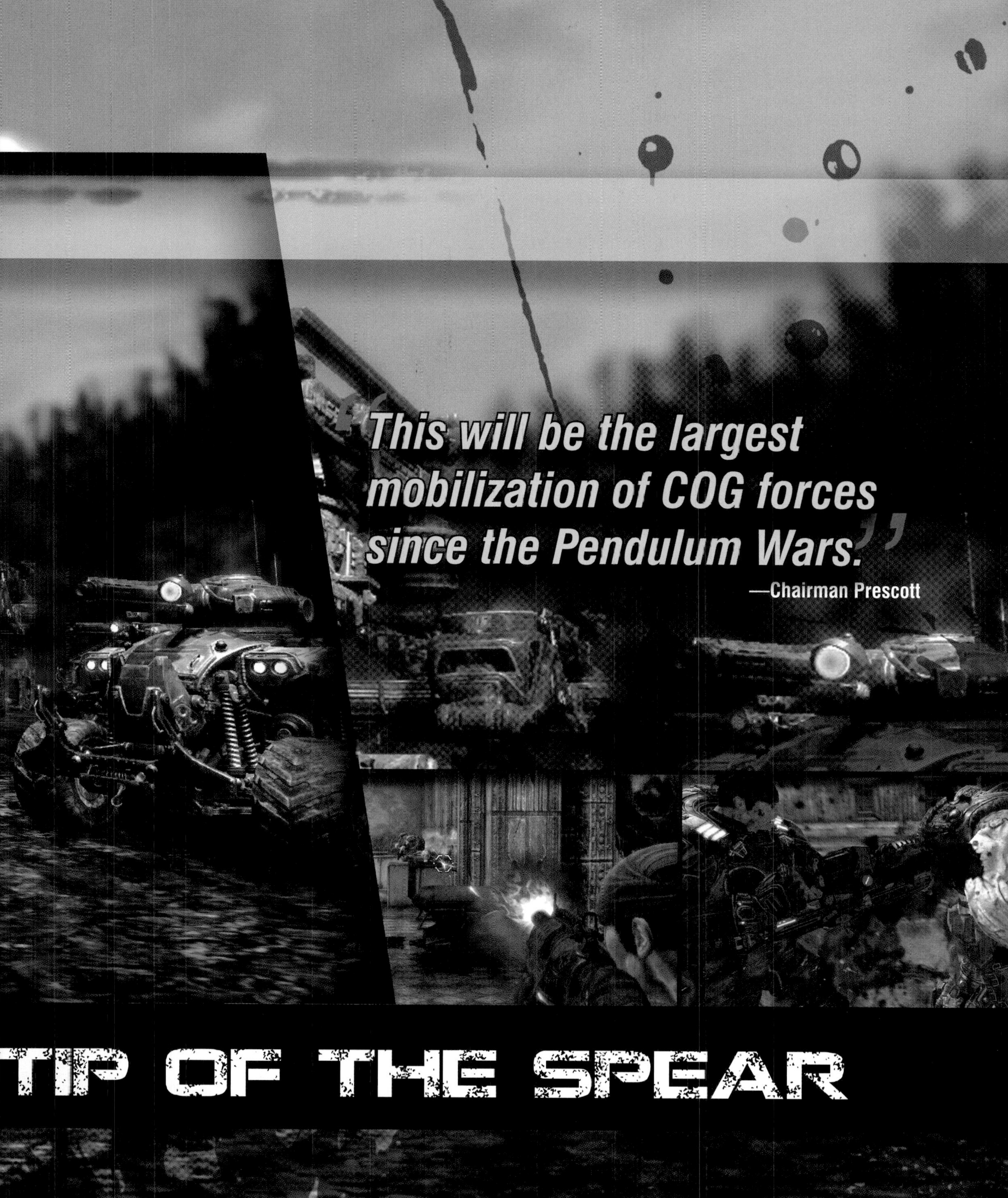

"This will be the largest mobilization of COG forces since the Pendulum Wars."

—Chairman Prescott

TIP OF THE SPEAR

CHAPTER 1: WELCOME TO DELTA

Six months have passed since the detonation of the Lightmass bomb. Six long months, while humanity has waited with hope that perhaps, finally, the grinding war against the Locust is finally over.

But it is not to be. The Locust have counterattacked with even more brutal weapons. Weapons so destructive that they can sink entire cities. The impenetrable stone of Jacinto Plateau has become a final protective shield against the assault of the Locust Horde.

As the story begins, Marcus and Dom are checking a hospital where Anya found word that Maria may be present, just before a Locust raiding party assaults the hospital.

MARCUS FENIX

Son of the scientist Adam Fenix, Marcus spent years imprisoned in a maximum security facility for the crime of desertion in a combat situation. Only Dominic Santiago's good word during the trial saved him from execution.

When he was freed from prison by Dom and re-enlisted into the COG military, he became part of a four-man team credited with detonating the Lightmass bomb and delivering a crippling blow to the Locust.

Now Marcus serves as leader of Delta Squad and is something of a war hero to the newer Gears.

INTEL

As Marcus discusses the war and Dom's search for Maria, he is introduced to a very green new soldier for Delta Squad: Ben Carmine.

BENJAMIN CARMINE

Ben Carmine is one of several Carmine brothers active in the Gears. His brother, Anthony Carmine, was killed during the events of the first *Gears of War* game, though it is possible to play as Anthony during multiplayer matches!

INTEL

After the introduction, you are given a choice: you can either go to training (Chapter 1) or directly into the conflict (Chapter 2). Training is very short, and it's a good refresher if you haven't played Gears of War in awhile. Plus, you may also want to zip through it to pick up the two collectibles in the training grounds.

Don't miss the first collectible at this point.

The Lancer

Standard COG-issue weaponry, the Lancer is an effective assault rifle with a brutal chainsaw bayonet attached on the front.

The Lancer easily can be your primary weapon for the bulk of the campaign. You nearly always have access to it, as well as ammo for it.

Snub Pistol

The standard issue sidearm for Gears, the Snub Pistol is a quick-firing semi-auto pistol with good accuracy. It also has a slight zoom, though it is less useful for long-range sniping—the zoom is best for targeting exposed bits of Locust behind cover.

COLLECTIBLE

01 The Eagle Newspaper

Just down the alley as you begin the training run, check the ground in the middle of the street for the first collectible, **The Eagle Newspaper**.

You can find the second collectible in this small room, opposite the direction that exits the tutorial area.

Frag Grenades

Frag Grenades are very powerful weapons, especially against large groups or Locust behind cover.

At the risk of exposing yourself to enemy fire, you can throw grenades with pinpoint accuracy if you take aim, or you can 'blindfire,' simply throwing a grenade without sighting its landing.

Throwing grenades by hand at nearby targets or enemies openly approaching your cover works extremely well.

You can also use Frag Grenades to close emergence holes. Or you can stick them to walls by tapping Melee when you're near a solid surface. This allows them to act as makeshift proximity mines.

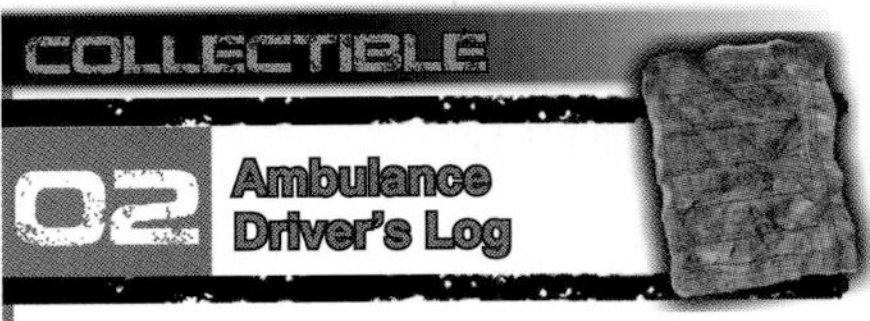

After you drop down the ladder near the end of the training course, turn to your right and make your way into the garage. Inside, you can find the **Ambulance Driver's Log**.

ACHIEVEMENT

GREEN AS GRASS

Completing the tutorial level awards this Achievement.

CHAPTER 2: DESPERATION

A Locust raid on the hospital and its surroundings changes a search for Dom's wife into the first conflict of the game.

Use this chapter to get comfortable with basic combat against Locust Drones. There's plenty of cover available, as well as ample ammunition and a few Frag Grenades here and there throughout the level.

There isn't much in the way of heavy-duty firepower, but you don't really need it.

Just after the mission begins, you are introduced to Tai Kaliso, a burly Gear who makes a welcome addition to your squad.

DEV TIP

If you get mixed up while exploring the hospital, just keep an eye out for the green lights—they always guide you in the proper direction.

—KEN SPENCER

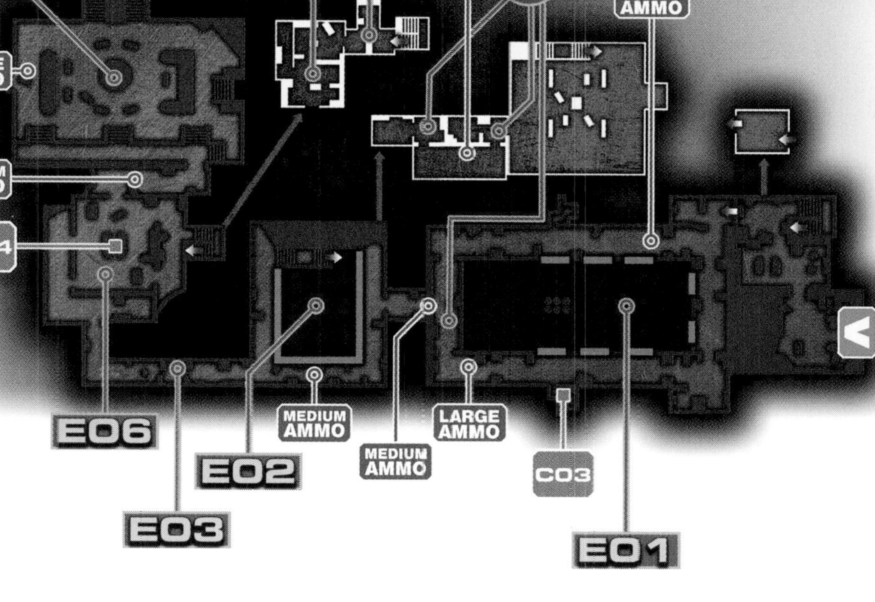

ICON KEY		
START	FINISH	LADDER
ENCOUNTER	COLLECTIBLE	

TAI KALISO

Tai is a burly Gear with a deeply spiritual side. His steady presence in combat makes him a solid and reassuring force in the midst of bloody battles.

Tai's fatalism gives him a certain calmness, as though he is comfortable with the prospect of his death, muting any fear he might have when battling the Locust.

You have the elevation advantage in this encounter, *and* the opposition occupies a ground floor littered with explosive tanks. Wait for the Drones to get close to the explosives, and then shoot them. The resulting explosion should decimate the entire Locust wave. If there are any survivors, use your superior vantage point to eliminate them.

A few drones in the hospital's upper floor don't present a serious threat. Your teammates may take out a few more on the bottom floor before you even spot them. If not, use the available cover and pick them off from a distance.

ACT I

A couple of Drones emerge from the end of the hallway as you enter it from the hospital's upper gallery, but they are quickly mowed down by a Raven hovering outside the hospital.

Note that it is possible to take the *lower* route through this area, skipping the Raven encounter entirely. Instead of going through the upper hall, descend the stairs to where you saw the Drones on the first floor, and you can follow Dom. This actually skips the next two encounters on the upper floor, but you wind up fighting the same number of Drones in the lower hall. Both paths end up in the same area at Encounter 6 in this walkthrough.

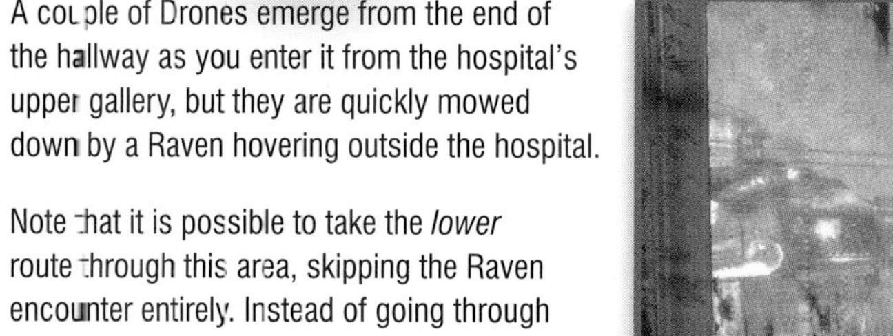

Hammerburst WEAPON

Taking out these Drones gives you your first opportunity to pick up the Hammerburst. A good complement to the Lancer, it has slightly higher damage and a lower rate of fire than the Lancer.

It can also be fired in semi-automatic mode, offering a potentially increased rate of fire over simply holding the trigger. The tradeoff is considerably worse recoil.

You do lose access to the Lancer's chainsaw, but the Hammerburst is slightly better at a distance due to its zoom capability. Plus, you almost always have access to it, as it is standard Locust weaponry.

COLLECTIBLE

03 Doctor's Journal

Once you've cleared out the second encounter, check the hallway on the left side of the room. A small room containing the **Doctor's Journal** is just off of the hall.

You find the first movable cover in this room. Slam into cover behind the table here, and you automatically flip over the table to use it as makeshift cover.

The Drone you encounter here is armed with a Boltok Pistol. This Locust weapon is stronger than the Gears' own Snub Pistol, though it's a bit slower and less accurate.

Take note of this Drone's unusual helmet. He's a bit faster and weaker than the usual Drone variety, and he always comes equipped with a Boltok.

Right in the center of the room is a reception desk for hospital employees. Check the ground to find the **Jacinto Medical Center File.**

The pair of Drones in this room isn't a serious threat, but you may have an opportunity to test out a meat shield. If one of the Locust is downed, approach it and tap the Cover button to pick it up as a body shield. While you are carrying your fleshy barrier, you move more slowly, and you can only use pistol-class weaponry, but you are protected from most frontal fire…for a short, messy time at least.

There's a small pack of Drones out in the courtyard, but there are also COG reinforcements nearby. Take cover up on the walkway above the courtyard, or behind one of the planters in the courtyard itself.

Once you finish the battle, a Reaver drops in from the sky. Don't worry, though; it sticks around for only a moment. Stay in cover and take some potshots. It's safe to move on once it departs.

Two Drones are roaming around the hospital in this lobby area—it's a brief fight.

A pack of Drones at the opposite side of the cafeteria make for a small firefight. Because there are several Drones present at a decent distance behind cover, you might get a chance to see injured Drones helped up by their buddies. Just like Gears, Locust can assist their downed teammates!

If you want to make a basic flank attack, head down the hallway beside the cafeteria—you can come in facing the Locust flank.

A small room containing the **COG Letterhead** is immediately beside the cafeteria.

REPORT

THERE IS AN EXPLOSIVE TANK ON THE ROOM'S LEFT EDGE, LOWER LEVEL, AND ONE BY THE DOOR ON THE UPPER LEVEL.

When you emerge into this courtyard area, a massive King Raven comes crashing through the glass ceiling, and a trio of Drones attacks from the gallery above the ground level.

You can either stay put on the ground, remaining behind cover, or you can make your way over to the stairs on either end of the courtyard and flank the Locust on the second floor.

Several Drones assault the hospital lobby as you enter the room. Given your elevation advantage, this is an easy battle if you stay above once you step down the stairs to trigger their attack.

After you take down the first wave, a few more Drones come in through the door that flashes with an emergency light. You can either stay up top or use the abundant cover in the middle of the room to engage them at medium range.

The **COG Proclamation** is located on the second floor of the hospital lobby, beside an ammo crate on the right as you enter the room.

As you exit the hospital, you're put into a siege situation with the largest Locust assault yet, located out in the street below the hospital. At the landing above the street, make a sharp right turn and check behind the pillar to find a COG Tag collectible. However, you have both Tai and Carmine assisting, so there's plenty of friendly firepower on your side.

Use the available sandbag cover on the upper level above the street to clear out the first pack of Drones. A Reaver shows up briefly—just avoid getting caught out in the street with it, and it flies off after a few moments.

Once you neutralize the first wave, a King Raven shows up and hoses down the street with its superior firepower, clearing a path before it flies away.

Make your way down onto the street and move forward until another group of Drones sets up a blockade down the street. When they do, you can go through a shop on the left side of the street to flank the Drones at the blockade.

Once you're past the blockade, there's one last pack of Drones at the end of the street, just past a ruined Rig off to the side.

Reavers shoot guns at you, but not rockets.

Just as you exit the hospital onto the landing above the street, make a sharp right turn and check behind the pillar to find the **COG Tags of Dylan Murphy.**

Anya is a tactical commander and the advisor for Delta Squad. Her intelligence is vital for combat operations carried out by Gear squads.

She was on-site at the hospital with Delta Squad in an effort to find information about a Jane Doe who matched the description of Dom's wife.

DOMINIC SANTIAGO

Dom is an old friend of Marcus and a longtime battlefield companion. Their personalities and temperaments match up well, providing a solid backbone for Delta Squad to lean on during brutal battles with the Locust.

Dom is tormented by the absence of his missing wife, Maria, and struggles to find any trace of her during the course of this campaign.

ACHIEVEMENT

ACHIEVEMENT: IT'S A TRAP!

Completing Chapter 2 awards this Achievement.

INTEL

The Locust forces retreat after the Gears push them from the hospital, behavior very uncharacteristic of the Locust Horde.

Dom has a chance to speak with Anya again after the fighting cools down, but it appears that Maria has been checked out of the hospital and is no longer present. Dom is furious, but there is nothing that can be done, as a major offensive effort by the COG to strike back against the Locust is beginning.

A huge force of COG troops, including Rigs equipped with Grindlifts to send infantry down into the Hollow sets out in a convoy toward the city of Landown, setting the stage for the next Chapter.

CHAPTER 3: ROLLING THUNDER

A massive Gear assault force has been assembled, as the COG plans to strike back against the Locust directly in their underground home.

Gears are to be dropped into the hollow in Grindlifts, which are tunneling 'drop pods' that can tear through the surface crust and deposit forces directly into the heart of the Locust-held underworld.

To do so, the attack must breach Locust defenses around the town of Landown. This was one of the towns taken over early in the war against the Locust, and has long been under their control.

Delta Squad begins the journey on the rig known as "Betty," piloted by Dizzy. You see a couple familiar faces, Cole and Baird, briefly during the long ride to Landown.

Most of this mission takes place on the Rig itself. You'll have to handle the Locust threats that periodically arise.

DIZZY

Dizzy is a conscripted Stranded. He took the Lifeboat assistance from the COG and Dizzy now drives a Rig for the Gear forces in exchange for food and shelter for his family.

Dizzy is a colorful character to say the least, but he's a good pilot and a skilled mechanic. He is charged with piloting Delta Squad's Rig during the assault on Landown.

COLLECTIBLE

08 Grindlift Spec Sheet

Find the **Grindlift Spec Sheet** directly on the Rig. Check behind you, stuck to the Rig's wall.

ENCOUNTER 01

ENEMY PRESENCE

NEMACYST MORTARS

A massive bombardment begins, with Seeders raining Nemacyst mortars down on the convoy. Ravens, Rigs, and Centaurs are all taken down, and even part of the canyon wall comes crashing down in front of the Rig on which Delta is stationed.

Get up on the turret mounted at the top of the Rig and prepare for directed Nemacyst bombardment. You need to shoot down the Nemacyst before they can critically damage the Rig. If you hold them off long enough, friendly Ravens silence the bombardment by killing off the Seeders in the distance.

Shotgun

WEAPON

A typical secondary weapon for the Gears, the Shotgun is ideal for close-quarters combat, and it's handy against the Wretches that so often accompany Locust Drone assaults.

DEV TIP

The number of Mortars that you have to destroy increases on each difficulty level, starting at one for Casual, then three, five, and finally seven for Insane.

Also, give the Shotgun a try against the Nemacyst—it can make your task easier than the turret does.

—DAVE NASH

Turret

WEAPON

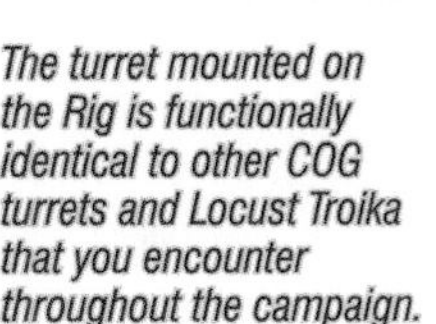

The turret mounted on the Rig is functionally identical to other COG turrets and Locust Troika that you encounter throughout the campaign.

A very powerful weapon, it does not need to be reloaded, but you can cool the barrel by holding the reload button to prevent it from overheating. This allows to you fire in long, sustained bursts punctuated by occasional cooling.

The turrets are powerful enough to be helpful against even heavy Locust forces, and they are absolutely lethal against normal Drone ground forces.

The next threat is a wave of Reavers that assaults the Rig. Again, stay up on the turret and hose down any Reavers that get too close with a spray of turret fire.

To get past this ambush, you need to fend off only a single Reaver that pulls up on the left. Just make sure you quickly dispatch it as it draws near. You can use the turret to take it down quickly.

As the Rig reaches the end of the narrow trail along the canyon ridgeline, the brakes give out. The Rig careens to a halt, damaged and smoking. Dizzy quickly gets out to commence repairs, but you must hold off the Locust while he does so.

There are two full crates of ammo and some Frag Grenades off to the left near Collectible #9. Grab the goods and then make your way over to the cover at the fallen pillars.

A Locust Emergence Hole pops up behind the cover. If you want to stymie the attack completely, you can move up to the second layer of cover (closest to the E-Hole) and toss in a grenade. If not, stay back behind cover and pick off the Drones as they emerge.

DEV TIP

The first two Emergence Holes overlap slightly. Killing roughly half of the Drones from the first causes the second hole to open.

After you clear out the holes, the Reaver causes the pillar to fall, and the ambush from the ledge above begins. You have to hold out for about 15 seconds before you can retreat to the Rig.

—DAVE NASH

Once you defeat the first wave, a second Emergence Hole opens behind the first. Again, if you have a grenade on hand, you may be able to shut the hole before any more grubs can get out of it.

After a short time, a Reaver flies past, causing a standing pillar to topple. This creates more cover, allowing you to deal with the enemies that flank you up high on the cliff to the right.

Friendly Rigs show up during the fight, and you get covering fire from Baird and Cole, which helps to take off the heat. More Nemacyst Mortars begin to land, and Locust emerge on the ridge above you. Hold out as long as you can. As soon as Dizzy says the Rig is good to go, retreat to the ladder to get out of here!

Ammo Requisition Form

Find the **Ammo Requisition Form** just to the left of the Rig as you hop down to defend Dizzy. It's near an ammo crate by the bushes.

CHAPTER 4:
THE BIG PUSH

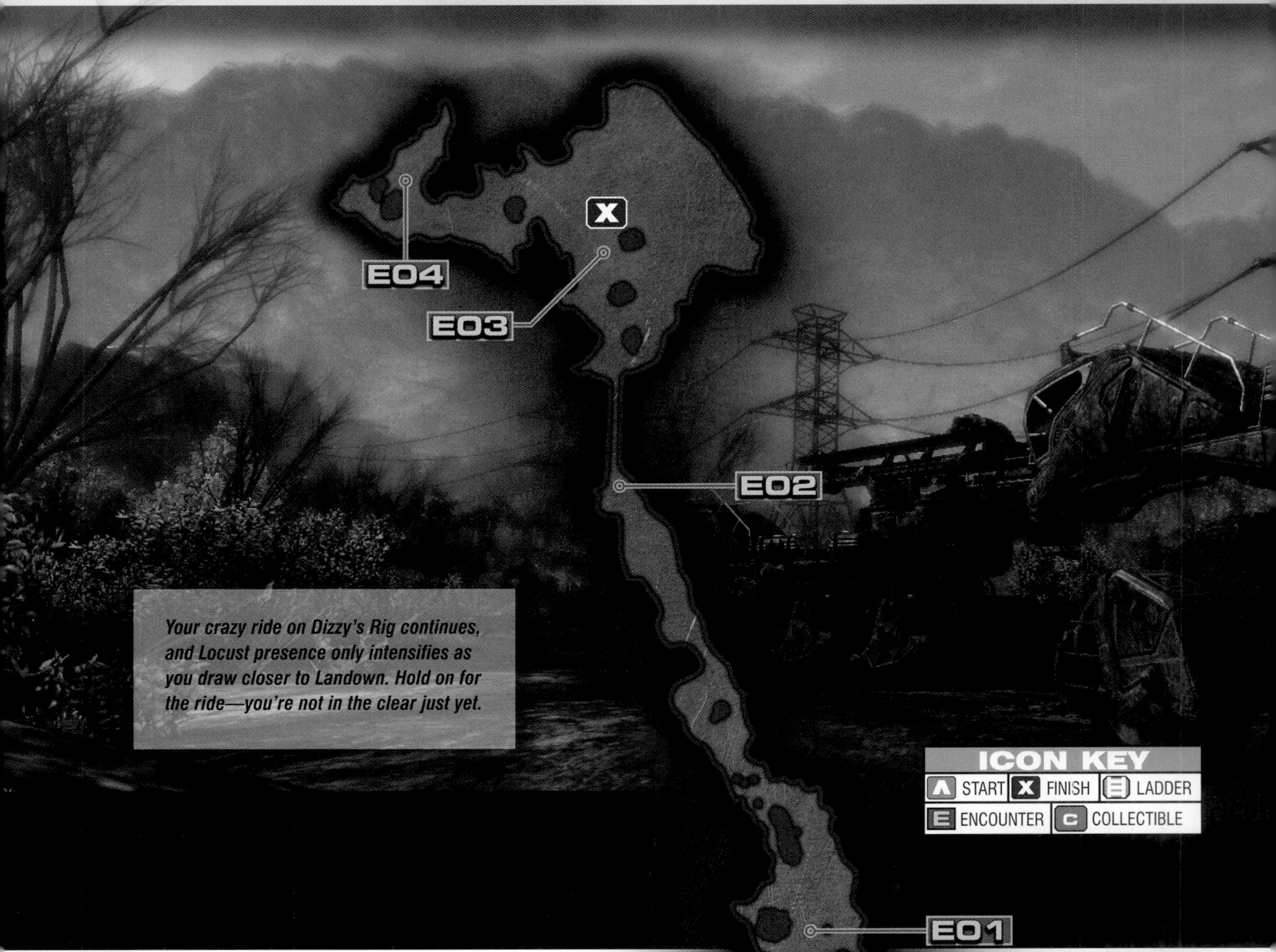

Your crazy ride on Dizzy's Rig continues, and Locust presence only intensifies as you draw closer to Landown. Hold on for the ride—you're not in the clear just yet.

After you remount the Rig, Dizzy takes off from the site of the ambush, but it quickly becomes clear that you aren't free of the Locust threat. Swarms of Drones pour out of holes in the ground, and a massive Brumak stomps by.

DEV TIP

Just to buy a bit of breathing room, you can attempt to shoot off the grapple hooks as the Drones climb onto the hijacked rig (as well as your own, later).

—*DAVE NASH*

The Drones begin to assault a nearby Rig, quickly grappling aboard and taking over the vehicle. There's nothing you can do to prevent them from stealing the Rig. However, you do have to deal with them once they hijack the Rig and use it to attack Dizzy's ride.

As the commandeered Rig comes within shooting distance, take cover on the sides to hide out from any Drones firing at you from the opposing Rig.

The fight with the hijacked Rig takes on new urgency as you draw close to a narrow bridge across a chasm in the road. You have to make sure that your Rig is the one that gets on the bridge—there isn't room for two.

As you get close to the bridge, two Drones leap down from a ledge onto the Rig. Then two grapplers climb up the sides. If you're quick, you may be able to take out the grappling hooks before the Drones can even climb up.

After you deal with the grapplers, Dizzy gives you a chance to take out the other Rig permanently. The Drone driver in the Rig is in a bulletproof chamber at the Rig's front, but Dizzy rams the hijacked Rig repeatedly, breaking the glass.

Shoot the Drone driver quickly. Once you take him down, the Locust-held Rig plunges into the chasm, while your ride makes it safely across. You *must* kill the enemy driver before you reach the bridge, or your Rig will be the one that falls into the pit.

As you near Landown, the Locust resistance intensifies, and you see the truly dangerous opposition emerge. Brumaks and even a Corpser assault the convoy as it approaches the city.

You can't affect the outcome of the battles that wage here. However, you can kill a Brumak about halfway along the ride. Get on the turret and attack it aggressively, as it shoots down a Raven.

Also about midway to Landown, a pair of grappler Drones attacks your Rig. If you're ready for them, you may be able to shoot them off the side of your Rig before they can even board it. If not, a chainsaw to the face also works well.

As you reach the end of the ride, a Corpser attacks the convoy, leaping on a Rig from above and sinking it. You can't help that Rig, but you have a bigger and nastier problem to handle, as a lone Brumak comes into view in your Rig's path.

The last danger you must deal with is a Brumak directly in your path. Man the turret on the Rig and mow it down. It's quickest to simply aim for center mass and unload as quickly as possible, rather than trying to aim for its arms and possibly missing while it bombards the Rig.

Once the Brumak is eliminated, the path to Landown is clear, and Dizzy takes Delta Squad in.

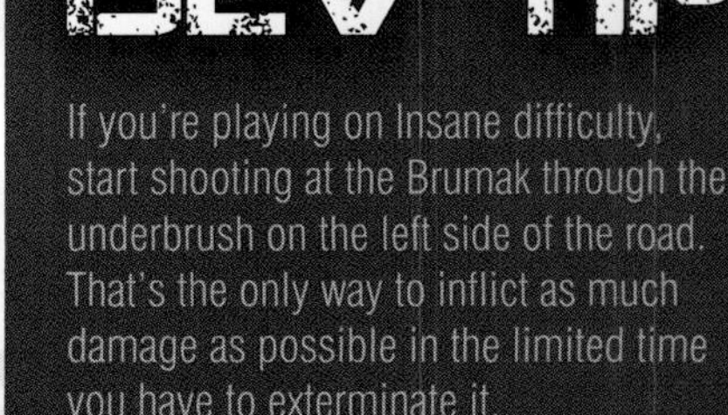

If you're playing on Insane difficulty, start shooting at the Brumak through the underbrush on the left side of the road. That's the only way to inflict as much damage as possible in the limited time you have to exterminate it.

—*DAVE NASH*

ACHIEVEMENT

ESCORT SERVICE

Completing The Big Push awards this Achievement.

CHAPTER 5: ROADBLOCKS

As the COG forces move into Landown, an attack by Locust Tickers cripples Tai's Rig and threatens your own.

Your team is forced to disembark and clear the path on the ground so that Dizzy can move the Rig and its cargo of Grindlifts into position.

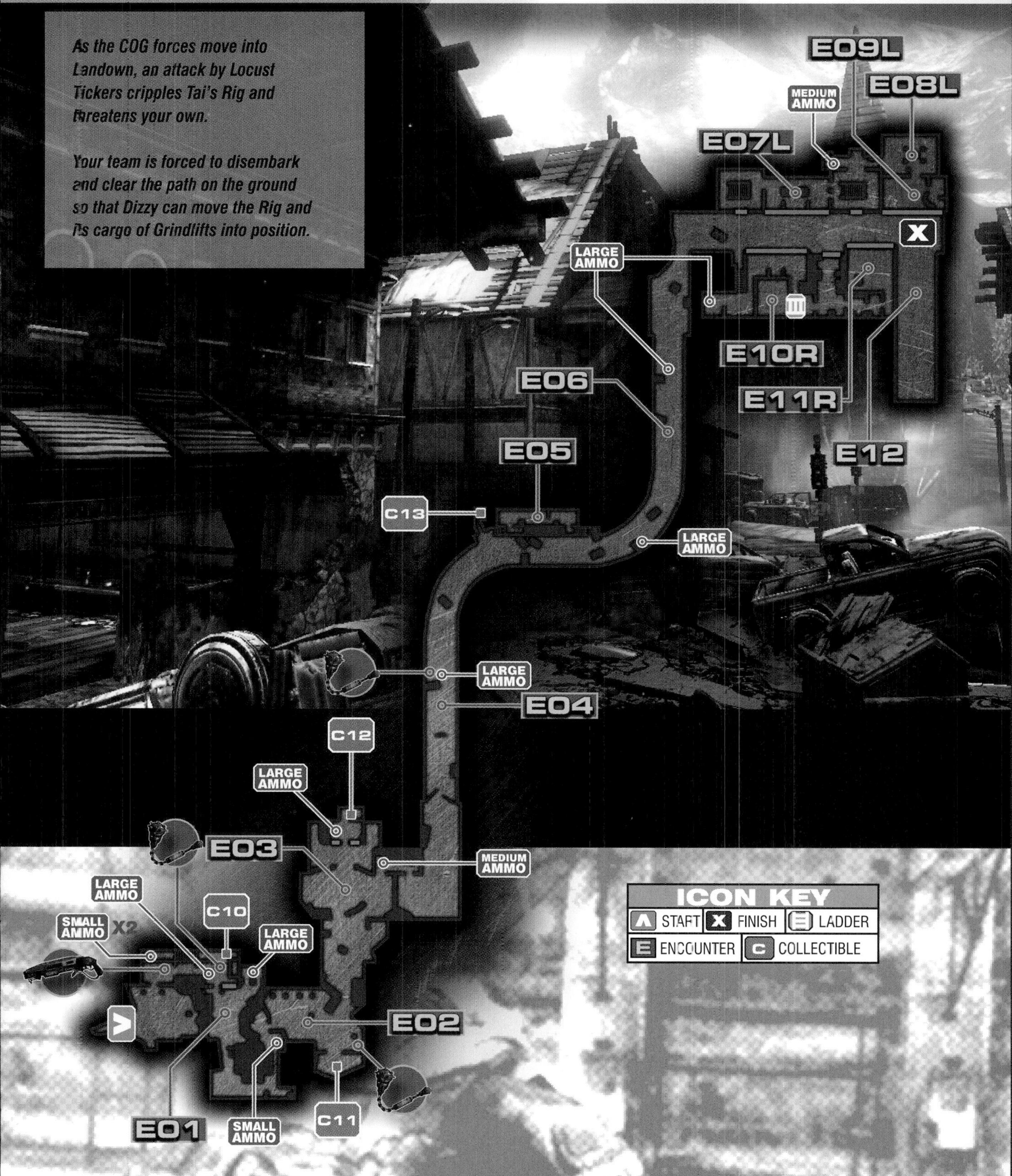

ICON KEY		
START	FINISH	LADDER
ENCOUNTER	COLLECTIBLE	

As your team moves into the ruined streets of Landown, Tai joins your squad from the wrecked remnants of his Rig…and his squad.

The town isn't heavily fortified, but Locust threats are definitely present. Make your way into the building across from your start position and check upstairs for a collectible. Then head back downstairs and proceed through the building to get into the open street outside.

As you go through the bottom floor, you catch your first glimpse of the Ticker. These agile Locust creatures have giant bombs strapped to their backs, and they are all too happy to rush your position and detonate.

Find the **Jacinto Sentinel Newspaper** upstairs in the very first building you enter. It's on the floor near some Frag Grenades.

When you get out into the street, the Tickers attack in earnest. Use your Shotgun to take them out. If they get too close, either roll away or melee them to knock them back before they explode.

Once you clear out the bulk of the Ticker pack, a final Ticker blasts through a fence at the other side of the street. Take it out, and then go through the fence to reach the next part of the street.

Once you clear the street, Control warns that the sky is filled with Nemacyst, meaning you won't be getting any air support. Grab the collectible over in the monument area, and then proceed up the street toward the gas station.

After you walk through the back alley and emerge onto the next portion of the street, be ready for another Ticker assault. You may want to hang back and let your squad mates take the brunt of the attack while you pick off the Tickers from the relative safety of the alley.

Find the **Memorial Inscription** by checking the wall of the war memorial area after you clear the Tickers from the yard. This place is a monument to the soldiers who fell during the Pendulum Wars.

ACT

The Locust have fortified this position at a rundown Imulsion station. Several Drones and Grenadiers are present on the ground, and a pair of Troika—one to your left and one ahead, atop the station—present a serious threat.

Stay in cover as you approach the fueling station. If possible, blow up the pumps when the Locust on the ground are near them.

Partway through the battle, a Nemacyst Mortar barrage comes down. Then a friendly Raven shows up and mows down the Troika on the roof, eliminating that unpleasant threat.

DEV TIP

On Hardcore and Insane difficulty, they're not kidding about the lack of air support. You *must* take out at least a few of the Nemacyst for the Raven to come down and eliminate the Troika on the roof of the gas station.

If you don't, you have to take out the Troika yourself, possibly with a grenade from the side.

Once the entire Locust force at the gas station is eliminated (including the Troika on the roof), your Centaur backup arrives to destroy the flanking Troika.

—DAVE NASH

Find the **Landown Delivery Driver's Note** at the back of the Imulsion station on the ground.

Finally, Baird and Cole roll by in their Rig, and a friendly Centaur crushes the Troika flanking you on the left, safely clearing your path ahead.

Check inside the station for another collectible, and then hop over the fence to the right of the station and move on.

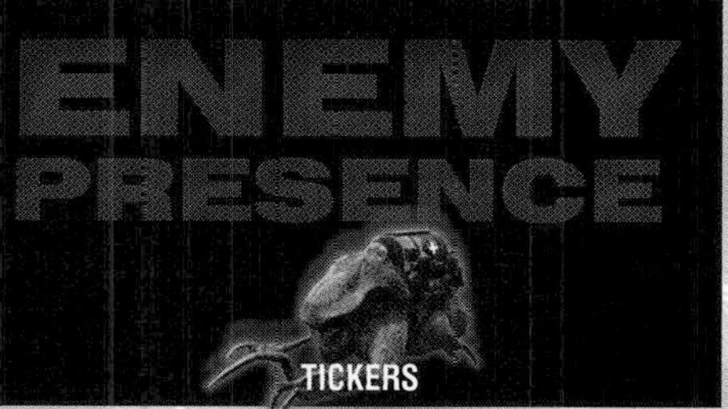

Past the fueling station, a dark and lengthy tunnel twists and turns toward your destination. Dizzy backs you up as you enter the tunnel, providing light from the Rig.

This is greatly needed, because shortly after you enter the tunnel, the Ticker parade begins. Small, organic bombs swarm out of the darkness to attack your squad.

Use the Shotgun, stay mobile, and use your teammates to sponge up some of the damage. Remember to melee these creatures if they come up next to you and prepare to detonate.

Once you reach about halfway through the tunnel, a pile of wrecked cars blocks your path. Before you enter the side hall where Encounter 5 is located, be sure to check just *before* the stairs on the left for another small room containing a collectible.

Find the **Pvt. Samuel Lee's COG Tags** in a small room off to the left side of the tunnel. This is *before* you ascend the very short steps into the side hall that leads around the cars blocking your path in the main tunnel.

A pair of Tickers emerges from the hole in the wall at the end of this small hallway. Don't go charging through unprepared!

Past the roadblock, more Tickers emerge from the darkness and attack your squad. Employ the same tactics that you've used to get this far, and you should soon see the light of day beyond the tunnel.

Don't get too eager, though—as you move toward the end of the tunnel, a Reaver flies in and lands in front of your squad.

The Reaver is a nasty threat. The mounted riders can fire down on you and the Reaver itself fires rockets. Plus, if it gets close to you, it raises one of its tentacles to strike, forcing you to move out of the way quickly.

Try to keep your distance and hammer the Reaver with fire. If you have any Frag Grenades left, use them here. If not, just be ready to back up from your cover should it approach too closely.

Once you eliminate the Reaver, exit the tunnel to reach your first path split. You can choose to head left into the hotel or right onto the rooftops.

These discrete branches always rejoin after a brief detour. In co-op play, you and your partner each take one of the routes. If you're playing solo and you want to see them all, no problem—just replay the chapter and pick the alternate path.

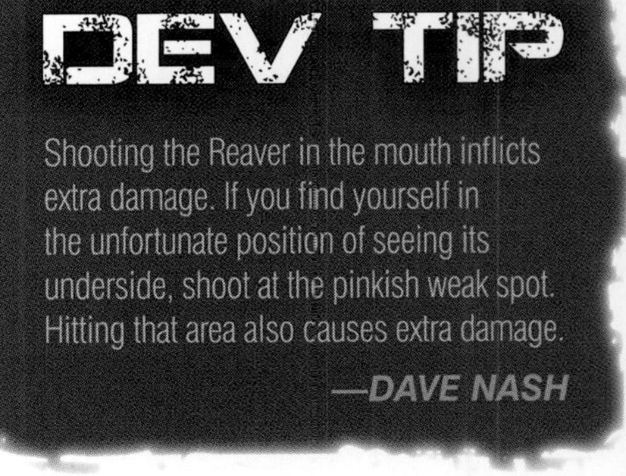

Shooting the Reaver in the mouth inflicts extra damage. If you find yourself in the unfortunate position of seeing its underside, shoot at the pinkish weak spot. Hitting that area also causes extra damage.

—DAVE NASH

LEFT PATH

ENCOUNTER 07

ENEMY PRESENCE

DRONES

Inside the hotel, head upstairs and you are greeted by several unfriendly Locust Drones. Take them down, and then wait for Dom on the opposite roof. The door into the next building is sealed; you need Dom to blast it open with a mortar.

Wait for Dom to shell the building. When the door is blown off, you can head inside.

DEV TIP

You can help out Dom and Tai on the opposite roof from here if you clear out your own Drones quickly enough.

Oh, and don't wait around on the rooftop here for too long. Mortar-wielding Drones a few rooftops down may start shelling you.

—DAVE NASH

Inside the bombed-out building, a Drone and a Grenadier quickly confront you. Use the column supports for cover to eliminate them both.

When they're cleared out, the door to the rooftop Mortar crew is on the right side of the room. However, you can actually shoot out through the windows rather than go through the door immediately.

Kill the pair of Mortar-wielding Drones here, and then pick up the Mortar to finish off the Mortar Drones on the opposite rooftop. If you hear a yell of 'Incoming!' from your partner, be sure to dodge back inside the building—you don't want to eat a full Mortar barrage.

Mortar

The powerful Mortar is a difficult weapon to use on the move, as it is too bulky and cumbersome to carry long distances.

In exchange, the Mortar is ideal for assaulting large groups of enemies at a safe distance. It is devastating in open areas, where you can range your target with your first shot and then rain down destruction from above.

Firing the Mortar from the hip is a bit of a desperation move. It reloads far too slowly to be used up close. Take advantage of it for eliminating nearby groups, and then ditch it when you need to get moving again.

Taking the right path, you initially deal with a lone Drone that climbs down a ladder from the higher rooftop above. Eliminate him and then climb the ladder to find some ammo and a Mortar.

If Dom is still fighting over on the hotel roof, you can use the Mortar to shell the Drones there. If not, use it to blast open the building that blocks Dom's path just across the street. Once he's in, you can ditch the Mortar and climb back down.

Jack rips the door here to allow you entry into the next building's rooftop. Take out the Mortar Drones on the rooftop, and then finish off any Mortar Drones on the hotel rooftop if they're still alive.

You can usually get line of sight on the Mortar Drones here from inside the building that Jack opens. Check from the windows; you may be able to shoot them without even going out in the open.

—DAVE NASH

No matter which route you take in the preceding path split, you end up on a rooftop armed with a Mortar...hopefully with a spare nearby. This is important, because a mighty Brumak comes stomping out of the nearby tunnel a few seconds later!

You need to take down this threat before it can destroy Dizzy's Rig, along with your chances of riding the Grindlift.

Shell it repeatedly with your Mortar. If you took the left path (hotel route), you may need to take cover as it comes out, because it fires a rocket barrage at the rooftop. On the right side, it usually ignores you, so you can fire more freely.

With two Mortars on either rooftop, you should have plenty of ammo to down this adversary. But if you run out, you can still use conventional weaponry to finish it off.

As long as you kill the Brumak before it gets to the street's intersection and fires on the Rig, you can clear this mission successfully.

The difficulty setting determines the number of Mortar hits required to kill the Brumak: one hit on Casual, two hits on Normal, four hits on Hardcore, and five on Insane.

—DAVE NASH

CHAPTER 6: DIGGING IN

Pushing past the Locust defenses, your Rig has finally arrived at the heart of Landown. As Dizzy prepares to deploy the Grindlifts, a final desperate push from the Locust threatens the deployment zone.

You must hold off the waves of Locust until the Grindlifts are ready!

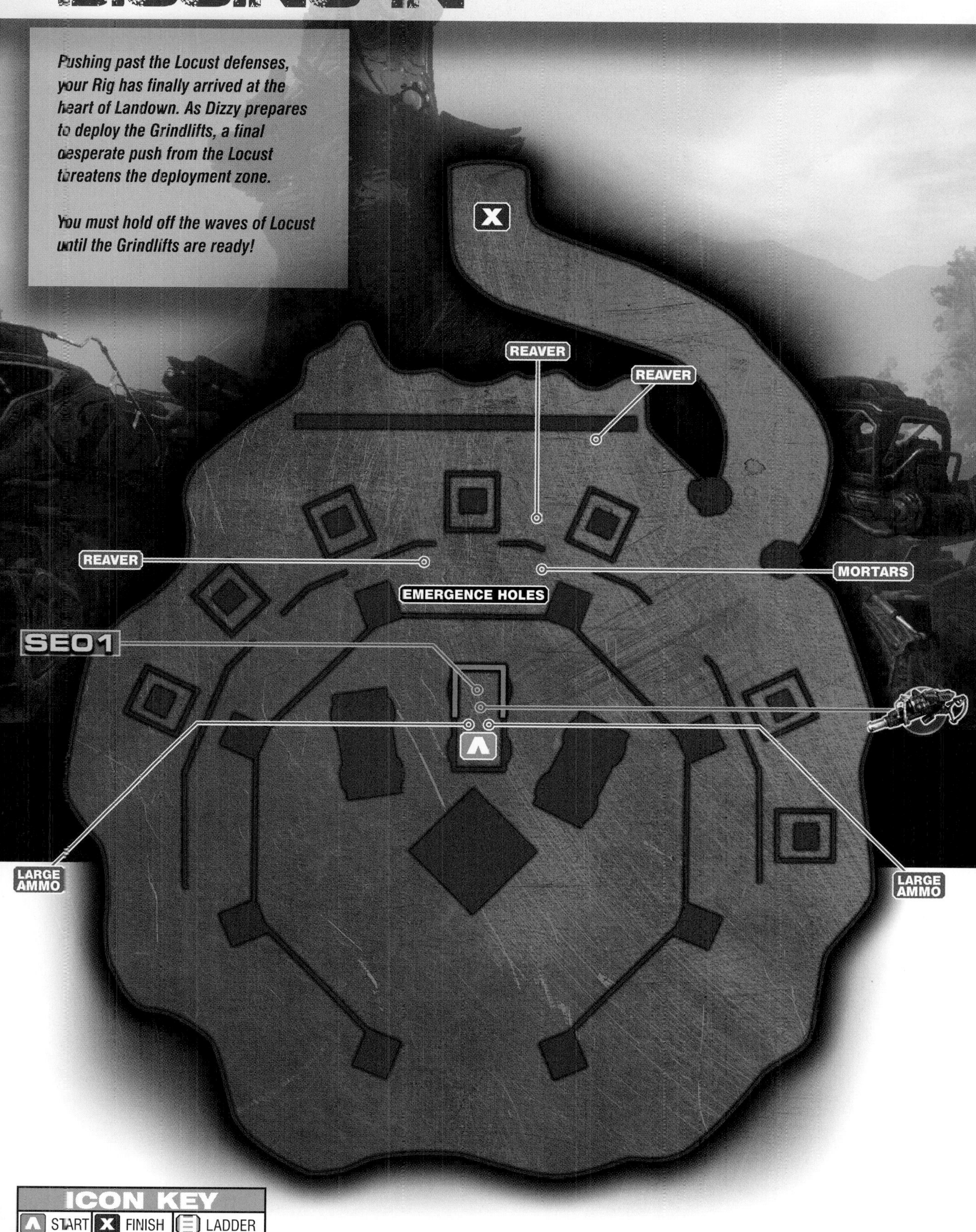

ICON KEY

START | FINISH | LADDER
ENCOUNTER | COLLECTIBLE

The final battle in Act One takes place entirely on Rig 314. You need to hold off the Locust long enough for Dizzy to ready the Grindlifts.

Until then, you have to deal with the Locust. All of the Locust forces attack from the front. There's no subtlety here, just lots of enemies!

The first wave consists of several Emergence Holes out in front of you. You can seal up the holes with a Mortar shot or grenade, or simply unload on them with the turret.

After you deal with the holes, Drones armed with Mortars move in on the right. Try to take them down swiftly. You really don't have any place to run from a Mortar shelling!

Once you eliminate the Mortars, Boomers stomp in from the right, far back in the field. You may be able to eliminate them at a distance before they can fully bring their Boomshots to bear on the Rig.

Be careful; part way through the fight, a few Grappler Drones try to sneak-attack your Rig directly! You should hear a yell from a squad mate and the clang of metal on metal when their hooks hit, so be ready to disengage the frontal battle and kill the Drones quickly.

Finally, the last attack comes from a pair of Reavers, one to the left and one to the right. The turret is likely gone by this point, but you may still have some Mortar shots left. If not, you can simply unload with your Lancer fire until you bag them.

Once the last Reaver drops, this chapter and this act are complete, and you hop aboard the Grindlift. Thus begins the true mission deep within the Hollow as you take the fight to the Locust!

DEV TIP

Because the turret eventually ends up getting destroyed, hop on it immediately and use it for as long as you can. Once it gets destroyed, you can switch to the Mortar for the last few enemy groups.

If you're going Mortar-happy, it's about four clicks of distance to hit the Emergence Holes and Mortar Drones. Try full range to hit the Boomers as they enter the battlefield, about one click short of max for the right Reaver, and four clicks for the left.

The Grappler Drones come up about a minute after the fight starts, so they could arrive during any stage of the battle, depending on how quickly you're eliminating the Locust forces.

—DAVE NASH

ACHIEVEMENT

GIRL ABOUT TOWN

Finishing Digging In awards this Achievement.

ACT II

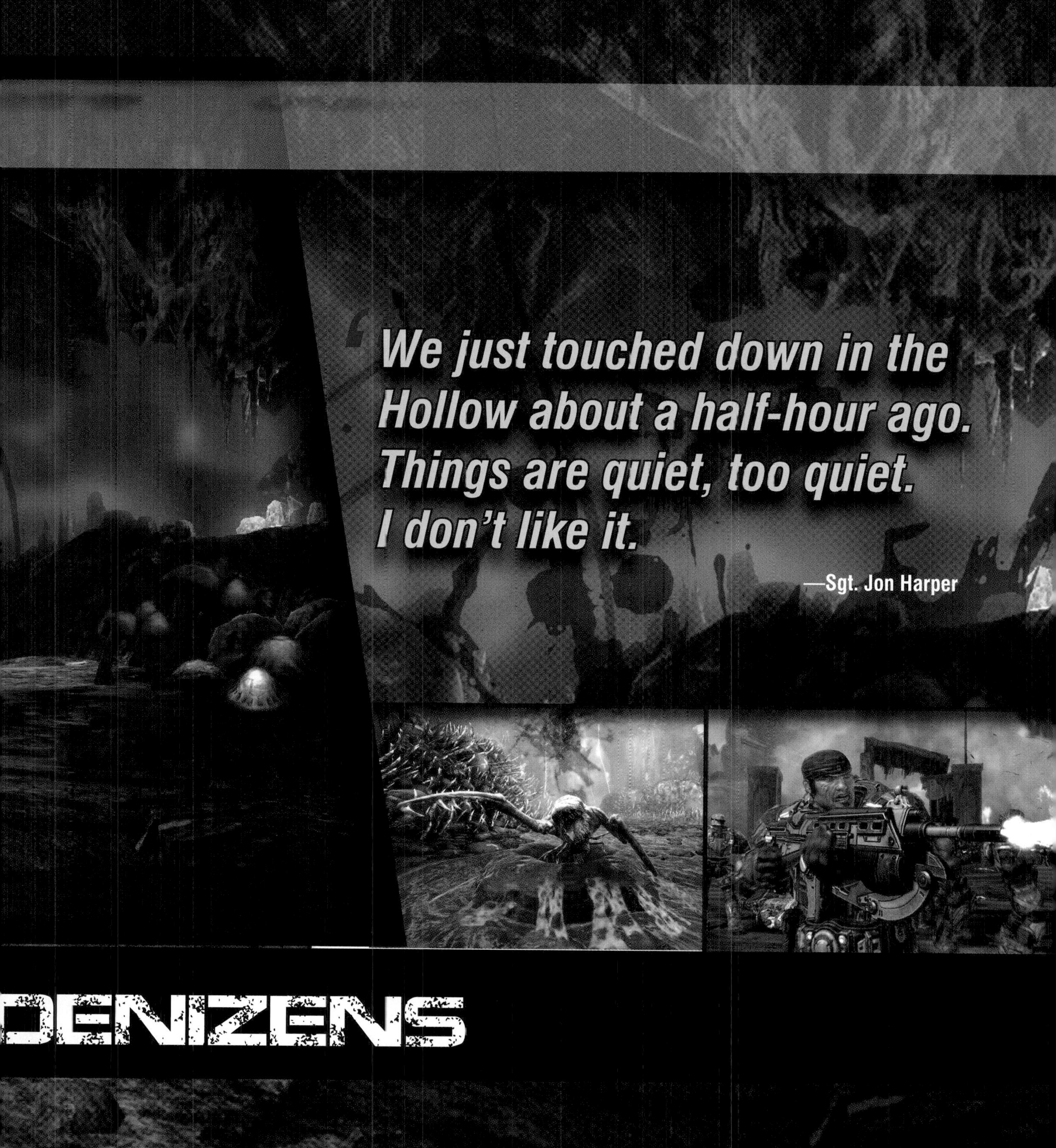
"We just touched down in the Hollow about a half-hour ago. Things are quiet, too quiet. I don't like it.
—Sgt. Jon Harper
DENIZENS

CHAPTER 1: SCATTERED

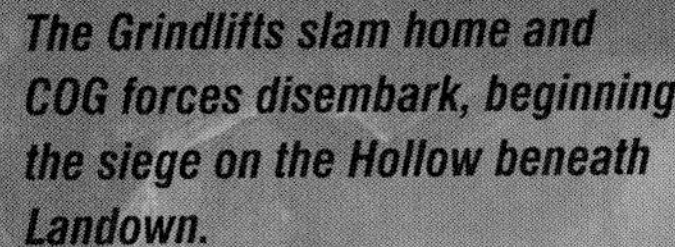

The Grindlifts slam home and COG forces disembark, beginning the siege on the Hollow beneath Landown.

This is the first concentrated assault that COG troops have made against the Locust on their home turf, and many unsettling discoveries await you beneath the surface.

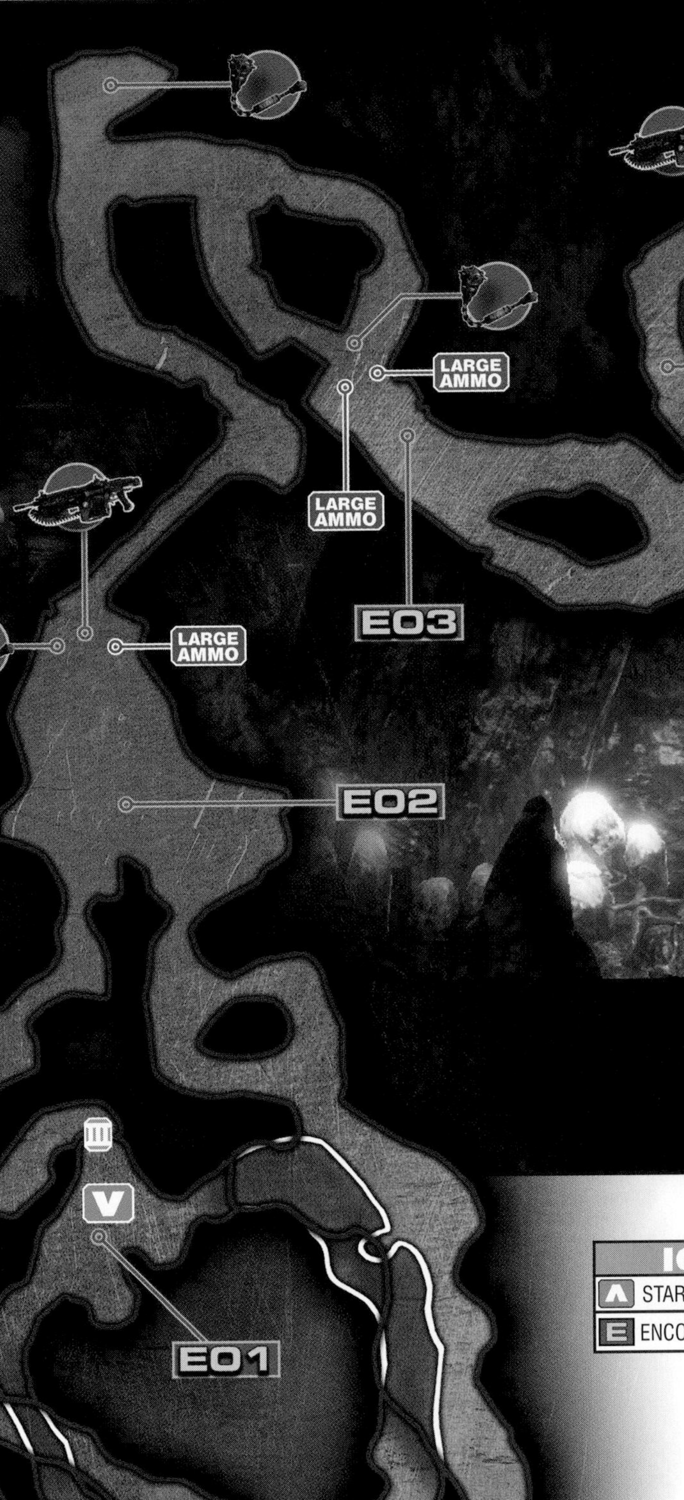

ACT 2

ENEMY PRESENCE

NONE

As the Grindlifts pound their target area, it quickly becomes apparent that most of the Gear assault teams have been scattered—including your own! Carmine radios in for assistance, and you set out to rescue him.

From the Grindlift with Dom, you can actually follow one of three routes: left, right, or up the ladder. All three eventually wrap back around and lead to the same point—some vines through which you have to bash or cut to reach Carmine's position.

On the way to the vines, you run across several Gear assault teams landing in their Grindlifts or, in one case, simply plowing through the ground near you. Move quickly, because Carmine needs your help.

When you reach Carmine, only a small group of Drones are attacking him. Clear them out from behind, and then move up to meet Carmine.

The next rendezvous point is about 30 meters away…through solid stone. Marcus gets Jack to repair and refit one of the Grindlifts for digging duty. While he does so, two Emergence Holes open and a wave of Drones and Grenadiers attack.

You must hold off the Locust while Jack makes the repairs. Concentrate on the Grenadiers, identifiable by their lack of helmets. You don't want them flinging grenades at your position.

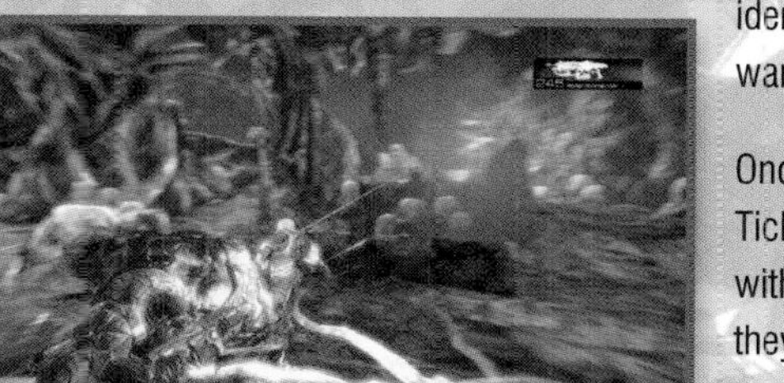

Once you down the first wave, a pack of Tickers attacks. Be ready to knock them back with melee attacks, and roll away from them if they get too close.

Past the freshly dug hole in the wall, you encounter Omega Squad in a desperate struggle against Locust forces.

Quickly make your way down the path to their position, and assist their squad against the Locust. Initially, you only have to contend with Drones. However, reinforcements soon arrive, including Grenadiers, more Drones, Tickers, and finally Boomers and Grenadiers.

Because the waves are staggered, you should have time to deal with each one individually. Keep your distance—there's no benefit to being up close to the enemy position as more Locust pour into the small combat zone.

A few well-placed grenades also serve you well to take out a few of the clustered Locust. The Boomers arrive late, and you may be able to mow them down with concentrated Lancer or Hammerburst fire before they really have a chance to make their impact felt.

After you deal with the Locust, you can move past the ambush point and up into the darkened tunnel from which the Locust emerged.

Boomshot

This is your first chance to grab the extremely powerful Boomshot. Ammo for this weapon is sharply limited, but keep in mind that you can find ammunition for the Boomshot in Locust ammo crates, which you frequently find within Locust territory.

Because the Boomshot is limited in ammunition, it's usually best to use it up on the first even remotely dangerous opposition you encounter. Then toss it and pick up a secondary weapon that has more plentiful ammo supplies. Carrying it around for several chapters doesn't do you any good if you don't use it!

The darkened passage is infested with Wretches. Try to stay near the light of the glowing plants or Jack's spotlight to take them out safely.

When you reach the end of the trail, you can chainsaw (or bash) your way through some viny overgrowth into the next portion of the cavern and the game's next chapter. There's a Lancer on the ground near the vines if you feel the need to switch, but it isn't necessary for cutting through.

Shotguns are by far the best way to deal with the Wretches—sticking near Jack and his light is the best bet.

—STUART FITZSIMMONS

CHAPTER 2: INDIGENOUS CREATURES

Reunited with Carmine, you set off into the Locust underworld. Resistance becomes stronger here as you encounter more fortified defensive areas and a larger Locust presence.

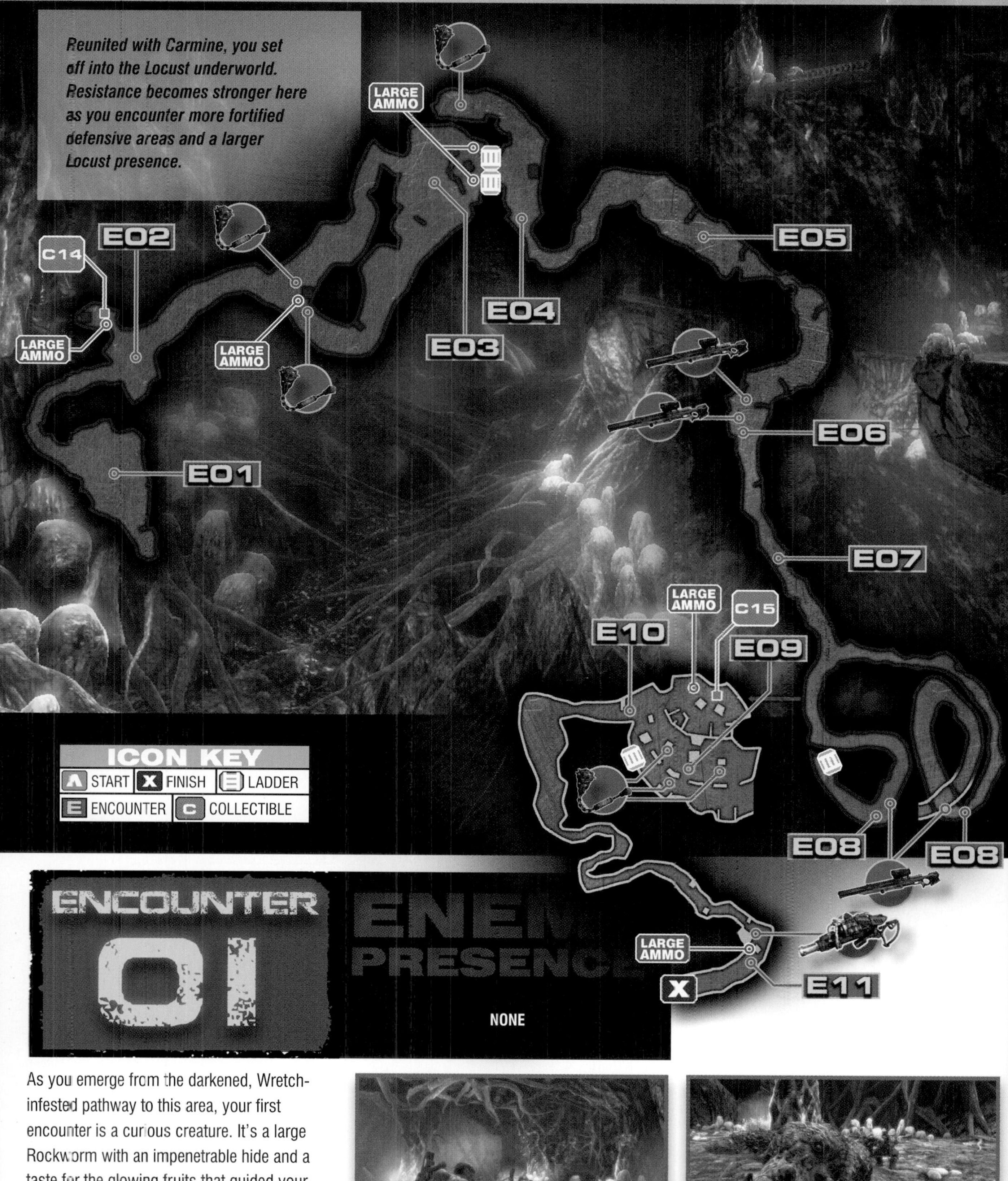

ENCOUNTER 01

ENEMY PRESENCE

NONE

As you emerge from the darkened, Wretch-infested pathway to this area, your first encounter is a curious creature. It's a large Rockworm with an impenetrable hide and a taste for the glowing fruits that guided your steps only moments ago.

Shoot down the hanging fruit on the ceiling above to make the Rockworm move. The Rockworm's stony exterior actually makes for great cover!

NONE

A second Rockworm is located here. Again, you can shoot the hanging fruit to make it move. Practice moving around behind the Rockworm or even mantling over it as it crawls around. You can use the Rockworms as mobile cover.

Before you leave this area, don't forget to pick up Collectible #14, through the vines in a small side chamber.

Find the **Gear Journal** just to the left of the second Rockworm. Cut or bash your way through the vines to find the journal by a Grindlift, along with a large ammo crate.

As the first organized Locust defense you've found in the Hollow so far, this small outpost presents a formidable challenge. A branching path leads to it. Grab the ammo crate and four Frag Grenades at the split.

If you follow the left path, you gain a slight elevation advantage and a few pieces of cover. As you move to the second low rock wall, a Rockworm crawls out of a hole on the left wall, making a convenient barricade just in front of the Troika at the sandbags.

Use this cover to close in, and fling Frag Grenades behind the sandbags at the Drones.

If you go right, a Rockworm crawling out of a hole in the wall provides a bit of mobile cover.

Shoot down the hanging fruit to make the Rockworm crawl forward far enough for you to Roadie Run into the bit of solid cover facing the outpost.

Once you're in position on the left or the right, toss the Frag Grenades behind the sandbags at the Troika gunner. There are too many grubs to suppress or kill them entirely, but you might get lucky and take out a few.

As you climb up to the higher tunnel via the ladder at the outpost, a small pack of Tickers rushes you. Also, an accidental detonation blasts open a path deeper into the cavern.

Just down the tunnel, another Rockworm crawls across your path. This provides some needed cover against an Emergence Hole that opens a bit further down the tunnel.

You can hang back behind the Rockworm and toss a Frag Grenade at the hole to close it. Then finish off the Drones and Grenadiers.

Continue to hang back and pick off the Drones as they expose themselves. When you clear the area of most opposition, you can then rush from cover and quickly get behind the Troika gunner. It's ideal to gut him with your chainsaw, but just getting close behind him is enough to make him hop off the turret.

The left path is definitely the easier of the two. While the right path lets Carmine and his Longshot take the high ground, it's more effective to have the Rockworm on the left path provide close cover for Frag Grenade tossing. If you go left and then double back, the second Rockworm won't come out, and vice versa.

Once you clear out the Drones, loot the area. There are three ammo crates lying about: two on the ground and another one on the second level. Plus, you'll find some Frag Grenades on the second level. Climb up the ladder and go left to reach them.

As you come around the corner, Marcus warns Carmine to watch for snipers. His fears are justified, as a Locust Sniper ambush awaits around the next bend.

Fortunately, your first chance to use the Longshot is also here. Grab the Longshot from the Grindlift. Then hit the cover and start picking off the Snipers on the distant platform. They're to the right of a narrow rock bridge that crosses the gap.

Once you clear off the first wave of Snipers, work your way down to the bridge. A Rockworm emerges, and you need to use it as cover to cross the bridge.

As soon as the Rockworm emerges, if the platform is clear, you can move down the trail to get behind it

Longshot

This potent rifle is an ideal long-range weapon. It's perfect for picking off distant Locust and for scoring instant kills with headshots.

Because you need only a few shots to down most Locust (sometimes only one if you're accurate), the Longshot can be a useful weapon to hold onto. It's not hard to reach more ammunition crates to refill before you run dry, unlike some of the other more powerful weapons.

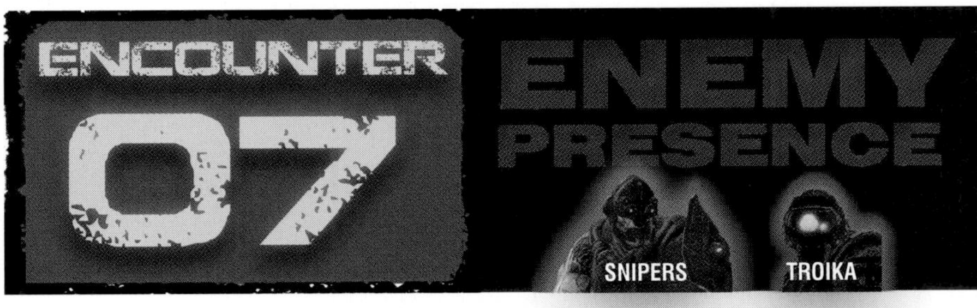

Follow the Rockworm across the bridge to avoid sniper fire. When you reach the opposite end of the bridge, a Locust Explosive comes into view on the platform where the Locust forces have been tormenting you.

One well-placed shot deals with that threat… permanently.

You don't actually need to kill the Locust out on the platform. If you hide out behind the Rockworm until the end of the platform, you can eliminate them all with the explosive.

—STUART FITZSIMMONS

After the rock bridge, you need to climb up the rock spiral tower to the top. No matter which path you choose (there's a branch at the bottom of the spire), you end up on a ledge overlooking a Locust patrol passing below.

Knock off five Locust Drones to hear a pleasant exclamation from Marcus.

On the higher difficulty settings, you need to hit headshots to score kills, and nail your active reloads.

DEV TIP

If you want a slim advantage, the lower path on the left side gives you a slightly better vantage point for sniping.

—*STUART FITZSIMMONS*

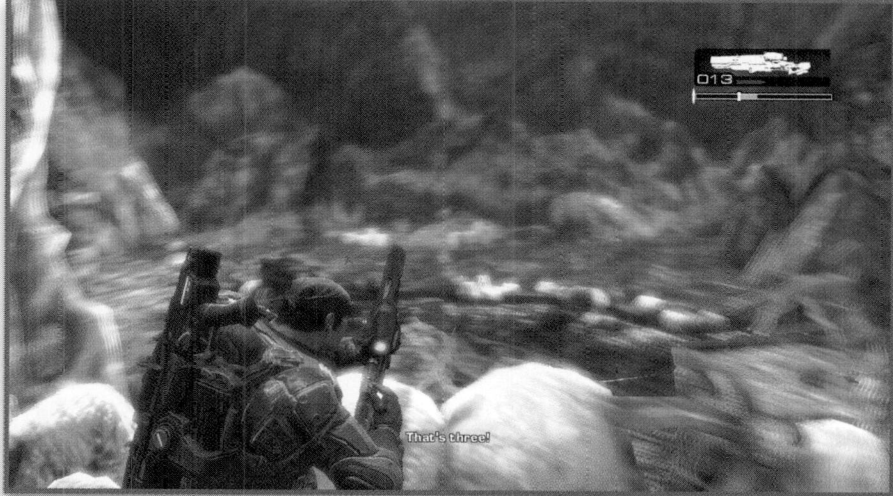

Once you reach the top of the spire, you're let out onto an open platform with a nasty Locust presence: several Drones and a pair of manned Troika.

Hit the cover and then SWAT turn across it to the center of the platform, where you can pick up some Frag Grenades. Once you have those in hand, you can slide forward into a piece of cover closer to the Troika. Toss in a grenade to clear out the turret nests.

You can also try to take out one Troika and then rush to man it immediately, turning it on the remaining Drones in the area.

Once you clear the platform of Locust, a Reaver comes crashing down. Stay on a Troika to mow it down quickly.

After you down the Reaver, take a moment to regroup. Grab Collectible #15 at the back of the platform behind the Troika. Then man the Troika closest to the closed doors at the edge of the platform.

After you finish mopping up the Reavers, find the **Kantus Scroll** at the back of the platform.

After a few moments of waiting on the cleared-out platform, a pair of Boomers and a pack of Wretches emerge from the door. Take them out using the Troika. Prioritize the Boomers because it's easy to deal with the Wretches once the Boomers are out of commission.

Be sure to hop off the turret if the Wretches manage to get too close. You don't want to get ripped up at close range.

The Boomers' twin Boomshots provide plentiful ammo, so you may want to ditch your Longshot for a Boomshot. It proves handy in the next several encounters.

Try grenade-tagging the door before the Boomers show up!

—*STUART FITZSIMMONS*

Heading down the ridge, Delta makes contact with the freshly dropped Alpha Two. They're under attack by a Mortar team up on the ridge that you're coming down—you're approaching the Locust team from behind!

Make your way down the trail. When you close in on the Locust presence, eliminate them from behind. There's a Troika there, as well as a single Drone manning a Mortar, and another Mortar on the ground.

With the Locust cleared off, grab the Mortars or use the Troika to help Alpha Two clear out the Locust contingent on the ground below.

If you're trying to shoot the Mortar, it's about 150m to the back edge of the field below. It's 100m to the closer side if you're up against the sandbags by the Troika.

Once Alpha Two is clear, the source of the seismic disturbance in the area is revealed. You can move on down the tunnel, directly into the next chapter.

CHAPTER 3: DISTURBING REVELATIONS

As you penetrate deeper into the Locust complex, you encounter a new and disturbing type of Locust: the Kantus. There's more to this unfavorable discovery; one might characterize these holy figures' impressive powers as "commanding," as they employ their voices to potent effect.

ICON KEY	
START	FINISH
LADDER	
ENCOUNTER	COLLECTIBLE

ENCOUNTER 01

ENEMY PRESENCE

KANTUS DRONES WRETCHES

As you meander your way through the tunnels, Carmine speculates on the origin of the Locust. There's not much time to discuss his wild theories though. Pick up the Longshot on the way up the distinctly unnatural staircase, and you are shortly introduced to a nasty new variety of Locust: the Kantus Priest.

This Locust holy figure can actually raise downed Drones, simply with the sound of his voice. Not only that, but his howls can also knock you down if you try to move in for the kill. He can summon Tickers and he's armed with the potent Gorgon Pistol and the very nasty Ink Grenades.

The room in which you engage him has several Drones in the battlements of a small fortified gate. Luckily, a convenient Rockworm meanders into the room from the right side.

Shoot the hanging plant on the ceiling to make the worm move across the room for you, thus providing extra cover. You need to take out the Kantus on the walkway above. Doing so causes the doors to open and a second Kantus to come out, along with a few Wretches.

Once you kill the second Kantus, the remaining Drones in the side battlements flee the scene. This leaves you free to head through the doors, where you can grab Collectible #16

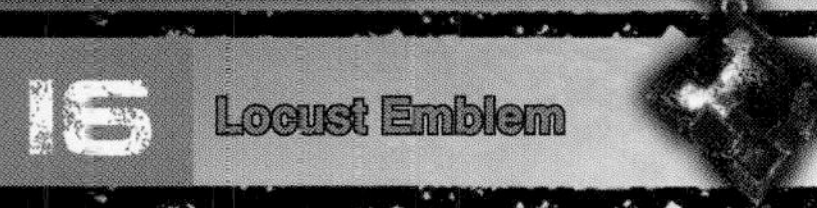

Find the **Locust Emblem** on the other side of the doors past the first encounter. It's just to the right, by an ammo crate.

Gorgon Pistol

WEAPON

The Locust burst pistol is a powerful weapon, though its lengthy recycle between eight-shot bursts and its relative inaccuracy beyond close-to-medium range make it a tricky weapon to master.

It's a nice weapon when you're using a meat shield though. It can deliver solid damage up close when you don't need to worry about your own safety.

Ink Grenades

WEAPON

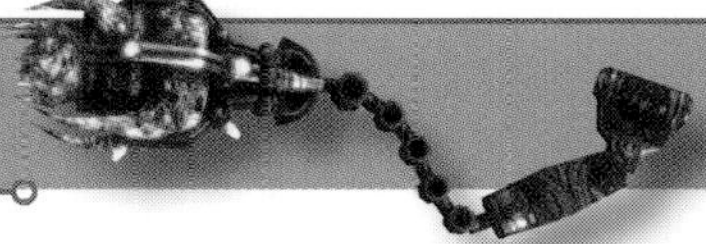

Ink Grenades are often carried by Kantus, and they are amazingly useful against enemies behind cover. The Nemacyst Ink cloud produced by an Ink Grenade's detonation completely envelops an area, causing blindness and inflicting toxic damage over time.

If you follow the right branch here, you have to crawl behind a Rockworm as it makes its way across the cavern floor. Your partner guides it from the ledge above, shooting plants down into the Rockworm's path, goading it to move.

You have to crawl behind the Rockworm because a pair of Troika covers the cavern. They'll tear you to pieces if you abandon the cover of the moving worm.

Once you reach the end of the Troika's line of sight, you can leave the cover of the worm and engage the Drones manning the turrets from the side.

After they're dead, pull the lever to open the door into the next room.

The left route is fairly simple, and you also get the benefit of a Longshot and an ammo crate if you take this path.

All you have to do is shoot down the dangling plants to move the Rockworm along below as Dom hides out behind it. Then move into the room containing a lever to open the door.

However, a pack of Wretches attacks before you pull the lever. Take them out first, and then use the lever to open the door into the next cavern room.

This encounter varies slightly depending on which path you took at the preceding branch.

If you come in from the right branch, you have to move along the ridgeline and ambush two Troika gunners from their flank in order to clear the path for your companion.

On the other hand, if you took the left path, you wind up facing the area where Encounter 5 begins. However, you have to wait for your companion to clear the Troika that are covering you.

A Kantus and several Drones are down on the cavern's ground floor. Take them out, preferably targeting the Kantus first. The doors at the end of the cavern then open, revealing a pair of Boomers and a pack of Grenadiers.

If you're on the ledge, you can turn the lower Troika to face the sandbagged cavern floor below. If not, hide out behind cover to deal with them at a distance. There isn't much else in the way of armament nearby.

Once you dispatch the last wave of Locust, this brief chapter is complete, and a discovery of sizable proportions awaits you.

ACHIEVEMENT

THAT SINKING FEELING

Completing Disturbing Revelations awards this Achievement.

CHAPTER 4:
SINKING FEELING

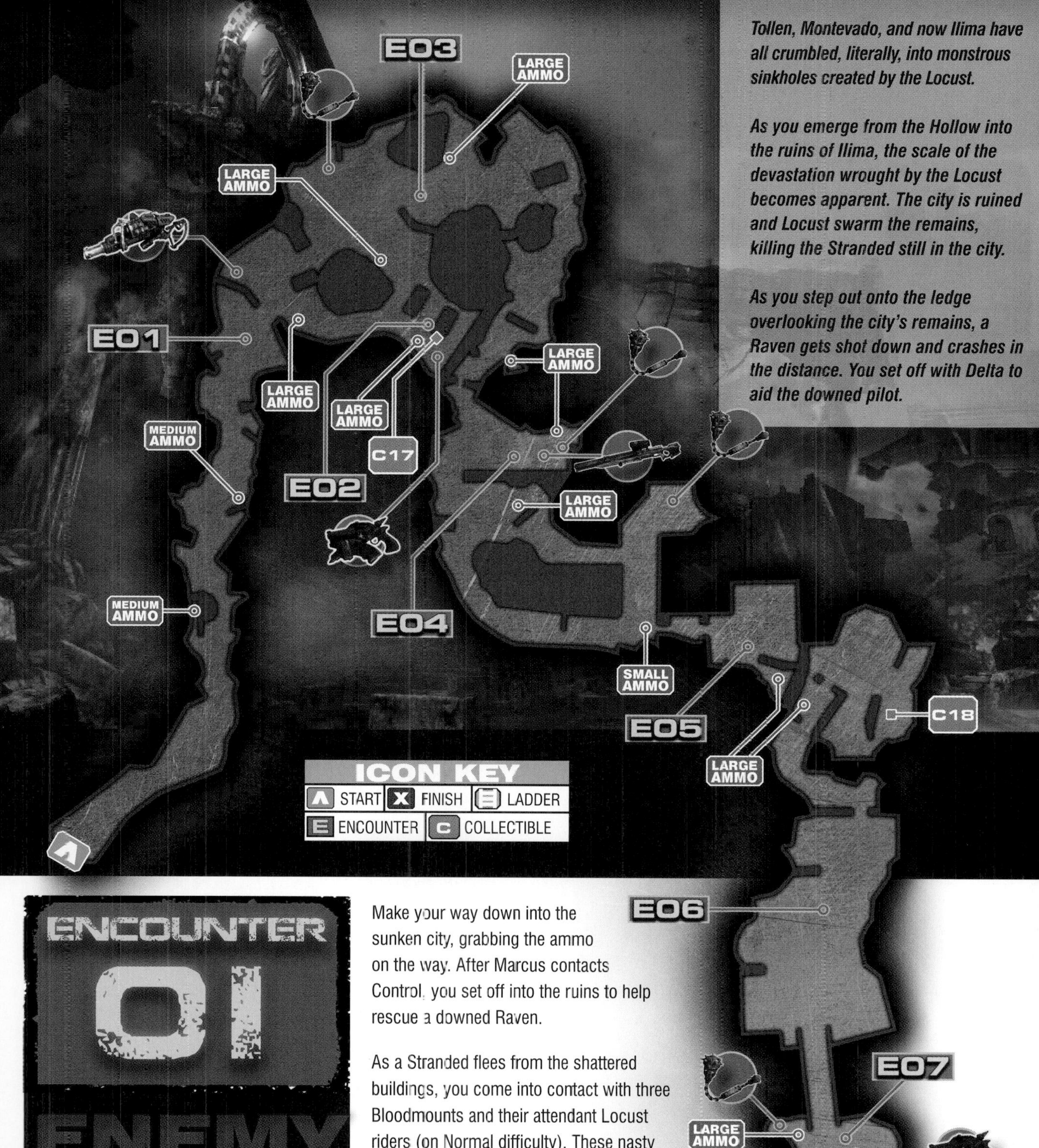

Tollen, Montevado, and now Ilima have all crumbled, literally, into monstrous sinkholes created by the Locust.

As you emerge from the Hollow into the ruins of Ilima, the scale of the devastation wrought by the Locust becomes apparent. The city is ruined and Locust swarm the remains, killing the Stranded still in the city.

As you step out onto the ledge overlooking the city's remains, a Raven gets shot down and crashes in the distance. You set off with Delta to aid the downed pilot.

ENCOUNTER 01

ENEMY PRESENCE

BLOODMOUNT GRENADIERS DRONES

Make your way down into the sunken city, grabbing the ammo on the way. After Marcus contacts Control, you set off into the ruins to help rescue a downed Raven.

As a Stranded flees from the shattered buildings, you come into contact with three Bloodmounts and their attendant Locust riders (on Normal difficulty). These nasty Locust beasts of burden are equal parts weapon of war and mobile elevation for their riders.

As a result, they are dangerous when you hide in cover. This is because the rider can shoot over low cover, and the mount is more than happy to run up and chew on you at close range.

Make the Bloodmount a priority target during any encounter. You can knock off the rider or kill the Bloodmount directly.

After you deal with the Bloodmount, you can pick up a Mortar on the ground nearby. Use it to shell the Grenadiers or save it for the next few encounters.

A few Drones secure the path ahead. You can engage them directly or take a detour to the right to find a collectible and a Gorgon Pistol.

From the Gorgon Pistol overlook area, you can shell the Snipers with the Mortar at about 150 meters from the safe area. Doing so frees up the route on the left, so you needn't worry about getting picked off while you deal with the Locust presence near Encounter 3.

Find the **Ilima Help Wanted Ad** beside the Gorgon Pistol, just up the path to the right of the Bloodmounts. It's on the overlook facing the Snipers.

A Reaver that swoops in and lands in the middle of the path bars your progress down toward the Raven. Back off immediately to get some distance whenever you hear the cry of "Reaver!"

If you still have Mortar shells available, they're effective. You can also use some Frag Grenades. Failing those options, pumping it full of bullets always works; just be ready to retreat and heal if necessary.

DEV TIP

If you clear out all of the enemies in this area and you *do not* engage the Reaver within roughly 10 seconds, more Drones come around the corner from the ruins and attack you.

Be ready to move up to the Reaver unless you want to deal with them!

—KEN SPENCER

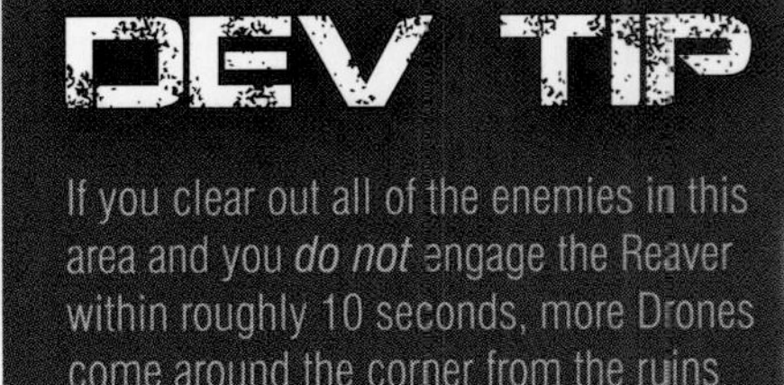

DEV TIP

After you engage the Locust troops that emerge from the Corpser hole, the Reaver drops into the battle about 15 seconds later. Try to be in position when this happens.

—KEN SPENCER

As you get closer to the Raven's position, a Corpser bursts forth from the wall of the sinkhole. This creates a hole from which numerous Drones, Grenadiers, and Snipers emerge.

Take cover on the wall facing their position. Pick up the Longshot and ammo nearby, and then settle in to pick off as many enemies as you can. A propane tank becomes exposed on the ground near the shelled-out building next to which the Locust take cover. Shooting the tank causes the building to collapse and take out some of the enemies.

Midway through the battle, another Reaver drops down to join the fun, so be ready. It lands near the right side of your cover, potentially leaving you dangerously exposed. Try to take out its riders quickly to reduce the amount of incoming fire.

Once you deal with the Locust in this area, make your way over to the building containing the crashed hulk of the King Raven. You can pick up some Frag Grenades and a tiny ammo pack just outside the building before you go inside.

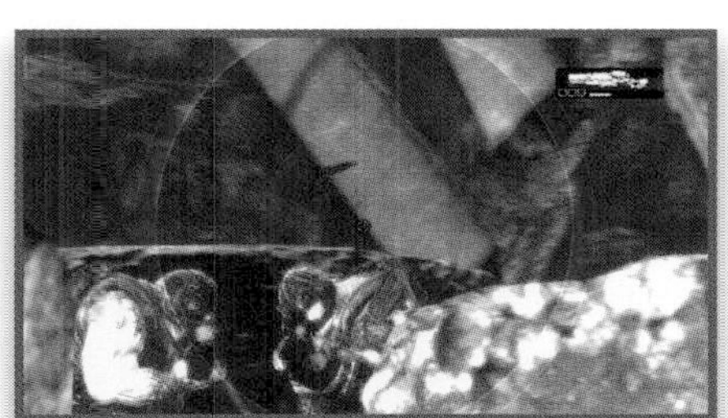

As you step into the building, it quickly becomes apparent that the crew of KR-54 is KIA. A Locust ambush provides an unpleasant answer to the question of who killed them.

Take cover and hold out. The Locust have an elevation advantage and there are too many to manage. Thankfully, you don't have to hang on for long. In spectacular fashion, Cole arrives, grenade-sticking, head-shooting, and just plain gutting the Locust above you.

When you rejoin Cole after he saws through the building's wall, you can continue deeper into the sinkhole in an effort to find Baird, who lost contact during the assault.

Don't miss Collectible #18 on the way out. It's just inside the building after Cole rescues you.

Find the **COG Tags of Hank Bissell** inside the building after Cole saves you.

AUGUSTUS COLE

The irrepressible Cole finally rejoins Delta, bringing some much welcome support to your team.

Cole is just as *enthusiastic* about fighting the Locust as he always was, and having him around to cover your back is good news.

It's apparent that Cole isn't all laughs. He lost most of his squad in the previous campaign. This time around, he has again lost his squad mates when he rejoins you. Cole wants this war over and done with just as much as Marcus does.

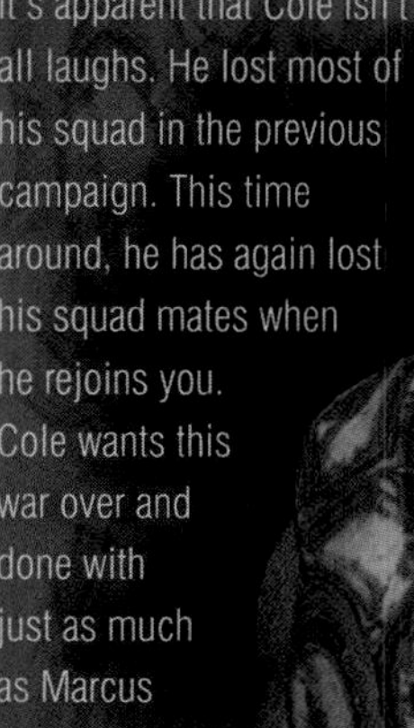

As you exit the building into a graveyard, another Reaver drops down to assault your squad. The headstones supply plenty of cover here. With your full squad, you have plenty of firepower to take down the isolated Reaver.

ENCOUNTER 07 ENEMY PRESENCE

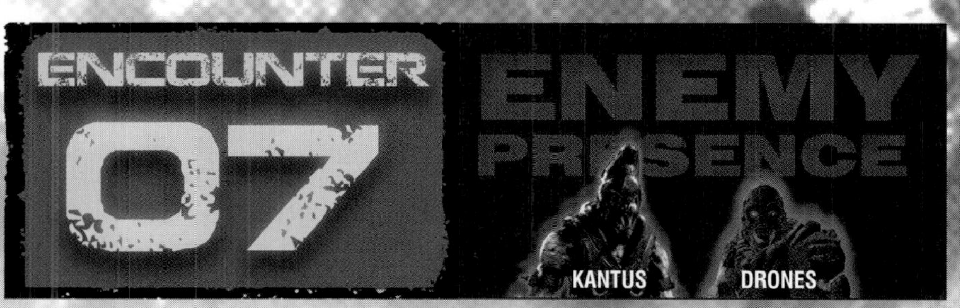

Up ahead, a bridge leads to a tunnel cut into the rock wall. But first you have to get past a small Locust force comprised of a Kantus across the bridge with two Drones in tow.

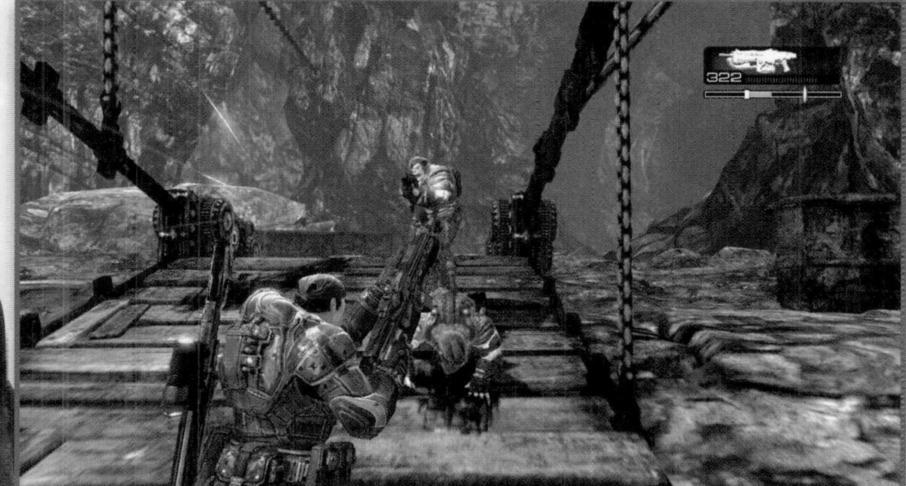

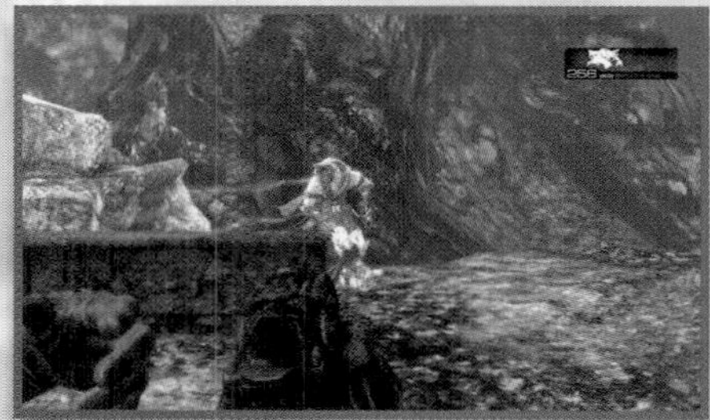

Don't let the Kantus hang back. If you still have the Longshot, take out the Kantus from a distance. Otherwise, be sure to kill his Locust escort fully or he may raise them with his chanting.

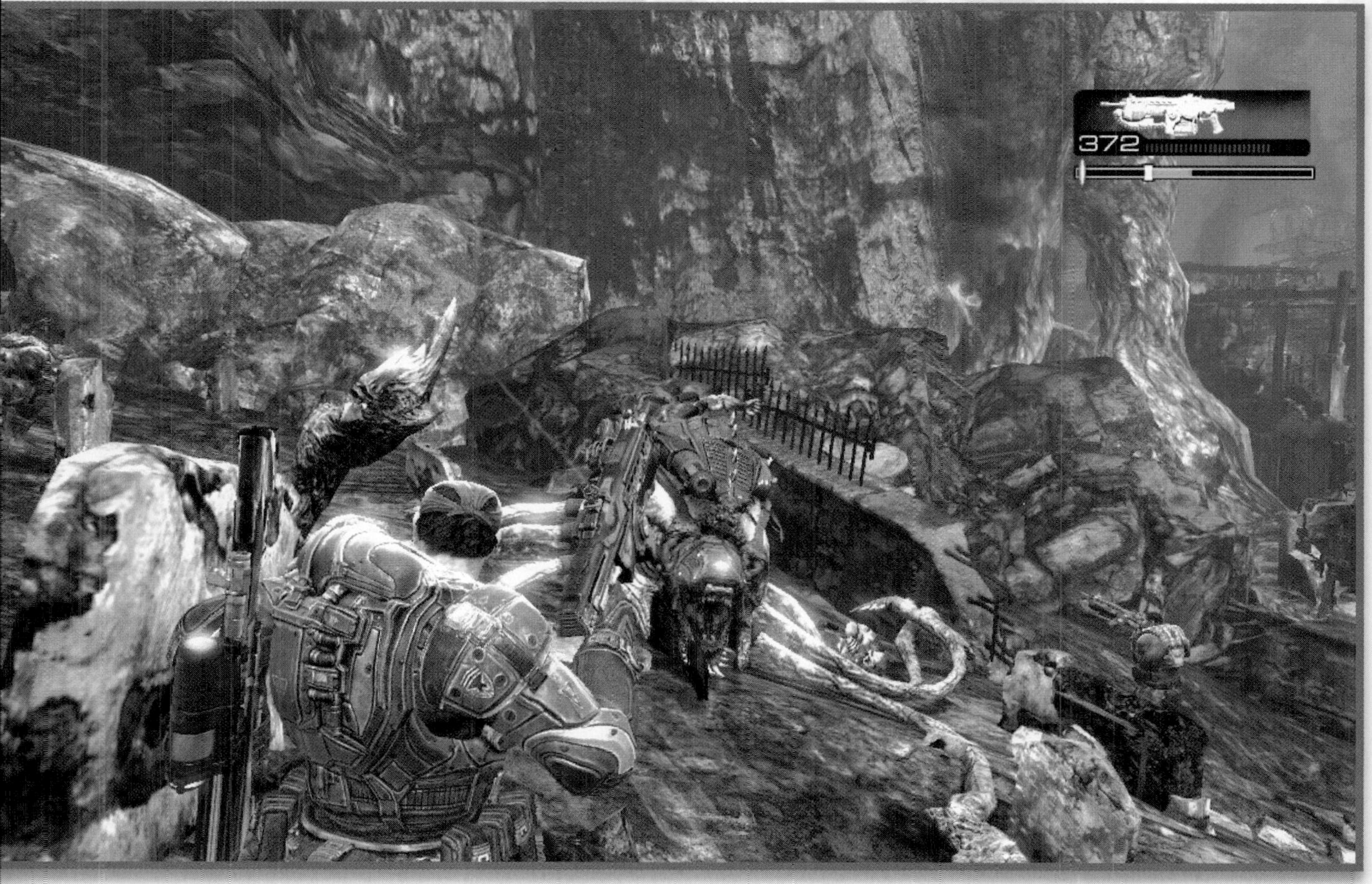

CHAPTER 5: CAPTIVITY

Beyond the ruins of Ilima, an unpleasant discovery waits to greet you. The Locust are capturing human prisoners for unknown reasons.

As you make your way through another cavern, you have to free some captured Gears before you can reach an evacuation point for a Raven to pick up your team.

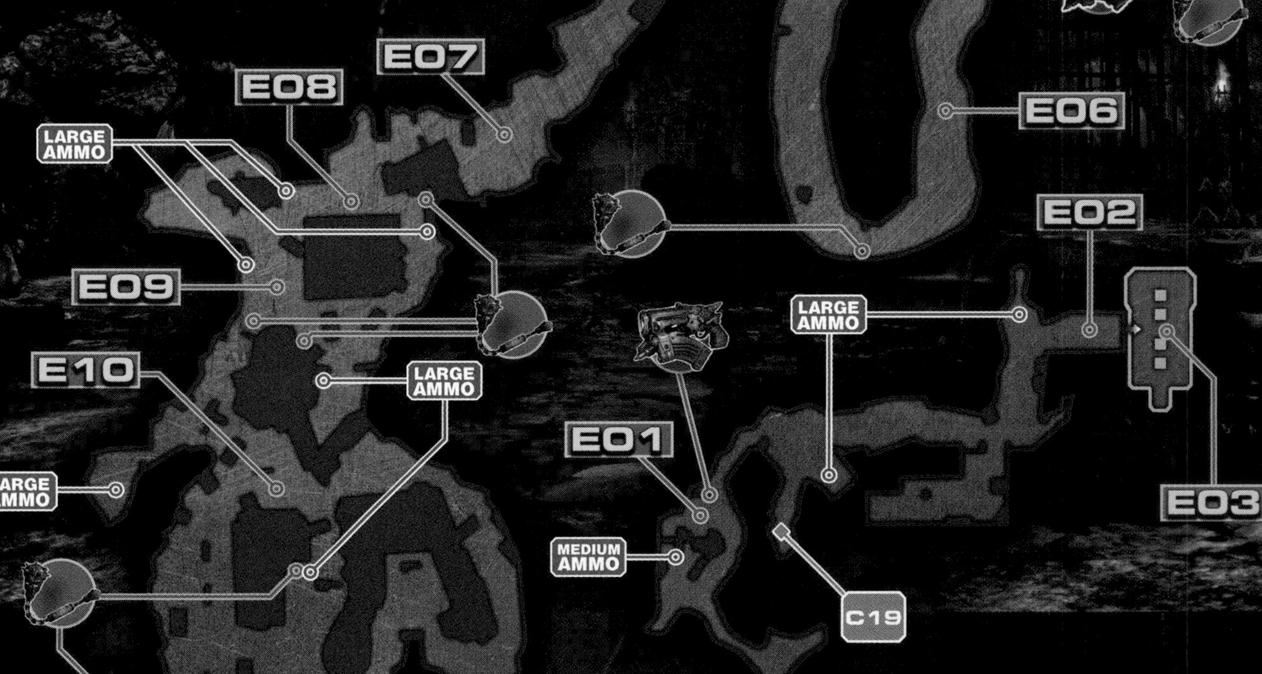

ACT 2

ENCOUNTER 01

ENEMY PRESENCE

NONE

As you enter the cavern, you run into some holding pen areas filled with strange containers. It quickly becomes apparent that humans are the cargo.

DAMON BAIRD

Spared from whatever horrors the Locust had in store for him in that prison, Baird is relieved to rejoin Delta.

Baird remains as cynical and sarcastic as ever, but his technological expertise comes in handy. Despite his constant griping, he's a steady hand in a firefight.

With Baird and Cole along for the ride, you now have a full-size team, much to the chagrin of any Locust that get in your way.

You can hear Baird shouting from within one of the containers. Get him out to add another combat-worthy Gear to your squad. Then move on, deeper into the cavern. Don't miss a collectible just around the corner to the right after you free Baird.

COLLECTIBLE

19 Stranded's Journal—Jennifer

Just after you release Baird from his prison, find the **Stranded's Journal** to the right, in a small rocky alcove.

ACHIEVEMENT

FREEBAIRD!

Free Baird from his captivity in a Locust cell.

ENCOUNTER 02

Make your way down the trail, and you soon encounter an unusual sight: a massive Locust creature fitted as a sort of mobile barge.

You have to hitch a ride to move deeper into the cavern. But first you need to deal with the Drones and the Boomer who really don't want you aboard their vessel.

You may want to take the Boomshot with you for the next few encounters. A nasty new Boomer type is coming up.

ENEMY PRESENCE

DRONES

BOOMER

Once you get on the barge, a Grinder comes down a lift from the barge's middle level. The Grinder is a Boomer variant that wields the mighty Mulcher instead of a Boomshot. Be ready for it to unload when you hear it yelling "GRIND!"

Take it down to secure its Mulcher, and then use the lift on which it came down to get into the heart of the barge.

Mulcher

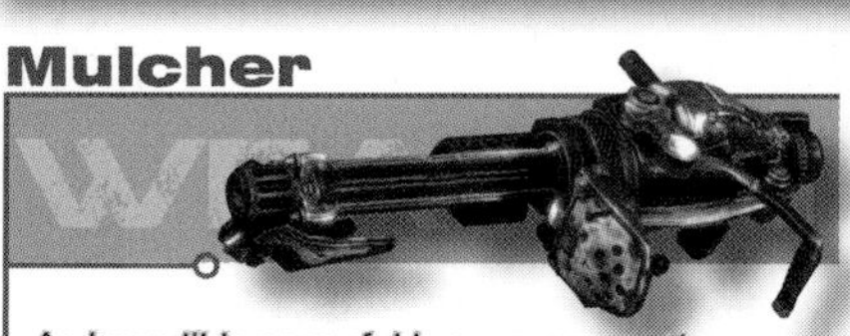

An incredibly powerful heavy weapon, the Mulcher is a chaingun that can unleash a blistering hail of bullets on any unlucky target in your path. Furthermore, rather than reloading, you must simply cool the barrel (by pressing the Right Bumper) periodically to continue firing.

Inside the barge, you can pull a lever to open the prison doors on the sides of the room, but there's no one in them. Head up to the barge's top deck, where you encounter several Grenadiers and a Troika.

Take down the Grenadiers and then pull the lever in the middle of the top deck to get the barge moving. As soon as it does, man the Troika to deal with the Reavers.

Inside the barge after you push the button, head up top and kill Drones. Then man the Troika to fight off the Reaver wave. Watch out for the Troika on the other barge nearby—there's a Locust Explosive beside.

After a short trip, you slam into another barge. Kill the Drones atop it and then board the barge. Pull the lever inside to reveal a gruesome discovery. Then proceed down into the barge to make your way back to solid ground...well, mostly solid.

As you leave the barge, you face a Locust defense of the docks comprised of more Drones and another Grinder. Use the barge for cover to take down the Grinder. Then secure his Mulcher and move on, toward an exit from the caverns.

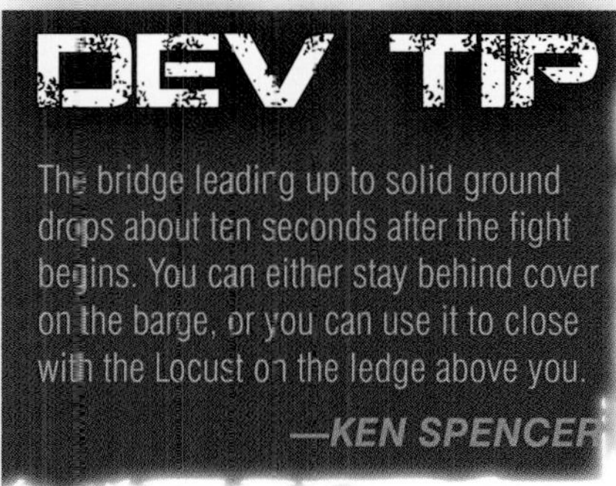

DEV TIP

The bridge leading up to solid ground drops about ten seconds after the fight begins. You can either stay behind cover on the barge, or you can use it to close with the Locust on the ledge above you.

—KEN SPENCER

As you make your way through the tunnels, the now familiar shriek of a Kantus announces his presence. More Drones and a pair of Bloodmounts join the party.

Lug along the Mulcher from the Grinder at the barge dock—it makes this encounter a snap. Mow through the Kantus and the Bloodmounts. Save the rest of the ammo for the next encounter.

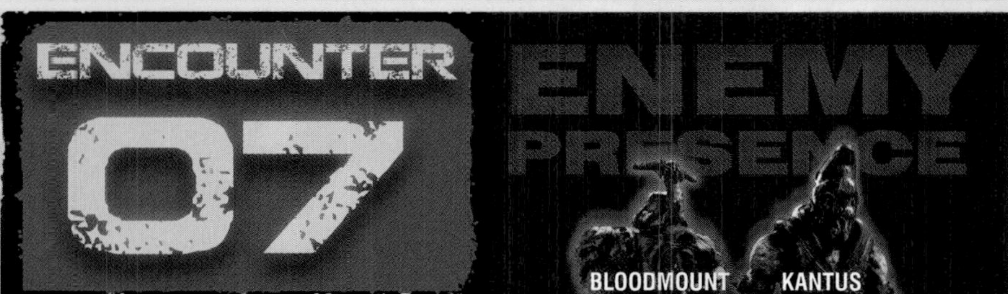

As you approach the exit from the cavern, another Kantus attacks with a Bloodmount (on Normal difficulty). You may still have ammo for the Mulcher to take care of them quickly. If you don't, just hang back and engage them at long range before they can close with you.

You do have plenty of squad support in this fight, so let your men fight for you. They make better bullet sponges than you do.

Once you leave the cavern, a handful of Drones oppose your entry into Ilima's ruined remains. There are several at the entrance to the ruins. A few more are to the left, where you can also find some Frag Grenades and a large ammo crate.

DEV TIP

The encounter here changes slightly depending on which way you go around the building. If you go left, you encounter a few more Drones. If you go right, you run into Drones accompanied by a Kantus. The left path is definitely the safer of the two on the higher difficulty levels.

—KEN SPENCER

A pack of Drones blocks a potential evacuation point for the Raven to pick up your team. You need to clear your path. Then you can head into the large building at the end of the street, either through the left or the right entrance.

Take down the Drones and then check the area. There's a large ammo crate in the doorway on the left side of the large building. You may also want to go around the right side to pick up some Frag Grenades on the way in.

It doesn't matter which way you take to the rooftop, but investigating both ways gets you a bit more ammo.

Once you make your way around to the right side of the building in the middle of the street, a Reaver slams down and engages Delta.

If possible, try to come at it from the entrance to the ruins. That is to say, go right where you first came to the split around the large building in the street. Doing so gives you a bit more room to back off. If you come at the Reaver from the left side, it lands nearly on top of you.

Once you dispose of the Reaver, don't miss the large ammo crate to the right.

The final fight here is simply an endurance test. Waves of Drones assault your position. You must hold out until the Raven lands.

DEV TIP

Although only the last thirty seconds are displayed on a visible timer, you have to hold out for a minute and a half. Don't overextend—you only need to survive!

—KEN SPENCER

There's plenty of ammo and a few Frag Grenades on the rooftop, but you don't want to get caught out in the open as Drones come from all sides.

Instead, hole up in the small, mostly ruined room where most of Delta usually ends up.

The major threat in this fight is the Kantus that comes up from the left staircase (where you entered if you came in on the left side from the street).

Try to take out the Kantus quickly. It's frustrating to kill Drones from a distance only to have them stand up again.

A meat shield is very useful during the fight. The extra bullet soaking it provides makes enduring the seconds until the Raven arrives that much easier.

Affix grenades to the walls near the entry points. There are a lot more Drones than you have grenades, and exposing yourself may not be worth the trouble. Nevertheless, you can at least cover the entrance nearest the ruined room with a few grenades.

Once the timer on the Raven's arrival counts down to zero, Delta is picked up and this chapter is complete.

CHAPTER 6: INTESTINAL FORTITUDE

When you wake up from your forced crash landing, it's apparent that your whole team is in the belly of the beast!

Most of the team favors getting out as quickly as possible, but Marcus has other plans. He wants their accidental host dead before they escape, so you set off to find the heart of the monster and rip it out directly.

*There is nothing conventional about the Intestinal Fortitude level. There's relatively little fighting, but you must deal with...*other *challenges to make it through in one piece.*

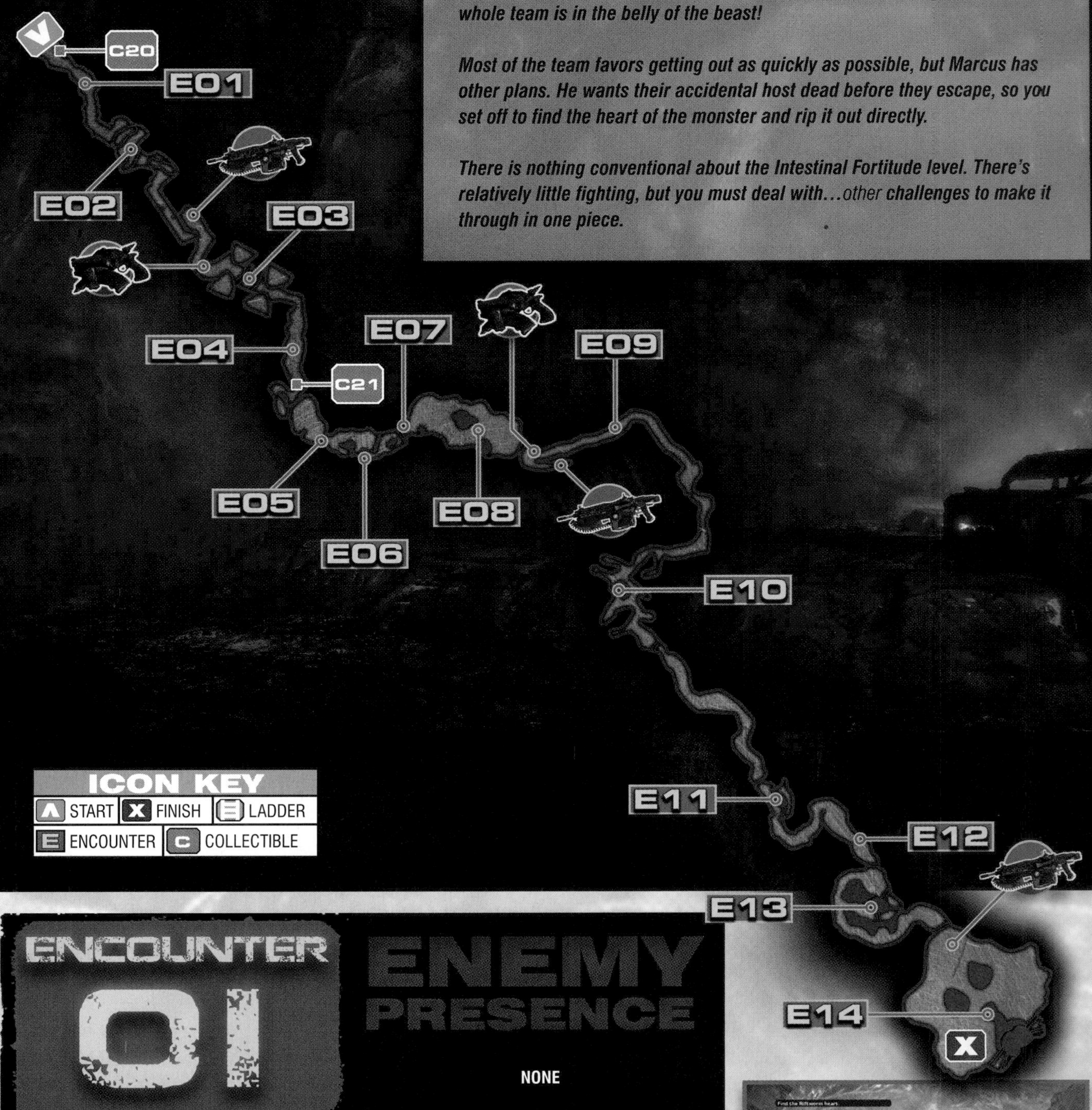

C20 E01 E02 E03 E04 C21 E05 E06 E07 E08 E09 E10 E11 E12 E13 E14

ICON KEY

START	FINISH	LADDER
ENCOUNTER	COLLECTIBLE	

ENEMY PRESENCE

NONE

As the groggy Delta Squad reassembles, it becomes apparent that Carmine is nowhere to be seen. There's nowhere to go except forward in the strange environment you now occupy.

Before you set off, look off to the left of the path to find a collectible. Then make your way through the nasty fluids ahead.

COLLECTIBLE

20 Car Gold Magazine

Just to the left of your start position, you can find the **Car Gold Magazine** on the ground.

ENCOUNTER 02

ENEMY PRESENCE

NONE

Your first real obstacles are massive, crushing digestive teeth. Time your running to skirt past them. Once you're past the first three, the next set is much lower, which prevents you from walking past them safely. You *must* Roadie Run to get under them safely.

ENCOUNTER 03

ENEMY PRESENCE

NEMACITE

After the short teeth, one final set of grinding teeth obstructs your path. Again, time your movements to slip between them.

As you pass the teeth, your first enemy appears. Nemacites are strange and parasitic creatures, all claws and teeth. Thankfully, they're not especially resistant to gunfire. Take them out on the move, as you would Wretches. Then continue down the 'path.'

More Nemacites oppose your entry to this foul chamber. Once you clear them out, you are reunited with Carmine.

After you speak with him, you have more pressing matters at hand. A massive wall of debris comes crashing down the tunnel behind you. If you don't start running, it can easily crush you—get moving!

As you run, you quickly reach an ascending ramp. Just *before* the ramp, check on the ground to the left to find a collectible.

These tags are extremely easy to miss. *Before* you reach the ramp, look carefully on the 'ground' to the left near the wall. The **COG Tags** are there. They're just so slimed up that they're darkened and difficult to detect.

Don't worry if you get squashed as you try to find them. You can simply reload the closest checkpoint and continue after they're in your possession.

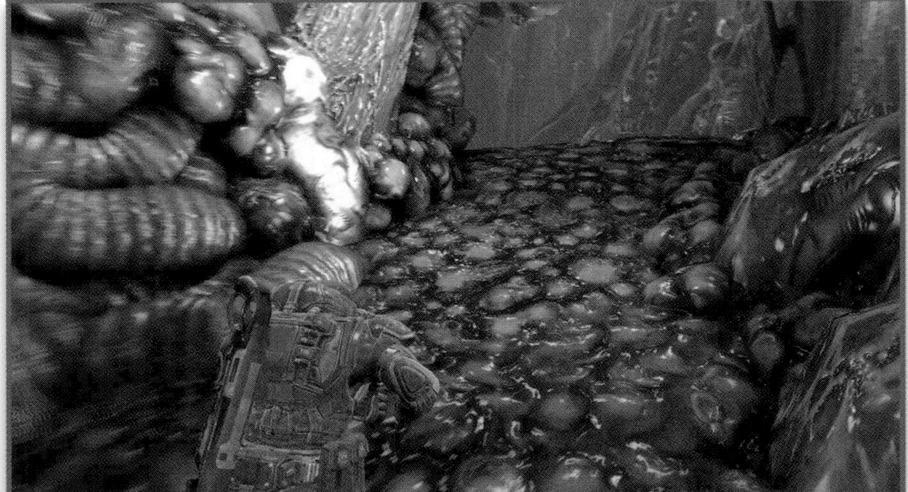

The next obstruction in your path is a membranous wall. You can't pass through the nearby cilia safely, so you must cut your way through this wall. Use the Lancer's chainsaw to carve a bloody hole, and then keep moving.

ENCOUNTER

05

ENEMY PRESENCE

NONE

As you flee from the rolling wall of debris, your first obstacle presents itself. A thick sphincter of muscle blocks the path. Fire at the center to cause the wall to retract, opening a route through it.

ENEMY PRESENCE

NONE

Another sphincter wall bars the path here. Again, quickly shoot it in the center to keep moving.

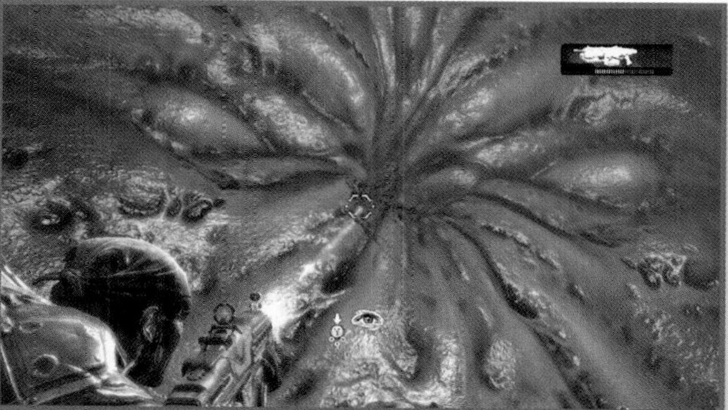

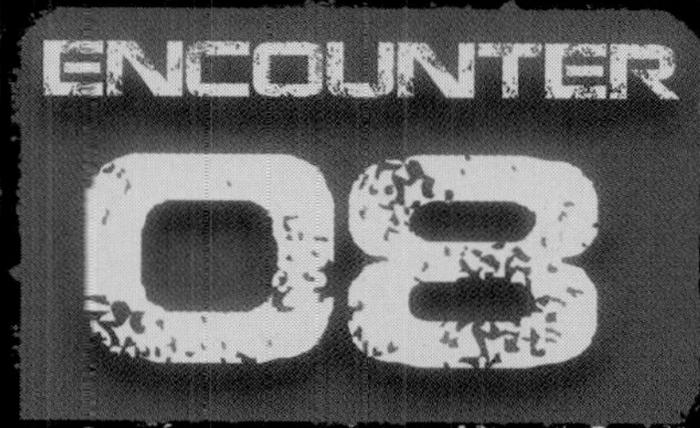

ENEMY PRESENCE

NONE

As you approach the end of your run, a few pools of nasty saliva block your path. Only the cilia can hurt you here. To get across one of the deeper pools, fire at a hanging car to knock it down. The car slams down and creates a makeshift bridge for your team to cross.

After you pass over the bridge, quickly run to the final membrane just ahead. Slice your way through, and you're safely away from the wall of debris crushing everything in its path.

DEV TIP

If you're playing on Hardcore or Insane difficulty, Nemacites are present throughout this run from the debris wall. *Don't* waste time on them. If they get in your way, fire from the hip. Otherwise, you don't have time to stop and engage them. Keep moving!

—DAVID SPALINSKI

Once you escape the immediate danger of the pursuing debris, you can relax for a moment and take stock of your situation. Your next obstacle is a pathway blocked by fleshy acid spitters.

To get past them, you must shoot the gleaming green orbs that are spraying the acid. When you fire at them, they retract momentarily, just long enough for you to sprint past. Continue in this fashion until you get past the walkway.

ENEMY PRESENCE

NONE

Beyond the acid spitters, you penetrate deeper into the creature's dank internals, and you must pass through a small mini-maze.

Avoid *darkened* passages. They're easily discernable as you move through the tunnels, even if you're not using the map for this chapter. As long as you skip the tunnels filled with what looks like a black haze, you won't waste any time here. If you take too long, your screen begins to blur. Eventually, you can suffocate and die—don't let that happen!

DEV TIP

On Insane difficulty, Nemacites are here to make things a bit more interesting…

The difficulty level determines how much time you get to traverse the maze safely. On Casual, you get 120 seconds. The allotted time decreases to 90, 60, and 30 for Normal, Hardcore, and Insane, respectively.

—DAVID SPALINSKI

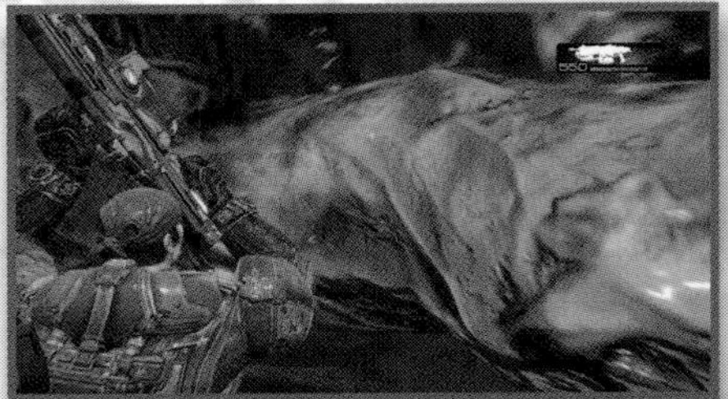

You've finally emerged at the heart of the beast—literally. Kill the Nemacites in the room. Then approach the heart and slice open the two arteries connected to it.

Completing this bloody work reveals that, while you have inflicted grievous injuries, there is still more grim cutting to do. You can hear the distant echo of another strong heartbeat in the distance, and you must follow it to its source.

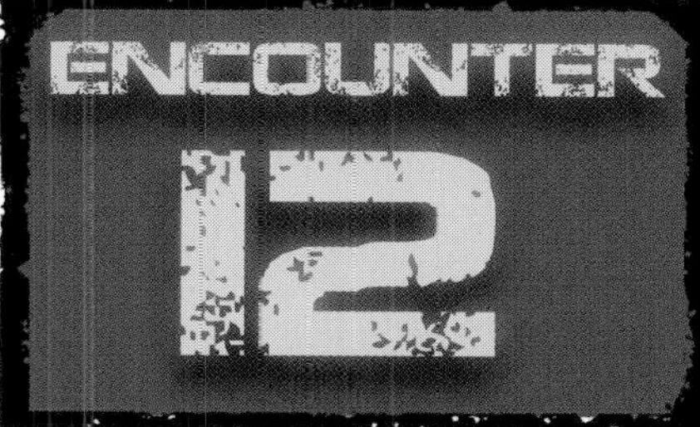

On your way to the second heart, an ambush of more Nemacites threatens your advance. Eliminate them before you move on to the next chamber.

There aren't any threats in this room, but you do have to slice open three arteries to sever the connections to this heart.

You're still not done! Keep moving to reach the final chamber.

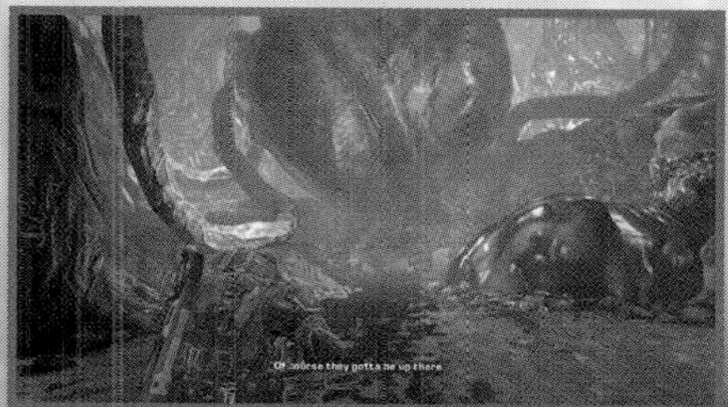

In this strange level's final battle, you must fend off waves of Nemacites while you attempt to cut *four* arteries connected to the largest and final heart.

Try to avoid wasting too much time fighting the Nemacites. As you cut the arteries, the room begins to fill with blood. When the level of the blood rises high enough, the Nemacites automatically begin to drown.

Once you sever all four arteries, your gruesome mission in this strange chapter comes to a close.

ACHIEVEMENT

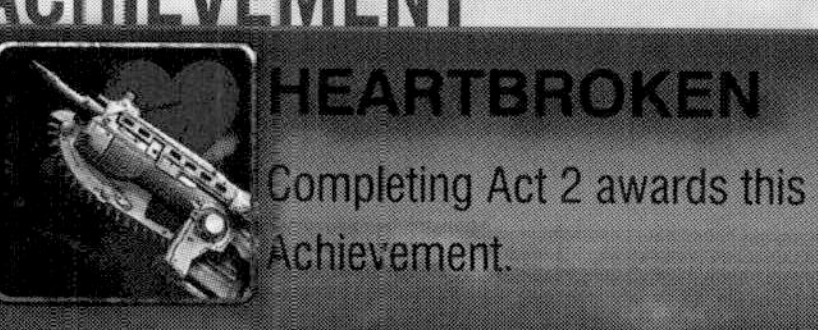

HEARTBROKEN

Completing Act 2 awards this Achievement.

ACT III

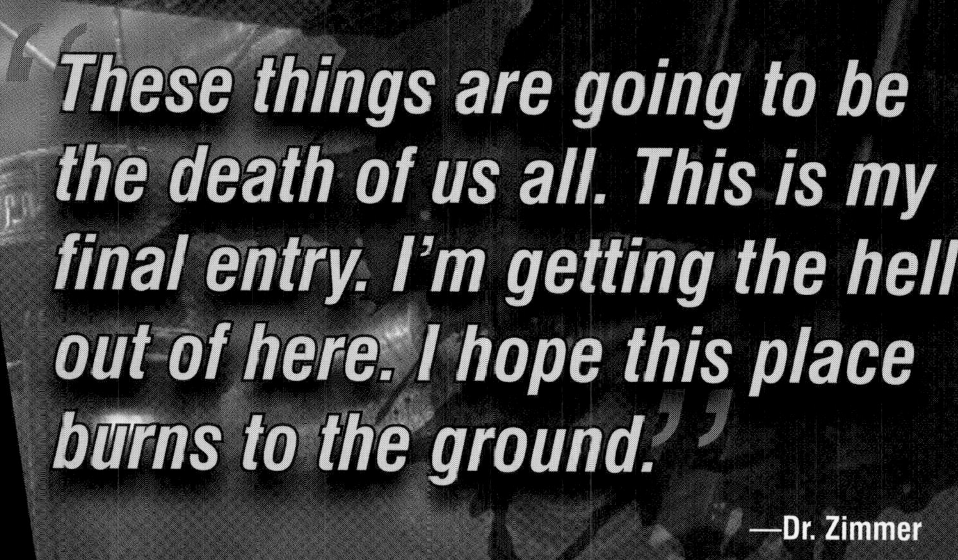

"These things are going to be the death of us all. This is my final entry. I'm getting the hell out of here. I hope this place burns to the ground."

—Dr. Zimmer

GATHERING STORM

CHAPTER 1: DIRTY LITTLE SECRET

After the unsettling conclusion to Chapter 2, you are given time to catch a breather, as Hoffman sends Delta on a mission to an isolated and abandoned research laboratory.

Command wants you to track down some information they believe is sealed within this crumbling wreck of a building, but they're not giving many details freely.

This facility is one of the largest areas in the game—its contents span three whole chapters! However, you don't have to worry about continuous conflict for most of the mission—you are mostly exploring the facility and learning its secrets.

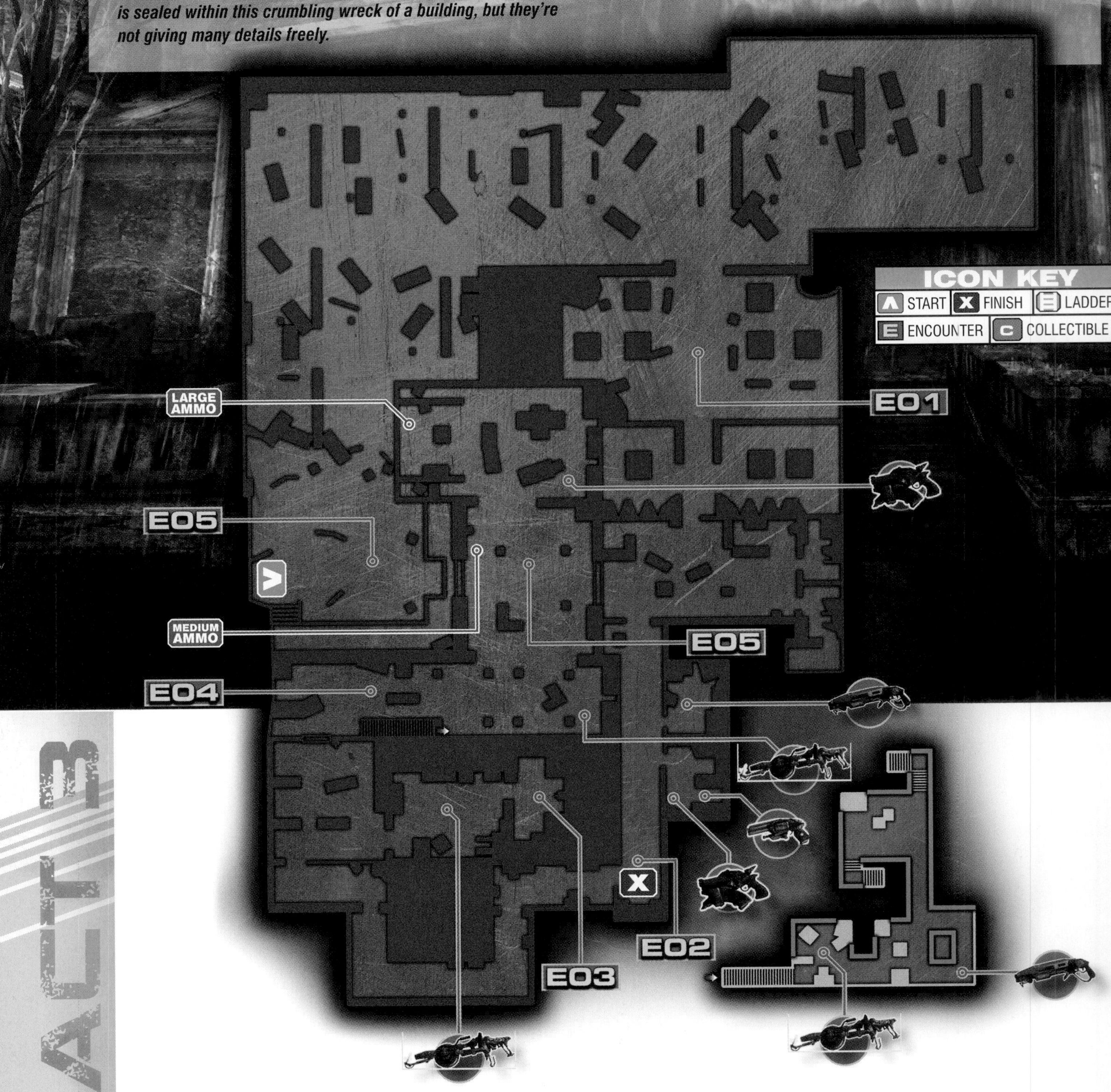

Delta arrives at the facility in a Centaur, and Marcus quickly orders Cole and Baird to secure their arrival point. Marcus and Dom enter the facility to investigate.

As you work your way around to the front of the facility, you spot a few Wretches running in the distance but no overt Locust activity—the place looks abandoned. Head inside.

Inside the decaying building, there is little evidence of what took place here. Mostly, the place is simply run-down and there's no power.

Work your way toward the end of the hall, grabbing any weaponry along the way that catches your eye. Pay particular attention to your choice of pistol—all three are present. Choose the one you're most comfortable with, as you'll need it in a moment.

When you reach the hallway's end, a massive, sealed vault door provides the first evidence that everything here is not as it seems. Your presence triggers a reaction from the monitors surrounding the vault door. An AI springs to life and requests your security codes for access to the facility.

Lacking such codes, you must *improvise*. Baird has precisely the *improvised* explosives you need to get inside. But first you have to restore the power…

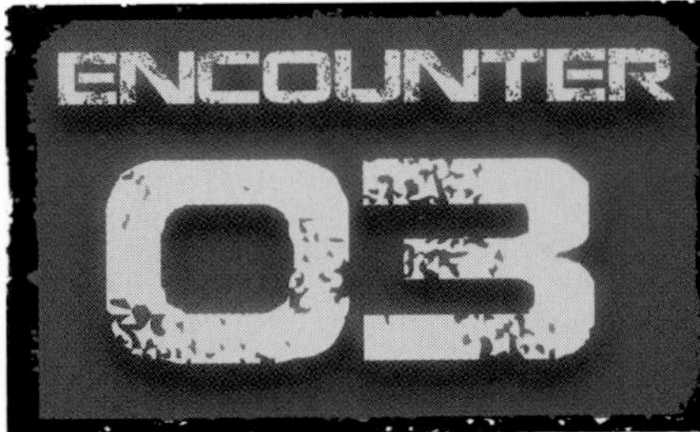

ENCOUNTER 03

ENEMY PRESENCE

NONE

The switch that reactivates the generators that power the facility is just past the Scorcher on the ground in this room. Pull the switch to get the juice flowing. Then return to the previous room and proceed through the now unlocked doorway. It leads to a loading bay, a room you must reach to get the explosives up from the Centaur.

Scorcher

WEAPON

This powerful flamethrower is an ideal weapon for close- and close/mid-range combat. It is extremely easy to hit targets with it, and decimates a number of weaker enemies, notably Wretches...

ENCOUNTER 05

ENEMY PRESENCE

WRETCHES

You must turn a wheel here to open the gate leading back to the yard where the Centaur is parked. But you can't turn the wheel safely until you take out the Wretches, unless you're playing co-op.

Finish off the remaining Wretches, and then open up the gate and drop down to meet up with Cole and Baird.

ENCOUNTER 04

ENEMY PRESENCE

WRETCHES

As you make your way out to the loading bay, your first real opposition appears: Wretches, and a lot of them.

Put your shiny new Scorcher to good use here. You can incinerate the charging hordes with ease. If you need more ammo, there's another Scorcher up on the catwalk above the floor, along with a Shotgun. Both are ideal for dealing with the swarm of Wretches.

Baird provides you with your custom made bomb, but it's a heavy, bulky, and unwieldy piece of equipment. And you really don't want to drop it. Dom picks up one side and Marcus gets the other, beginning a very unusual challenge.

You have to walk back over to the loading bay lift to get into the facility again (where you just came through), and the lift is raised to get you back inside.

From where you come into the loading bay, you just have to go straight forward, then right and up the hall (directly toward Encounter 2) to reach the door.

Of course, you're carrying the bomb with one hand, leaving only one hand for a pistol... Oh, and your maneuverability is severely limited, making it very awkward to turn.

Take your time making your way to your target. You don't want to get overwhelmed by the packs of Wretches that attack while you're burdened with the bomb.

Once you reach the door, Marcus sets the timer, and the path is cleared into the next chapter!

CHAPTER 2: ORIGINS

Penetrating into the secured heart of the facility, disturbing revelations await Delta. There is still relatively little combat in this chapter, though you do need to stay alert for automated defenses.

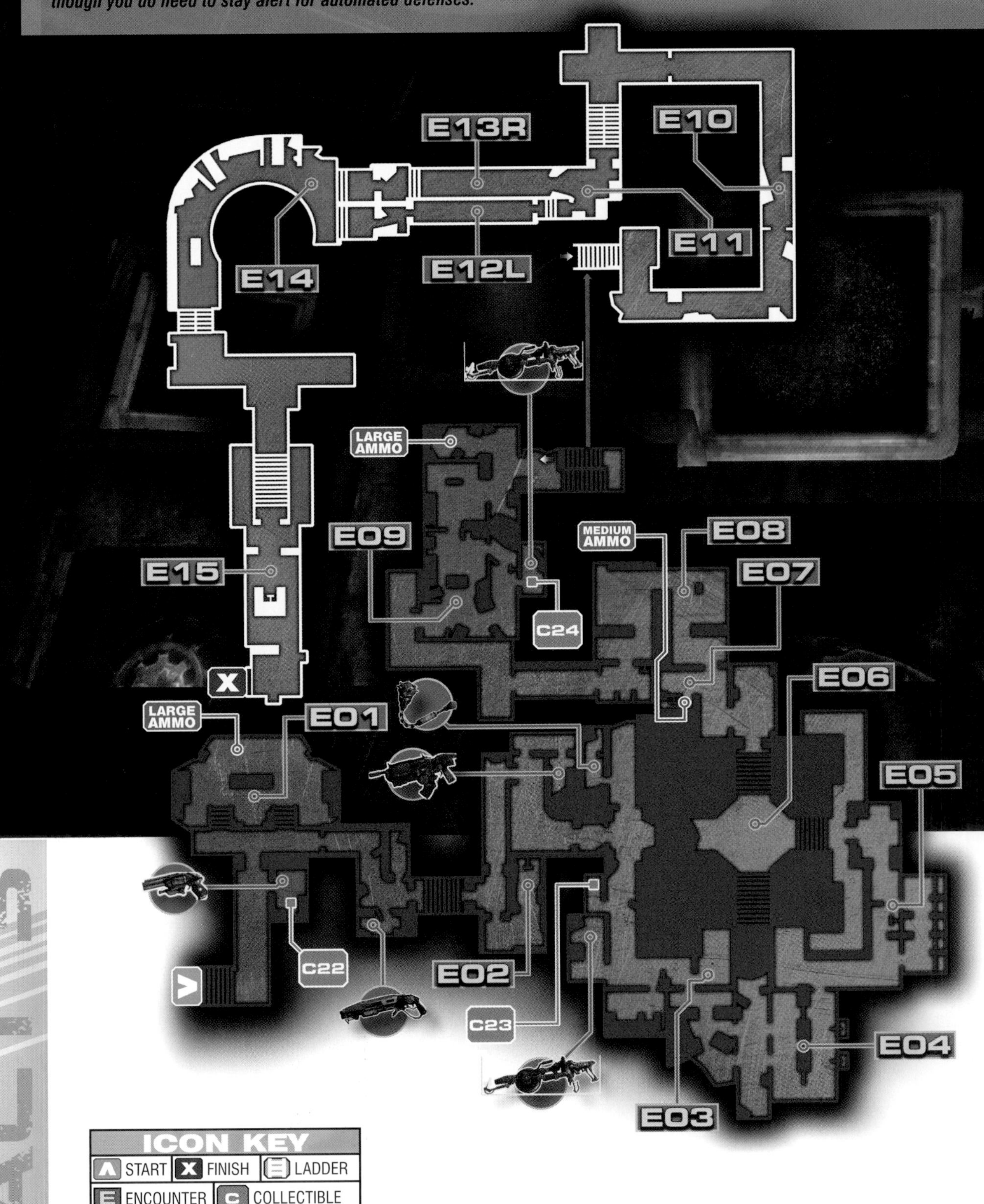

ICON KEY		
START	FINISH	LADDER
ENCOUNTER	COLLECTIBLE	

As you step into the facility's interior, the AI known as Niles continues to communicate with you. He seems slightly...*off*, but he has not acted in an aggressive manner. Step over to the windows to trigger a brief communication with Command.

Command wants you to proceed deeper into the facility and continue your investigation, so keep moving. Don't forget to grab the collectible here, and you can pick up a Boltok and a Shotgun if you wish.

Find the **New Hope Computer Printout** tucked away in the small office. It's to your right as you enter this larger room, just beside a Boltok pistol.

As you enter this small hallway, a pack of Wretches appears. Thankfully, they're on the other side of a thick window and can't get at you unless you open the door.

Don't open the door just yet. Make your way around to the right, open the door, and flip the switch inside the control room that looks into the room with the Wretches. Doing so activates an automated sentry turret, which quickly mows down the Wretches.

Once the room is clear, turn off the sentries, and you can proceed safely.

Find the **New Hope Memo** in a small room off the main hallway. You have to enter the room and then kick open a door to find it resting on the ground.

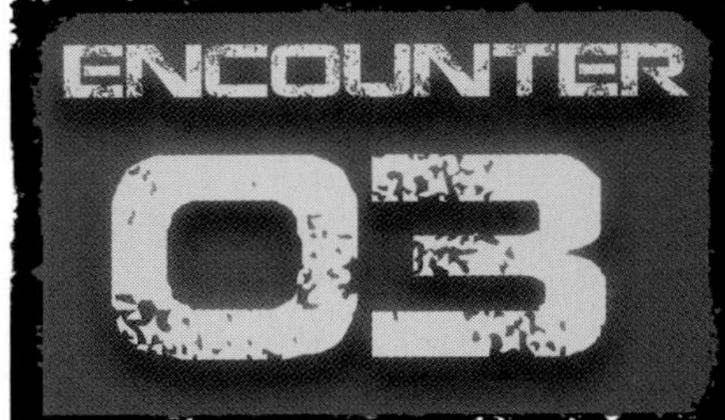

Encounter 03

Enemy Presence

NONE

A single turret watches this hallway. You can't deactivate it as easily as the previous one, so you must dodge past it to get into the next room. Just watch the sweep of its sighting laser and Roadie Run past it when it moves away from you.

You can also use cover to avoid damage. If you start getting hit, you can still usually evade the line of fire or dodge into cover before it downs you.

Encounter 04

Enemy Presence

WRETCHES

Several active flame turrets occupy the wall in this small room. Wait for the Wretches down the hallway to enter the room and attack. Then use the turrets to your advantage. They can easily char the Wretches, leaving them weak and easy to finish.

Encounter 05

Enemy Presence

NONE

This hall is heavily guarded by security turrets. Watch their targeting carefully, and then dart past them into the bathroom adjacent to the hall.

Inside the bathroom, sneak through to another doorway opening into the hall. The switch that deactivates all of the turrets is just outside the doorway to the left, allowing you to proceed safely.

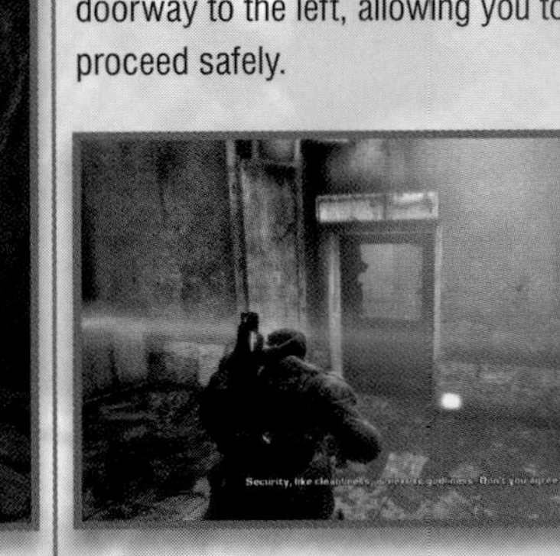

Out in the open courtyard, the area initially appears to be safe. But the instant you climb the steps and open the door into the next portion of the facility, a large pack of Wretches attacks.

Be ready with your favored anti-Wretch weaponry. Once you clear out the pack, you can proceed.

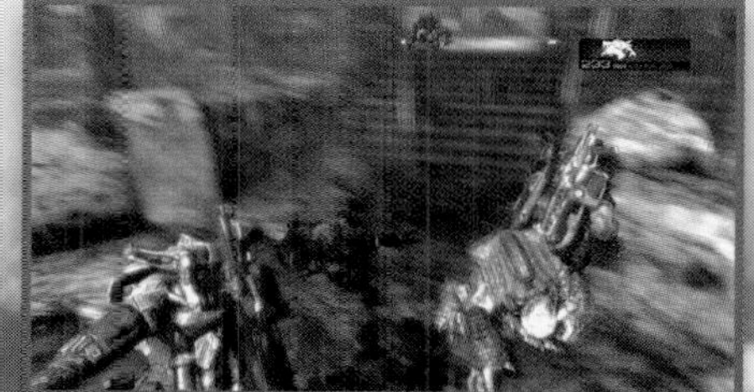

There's a single turret in this hall. You can evade it completely and continue moving. Alternatively, you can roll past it to pick up some ammo and find a switch to deactivate it.

There are several active turrets in this room. The switch to deactivate them is in the next hallway, so you have to dodge, roll, and run past them.

However, there are also several Wretches in the area. Let the turrets do most of the work for you, and then make your way past them.

A few security turrets on the ceiling here provide more supplementary firepower for your squad. Let them assist you against the Wretches. Then roll past them and trigger the switch at the back of the room to deactivate them.

Don't miss the collectible in the small room behind the switch! Also, there is a flamethrower in this same room.

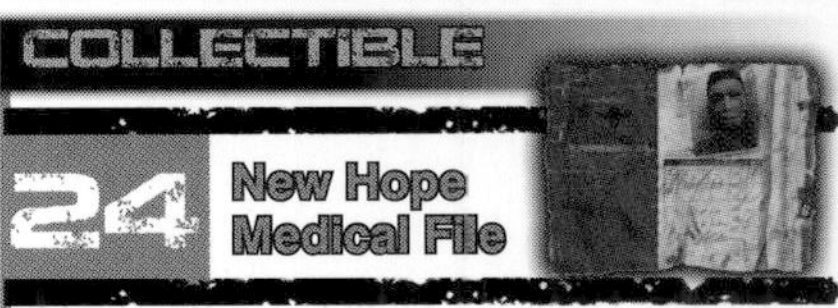

Find the **New Hope Medical File** just off the main room, behind the switch that deactivates the turrets.

After you clear out the ground floor, you have to head downstairs. Down there, you find a long hallway filled with more of the stationary flame turrets, along with a large pack of Wretches charging you!

The Wretches are very easy to dispatch, thanks to the tight quarters and help from the flame-throwing turrets. When the Wretches are dead, you can roll or Roadie Run past the turrets to get to the end of the hall.

The path branches here, though it is a *very* short branch. If you're playing solo, follow the left path, as it's a bit quicker. However, both are safe and easy.

LEFT PATH

ENCOUNTER 12

ENEMY PRESENCE

NONE

This hallway's left branch puts you in charge of a series of switches that disable the turrets in the hallway adjacent to you. Press them in sequence to allow your partner to slip through the hallway safely.

RIGHT PATH

ENCOUNTER 13

ENEMY PRESENCE

NONE

The right branch is only marginally more complex. Wait for your partner to flip the switches, and then slip between the next set of turrets until you reach the end of the hall.

ENCOUNTER 14

ENEMY PRESENCE

NONE

Rejoining your partner after the final security hallway, you emerge into a quiet section of the lab. Strange *things* reside within stasis tanks. It's clear they were conducting experiments on the specimens inside, but exactly what, or who, or why remains unclear...

ENCOUNTER 15

ENEMY PRESENCE

NONE

When you reach the computer room, many answers await you in the databanks. Flip the switch to restore power and wait for Jack to access the database to reveal some startling discoveries. This completes the chapter.

CHAPTER 3: RUDE AWAKENING

Reactivating the computer systems has had an unintended side effect. The creatures within the stasis chambers have begun to wake up...and they aren't friendly.

You must fight your way back out to the Centaur, where Cole and Baird are waiting, and escape the facility with a new destination in mind: Mount Kadar.

E01
MEDIUM AMMO
E02
E03
E09
E10
E04
LARGE AMMO
LARGE AMMO
E08
LARGE AMMO
C25
E05
E06
E11
E07
E12
E13
LARGE AMMO
C26
E14
LARGE AMMO
E17
E15
E16

ICON KEY

START	FINISH	LADDER
ENCOUNTER	COLLECTIBLE	

Unintended consequences or no, the *things* contained within the stasis chambers have awakened. As you exit the computer room, it quickly becomes clear that they are aggressive and dangerous.

The only bright side to the mass of emerging teeth and claws is that these beings are a threat only at close range in melee combat. They're also soft, fleshy, and perfect for ripping to shreds with the Lancer chainsaw bayonet.

You *can* shoot them down. But they frequently stand right back up and come after you again! The safest way through is often simply chain-sawing every one in sight until the area is clear.

They're fairly quick, but you can Roadie Run and fire on the move to down them if you're simply moving from area to area. There is a medium ammo box to the side of the door that leads to the next encounter.

Before you enter the next room, there is a flamethrower and a medium ammo box to the left. You don't have a choice about fighting in this next room. There's a sealed gate, and *two* wheels must be turned to open it. Because you and Dom both must operate the wheels, you must first exterminate the creatures in the area before it's safe to open the gate.

Fight near the doorway and chainsaw as many of them as you can. When the area is quiet, open the door and continue.

While this excitement carries on, a storm brews outside—a razorhail storm. This vicious atmospheric threat is just as dangerous as the creatures attacking you inside the facility. The blowing storm brings a rain of tearing shards from the sky. Baird and Cole are pinned down, and getting back to the Centaur will be problematic.

You reach the heart of the security system in this room. The Niles AI must be shut down, as he's acting against your team. You can't have a rogue AI causing problems while you're dealing with everything else. Find the main switch inside this room and shut him down.

After you leave behind the computer center, a new threat arises. Locust forces have arrived at the facility. As you enter this room, the vanguard of their force smashes through the wall. If you need it, this room contains a large ammo box

This is your first encounter with the Scorcher-wielding Grenadiers. These flamethrower-brandishing foes are a dangerous threat in close quarters—exactly where you're forced to fight them here!

However, there is a tactical advantage you can employ. Check the back room for a switch that controls the security turrets in the room where the Locust arrived. Turn it on and watch the fireworks. Then flip it off so you can safely leave the room.

More Drones and Scorcher users here; keep your distance and focus fire on the Scorcher wielders first. They're more dangerous than the Drones. If you like using the Scorcher, use this opportunity to stock up on ammo from their dropped weapons.

The next room has a nasty ambush, featuring more Drones and Scorcher Grenadiers in the hall. This makeshift battlefield is made up of three parts: your side of the hall in a few rooms, the central hallway, and the opposite rooms. Each area is exposed to fire through windows.

More critically, a security turret in the central hall makes passing through the middle hazardous. You can turn this to your advantage. Rather than engaging in head-on conflict with the Locust here, sneak around into a back room on your side. Find a switch and pull it. The security turret drops down from the center hall, and a new one pops up over on the Locust side!

With the help of the turret, you can easily clear out the remaining Drones and continue down the hall.

A Drone and a Scorcher Grenadier lie in wait down this hall, making for a brief fight. Keep your distance, pick off the Scorcher user first, and then keep moving.

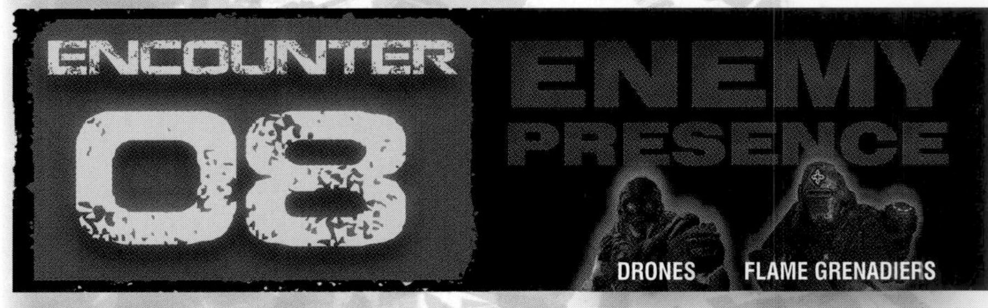

The exact same battle calls for the same remedy—hang back and take down your foes from cover at a distance.

If you've picked up a Scorcher of your own, there's one point worth mentioning: going after Scorcher-wielding Grenadiers is not a recipe for success. You eventually end up badly burned no matter how you engage them.

As you enter this sizable room, a larger Locust force comes in from the door that leads outside. There are Drones, Flame Grenadiers, and a Grinder in the mix.

DEV TIP

You can either kill three Locust here or wait about 15 seconds. Either way, the razorhail smashes through the ceiling and shreds them!

—ADAM BELLEFEUIL

Quickly take cover and try to pick them off. You don't have to actually kill them all. After a short time, the glass ceiling breaks under the battering from the razorhail storm. This inclement weather makes quick work of the Locust out in the middle of the room!

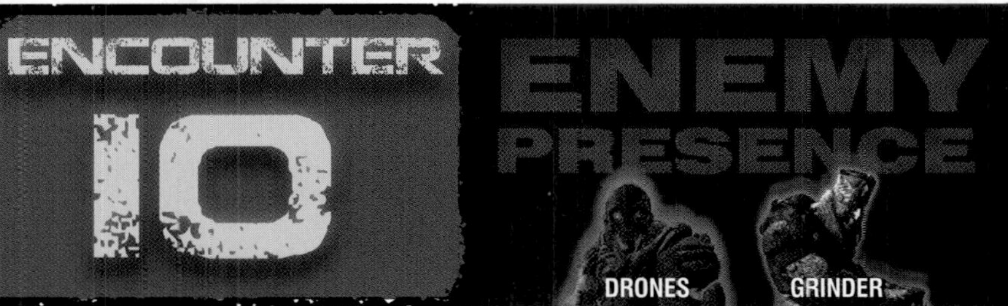

Once you get outside the facility, the razorhail storm's full force and fury become apparent. Walking directly back to the Centaur is not an option, at least not without the storm cutting you to ribbons.

You must exploit the scant cover afforded by the ruined buildings and the rusting train hulks in the yard.

Before you get moving, head into the nearby building to pick up the collectible, and then hop into the train.

Inside the train car, you can pull the lever to get it moving. As you do, several Drones arise from an Emergence Hole outside the train windows. As the train car moves, you also pass a Grinder and more Drones. None of this is a problem, though; just keep your head down until the train reaches its destination.

After you emerge from the facility, you can go left into a building and then hop onto the train—but don't do this! Instead, turn right, and run into the small building. You can find the **New Hope Journal** on the ground at the back.

Once you disembark the train at the covered platform, you're safe for the moment. That is, until you step forward and an Emergence Hole appears out in the open.

Several Drones and Snipers arise from the hole and take up positions under a covered walkway. Two waves of Locust originate from the hole if you don't close it.

DEV TIP

It *is* possible to hit the Emergence Hole just after you disembark from the train. You must make a long and high grenade throw to do it!

—ADAM BELLEFEUIL

There are a few ways to deal with this situation. You can stay put and try to pick them off from a distance, or you can move down the covered walkway and try to flank them—it's comprised of several sharp L turns.

In either case, once you deal with the hole, use the walkway to reach the next building safely.

There are two Locust inside the garage building: a lone Sniper and a single Drone. Deal with the more dangerous Sniper first.

Once you deal with the Locust inside, turn the wheels on the garage doors to move them up and thus provide cover from the razorhail.

DEV TIP

Pick up a Longshot, either from this building or from the Snipers at the Emergence Hole. You can use it to easily dispatch the Drones outside the garage.

—ADAM BELLEFEUIL

You can move from door to door this way until you reach the last door, which is outside the garage and covered by several Drones outside. Take them down, and then use the last garage door to reach the next train car.

ENCOUNTER 13

ENEMY PRESENCE

DRONES, BOOMER, GRINDER

Once you're past the garage, be sure to stop in the nearby building to pick up the collectible. There is also a large ammo box in this building. Then hop onto the second train car.

Inside, pull the lever to get your ride moving. You pass several groups of Drones, a Grinder, and, of greater concern, a Boomer. You can easily avoid the Drones and Grinders by keeping your head low in cover, but the Boomer can hurt you with splash damage. Concentrate your fire on him as the train car moves.

When the train ride ends, you can climb up a ladder to a covered walkway. It leads back to the courtyard out in front of the facility—you're nearly home!

COLLECTIBLE

26 Captivity Marks

Before you board the last train, turn 180 degrees and face the building at the back of the train yard. Run inside and check the wall to find the **Captivity Marks** scratched into it.

ENCOUNTER 14

ENEMY PRESENCE

DRONES

Back down in the courtyard, a series of covered areas leads back toward the Centaur.

As you reach the first, an Emergence Hole opens, spewing forth Drones. Use the plentiful cover in the area and take them down. Or simply grenade the hole if you have any frags handy.

DEV TIP

There are only five Drones in this hole. They come out in pairs until you eliminate them or the hole is closed.

—ADAM BELLEFEUIL

ENCOUNTER 15

ENEMY PRESENCE

DRONES, MAULERS

Sprint from the safety of the covered roof, get past the razorhail, and reach the next bit of cover. When you reach it, another Emergence Hole opens and more Drones rise to attack.

The Drones are just a sideshow. Shortly into the battle, a pair of Maulers shows up. These massive Boomer-sized Locust wield close-range explosive flails and carry the powerful Boomshields.

Normally, the Boomshields provide almost perfect frontal defense for Maulers. But in this case, they use them as mobile protection from the razorhail!

Take advantage of this momentary weakness, concentrating all of your firepower on the Maulers when they show up.

Once you down the Maulers, you can sprint out and pick up one of their Boomshields. Then you can easily walk in the razorhail with the shield over your head.

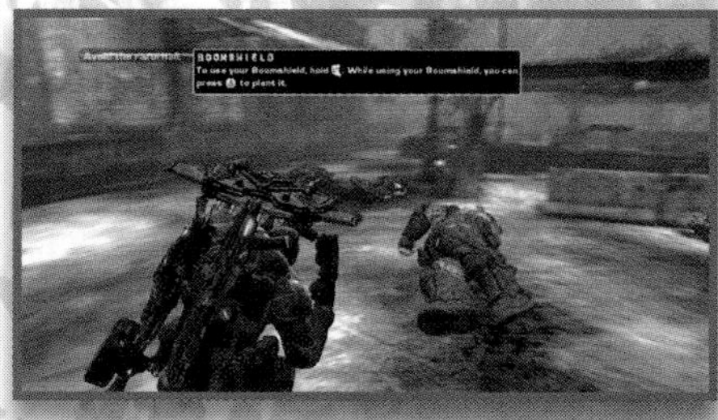

Killing two of the Drones from the hole makes the Maulers show up. Once they do, let them get close enough that you can run out and grab their shield safely.

Don't worry if you kill them far away, though. If the Boomshields are too far to reach, the razorhail does eventually cease.

—ADAM BELLEFEUIL

While not strictly a 'weapon,' the Boomshield is nonetheless a very powerful defensive tool. Much like a meat shield, you can use the Boomshield to block fire from the front.

However, unlike a meat shield, the Boomshield does not wear out. You can continue using it for as long as you like. You're still restricted to pistol-class weaponry, but you can move more quickly.

One last thing: the Boomshield can be planted as static cover and then picked up again. This lets you to bring your heavier two-handed weapons to bear and still enjoy the benefit of mobile cover when you need it!

Your next fight is nearly a freebie. Use your newfound Boomshield's awesome protective power against the Emergence Holes that spring up here. The Drones that come out don't have the firepower to penetrate the shield, and you can take them down easily and safely.

As the razorhail dies off, your path to the Centaur is clear, and you can proceed without danger from the storm.

Last stop. Once you reach the Centaur, Baird has to work on repairing it from the damage caused by the storm. This would be fine…if Reavers didn't show up!

Two Reavers come after you here. Your Boomshield is still plenty useful to block their shots. You may simply want to plant it and use it as stationary cover so you can break out your heavier weapons.

Be careful about letting the Reavers get too close to you. You don't want them spearing you with their talons, whether you're behind hard cover or Boomshield cover.

Once you deal with the two Reavers, Delta sets off in the Centaur for a new destination.

CHAPTER 4: ASCENSION

The databank at the New Hope facility has revealed that the source of the Locust may be located deep within Mount Kadar. Delta Squad sets out in their Centaur to reach the interior of the mountain, but Locust resistance to their intrusion is fierce.

This mission is very different from the on-foot combat you've experienced up to this point. Instead, you get to raise hell in the Centaur. Your objective is simply to reach Mount Kadar, so you don't get any rewards for taking the long route or clearing the map of all Locust presence. Keep that in mind while you pick your path through the passes leading to the mountain. This is doubly true on the higher difficulty levels. On Casual or Normal, you can fairly well blitz through the encounters. But on Hardcore or Insane, you need to eliminate priority targets quickly and hang back at a distance to avoid fire whenever possible.

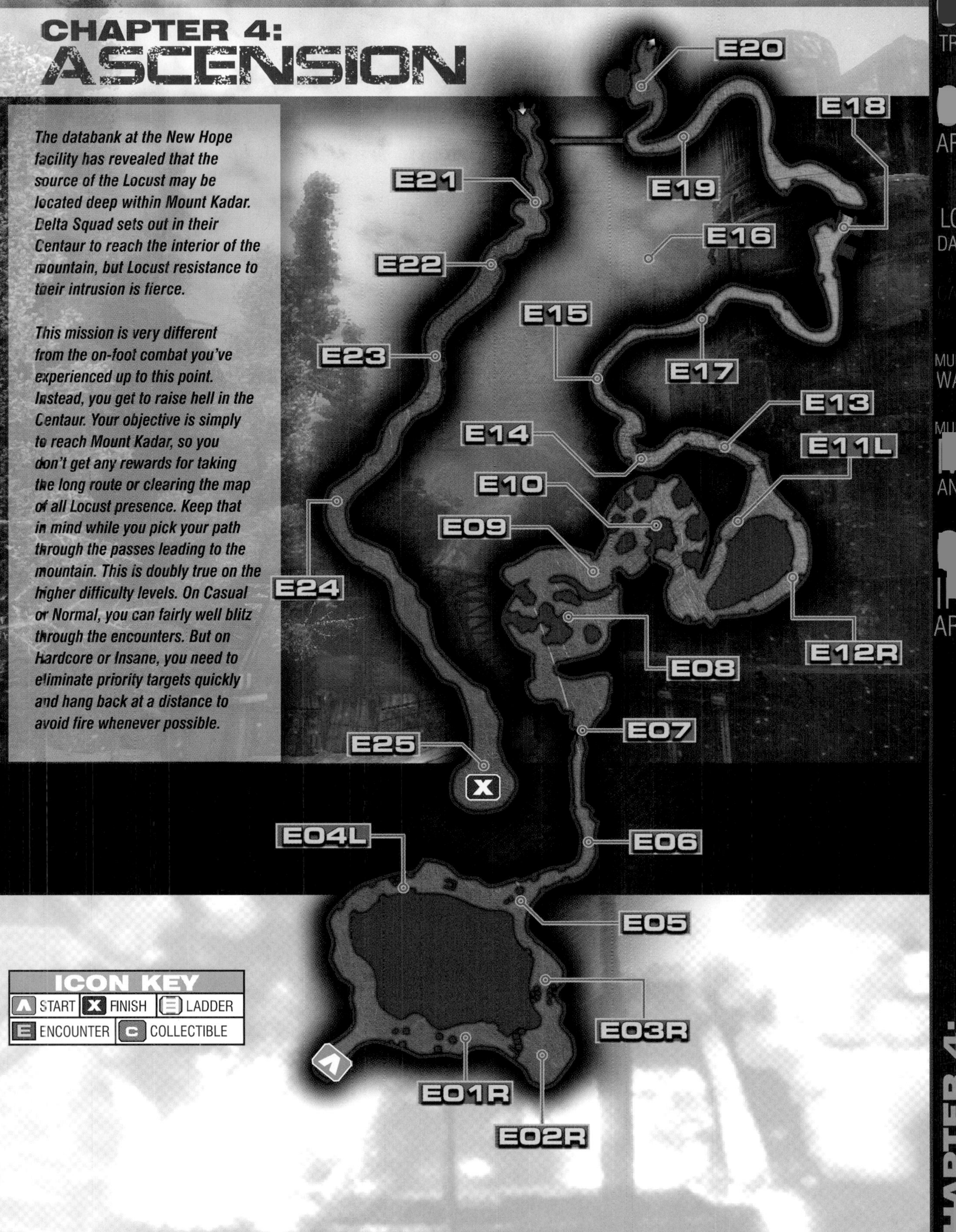

The Centaur

VEHICLE

The Centaur is a powerful COG vehicle, a battle tank capable of taking on Corpsers or Brumaks on nearly even footing. Of the more common Locust ground troops, only Reavers present a serious threat. Troika and Boomers can be dangerous, but the powerful main turret makes short work of lighter Locust troops.

You can Active Reload the Centaur's turret for a quicker fire rate. Hitting Perfect Active Reloads is very helpful for eliminating the heavy Locust resistance you face on the road to Mount Kadar.

You can tap 'run' in the Centaur to get a speed boost, which is useful for outrunning pursuing Locust or jumping over ramps.

Your first encounter consists of an easily dispatched Boomer and then a barricade that you can blast open. Beyond it, Drones and a Troika provide you with some target practice.

Blow them away with the Centaur's cannon, and then make your way across the bridge just ahead.

Boost-jump across the ramp on the right side of the road here. When you land, be ready for two Reavers that drop in. You may want to fire off a few shots and then do an Active Reload before you encounter them, just to have a slight edge in the battle.

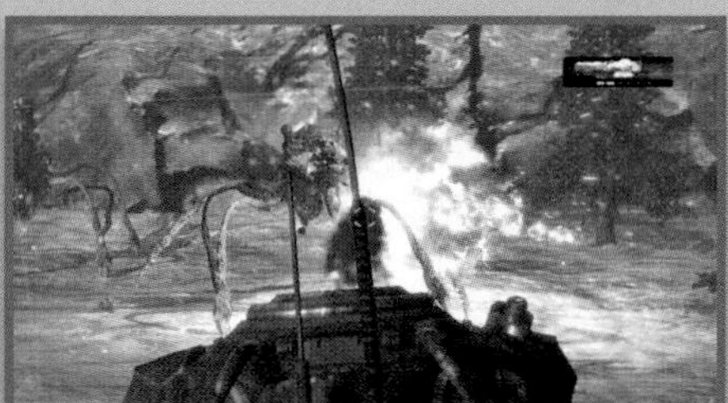

No special tricks in this encounter, swarms of Drones and a few Boomers litter the road. A few precise applications of the Centaur's cannon, and they end up *littering* the road.

ENCOUNTER 04

ENEMY PRESENCE

BOOMERS · DRONES · TROIKA · REAVER

If you take the left branch from the start point, you have only one encounter to deal with before the path rejoins the right split. But the enemy presence is more substantial than the smaller encounters on the right route.

In this case, treat the Boomers, Troika, and the Reaver as priority targets. Don't pay much attention to the Drones—you can even run them down if you wish.

On the bright side, once you clear out this checkpoint, the road is clear to the next encounter.

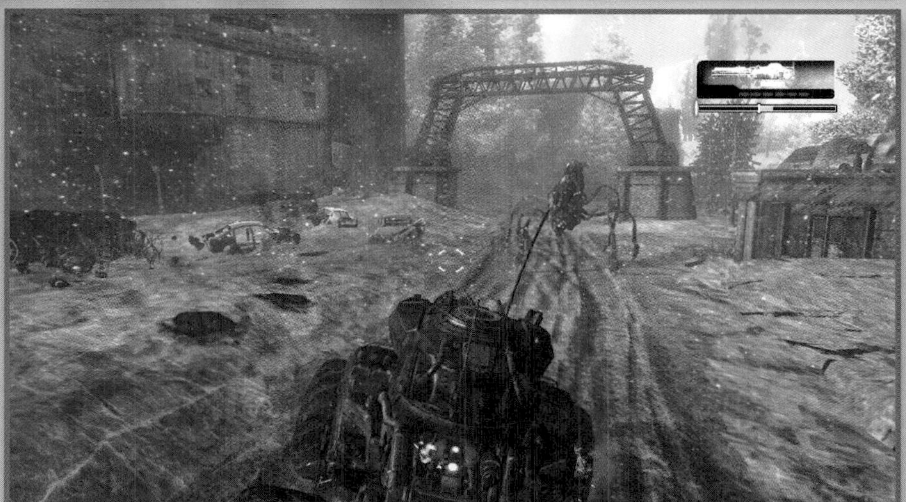

As the path reconnects the two split routes, a small Locust force opposes your ascent up the mountain. First take down the Troika up on the building. Then you can either dispatch the remaining Drones or simply ignore them and continue driving.

As you approach the building, a substantial Locust ambush faces you: multiple Boomers, a Troika on the building, and a Reaver, along with plenty of Drones.

Keep your distance and pick off the primary threats first. When little more than Drones remain, you can shoot through the barricade blocking the road and continue driving.

No enemies here, just a sharp drop! Boost and fly over the edge to land in style.

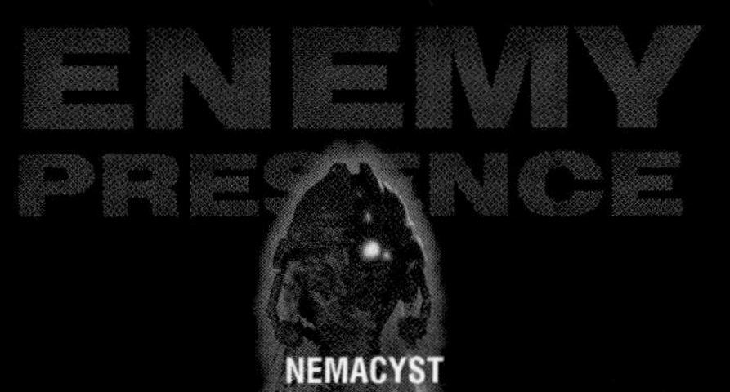

Your next obstacle is a frozen lake. Carefully, slowly drive out onto it. As you do, Nemacyst mortars blast holes in the ice! As long as you take it slow, you can navigate between the holes and come out on the other side. Check the map for a glimpse of how the holes end up covering the lake.

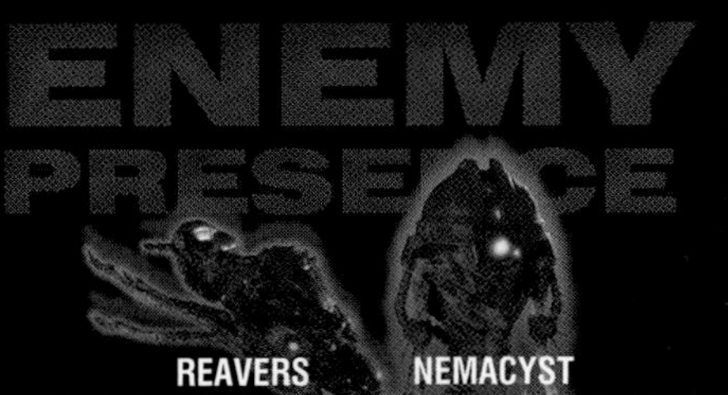

Getting across the lake provides no rest, as two Reavers drop onto the narrow strip of land between the first lake and another just ahead.

Down them both before you attempt to move on—you can't cross the lake safely with Reavers firing on you.

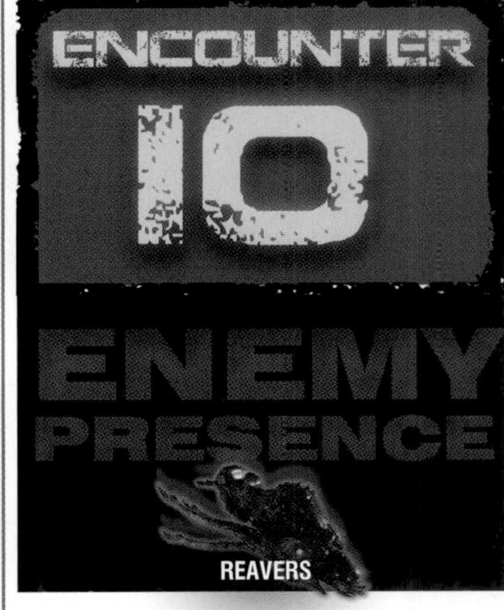

Another frozen lake, but this time you have to deal with Reavers dropping in on you as you try to cross. Keep an eye out for them. When they swoop in to land, greet them with thunder from the Centaur's cannon.

The left route is more direct, but you have to deal with a pair of Reavers as you drive up the road. Focus your fire on one, then down the second as the first one falls.

If you follow the right route at the branch here, you must dispatch a few Boomers near the building and then jump a gap out onto a stretch of road.

There are two Reavers past the jump. Because this route is a bit longer and has more enemies, there's little reason to go this way.

Regardless of which path you take, they both end up here. You must blast out a barricade in the road to continue.

Then blow out the Troika protecting the split in the road. Drones swarm the area; you can blow them into small Locust chunks or simply drive over them.

Two more Reavers drop in as you make your way up the mountain trail. You should have plenty of practice dealing with them by this point—take them out and keep moving.

A single Reaver here isn't a major threat. Blow it apart and continue driving up the road.

A rare encounter with Seeders, presumably these were the ones launching Nemacyst to the ice lakes. They're both perched on a distant ridge. Shoot them down before you continue up the road.

Another pair of Reavers attempts to stop you here beneath this icy bridge. Blow them apart and drive under the bridge to continue.

There aren't any enemies here, but there is a tricky jump. The main bridge across this chasm is destroyed, so you must take advantage of a small ramp to its right.

Before you do, you can run over the trees in front of the ramp to clear a straight path. Then drive back up the road to reach full speed. Boost as you approach the ramp and make sure you're going straight. If you do this properly, you should land safely in one piece on the other side.

You're getting near the end of the road, and the resistance gets slightly tougher. Two Reavers hit you on the road, and a final one is up on the ridge to your right as you drive up the road. Take your time driving so you don't have to deal with all of them at once.

As you approach the tunnel that leads into Mount Kadar, you must pass this final Locust stronghold. As you approach it, you face Reavers, mounted Troika, and Boomers on the ground, as well as a healthy dose of Drones.

Prioritize the Reavers as you edge up to the facility, but don't rush in. Try to snipe as many targets as possible from the mountain road before you close the distance.

Once you down the major threats, you can blast the tower to the left of the gate blocking access to the mountain tunnel. As the gate falls, your path into the heart of Mount Kadar opens; drive into the darkness.

As you enter the tunnel, it begins to dim until the lights are gone. The Centaur's lights provide some illumination, but it is still a gloomy venture.

As you get near the wall at the back, a Corpser bursts through, menacing you only a moment before withdrawing. This opens a route deeper into the mountain—follow it!

A steep drop from your level to a lower passage makes for a bumpy drop. But there's no danger here, so just keep moving.

Another drop, this one is hard enough to make the Centaur's lights flicker. After you reorient and continue moving, you can see an unpleasant sight: a Brumak stomping along, parallel to you on the right side. As it tramps along, some of the rock columns to your right collapse. Carefully drive under the arch that remains.

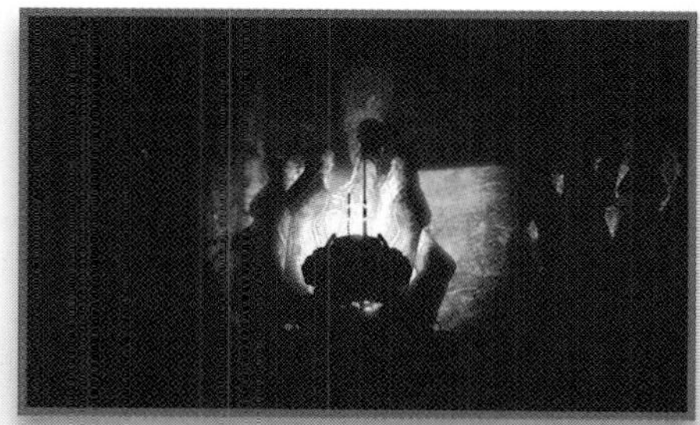

A long drop here slams and shocks the Centaur, knocking the power out...along with your lights. The gleaming light of a Corpser's eyes is not a comforting sight.

The instant the power comes back, target and fire! Three Corpsers surround you, and you need to eliminate them quickly. Aim for the Corpsers' faces to kill them swiftly.

If the Corpser encounter wasn't bad enough, the grand finale when you arrive in this cavern is not one, but *two* Brumaks. They aren't happy to see you on their turf.

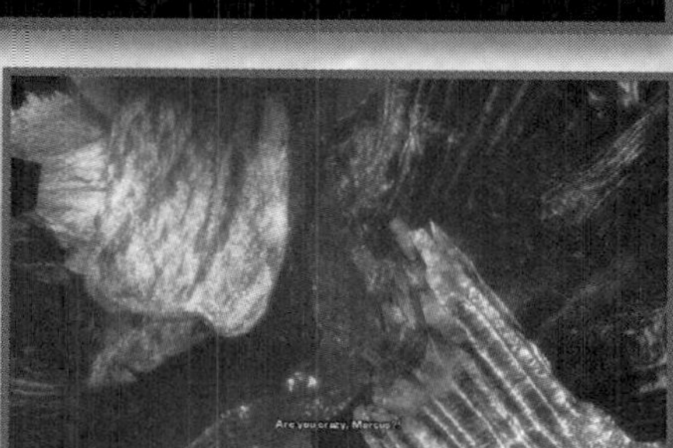

You have plenty of room to maneuver in the large cavern where they attack. Be sure to keep your distance, and take any opportunity to mess with their line of sight.

If at all possible, focus your fire on one of the two Brumaks. This cuts down on the incoming fire you receive.

To gain a small edge, you may wish to empty the Centaur's ammo load and then perform a Perfect Active Reload before you engage here.

Once you take down the Brumaks, you must make a final long jump to finish this chapter and penetrate deeper into Mount Kadar!

CHAPTER 5: DISPLACEMENT

Delta arrives to find a group of Stranded hiding within the mountain. Marcus orders Cole and Baird to take them back to the surface, while he and Dom attempt to find the Nexus of which they speak.

Dom questions Chaps about Maria, and he indicates he may have seen her. Now Dom wants to go looking for her.

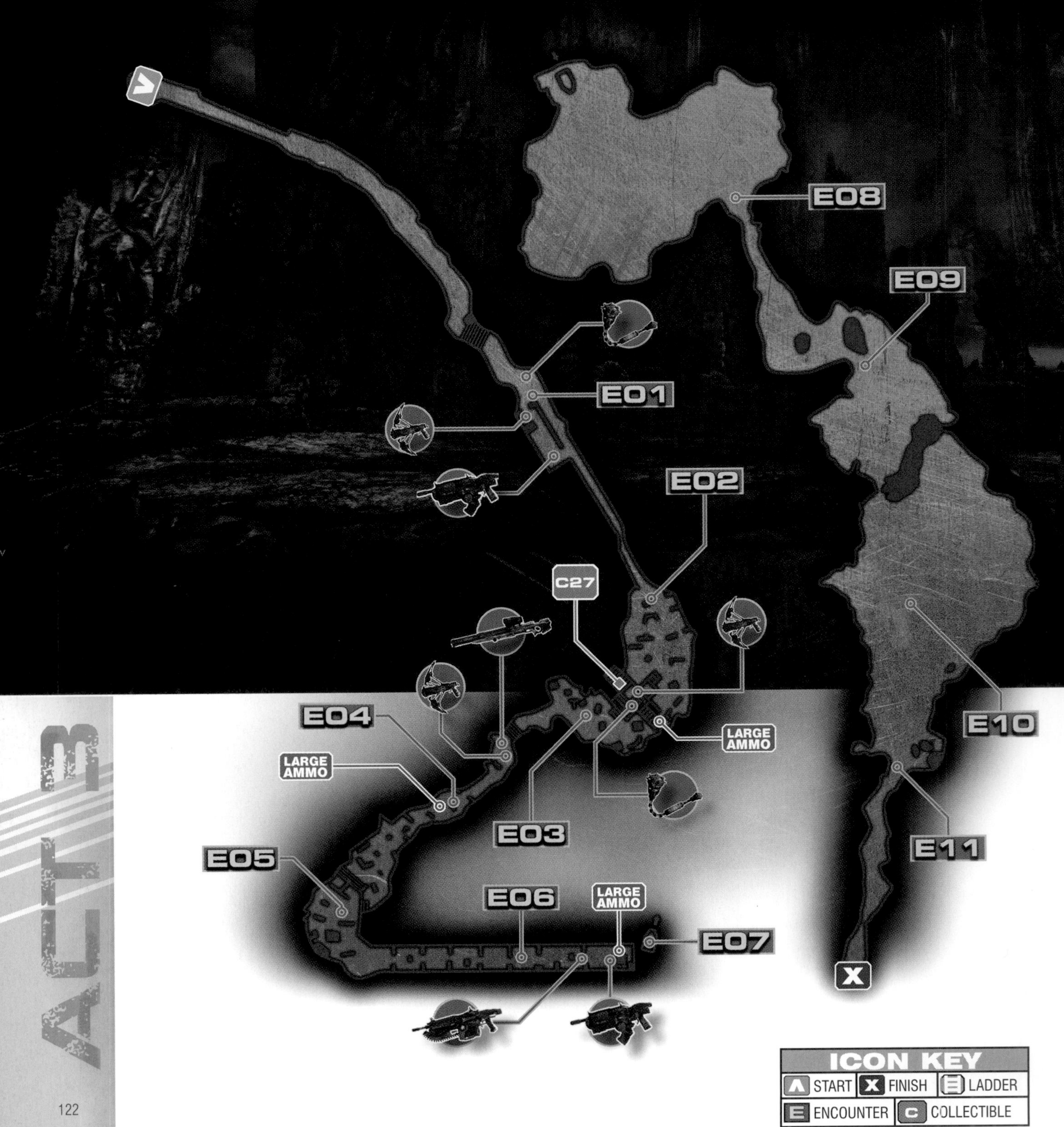

ACT 3

Prepare for your first encounter with the Theron Guard. If you're a *Gears of War* veteran, you already have a healthy hatred for this foe. If not, be warned. Theron Guards are tougher, smarter Drones, and they are often armed with the lethal Torque Bow.

Depending on your difficulty setting, a Torque Bow in the hands of a Theron Guard ranges from very dangerous to instantly lethal. Don't give them a chance to fire. If you see the glow of a charged Torque Bow, stay under cover.

Skirt the Theron Guard's clean lane of fire by going through the tunnel on the path's right side. Sneak your way down and grab the Torque Bow on the ground. Then flank and eliminate the Theron Guard to get some additional ammunition.

Torque Bow

WEAPON

The Theron Guard is a dangerous foe, but this adversary is also your first opportunity to acquire the lethal Torque Bow. One well-aimed shot can take down any basic Locust infantry or deal heavy damage to even Boomers and Reavers.

As you reach the 'docks' area by the water, the first sign of heavier Locust resistance arrives. A wave of Drones and several Wretches appear as you get closer to the ruins further along the trail.

Be careful about moving too far forward here. You don't want to end up in cover near Drones when the Wretches attack. That wouldn't give you enough room to dispatch the Wretches without taking an unhealthy amount of fire from the Drones.

DEV TIP

If you're playing on Hardcore or Insane, watch out for the Theron Guard that accompanies the Drones in this encounter.

—ANDREW BAINS

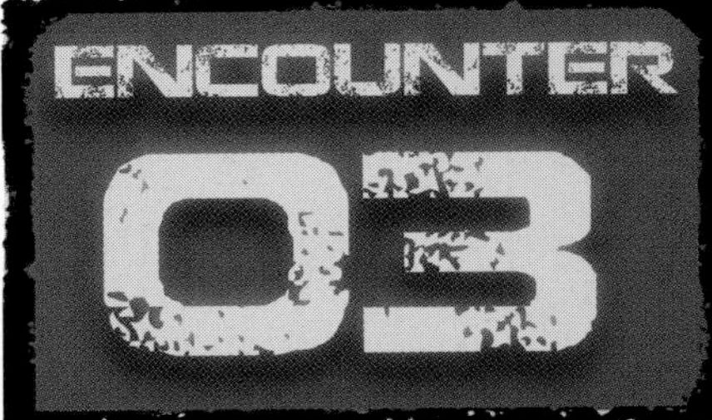

If you're playing on Hardcore or Insane, there's a Kantus here. Make him a priority—you don't want to deal with Tickers or rising Drones!

—ANDREW BAINS

27 Stranded's Journal

A short, worn-down flight of steps is in the center of the ruins. Check the top of the steps to find the **Stranded's Journal**.

As you approach the center of the ruins, a Drone and a Flame Grenadier attack from the front. Simultaneously, a Locust gunboat strafes you from the shoreline.

Take cover and deal with the immediate threat from the Drones. Then turn your fire on the Locust explosives conveniently located on the gunboat. Detonating them causes the gunboat to crash, eliminating the threat and creating a makeshift platform to reach the next section of the 'docks' area.

Before you leave, don't forget the collectible in the center of the ruins.

Several Drones and a Kantus resist your approach down this stretch of the shore, but you have access to some handy firepower. A Longshot and a Torque Bow are on the ground as you cross over the wrecked Locust gunboat.

Pick up your favorite of the two, and use it to dispatch the Kantus before you deal with the Drones.

A nasty encounter here, a Bloodmount charges from the ruins ahead. Deal with it first, and then slowly approach the raised platform ahead.

You have to deal with several Grenadiers and a Kantus. If possible, take out the Kantus with your heavy firepower. After you bring him down, mop up the resistance and move on.

A Locust gunboat is docked at the end of the long pier leading out to the water. Make your way down the pier and clear out the resistance.

There are several speedy Drones here, a Grinder at the end of the pier, *and* a Troika on the gunboat.

There's plenty of cover on the approach, though. If possible, pick off the Grinder from a distance. Once the Locust on the pier are gone, the gunboat flees from your approach.

As you reach the end of the pier, you find a tiny boat but it has been sunk by the Locust. A gunboat then slams into the pier, separating the end of it from land—with you on the makeshift raft!

As you float helplessly, the gunboat comes in close enough for you to retaliate. Dispatch the Drones on the gunboat. Then you can do little but wait as the current catches your raft and carries you down the river.

As you float, a second gunboat attacks but soon retreats…strange.

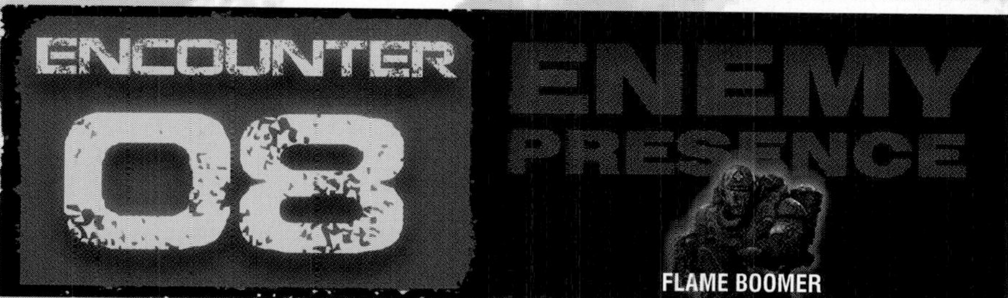

As you drift down the river, you slowly float through an area covered with Imulsion fumes, perhaps the reason the Locust broke off the chase.

While you float through the fumes, something disturbingly large bumps into your raft from below and then vanishes…

When the raft finally leaves the fumes, another gunboat attacks. Kill the Flame Boomer aboard the gunboat, and you can finally hijack a real ride. Board the gunboat as the 'raft' sinks behind you.

ENEMY PRESENCE

GUNBOAT

Now you have a real ride, but the Locust resistance to your presence on the river intensifies as multiple gunboats come after you.

You can use the heavy Troika mounted on the front of your boat against a few of the Locust boats that come near your own.

In total, four boats attack: first from the right, then two from the left, and finally a last one on the right.

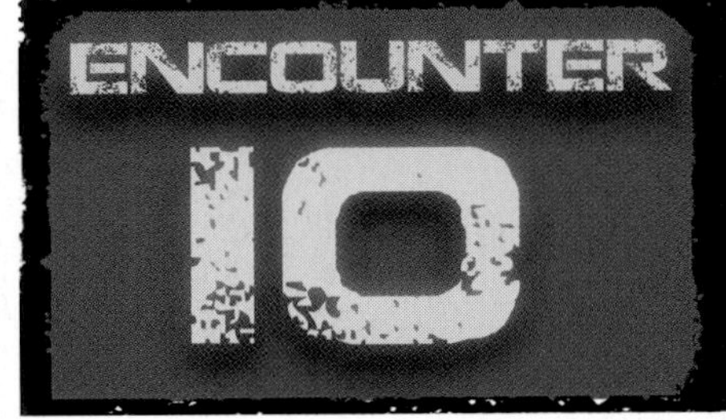

ENEMY PRESENCE

NONE

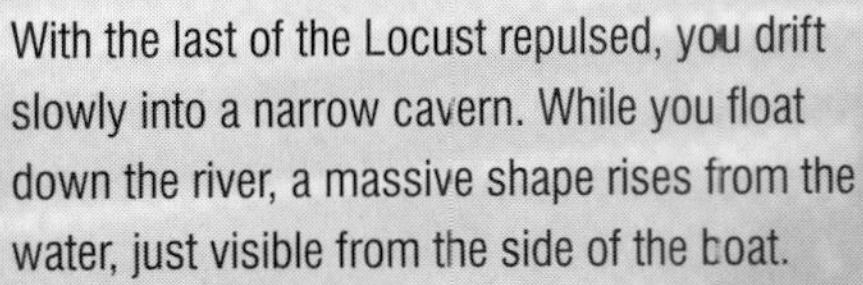

With the last of the Locust repulsed, you drift slowly into a narrow cavern. While you float down the river, a massive shape rises from the water, just visible from the side of the boat.

Before you have a real chance to identify what the shape is, your craft plummets over a waterfall!

The first gunboat has Drones armed with Hammerburst. The second carries Lancers. The third brings a Grinder with Grenadiers. Finally, the last has Grenadiers and a Theron armed with a Lancer.

Use the Troika when you can. The rest of the time, use the gunwales on the vessel's side to shield you from Locust fire.

CHAPTER 6: BRACKISH WATERS

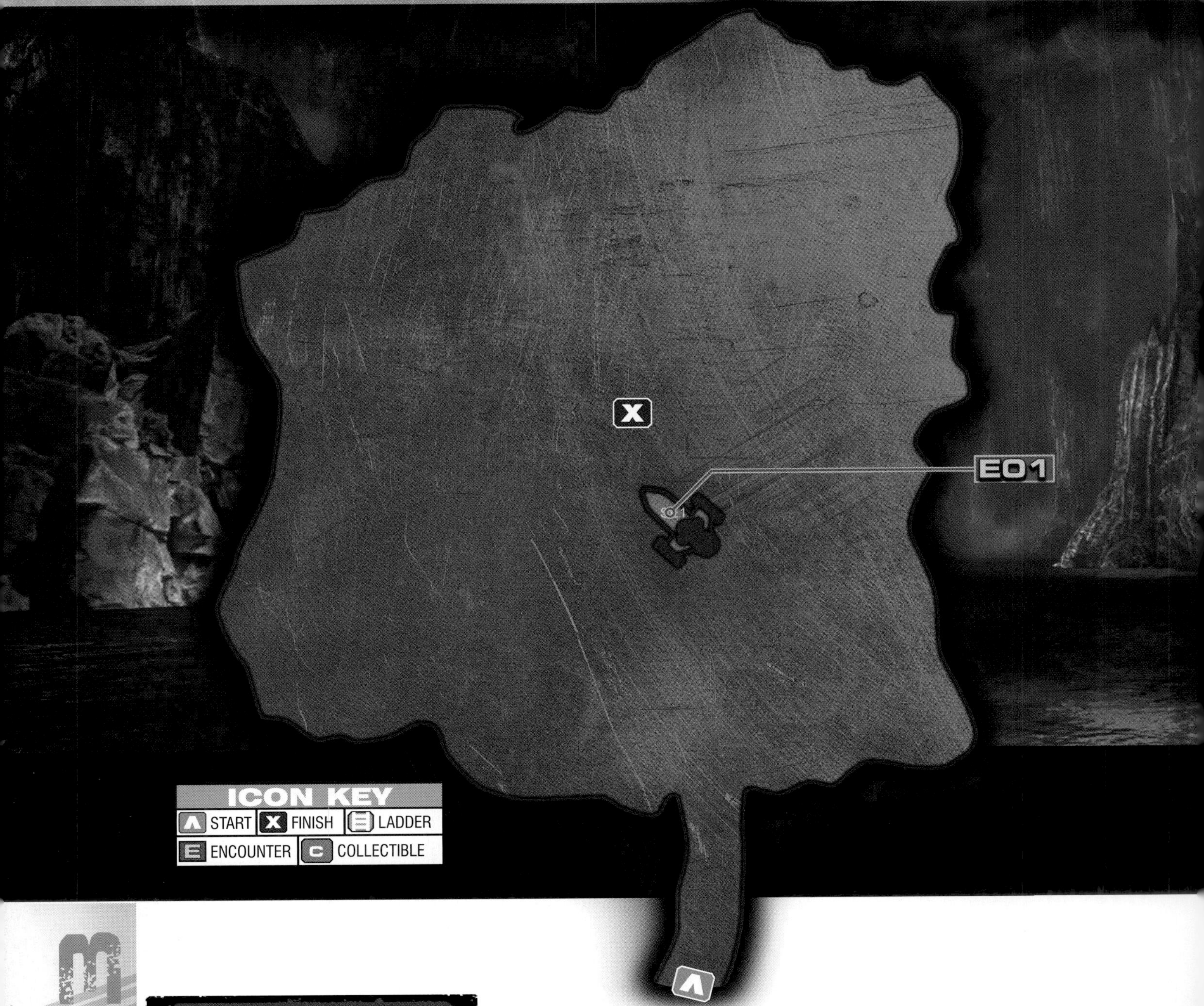
E01
ICON KEY
START
FINISH
LADDER
ENCOUNTER
COLLECTIBLE

CHALLENGING ENCOUNTER 01

ENEMY PRESENCE

LAKE MONSTER

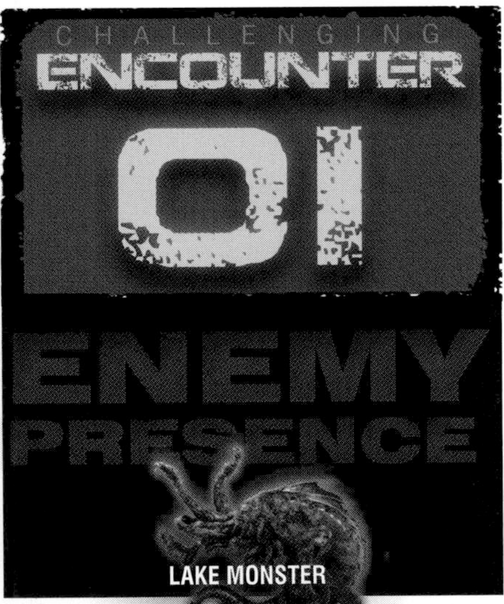

The shadow that has trailed your movements across the underground waters finally reveals itself—and it is a horror.

The Lake Monster is a monstrous aquatic beast, and you are confined to the very limited space aboard the drifting Locust vessel that brought you here.

The Lake Monster first makes its presence known by lashing the boat with its tentacle. You must quickly rush the tentacle and chainsaw it. This causes the Lake Monster to retract the severely wounded appendage...and enrages it further.

The Lake Monster repeats the tentacle attack on the boat three times. Each time the process is the same; watch for the tentacle to rise, dodge if it comes down near you, then charge and chainsaw.

Once you've wounded the Lake Monster badly enough, it withdraws for a moment. Dom draws your attention to it rising from the water off to the side of the boat, and then it goes under.

When the Lake Monster reemerges, it doesn't waste any time. It goes straight for a kill, rising from the depths and gnashing the end of the boat in its mammoth maw.

To make it retreat, shoot it in the eye, which is its only vulnerable area. When it retreats, wait for a moment and stay back from the end of the boat! When it returns, it bites the boat again. This time, shoot it in the eye—it opens its mouth wide. Go inside!

Seriously, you must get into its 'softer' regions. Rush inside the mouth before it snaps shut. Inside, several tentacles surround an orifice in the middle. Shoot the moving tentacle to make the Lake Monster 'open up.' Then toss a Frag Grenade into its exposed maw. You don't have to be perfectly accurate; just get it roughly in line with the opening to cause a devastating and damaging explosion.

The Lake Monster withdraws after you land a damaging hit. As it does, you should find several Frag Grenades to pick up on the boat. Grab them if you need them.

You have to score three grenades down the Lake Monster's gullet to end its assault. If you miss, the Lake Monster continues to assail the boat. Once you nail the third toss, the Lake Monster goes down and this act is complete.

With the Lake Monster down, you can take stock of your situation. You're now deep within Locust territory under Mount Kadar. The Stranded spoke of a Locust 'highway' in the region, possibly leading to a location known as the Nexus, and that's your next stop.

ACT IV

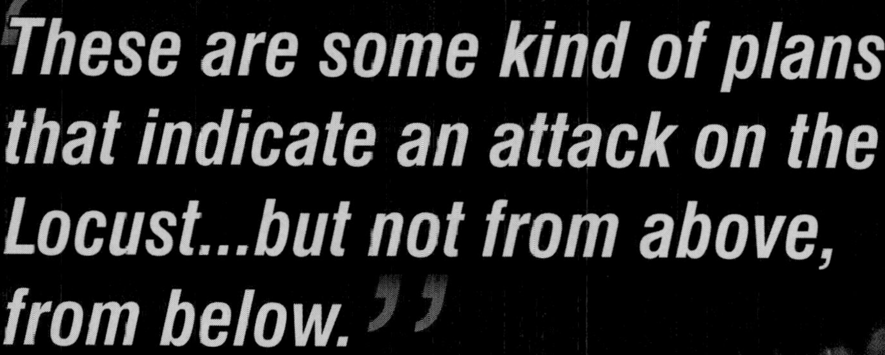

> *"These are some kind of plans that indicate an attack on the Locust...but not from above, from below."*
>
> —Baird

HIVE

CHAPTER 1: PRIORITIES

After the draining battle against the Lake Monster, Marcus and Dom have a brief chance to cool down during the next two chapters. Dom convinces Marcus to aid him in searching for Maria.

There isn't a lot of conflict during either Priorities or Answers, but be grateful for the breather. As you travel deeper into Act 4, the combat gets progressively nastier.

Make your way along the back route into the Locust highway. On the way, you run into a huge train of marching troops. Marcus wants to follow them, but Dom wants to search for Maria, based on Chaps' intel.

Marcus reluctantly agrees and the two set off. Make your way up the walkway toward the dam, where you can take an elevator up to the next level. From here, you spot a Brumak on the highway running past the dam. More importantly, down below the dam, you see a slave camp of imprisoned humans. There may be some hope for finding Maria in this area after all.

Make your way along the ledge to another elevator, this one leading to the dam's interior.

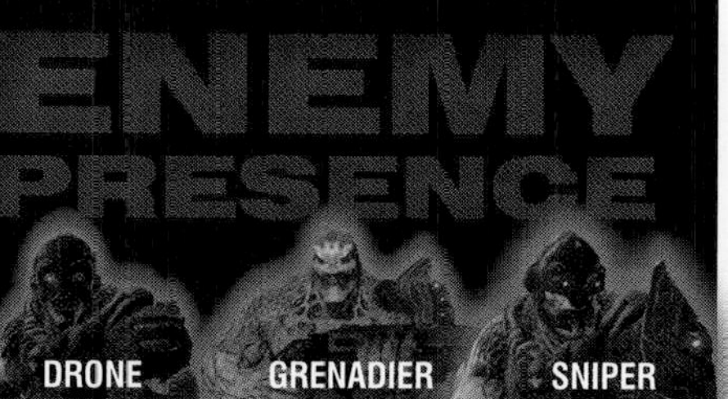

When you enter the dam room, the flow of water is too high to cross. Rotate the wheel at the side of the chamber to lower the water level enough to cross.

Unfortunately, as soon as you start to cross the water channels, a pack of Locust rushes into the room: a Drone, a Grenadier, and a Sniper.

You can't worry about them though, as a Drone Engineer heads for a valve on the opposite side of the room, attempting to increase the water flow again! Shoot him quickly—if he succeeds, you and Dom won't survive.

Once you deal with the Engineer, pick off the other Locust. If you have any Frag Grenades, one well-placed throw can remove them. If not, just use the water channels as cover and finish them off.

After the water chamber, you descend another elevator to reach the ground floor. Grab the ammo pack and the Longshot located just down the hall from the lift, and then make your way out into the cavern.

When you emerge, a Mauler and a pack of Wretches attack. This is actually a blessing in disguise, as the Wretches are easy to dispatch, and the Mauler's Boomshield is very useful for the next fight. Pin him between you and Dom to take him down. Then grab the shield and the nearby Frag Grenades before you step onto the bridge.

When you set foot on the center of the bridge, a Locust searchlight illuminates your position and a pack of Locust attacks. Hopefully you have the Boomshield up and ready, as the Theron Guard, Sniper, and Troika are serious threats. With your shield up, they're more of a minor inconvenience.

You can handle this fight two ways. One option is to advance slowly with the shield, picking off the Locust as you close with them. Alternatively, you can proceed midway up the bridge, plant the shield, and use the cover to lob a few grenades at the Locust in the open.

DEV TIP

The searchlights don't directly hinder you in any way, though they may obscure your vision a bit. You can take them down with just a few direct shots.

—WARREN MARSHALL

Once you deal with the Locust, step up and search the room to find an ammo crate where the Sniper was. There's a Torque Bow near the Locust Terminals on the room's left side.

Don't hit the primary Terminal to search for Maria just yet. Check the second active Terminal to find a collectible.

COLLECTIBLE

28 Locust Terminal

The **Locust Terminal** is the second active Terminal on the room's left side—*not* the one indicated as your objective target.

ACT IV

CHAPTER 2: ANSWERS

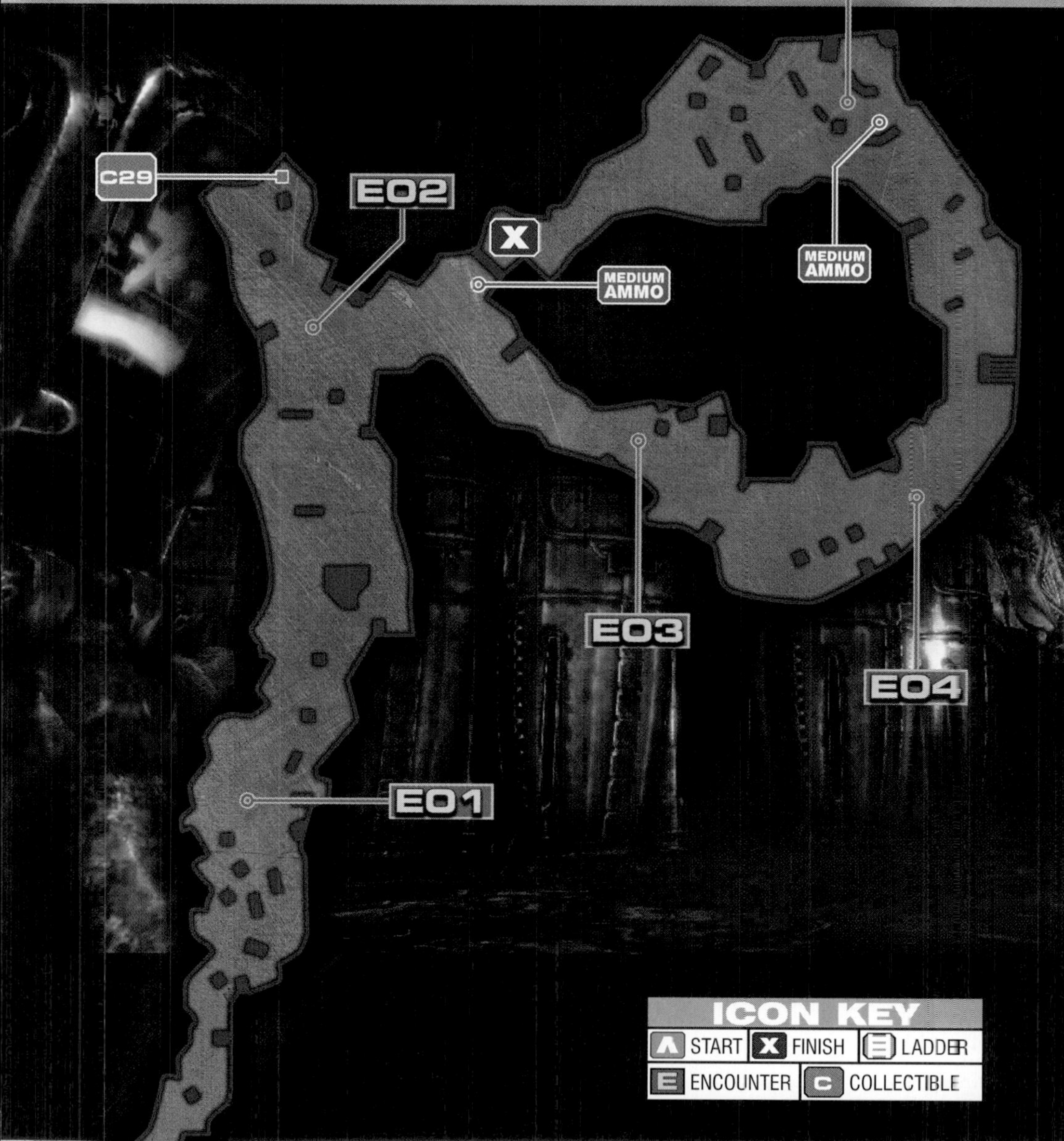

E05
C29
E02
X
MEDIUM AMMO
MEDIUM AMMO
E03
E04
E01

You pick up only a few feet from the end of Priorities. Dom finds a clue that may lead him to his missing wife. This is a short chapter with little combat. Most of the focus is on helping Dom.

ICON KEY

START | FINISH | LADDER
ENCOUNTER | COLLECTIBLE

ENCOUNTER 01

ENEMY PRESENCE

NONE

After searching the Locust database for a reference to Maria, you end up in this gruesome Locust prison camp. Hundreds of humans are locked up in the Locust cages.

However, Dom has his mind set on finding Maria so he takes point while you follow. You need to locate a Locust Terminal that has a symbol matching the one that indicated Maria's presence.

The first Terminal is just up the path from your starting position. There's no enemy presence, so run up and trigger it.

As you approach the second terminal, a Locust patrol comes into view. Drones accompany the much more dangerous combo of a Mauler and a Theron Guard.

However, you can *entirely* avoid combat with these enemies if you wish. They won't spot you unless you get too close. So, if you're patient, you can simply follow them around the prison camp as they make their circuit.

After they wander off but before you check the second Terminal, run around, into the alcove on the left, to find a collectible for your journal.

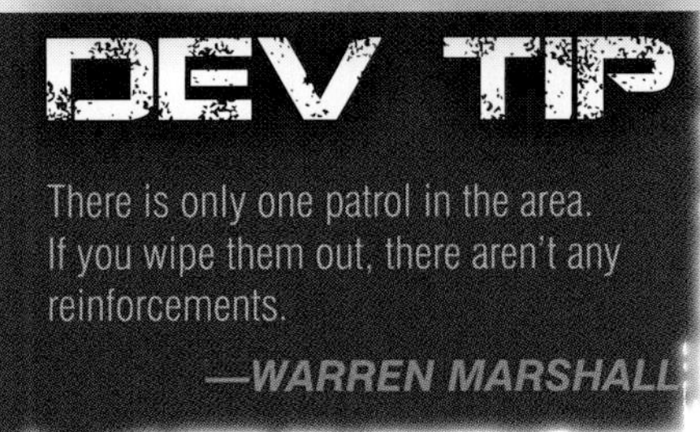

There is only one patrol in the area. If you wipe them out, there aren't any reinforcements.

—WARREN MARSHALL

Find the **Locust Prisoner's Journal** just to the left of the second Terminal, back near the cavern wall.

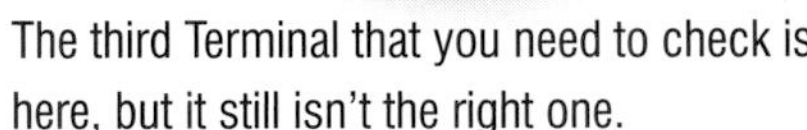

The third Terminal that you need to check is here, but it still isn't the right one.

This is the second-to-last Terminal, and again it's not the correct one.

ACT IV

Finally, at this location, you discover the correct Locust Terminal. After you find the right prison, Jack sets to work to open it.

Unfortunately, your infiltration of the prison is discovered. A pair of searchlights bursts into view as waves of Locust begin their assault. You have to hold out until Jack finishes his task.

The first attack comes from the right side, as a Bloodmount and its rider, along with two Wretches, come after you. Try to take out the Wretches quickly. You don't want them chewing on you from behind while you're trying to dodge the Bloodmount.

Once you take down the first wave, a Bloodmount and yet more Wretches attack from the left side. Use the same strategy to take them out. The next group comes from the right side: a Grinder and two Drones.

The final two waves consist of Drones and Theron Guards. On the higher difficulties in particular, be careful about showing your head from behind cover when you see the glow of the Theron's Torque Bow. If you've saved the Torque Bow or Longshot from the last chapter, or you have the Mulcher, you can take them down quickly.

When you finish the battle, Dom finally gets his answers. He and Marcus move on down the Locust highway toward Nexus, the heart of the Locust presence in the Hollow.

Kill off one of the Drones accompanying the Grinder, and let the Grinder close on your position. Take down the Grinder when he gets closer, and then grab his Mulcher and finish off the second Drone.

The next wave of enemies doesn't arrive until you finish both Drones, so you can have the Mulcher in place and ready to cut them down in time.

—*WARREN MARSHALL*

CHAPTER 3:
HORNETS' NEST

After your excursion to assist Dom, you both head out along the Locust highway to reach Nexus—the source of the Locust leadership. Nexus is an amazing sight, but it is a very unfriendly area. Locust resistance really kicks up in this chapter, and it only gets tougher as you progress toward the end of the act.

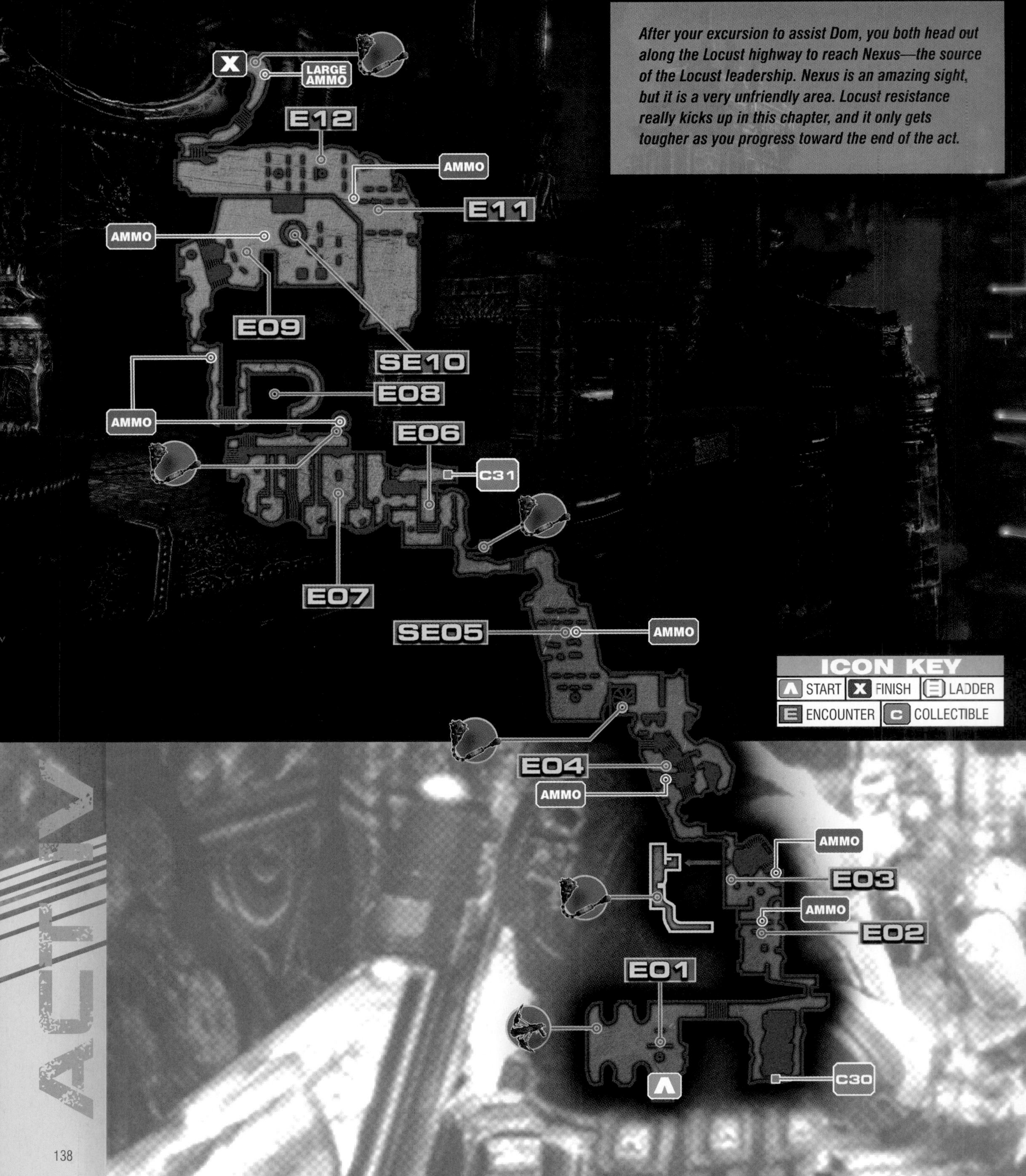

ACT IV

ENEMY PRESENCE

NONE

Your arrival at the heart of the Locust presence in Nexus provides some impressive vistas. However, no one here is friendly, which spoils the ambience.

You must work your way through the Locust grounds here, with your sights set on the largest, most impressive building in the 'city,' the Locust palace.

The starting room provides a useful lesson—pull the lever just in front of you and watch as low walls rise up from the ground. This pop-up, collapsible cover is a staple throughout the Locust areas for the remainder of the act, so get used to using it. In some encounters, the Locust can pull levers to lower your cover.

Just down the stairs from the entry room, turn to the right to go down a narrow hallway (rather than going out into the open through the door). In the hall, you can find the **Locust Jailer Document**.

As you emerge into the open cliff-side area, you face your first real opposition. The small combat area has bits of cover scattered on the ground. There's an elevated walkway with a bridge section that crosses just in front of you as you enter the area. In the distance, a spiral staircase wraps around a small tower: your path to the upper walkway.

Drones are on the bridge and a Theron Guard up in the tower also poses a threat. Try to take out the Drones before you advance, but keep an eye on the Theron. If you see the glow of his Torque Bow, stay under cover.

When you pass the bridge, more Drones emerge from a door behind the tower. Drones and a Sniper descend the tower's spiral stairs.

Keep your distance, using the cover around the bridge section to pick them off. Once you deal with them, proceed into the tower and pull the switch to open the door behind the tower.

After you pull the switch, the door leading out of this area opens...but not without Flame Grenadiers and a Theron Guard to oppose you.

Stay on the upper level. You can even use the bridge that overlooks the ground level to pick off these foes with ease. Don't descend the stairs just yet; remain outside the flame-throwers' range.

DEV TIP

Slap a grenade on the door before you pull the switch. It's a nasty surprise for the Locust who try to come through.

—DAVE EWING

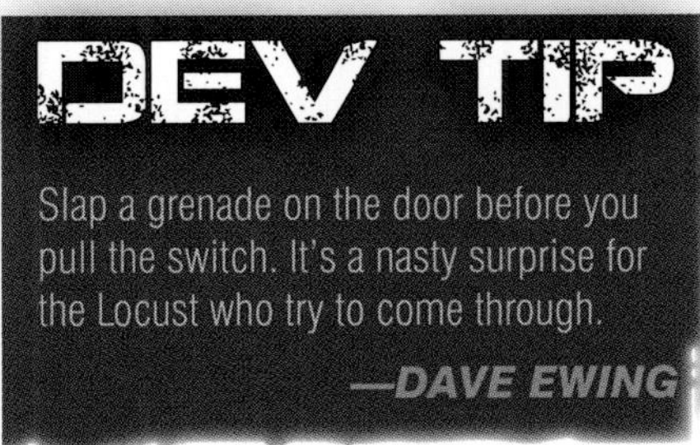

Past the door, you're still out on the cliff-side, this time on a series of terraces connected by shallow stairs. As you enter this area, you will find an ammo box. Your first concern is a Bloodmount. Deal with it before the other Locust—Drones and Grenadiers—become a problem.

As you emerge from the cliff edge, you encounter your first really substantial battle. You reach a wide-open courtyard with pop-up cover on each end. Quickly move over to 'your' side (the closer area of cover) and pull the lever there to raise more cover. The courtyard's opposite end is too far to reach, as Locust Drones and Snipers quickly infest the area.

As you fight, a Drone emerges on an upper ledge to the right as you face the enemy forces. It attempts to pull a lever to lower your cover. Don't let this happen! Make him a priority target and take him down.

After you solve that problem, a Reaver landing in midfield is your next challenge. If you can take it down before it closes on your position, no problem. Just make sure you don't stay in place if it approaches and tries to spear you.

A bit later in the battle, another Reaver flies by, knocking over a pillar and creating a mess of cover in the center of the killing field. This gives you enough protection to start pushing forward to break the Locust defensive line.

There's actually some pop-up cover here, along with a lever that can lower it. Its position is such that moving forward to lower it isn't especially helpful.

Once you clear the area, head inside the building. You have to fight your way through this Locust complex's interior to get closer to the palace.

As you push forward, a large pair of doors opens and two Grinders move out. Stay in cover and take them down before they get close enough to threaten you. The Mulchers they drop can come in handy in the next area. However, see the note on the collectible in Encounter 6—you can't take the Mulcher if you're trying to get the collectible there.

ENCOUNTER 06

ENEMY PRESENCE

NONE

DEV TIP

If you're playing co-op, have one player bring a Mulcher while the other goes for the collectible and the Troika.

—DAVE EWING

This small room is curious. It's basically a transition to the next chamber.

It's worth noting that the Troika in the collectible room is very helpful for the next chamber. So, even if you aren't concerned about the collectible, running into its room is still tactically advantageous.

If you don't want or need the collectible, bring along a Mulcher from the previous room. It serves nearly as well as the Troika for mowing down the Locust in the next room.

COLLECTIBLE

31 Human Finger Necklace

The **Human Finger Necklace** is one of the easiest collectibles to miss. In order to pick it up, you *must* run through the room here to reach the adjacent chamber containing the collectible.

As you enter the room, you can see two doors slowly closing. The door in front of you drops too quickly for you to get past. However, if you Roadie Run swiftly up the steps and across the room, you can get under the second door before it closes.

The collectible is at the back of the room, behind a Troika that overlooks the next room—a very advantageous position.

If you *do* miss this collectible because of the closing door, no problem. Just replay the chapter—it's fairly near the beginning.

ENCOUNTER 07

ENEMY PRESENCE

DRONES BUTCHERS FLAME GRENADIERS GRENADIERS

This curious chamber turns out to be a Locust feeding room. Butchered Rockworms reveal at least one part of a Locust healthy diet.

You also get to meet their chefs, massive Boomer-sized Locust wielding cleavers! They aren't particularly dangerous unless you let them get close to you—they can kill you in two chops!

The other opponents are more familiar: Drones, Flame Grenadiers, and Grenadiers. The 'feeding channels' create helpful, ready-made trenches along this room's length. If you're packing grenades it's easy to toss one into the gap with a few Locust.

As you emerge from the feeding room, you arrive at the meat grinding room. There's a large set of grinding gears at the room's base, around which a walkway spirals to an upper level. There is an ammo box and Frag Grenades past the entrance to the grinding gear room.

A flimsy wooden bridge projects directly out over the gears, and a few Locust are standing on it... Target the Locust explosives on the bridge. Or, if you can manage it, shoot the backpack that the Flame Grenadier on the bridge is wearing. Hitting either target causes the entire bridge to collapse, sending the Locust down into the grinder.

Beyond the few Locust on the bridge, you have to deal with some Drones and a Butcher on the walkway. Drop the bridge first, and then stay under cover to pick them off from a distance. There is an ammo box on the way to Encounter 9.

DEV TIP

Be careful—the Drones here have Lancers. Don't get close!

—DAVE EWING

When you emerge from the Locust feeding chambers, you come out into a large, wide-open area. You can pull a lever here to raise some cover. The initial opposition is fairly mild—some Grenadiers and Drones. However, be careful of the Sniper that is also part of this encounter. Don't worry, it gets tougher. Mop up the opposition and then move out into the open yard's center.

The yard's center is deep enough in Nexus for Jack to transmit the positional data to begin a Grindlift assault. You must hold off Locust forces in waves as Jack transmits the position.

A circular area of cover is in the center of the yard. You can move around inside it and deal with threats from all sides.

Once Jack starts transmitting, you're in for a fight. The initial wave consists of Drones, Grenadiers, Snipers, *and* Tickers. There aren't any magic tricks to this fight. Don't go saving ammo for your heavy weapons, and use your grenades liberally.

As you fight, you may catch Reavers flying by overhead. If you have even a moment to breathe, try to send some fire up their way. The Reavers are surprisingly vulnerable in the air, and any damage you inflict helps when they finally land. Landed Reavers can put you in a sticky situation. You may very well have to evacuate the central area to avoid getting stabbed by Reaver talons.

There are some Locust explosives near a column as you approach the center of the yard. You can destroy them to topple the column and create some cover.

—DAVE EWING

Another wave of Drones follows the Reaver assault. Finally, the wall at the other end of the room drops and a Drone armed with a Mortar appears. Don't give him a chance to shell you. Rush him, take him out at close range, and grab his Mortar.

Once Jack completes the transmission, the COG assault on Nexus begins. While Grindlifts dig through the roof and plummet into Nexus, you must keep moving to find a way into the palace.

An open yard is just beyond the wall that opened for the Mortar-using Drone, again near the cliff edge. Pull a lever out here to raise some cover. Another wall drops down, revealing Mortars and Grenadiers.

Use your Mortar to pop them—they're at roughly half range from the first cover. But watch out for a single Mortar Drone. Quickly shift positions if you see him fire. When you clear this fight, grab his Mortar and lug it along to the next encounter.

ENCOUNTER 12

ENEMY PRESENCE

DRONES GRENADIERS TICKERS GRINDERS

This outdoor area's final section consists of another open yard and another lever to raise pop-up cover. In the distance, Drones and Grenadiers come at you, accompanied by some Tickers. Note that one of the Drones is armed with a Mortar. You can use nearby Locust explosives to thin out some of the onslaught. In combination with your Mortar, you should be able to down them fairly quickly.

More of the dropping walls are in the distance. When the last one drops, Grinders emerge. Be careful about using the Mortar on them. Taking a shot exposes you for a while. If you're still at a distance, give it a try. If not, stay behind cover and take shots when they aren't hosing you down with bullets.

When this battle concludes, you can climb some stairs at the yard's edge. A pleasant surprise greets you—Cole and Baird have made the drop successfully and Delta is reunited. Grab the nearby ammo and grenades, and drag a Mulcher along. Then head up to the gondola and flip the switch. The gondola can take you directly across the yawning gulf to the Locust palace.

DEV TIP

Rather than moving forward from Encounter 11, you can hang back and lob Mortar shots at maximum range to down the final encounter.

—DAVE EWING

CHAPTER 4:
NO TURNING BACK

The perilous gondola ride across the chasm from Hornet's Nest leads you here, the palace's upper reaches. Somewhere within, the Locust Queen lies in wait. But first, you must penetrate the defenses guarding the approach to the palace itself.

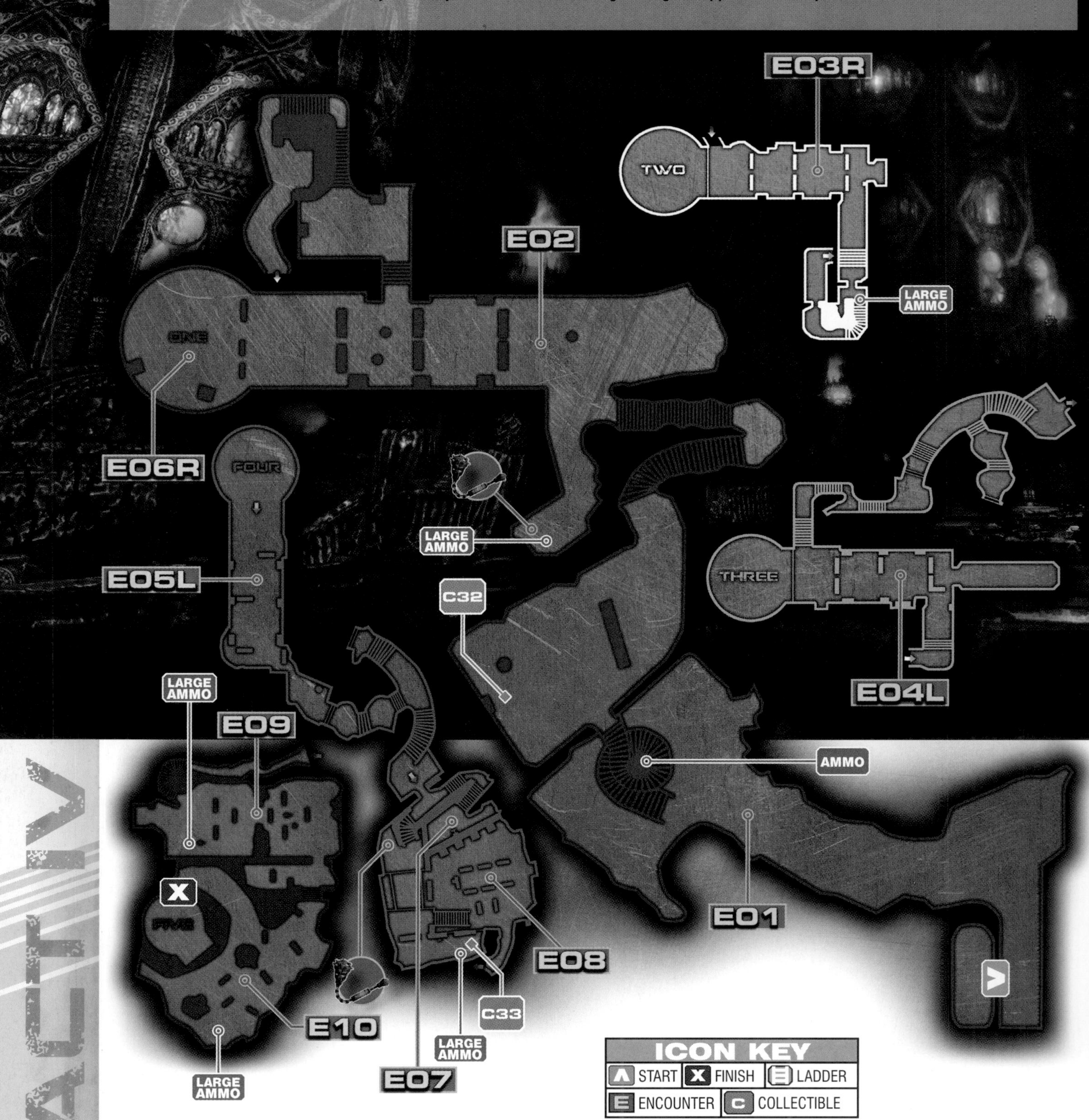

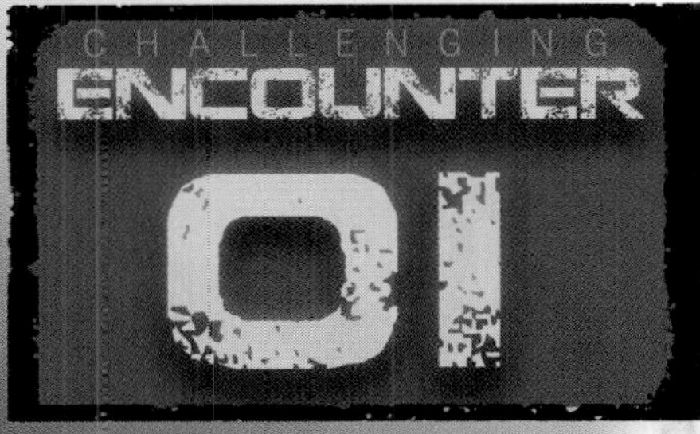

DEV TIP

You can survive the Reavers as long as you don't get hit by three of the four that attack the first gondola, or both of the Reavers that attack the second. As long as you shoot them down before they fly past the gondola, you're safe.

—DAVE EWING

Once you board the gondola that leads into the palace heart of Nexus, your approach does not go unnoticed. The Locust respond in force.

First you must eliminate waves of Reavers attempting to bombard the gondola in which you're traveling. Hit them at a distance, before they get close enough to damage the gondola. You get a visual prompt the first time they show up.

COLLECTIBLE

Find the **Locust Calendar** just up the stairs from your entrance to this chapter. It's a strange-looking pedestal against the back of the room.

After you deal with the Reavers, a second gondola comes alongside, and you must eliminate the Locust onboard. As your gondola gets damaged, you can hop over quickly to finish the trip in your hijacked ride. Two Reavers show up after you jump onto this gondola. There is an ammo box under the spiral stairs after this encounter.

As you arrive at the palace proper, you must begin to work your way into the belly of the beast, where the Queen lurks.

From the upper level, you come to a path split, where you must descend into the palace. Both routes lead down, so it's just a matter of how hard you want the descent to be.

However, before you can go down, you have to deal with the Locust forces here. There's also an annoying Troika in the distance. Hit the lever to summon some pop-up cover. Use it to move forward and engage the Locust. When your teammates distract the Troika, you can run forward and flank it or you can lob a grenade beside it.

When you clear the platform, descend the steps to the right and pull the lever. Doing so triggers a branch choice: left down the stairwell or right onto the lift with the Troika. The Troika lift is considerably easier, which is handy if you're playing solo on a higher difficulty. The Stairwell route serves up a lot more straight combat.

Use the Locust explosives on the platform to aid in the fight. The heavy firepower from the Troika as Baird and Dom come down on the elevator should make this a fairly easy battle. Just don't rush past the cover with an active explosive near you!

You face slightly tougher enemies here. But again, as you approach from above, hang back and let the Troika soften the forces before you approach them. The two Boomers in particular can be dangerous. Just don't stick your head up when they loudly bellow "BOOM!"

Don't miss your chance to pick up the Boomshot here. The Locust ammo packs in this area provide Boomshot ammunition—and Torque Bow ammo, for that matter.

Last stop. Stay in cover on the staircase as the elevator comes down. When the Locust turn their attention to the Troika elevator, pop up and hit them with flanking fire.

The Troika route takes you past each floor with all of the enemies in front of you. It's still a safe and fairly easy route to take. The Troika gives you supreme firepower. The ready explosives on each floor give you an added punch to take down the Locust groups that emerge to oppose you.

Dom flanks the Locust on each platform as he moves down to flip each switch. His actions allow you to get through this section fairly quickly despite the heavy enemy resistance.

No matter which route you take down, the switch at the end of the platform on the right path (Troika elevator) opens both doors to the next area. Once you trigger it, both parts of Delta can meet in the next hall.

Grab the ammo before you enter this area and then get ready. A large pack of Locust who just fought off a group of Lambent occupy this room. Fortunately, Delta Squad has the elevation advantage, and you can fire down on the Locust, nullifying most of their cover advantage.

Once you clear out the Locust, pull the lever on the ledge to extend a bridge across the room. Don't miss the collectible across the bridge.

Grab the collectible and yank the lever on the wall to raise a set of stairs connecting to the bridge to the ground floor below.

DEV TIP

If you wait around long enough, Dom hits the switch to extend the bridge here.

—DAVE EWING

After you pull the lever to extend the bridge above this room, run across it, turn left sharply, and proceed to the end of the hall to find the **Locust Defensive Plans**.

Once you're down on the ground floor, Delta takes a moment to prod the possibly toxic remains of the Lambent on the ground. There isn't much time to discuss the autopsy, as a pair of Grinders emerges from a large set of doors at the end of the room.

After you down the Grinders, a Grenadier bursts through a door at the side of the room. Take him down to clear your route into the next area.

As you come down on this room from above, there are only a few Locust to exterminate. If you dragged along a Mulcher from the Grinders in Encounter 8, this should be a quick and bloody clearing.

Regardless of what you use, clear the room and follow the splattered Lambent trail into a rocky cavern beyond the two rooms filled with pop-up cover.

As you enter the cavern, an elevator arrives with a very nasty cargo: two Maulers, a Kantus, and two Palace Guards armed with Torque Bows.

Use the available cover. If possible, exploit the Locust explosives in the area to help your cause. It's worth using any grenades you have on hand during this fight. As you deal with the Kantus and the Palace Guards, 'tap' the Maulers with fire just to force them to raise their shields and slow their movement.

After you down the Locust, grab one of the Mauler's Boomshields and hop on the elevator to trigger a cut-scene and reach Chapter 5. You're drawing ever closer to the palace and the Locust Queen within.

CHAPTER 5: THE BEST-LAID PLANS

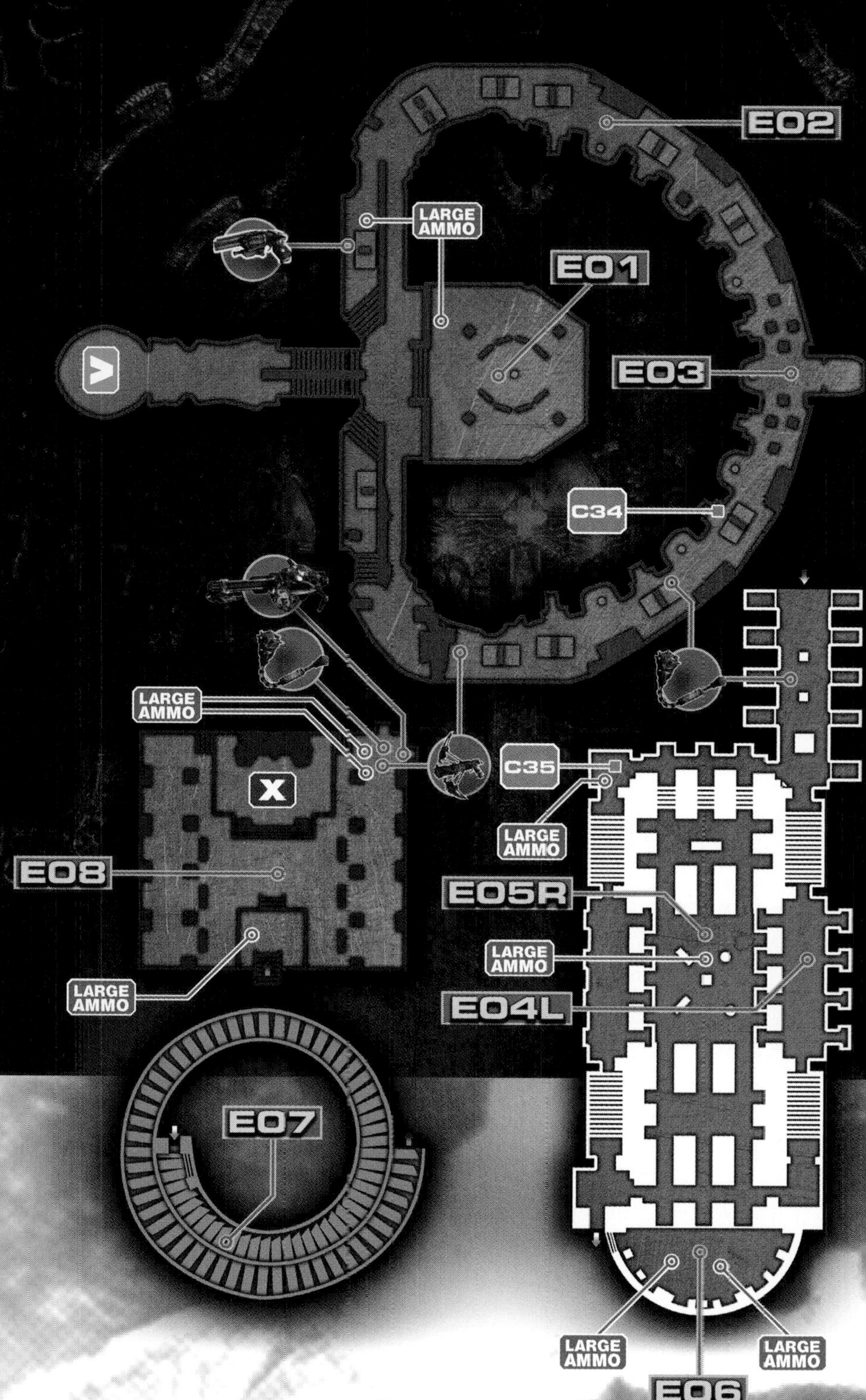

ICON KEY

START	FINISH	LADDER
ENCOUNTER	COLLECTIBLE	

As you approach the main gate to the palace, a trap springs. The gates close and the windows above the yard open up, revealing Drones in elevated positions surrounding your squad.

If you still have a Boomshield from the last encounter in Chapter 4, you may have an easier time here. If not, use the available cover in the middle of the yard, and quickly change sides when more Drones emerge from the opposite windows.

A switch in the center of the floor raises the cover again when the Locust retract it midway through the battle.

Once you dispatch the Locust, you have to back off and find an alternate entrance.

DEV TIP

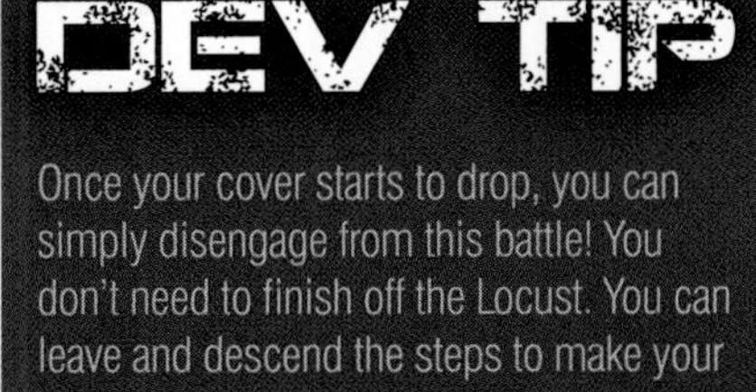

Once your cover starts to drop, you can simply disengage from this battle! You don't need to finish off the Locust. You can leave and descend the steps to make your way around the outside of the palace.

—PHIL COLE

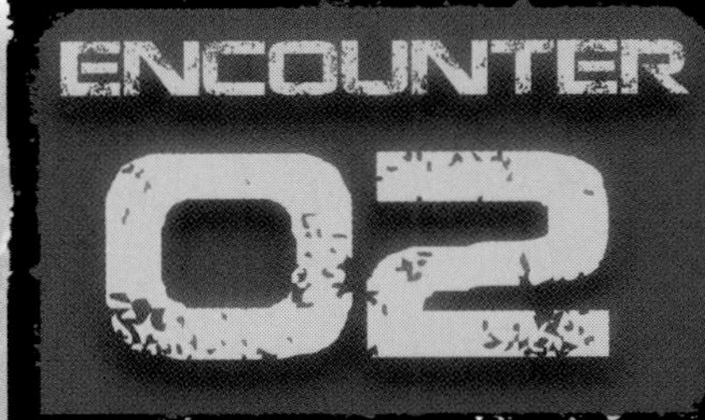

Once you leave the entrance, you have to walk around the palace's outskirts to the left side of the entrance. As you round the first corner, a Locust force of a Bloodmount (with a mounted Palace Guard!), more Palace Guard Drones, and some Tickers are your first opposition.

Use the pop-up cover to your advantage. When you step on the glowing platforms, barriers rise. You can use them as temporary cover as long as you stay put.

Just about everything here is nasty, but make the Bloodmount your priority target. You don't need it chewing on you while you deal with the other targets.

A short ways around the palace, you encounter a Locust lift that leads to a back entrance—exactly what you need. Of course, first you have to deal with the Guard and the Kantus that ride up on the lift.

Take both of them out. Before you hop on the lift, continue around the palace's outskirts to pick up the collectible. An additional Torque Bow is at the end of the path if you need it.

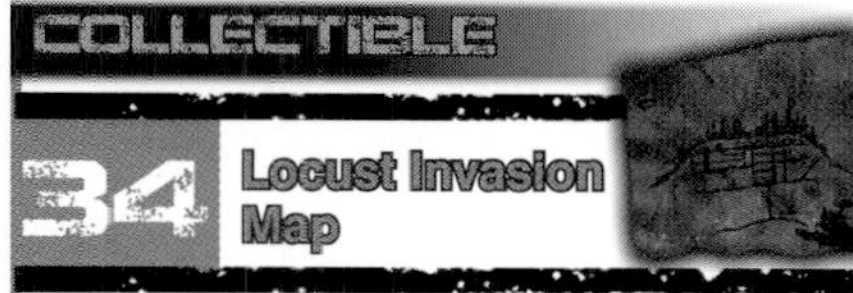

COLLECTIBLE

34 Locust Invasion Map

The **Locust Invasion Map** is tucked away in a small alcove on the right side of the path, just beyond the lift.

LEFT PATH

ENCOUNTER 04

ENEMY PRESENCE

MAULER FLAME GRENADIER GRINDER BLOODMOUNT

Following the left path is a little safer. You end up on the upper level after you climb a staircase, giving you clean line of sight on the enemies below.

The only substantial threat to you is the Grinder on the room's opposite side, on the same level as you. Take him out quickly, as he's a threat to you and your squad mates on the floor below. On this path, you have to hit a floor switch to let others join the group.

RIGHT PATH

ENCOUNTER 05

ENEMY PRESENCE

MAULER FLAME GRENADIERS GRINDER BLOODMOUNT

DEV TIP

The Bloodmount emerges after you take out the Mauler and Flame Grenadiers—be ready for it!

—DAVE EWING

The lower route is a bit tougher, as you have to deal with the enemies face-to-face. However, there's only one of each, so if you have grenades of any sort or any power weapon, you can down them quickly.

ENEMY PRESENCE

NONE

The two branches quickly meet up at the same location on the room's opposite side, near the palace's outer edge. From here, you can start down a spiral staircase that leads into the palace's interior.

Before you do, be sure to climb the *right* staircase. This is the area from which the Grinder fired. If you followed the right branch, it's where the grating slammed shut in your face. You can pick up the collectible and some ammo before you continue deeper into the palace.

Don't forget to pick up the Mulcher or Boomshield here. Either item makes the next area considerably easier.

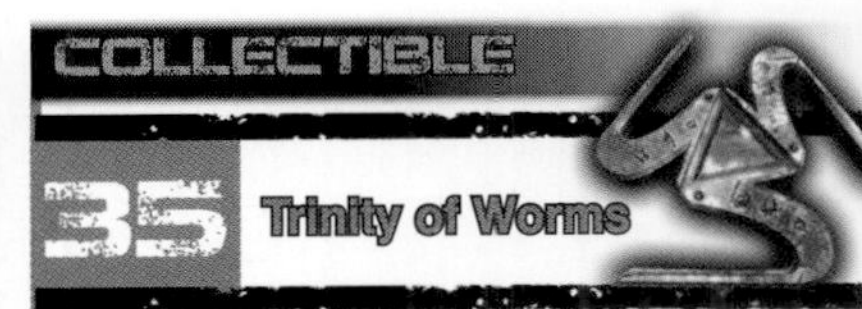

An ornate pattern is on the floor at the end of the hall, past the stairs. Investigate it to find the **Trinity of Worms**.

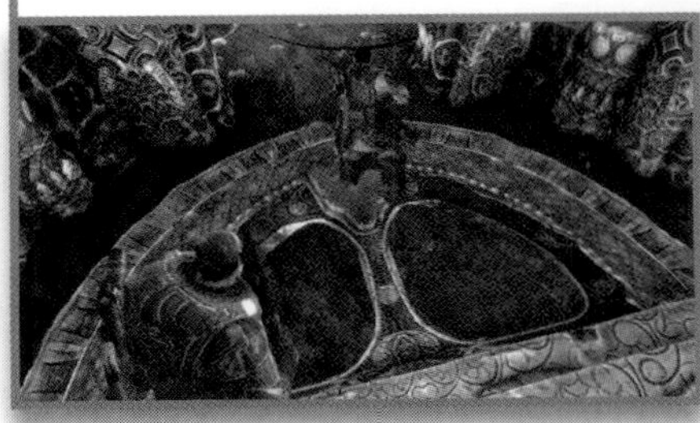

The long, spiral staircase down into the heart of the palace is positively infested with Palace Guards. Many of them wield the deadly Torque Bow.

Use the abundant cover provided by the columns on the staircase's edges. Stay out of sight when you see the burning glow of the charged Torque Bow.

The Ticker assault midway down may throw off your rhythm. Be ready to beat them back, or roll away when they're ready to detonate.

The chapter's final encounter takes place in a strangely high-tech chamber filled with terminals and computer displays. Hang back at the opening doorway to give yourself some time to size up the opposition and hit them from a distance.

Once you clear out the entryway, you can move in and eliminate any guards that are reluctant to show their faces. Be sure to take down the Kantus quickly. You don't want it hanging back and repeatedly summoning Tickers, or worse, raising downed Guards.

CHAPTER 6:
ROYAL INQUISITION

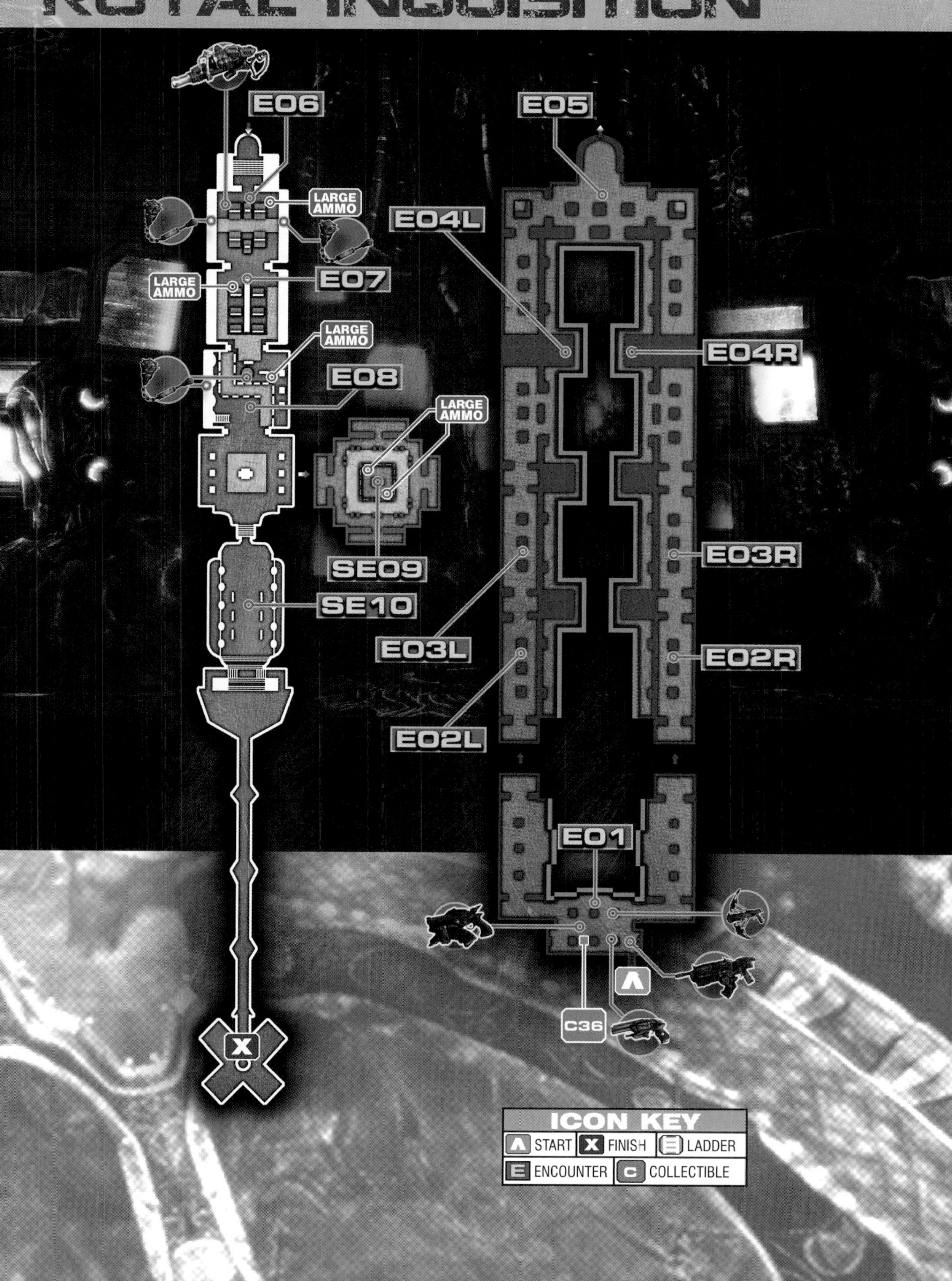

Encounter 01

Enemy Presence

NONE

Collectible

36 Locust Tablets

The **Locust Tablets** are on the ground between two of the columns in the room. They're near the corner to the left as you exit the computer room.

Before you even get started, choose your weapons from the huge array available in these rooms. Then pick up the Locust ammo crates to top off your supply. Consider bringing a Mulcher—it really helps.

You have to prepare, because as soon as you approach the balcony looking down into the palace's heart, you must choose a branch. It doesn't matter which route you select—they're identical branches into the palace. But you are separated from half of your squad as you work your way to the palace's opposite end.

The path divides here, but curiously, both paths are completely identical. It doesn't matter which side you take, and they both end up in the same place.

You face a Mauler and two Palace Guards in your first battle here.

Depending on how the situation plays out, you may want to take down either the Mauler or the Guards first. If you lugged along the Mulcher, you can mow them all down before they have much chance to engage you.

Once the Mauler goes down, you can take his Boomshield. It proves invaluable during the mess of fighting you endure as you push deeper into the palace.

This time, you have to deal with a mix of Palace Guards and Tickers. The Tickers are your first priority. If you engage them quickly at long range, you can destroy them before they get close enough to pose a threat.

Don't forget you can melee them to knock them back if they do get close. One other thing: watch out for a Lancer-wielding Palace Guard. Don't let him get close, or you may end up in bits.

Say hello to another Mauler with Palace Guards. This time, watch out for the Torque Bow in the hands of the guards.

The Mauler can put pressure on you by moving up while the Palace Guards stay back. If you're still packing grenades, you may want to use them here.

Don't hesitate to plant the Boomshield and go mobile if you need to. You can always pick it up again after you clear out the opposition.

As the path branches rejoin, you must face *two* Maulers accompanied by Palace Guards, two again armed with Torque Bows.

Keep your distance. Depending on how quickly Dom (or your co-op partner) clears the other side, you may have to deal with only part of the forces.

Just past the Locust forces, a large elevator leads down into the palace's depths. Once you clear out the opposition here, grab a Boomshield and head down.

There's no Mortar present on Insane difficulty—sorry!

—PHIL COLE

On the bottom level, it's a straight shot to the Queen's room. But first you have to deal with the extensive Palace Guard contingent here. A few defensive mechanisms are also in place.

The room you land in from the elevator is very large and wide-open, but there is pop-up cover. Here's the trick: as you get near the cover, the floor ahead literally drops away, preventing you from progressing. A swarm of Palace Guards emerges on the other side of the gap.

There are a few ways to deal with this situation. Firstly, a Mortar here makes taking down the Locust a snap—fire at about 100m from cover. The nearby Torque Bow also helps.

The levers at the sides of the room present another option. These levers raise staircases to upper galleries on the room's sides. Both contain Frag Grenades. You can make your way up and lob grenades down at the Locust or simply fire at them from above—it's your call.

In any case, once you defeat the Locust, the floor rises and you can move forward again.

The second encounter on the bottom floor is very similar to the first. The floor drops out and you must deal with more Palace Guards on the opposite side.

However, this time there's a curious bit of pop-up cover. A central barrier bisects the middle of the room. On each of its sides, pressure pads raise cover as you move across them. You must move from pad to pad to get forward far enough to threaten the Locust on the other side of the pits.

If you still have Mortar shots, you can again nail them from about 100m. If not, move up in cover and pick them off.

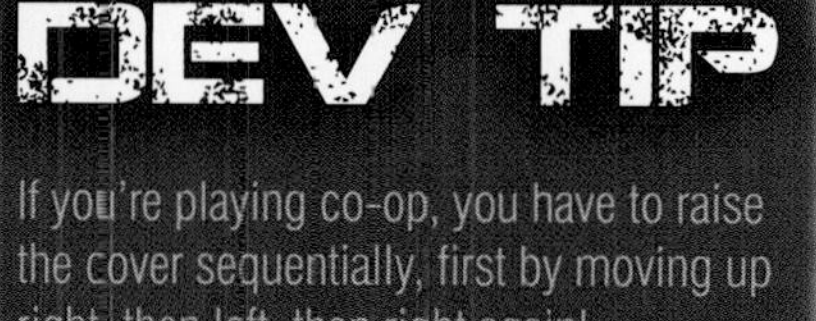

If you're playing co-op, you have to raise the cover sequentially, first by moving up right, then left, then right again!

—PHIL COLE

You reach a final cover fight across a dropped floor. Again, more Palace Guards resist you. This time, watch out for their Torque Bows.

If you have any Mortar rounds left, burn off the last of them here. The cover on your side may drop. If it does, step on the switch in the center of the room to raise it up again.

The Locust on the other side try to raise a staircase on the right. This is their attempt to reach the side gallery and fire at you from an elevated flanking position—not good. Focus your fire on any Locust that makes a move to climb the steps.

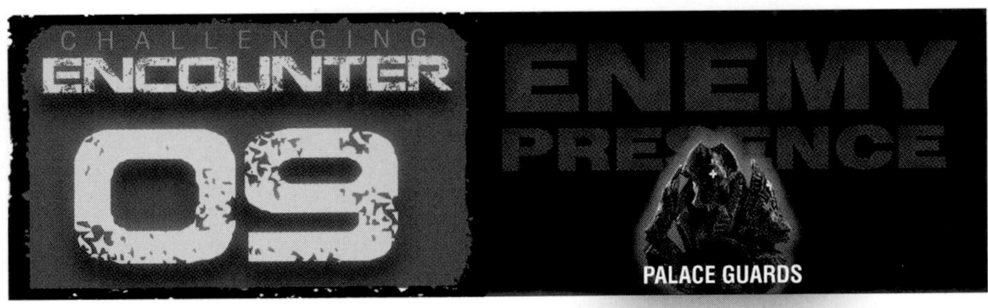

The last room at the bottom of the palace contains a brutal trap. When you reach the middle of the room, the entire floor drops down with you on it.

You end up on a square platform separated from the room's edges by pits. Each of the four cardinal directions has a door. Each door has a pack of ravening Palace Guards behind it.

The enemies come out from the north and then the east. These foes are 'polite' in that they wait for you to wipe out most of the Locust before the next door opens. However, the west-to-south transition is not so accommodating, as the doors quickly open in sequence. Be ready for the onslaught.

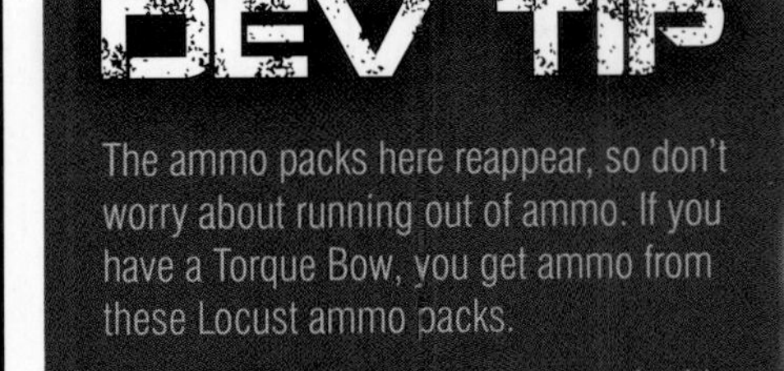

DEV TIP

The ammo packs here reappear, so don't worry about running out of ammo. If you have a Torque Bow, you get ammo from these Locust ammo packs.

If you're playing co-op, have your buddy drag a Boomshield down here. He can cover you as you use the crank to get up out of the pit!

—PHIL COLE

Success! Your persistence is rewarded with an exceptionally rare event: a face-to-face meeting with the Locust Queen. Curiously, she seems unbothered by your presence and is rather talkative. Of course, the presence of her bodyguard, Skorge, sort of spoils the *polite host* effect.

To get out, you have to use a wheel mounted on the central pillar. Turning it while you're under fire is dangerous, especially because raising the platform elevates you above the level of cover! You have to clear out the Locust to get back up safely.

If you brought along your Boomshield, it's difficult to use it effectively. But there is cover along the edges, so you can bring your heavier weapons to bear.

After a lengthy and revealing conversation, the Queen departs and orders Skorge to kill you. Marcus sends Cole and Baird in pursuit of the Queen, but you have to deal with Skorge in a straight-up fight.

Skorge is a brutal fighter, and he slams into Marcus with his twin-bladed chainsaw staff—how do you like that for a weapon? You have to mash the melee button repeatedly to come out of this in one piece, just as if you're fighting a Lancer duel.

When Skorge gets knocked away, he begins to attack you in earnest. Skorge comes at you with a variety of attack patterns.

When he leaps away and runs along the room's sides, he sprays Gorgon Pistol shots and tosses Ink Grenades down at you. Stay mobile, quickly moving around the room to avoid the ink clouds.

Occasionally, he summons nasty glowing Tickers from vents at the floor's edges. Deal with them quickly while you're on the move—losing sight of Skorge can be fatal.

He may also leap up into the blackness of the roof and send stalactites plummeting down toward your head. Watch for the falling dust and move quickly to avoid the projectiles!

Skorge can also slice down one of the room's support columns. If he does this, watch for the column to start falling and wait for Dom to yell. When he does, quickly roll to the side to avoid getting pulverized!

After each pillar collapse, Skorge attacks you directly. He leaps down and engages you in a brutal chainsaw match. Mash the melee button to come out ahead and damage him. You have to repeat the duel three times to come out victorious.

Unfortunately, victory does not lead to Skorge's death. He summons the Hydra, his massive and mutated Reaver mount, and flees the scene.

You must chase after him! Run through the doors at the end of the audience chamber to reach a long bridge. You can run across the bridge to the Reaver pens. That's right, you get to mount up on a Reaver to pursue him!

ACT V

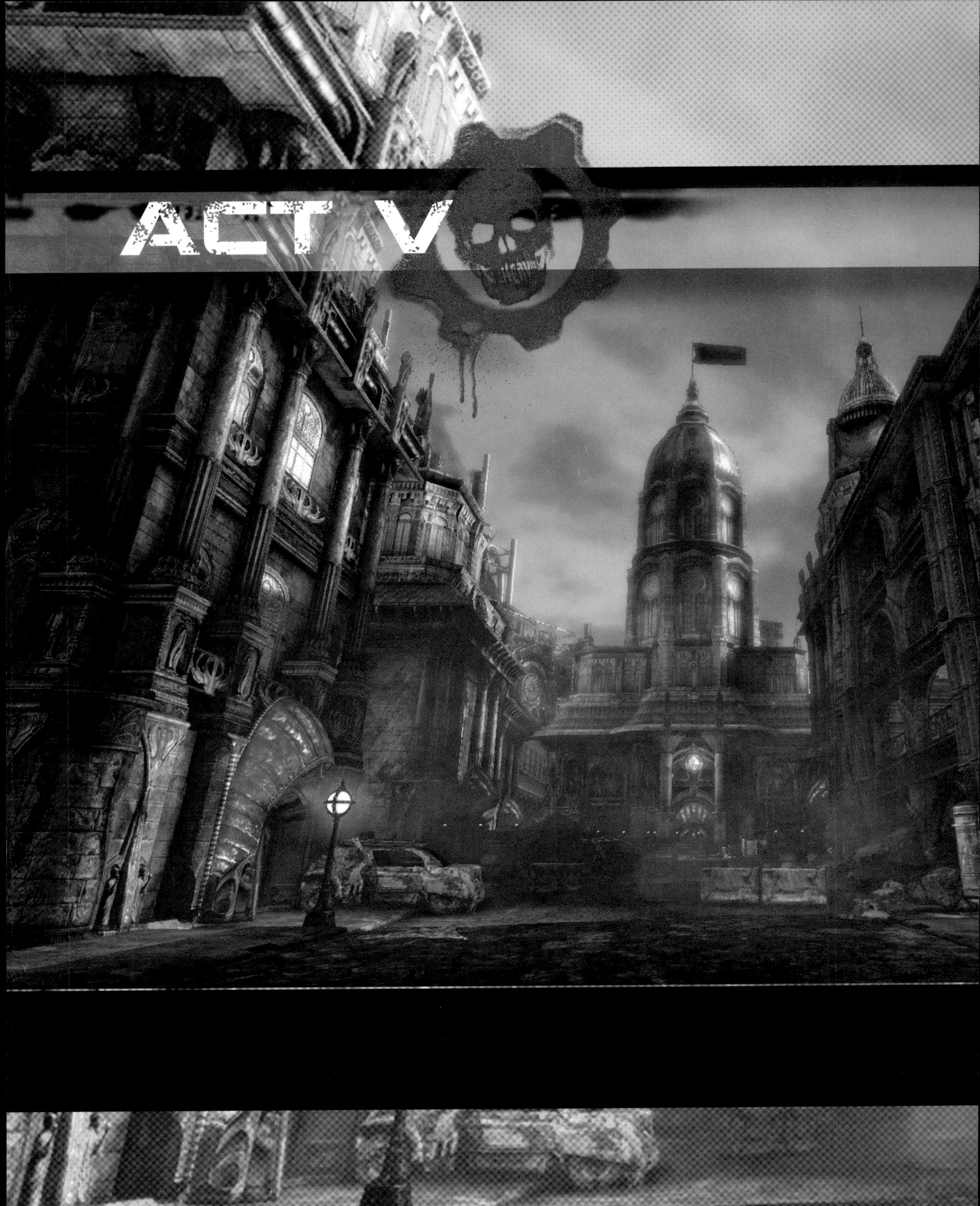

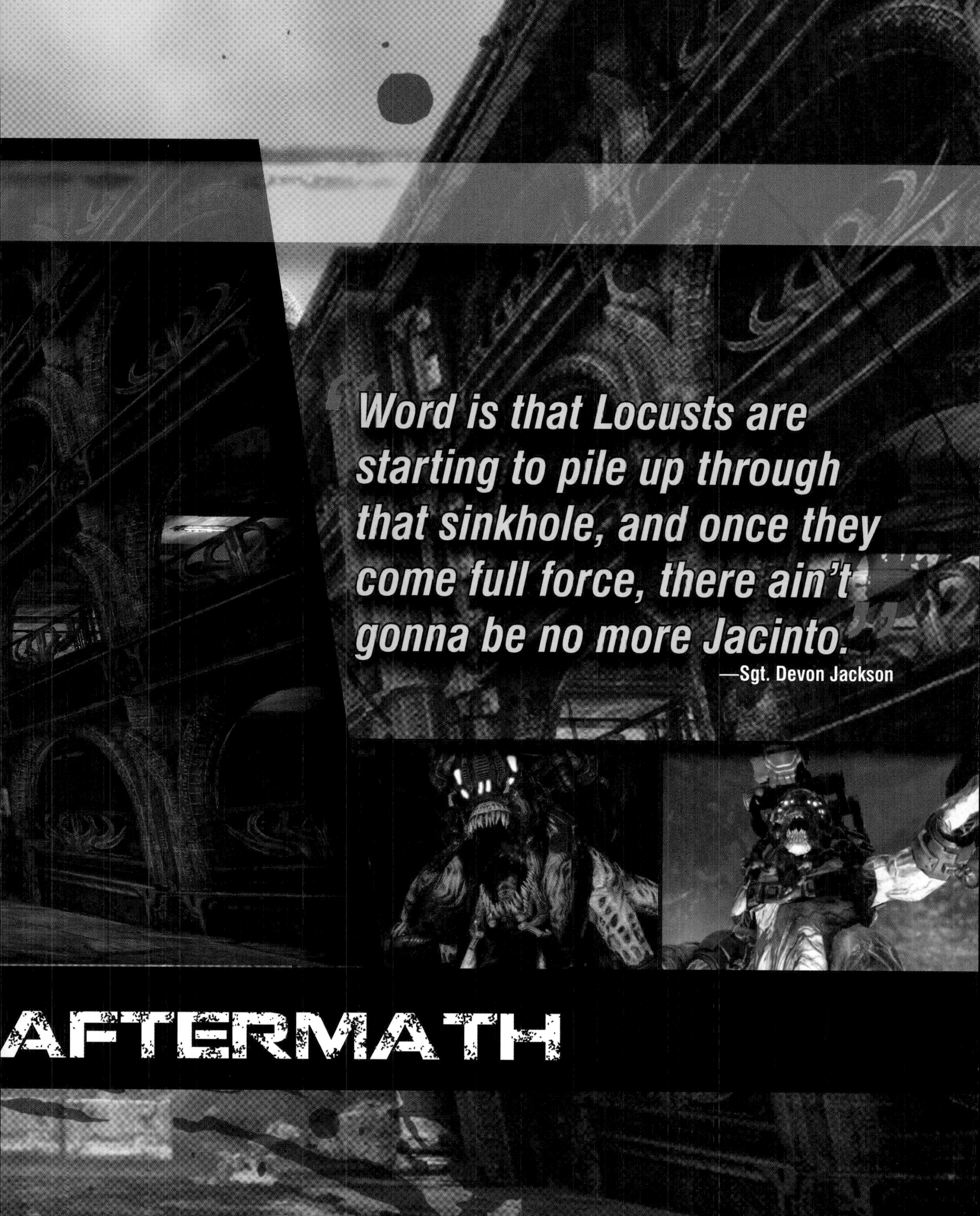

"Word is that Locusts are starting to pile up through that sinkhole, and once they come full force, there ain't gonna be no more Jacinto."

—Sgt. Devon Jackson

AFTERMATH

CHAPTER 1: ESCAPE

Delta Squad has escaped from the palace and the pursuit of Skorge on the Hydra. Now they must flee the underground and get back to Jacinto. They must help in the last stand against the Locust onslaught...and to sink Jacinto to wipe out the Locust in the Hollow beneath the plateau.

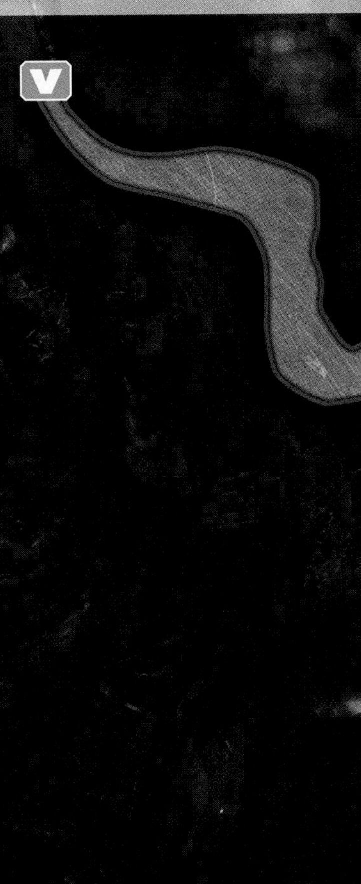

SPOILER WARNING!

As much as possible, we've endeavored to avoid spoiling key story moments. But there's no avoiding certain events that happen in the game's final act. If you haven't finished playing through the game up to this point, resist the temptation to look further ahead than your current spot!

The first section of Escape gives you a chance to get your bearings on your new Reaver mount. You can face forward and fire powerful rockets to destroy turrets and damage the Brumaks taking shots at you. You can also tap the X Button to reverse your facing and fire the chaingun behind you. If you turn to face from front to back (or vice versa), you automatically switch weapons; pressing X is just a shortcut to instantly change sides.

The targets marked on the map are major danger points. Take out the three turrets and repeatedly shell the Brumaks as you make your way toward the second encounter.

While you're in the air, you don't have a full range of motion. But you *can* dodge incoming rockets. On higher difficulties, you *must* do so, as you can get taken out very quickly.

Don't worry about ammo or overheating with the front-mounted rockets. Cut loose and blast everything in sight as you fly through this level's first portion.

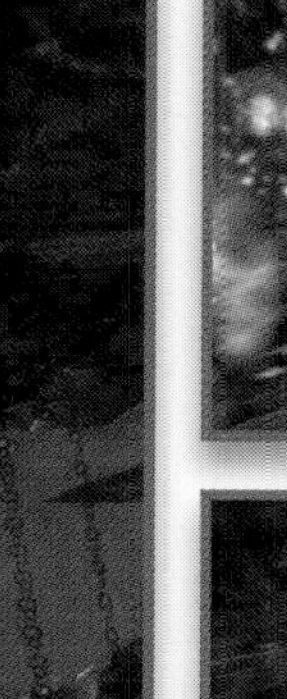

A group of embattled Gears draws Marcus' attention as you fly toward the exit. Marcus refuses to leave without assisting them, so Delta quickly lands in the area. Target the Locust ground forces and pummel them with rockets until they're pasted. Once you clear them out, a Brumak bursts through the wall just to your left. Hammer it with rockets until you down it.

When you've sufficiently relieved the Gears, Skorge appears on his mount, the Hydra. You quickly take to the air, flying into the tunnel that leads to the surface with Skorge in pursuit.

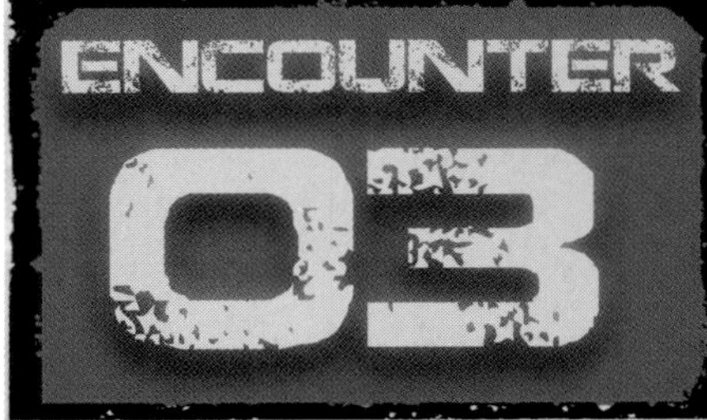

DEV TIP

It takes three hits to the turret to knock out the Hydra in this fight.

His attack pattern consists of the turret, then rockets, his lunging bite, rockets again, and then the cycle repeats.

—MIKEY SPANO

As you enter the dark, spiraling tunnel that leads back to the surface, Skorge catches up to you on the Hydra, his massive and mutated Reaver mount. You have to keep him at bay with the chaingun.

As he chases you, he periodically fires volleys of rockets in a spread pattern. Move to evade them—you have good mobility in the tunnel.

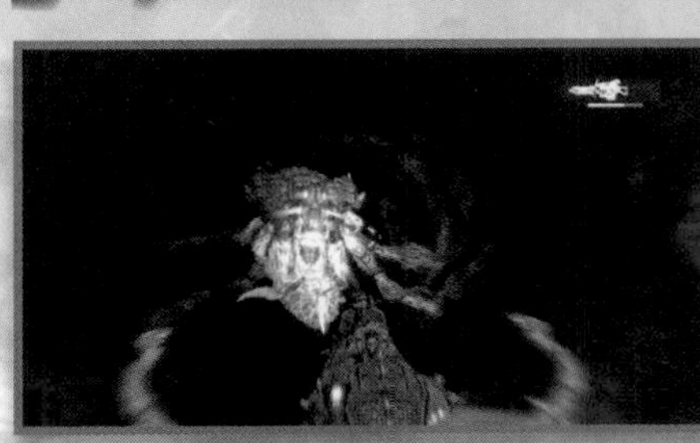

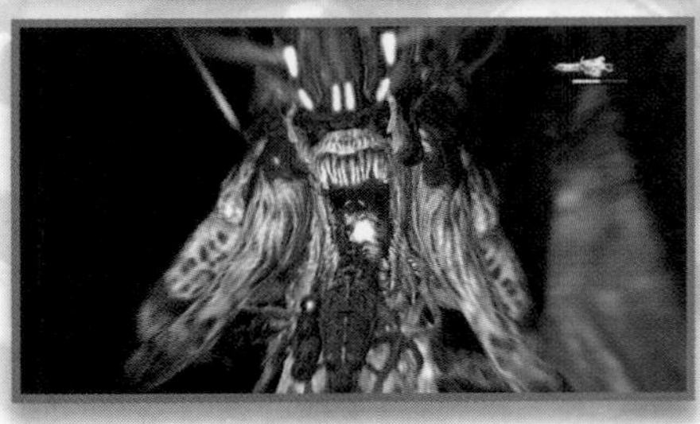

Occasionally, Skorge attacks with the turret mounted atop the Hydra. When he does, direct your fire at the turret to ward him off.

The final and most dangerous attack is the Hydra itself biting your Reaver with its massive jaws. When it comes at you with this attack, its mouth is open. Direct your chaingun fire into its gaping maw to shut it up and keep it away.

You can't actually kill Skorge here, but you have to survive long enough to get through the tunnel. Once you reach the surface, the final phase of Escape begins.

When you burst forth from the Hollow, packs of Locust Reavers rise from the forest below and pursue your hijacked mounts.

Mow down these enemy Reavers with the chaingun. Try to fire quickly and accurately at each Reaver group. Then fully cool the chaingun to prepare for another burst of fire as more Reavers emerge from the forest to pursue you.

After you fight your way past the Reaver patrols, Skorge dispenses with the cat-and-mouse tactics and comes in for the kill.

As Skorge attacks, the Hydra lunges from behind and grabs your Reaver with one of its powerful tentacles. Quickly shoot the tentacle right where it's grabbing your Reaver to prevent the Hydra from taking a vicious bite out of your mount's rear end.

When this gambit fails, Skorge backs off and then swoops to the front. Quickly switch sides to target him and *wait*. Dodge any rockets he fires at you. Then, when he lunges toward you, fire at the Hydra's mouth. If you fire too soon, you can't stop the rush. If you fire too late, the brutal lunge will hit you.

This pattern repeats until you finish off Skorge's mount by blasting it enough times in the mouth. When this happens, the Hydra goes down in a spectacular crash, and the route is clear for Delta Squad to fly to Jacinto.

Skorge tries to grab your Reaver with the Hydra. He then flies around a bit and fires rockets. Next, he moves in front to ram you.

You can fire at the Hydra the instant his mouth opens before he charges. But you may want to wait for him to lunge to increase your chances of hitting him!

—MIKEY SPANO

CHAPTER 2: DESPERATE STAND

The siege of Jacinto has begun. While Command scrambles to evacuate the city and formulate a plan to sink it, Delta Squad, accompanied by Colonel Hoffman, must defend headquarters against a Locust assault force. The bulk of this mission takes place on the headquarters' fortified battlements.

ACT V

COLONEL HOFFMAN

The hardened commander of the Gear forces, Hoffman has seen many battles in many places, but none worse than the Locust conflict.

Now he joins your side to defend Jacinto. He refuses to sit on the sidelines and watch while the Locust sack the last refuge of humanity.

ENCOUNTER 01

ENEMY PRESENCE

As you exit the courtyard onto the battlements, the first wave of attackers comes up on the platform outside the walls. Grappling Drones begin making their way onto the platform. Hang back and snipe them with the Longshot, or try to shoot down their grapples to prevent them from climbing up.

After the first several groups of Drones attack the platform, a Reaver lands and begins shelling your position with rocket fire. Shortly after, KR-36, a heavy attack gunship, strafes the platform, clearing it of any remaining Locust resistance. Grab ammo from the nearby halls if you need it, and then move on to follow Hoffman.

COLLECTIBLE

37 **COG Recon Report**

After the Raven clears the platform, go to the right and then down a short set of stairs to reach the lower platform. You can find the **COG Recon Report** here.

ENCOUNTER 02

ENEMY PRESENCE

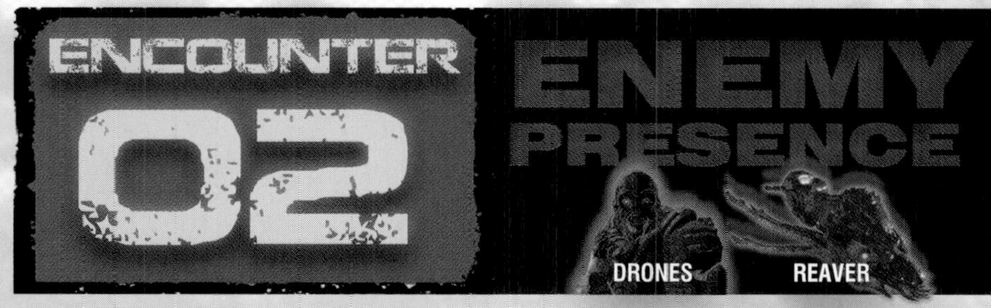

This encounter is similar to the first platform battle. But this time, a Reaver takes out your air support. Finish off the Reaver as soon as it lands. You can snipe its riders fairly easily and then eliminate the unmanned Reaver safely.

Once the platform is cleared, you move on to a small parking garage area for the next battle.

As you enter the parking garage's second floor, there's a large weapon cache to your left, including *two* Mulchers, two ammo crates, a Longshot, and Frag Grenades. Load up, drag a Mulcher over, and set up camp on the edge of the garage.

A huge wave of Drones comes in from below, followed up by a Boomer. But your elevated position and superior firepower give you a marked edge in this battle. Mow them down until the Reavers show up. This shouldn't be a problem with your two Mulchers, but save your ammo.

KR-32 arrives and blasts the street, eliminating the Reavers for you. Unfortunately, KR-32 gets shot down shortly afterward, but at least the sacrifice saved you a fully loaded Mulcher…

In the next section of the battlements, the Communications Array comes under Reaver attack. Man the turrets on the wall and shoot down at least six of the attacking Reavers to prevent the Array from getting damaged. Without it, Gear forces can't communicate with Command, crippling the COG contingent.

You don't have to use much finesse here. Just cool down the turret between Reaver attacks and gun them down on the approach. Once you eliminate the Reavers, move on to the next encounter.

During the last encounter, check the ground to the right of the Longshot, over on the platform's right edge, to find the **COG Tags** of Sgt. Devon Jackson.

The final battle to defend headquarters takes place here as the Locust perform a full ground assault.

Again, there is plenty of weaponry and ammo: a Mulcher, two Mortars, a Longshot, and ammo for your weapons. Exploit the heavy hardware to devastate the encroaching waves of Locust.

The initial attack is simply Drones, followed by Grinders, and finally a pair of Brumaks. You can take out the Drones and Grinders easily with the Mulcher or Mortar, saving at least two pieces of heavy hardware for the Brumaks.

The Brumaks move in and set up shop anywhere between 100m and 150m from your cover, depending on where you're positioned. Once you dial in their range, shell them repeatedly with Mortars to take them down.

When you finish decimating the Brumaks, the defense is a success. You move into the streets to head toward the Locust sinkhole, deeper in the city.

CHAPTER 3: FREE PARKING

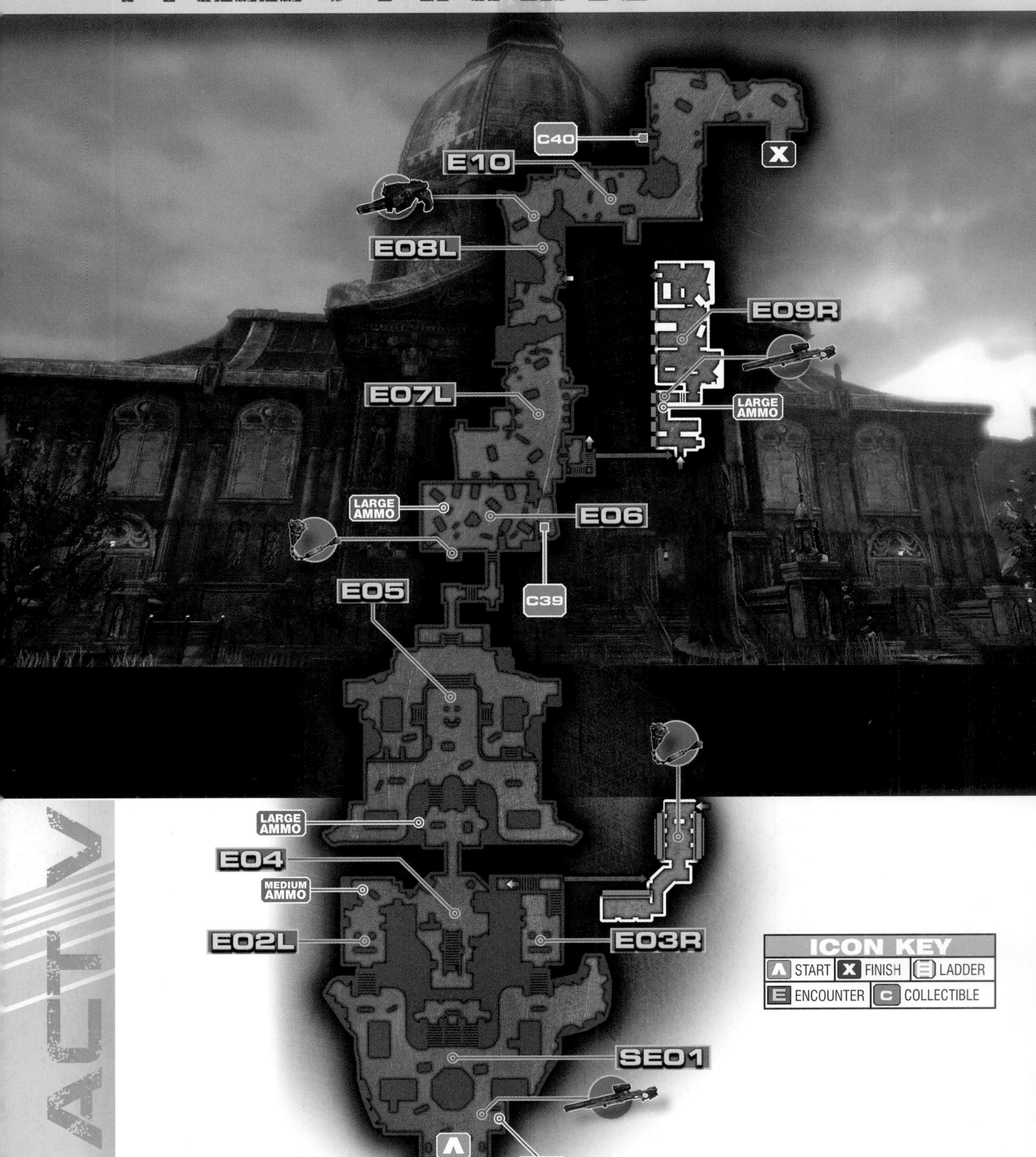

ACT V

CHALLENGING ENCOUNTER 01

ENEMY PRESENCE

DRONES FLAME BOOMERS SNIPERS

The initial battle in the courtyard is pretty fierce. Before you engage the patrolling Locust in front of the mansion, move over to the right of your starting position and grab the Longshot and the ammo there—you'll need it.

When you're ready, pop the head off a Sniper to get the Locust's attention. A pair of Snipers shows up on the mansion's second floor balcony. Make them a priority; you can't have them sniping from an elevated perch while you try to fend off Drone assaults from the courtyard's left and right sides.

Once you deal with the first force of Drones and Snipers, the mansion doors open and two Scorcher-wielding Boomers emerge. Dispatch them from a distance before they can close on your position. Then grab their weapons, which prove handy in the close quarters combat inside the mansion.

You can choose routes here, though it isn't an explicit branch choice. You can enter the mansion through the left door (ground floor) or the right door (second floor). Both areas are accessible from the other side of the building, so you can clear out both or ignore the alternate route as you see fit.

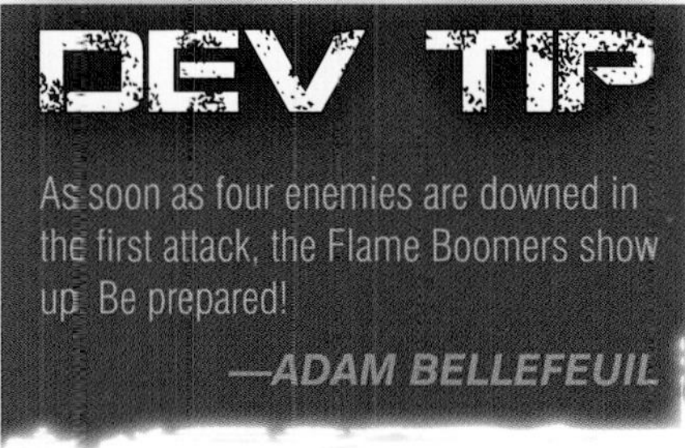

DEV TIP

As soon as four enemies are downed in the first attack, the Flame Boomers show up. Be prepared!

—ADAM BELLEFEUIL

LEFT PATH

If you decide to use the left door, a Grenadier and a Scorcher-wielding Grenadier oppose your entry into the mansion. Down them to hopefully grab a few extra Frag Grenades before you set foot in the mansion's center room.

Note that if you take this route, you might have to deal with Snipers still alive on the second floor *and* the Kantus from above. This is not a desirable situation. It all depends on how fast Dom (or your co-op buddy) is.

RIGHT PATH

The right door is fairly heavily defended. The ground floor has a Grenadier and a Flame Grenadier, while the second level has a pair of Snipers leading into a Kantus.

Thankfully, you can hang back at the doorway to deal with the ground-floor Locust. Then move in to assault the Snipers. If you time your approach properly, you can rush the stairs to get up close to them. They're ill equipped to take on an angry Gear in close combat.

The Kantus is a bit farther back on the second floor. It's just before you reach the master staircase that leads back down to the mansion's center. Eliminate the beast and then move in to the heart of the building.

This right path is slightly tougher to get through than the left. However, it gets much easier once you're into the center of the mansion. This is something to consider if you're playing solo on a higher difficulty level.

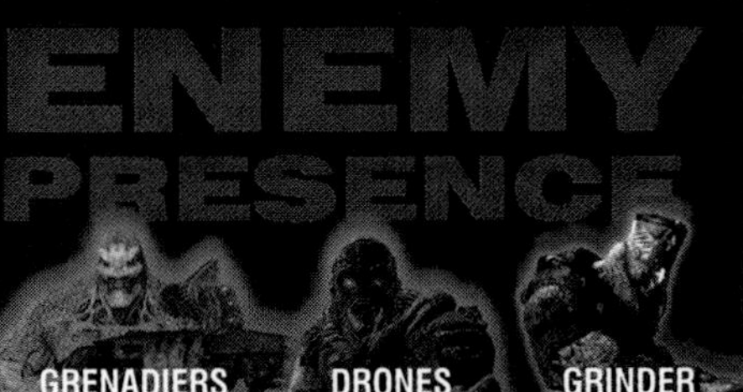

The center room holds a few basic grub grunts, but once you down them, a Grinder bursts through the door that leads out of the mansion. Be sure you're behind cover when this happens!

Take him down and grab the Mulcher he drops; it's useful in the next encounter.

There's a cool trick here: If you come in fast enough, you may spot the Kantus on the upper level. The Kantus moves under a chandelier hanging from the ceiling. Fire at the fixture to make it fall and crush him!

—ADAM BELLEFEUIL

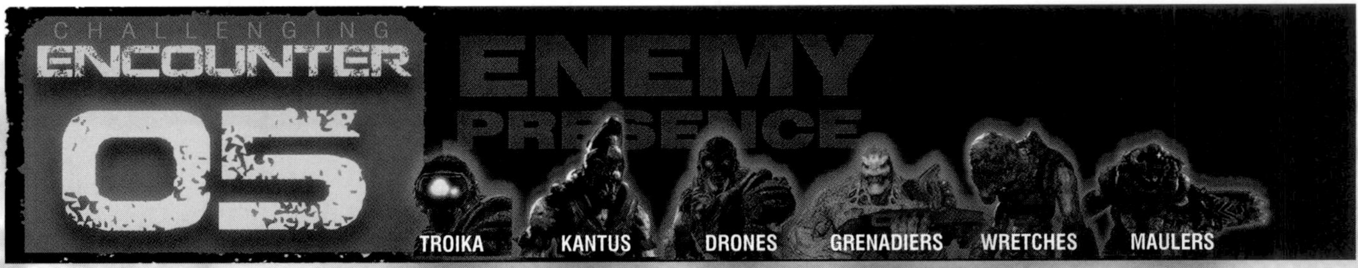

A Troika is planted in this huge courtyard's center. It covers your approach and most of the courtyard in a most inconvenient fashion.

A Kantus also roams around as you enter the yard, so be sure to kill him quickly to avoid resurrection problems.

The best way to take out the Troika gunner is to use the Longshot. He is vulnerable to sniper fire. Failing that, if you managed to secure any Ink Grenades from the Kantus in the mansion, they're great for eliminating the Troika gunner.

On Hardcore and Insane difficulty, Bloodmounts also appear in this battle.

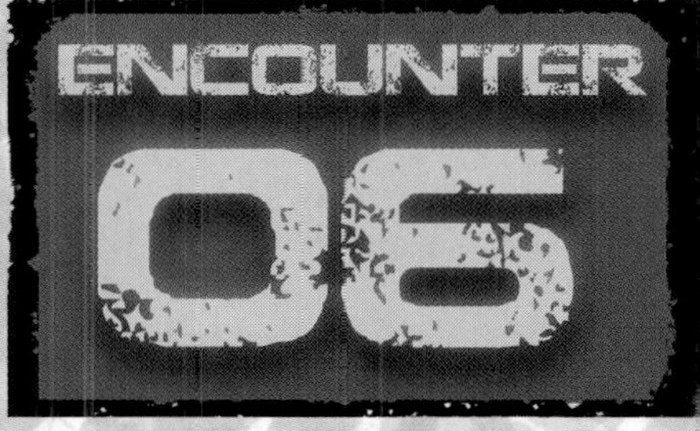

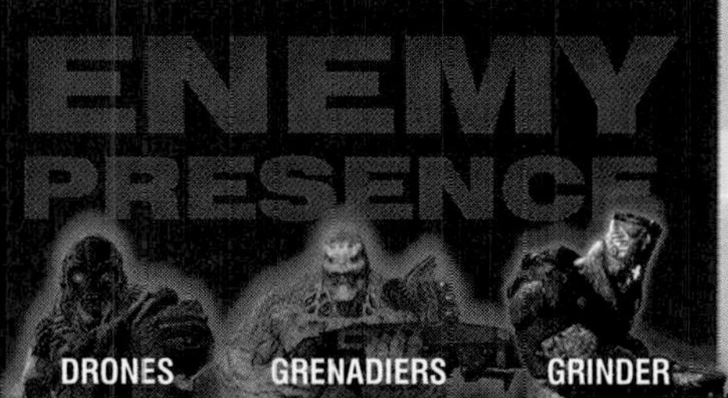

Encounter 06

Enemy Presence

DRONES GRENADIERS GRINDER

Collectible

39 COG Recon Report

Find the **Jacinto Sentinel Newspaper** behind the wall to the right of the Grinder.

This is a nasty street fight. The central Grinder Boomer presents a major threat. The Grenadiers around him can close in on you fairly easily in the awkward cover provided by the cars.

At the start of the fight, some Reavers strafe the street, blasting several of the cars. To avoid eating the explosions, stay away from the right side of the street as you emerge.

Try to back off to the end of the street opposite the Grinder to pick off the Locust grunts more easily. On the upshot, once you down Grinder, you get a shiny new Mulcher to take to the path branch ahead.

Use your Mulcher to mow down any opposition that readily presents itself. Then dive down to the left or right to quickly evade the Troika's line of sight.

From either side, you can then move up onto the ledges overlooking the Troika. Either toss down a regular Frag Grenade or simply close with the gunner and take him out at close range while Dom distracts him. A third option is to down a Drone on either side and use him as a meat shield.

Finally, you can also make your way to the back of the yard where several Wretches and a pair of Maulers attack. Taking out a Mauler gives you a Boomshield. This provides a ready answer to the Troika, letting you simply walk up and remove the gunner while you're shielded.

Once the Troika is clear, man it to mow down the two Bloodmounts that emerge from the doors at the end of the yard.

Once you fully clear the yard, go down the hall where the Bloodmounts emerged. You can turn a pair of hand cranks to open the gate that leads to Cooper street.

The first threat is a pack of Locust in a building on the street's left side. Shoot the fuel tank outside the building to trigger a chain reaction that results in a massive explosion, clearing out the building's interior and removing the Locust infestation. It also causes a sign to drop from the building, providing a wall of half cover.

Next, turn your attention to the street ahead. There are more Drones in the street, along with a single Reaver for you to dispatch.

As you move down the street, a car comes flying over the top of the garage, presumably dislodged by a Reaver. It slams into the street, providing another piece of usable cover. Unfortunately, the car is quickly followed by the Reaver itself. Keep your distance and take it down. Dom can kick down a dangling car from the garage to provide more cover once the Reaver is toast. This gives you another position to advance to as you clear out more Drones in the street ahead.

Once you hit the street's midway point, you have to mop up the remaining Drones. You also have to shoot another explosive fuel tank on the right side of the street.

Doing so dislodges a weakened portion of the garage, causing a few cars to roll out. More importantly, it creates a sloping path for Dom to rejoin you.

When you meet at the end of the street, a Grinder bursts through the barricade. Stay behind cover and eliminate him. Then grab the Mulcher and move on.

RIGHT PATH

ENCOUNTER 09

ENEMY PRESENCE

SNIPER GRENADIER FLAME GRENADIER

There are two parts to the garage route. The first is simply eliminating a lone Sniper at the top of the steps. You then grab the nearby Longshot and ammo to cover Dom in the street below.

Clear the Locust and the lone Reaver from the first portion of the street. Then move through the building to reach the parking garage's second floor.

From here, you have to eliminate a pair of Grenadiers and a Flame Grenadier. Once you take them out, walk over to the left side of the garage and push a dangling car out the window. This provides some ground cover for your partner below.

Mantle over the cover to the back end of the garage. A partial collapse in the building provides a convenient path back down to the street, where you can rejoin Dom.

Just after you clear the Grinder at the end of the split path, you can pick up the mighty Hammer of Dawn. This potent weapon provides supreme firepower, making it easy to sail through this area's last encounter.

Stay behind cover and incinerate the Locust forces with an orbital bombardment. After the first Reaver lands, a shockwave rocks the area as a building at the end of the street collapses, showering you with a wall of dust.

After the building falls, a Mauler and a few more Locust emerge. Again, they're no match for the Hammer's power. Once you eliminate them, make your way down the street to the end of the chapter. Be sure to pick up the second-to-last collectible on the way.

This is the final weapon you acquire in the campaign, and it's easily the most powerful. The Hammer of Dawn allows you to tap into the orbital satellite network and rain down hell from above.

You don't get to use it for long, so make the most of it while you can! It makes the remaining encounters here much easier.

As you approach the end of the level, find the **COG Tags** in the ruined building on the left side of the street.

CHAPTER 4: TENUOUS FOOTING

Having made their way to the Locust sinkhole, Delta attempts to descend to the bottom, where they can clear the area for a drop of the Lightmass Bomb. The objective is to sink Jacinto and flood the Hollow.

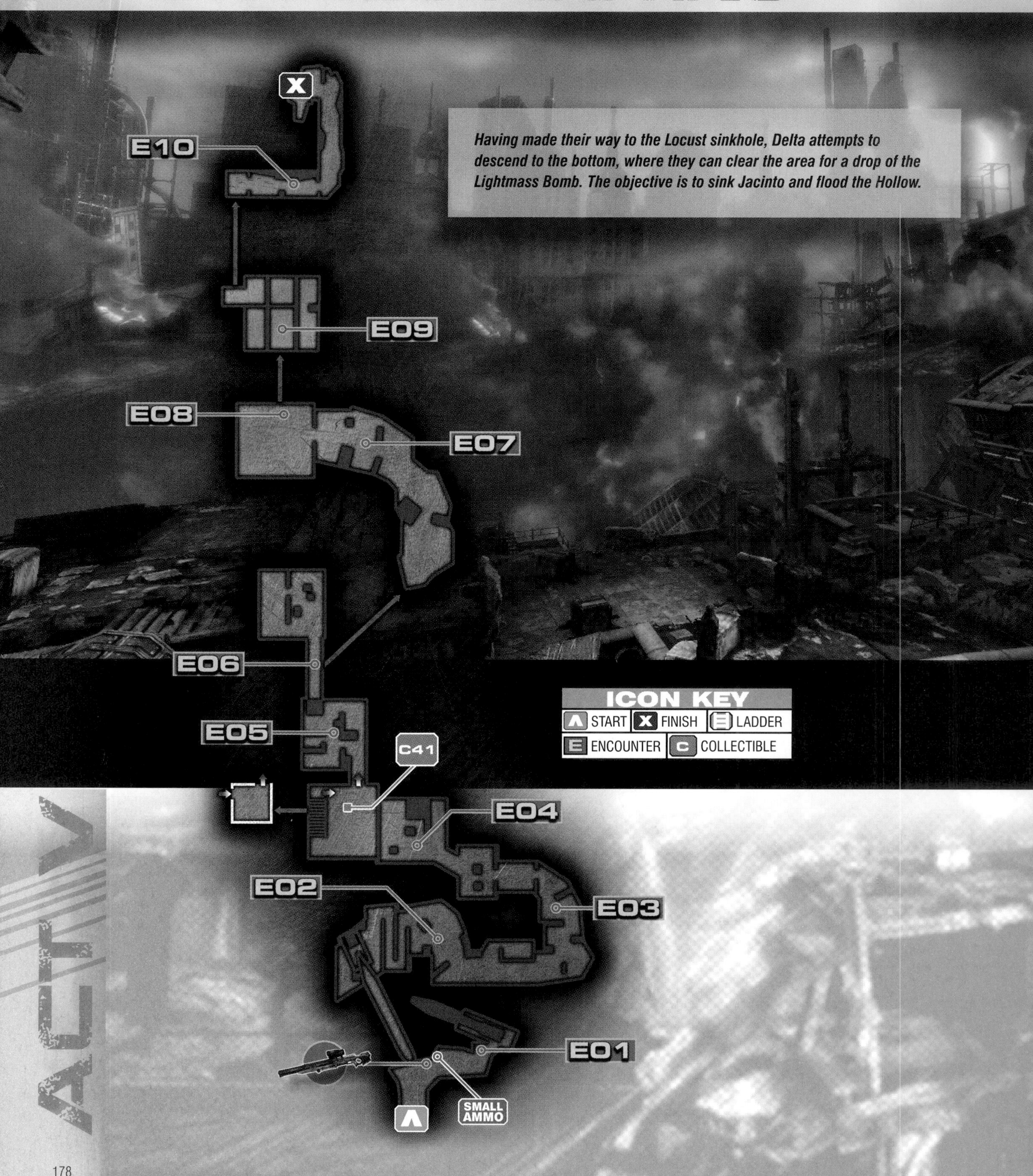

ACT V

Before you can make your way down, you have to cross a huge, open-air gap to the buildings visible below. To accomplish this feat, hop into the crane just to the right of the starting position.

From here, move the crane's platform load over to the left side of the gap and drop it down so that Dom can hop aboard.

Next, move the load all the way to the right and deposit Dom down on the building in the roof's large, open area. If you're playing co-op, you may want to delay the drop a bit so your buddy can clear the area from above. If you're playing solo, Dom moves quickly to the crane on the other side to get you across.

Once you make the drop, hop out and move over to the left side of the ledge. Dom attempts to use the crane on that side, but the crane arm crashes down, forming a makeshift bridge… whatever works.

If you wish, pick up the Longshot beside the small ammo pack before you move across the crane arm to the rooftops. Snipe some of the Locust below before you come within their weapon range.

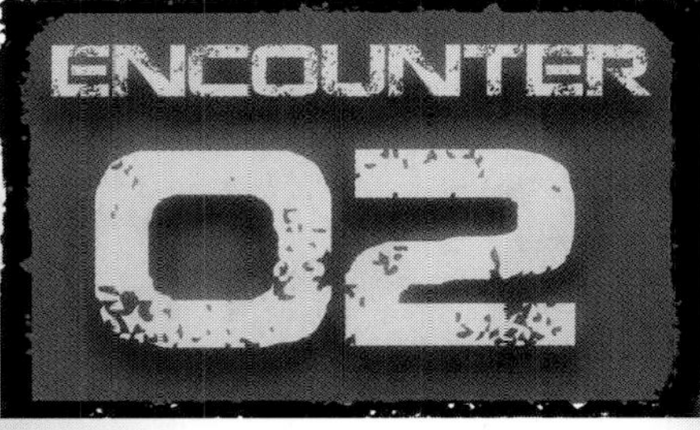

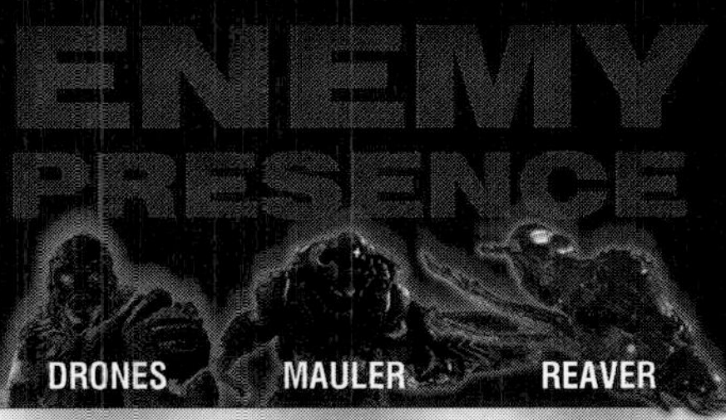

There are a few Locust on the rooftops, though nothing too major. However, once you hit the encounter marker at this point, a Mauler stomps out onto the roof.

Take him out with Dom's help and then grab the Boomshield. It comes in handy as a Reaver crashes down on the opposite building. You can easily use the Boomshield as cover and eliminate the Reaver with the Hammer of Dawn. If you aren't carrying the Hammer for some reason (loading a checkpoint), you can still use the Boomshield or regular cover to eliminate the Reaver, but it costs a bit more ammunition.

As you round the corner, a Flame Grenadier and several Tickers rush you. If you're quick, you may be able to detonate the Tickers near the Flamer. The resulting explosion should clear out most of your opposition.

If not, stay back—both the Flamer and the Tickers are dangerous only at fairly close range. Once you finish them off, move through the short hall onto the next roof, where a few more Drones and Tickers are waiting.

When you reach this building, numerous grappler Drones start ascending up the sides. If you're quick, you can shoot down many of them before they even reach the rooftop, saving some time and ammo.

After a few rounds of grappler Drone assaults, the building's roof finally can't handle the strain. It collapses, sending you and Dom plummeting to the bottom.

When you hit the 'ground' level, you can mantle out of the building to a small area containing the game's last collectible. But you also meet a Boomer using a Scorcher and a few more Drones.

For the time being, hang out inside the collapsed building. It's safer than going out onto the next building top, as the cover out there is destructible (a few pieces of furniture). Instead, you can easily gun down the Locust while you remain safe behind thick walls.

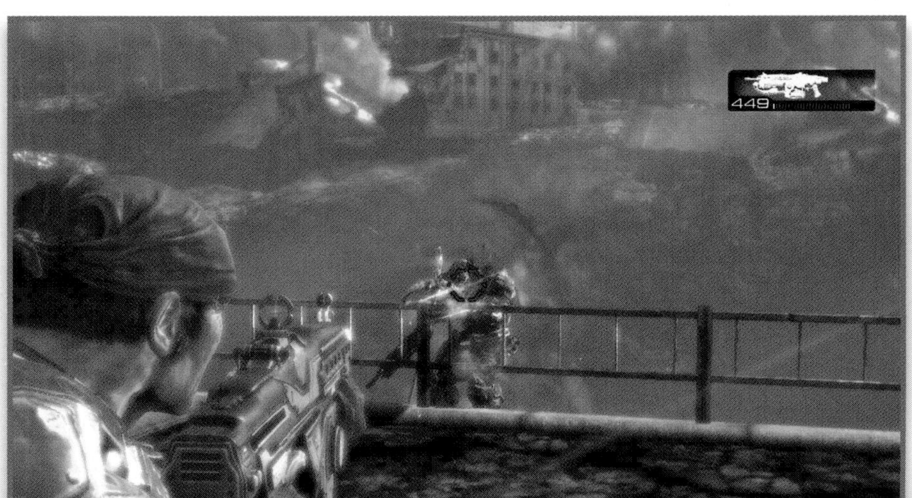

DEV TIP

Use the Shotgun on the grappling hooks to take them out easily. Once five Drones come at you, the floor drops out.

—*ADAM BELLEFEUIL*

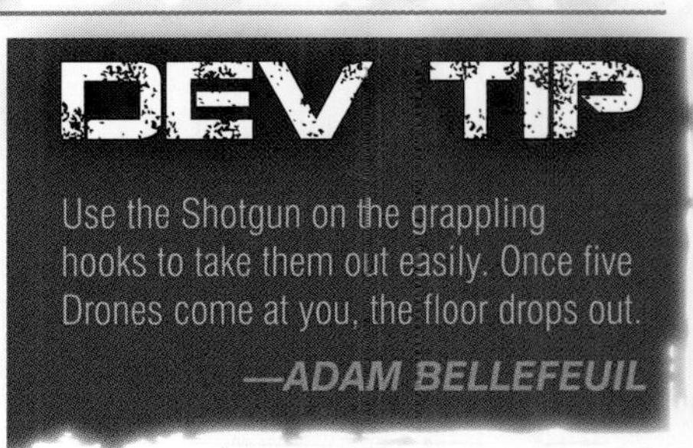

The game's final collectible is nearly in plain sight. After the building collapses, check the room's corner behind the destroyable desk to grab the **Stranded's Journal**.

ACT V

Be careful approaching this building. There are only a few Drones here, but they're armed with Lancers. The close quarters mean that one misstep on an approach gets you gutted. Take them out from a distance.

When you clear the Locust, you have to slice a pair of steel cables with your Lancer. Doing so drops a steel cage as a makeshift walkway onto the next building's roof.

Only two Drones occupy the opposite roof. But as you step into the cage, it loses its grip on the rooftops. You and Dom plummet to the ground below inside the cage.

A lone Kantus and a few grappler Drones guard the approach to the building behind them. If you're fast, you may be able to knock down the grappling hooks before the Drones can even reach solid ground to attack you. Of course, if you're still carrying the Hammer of Dawn, this is a short and messy encounter.

Once you kill all three, a debris slide occurs, giving you a way into the next building through the windows.

Inside the building, you get a clear view of a huge wave of Drones and one angry Brumak on the ground below. The Brumak blazes away at the building you're in with all its massive firepower.

If you have the Hammer of Dawn, unleash a blast to immolate the Locust below. But regardless of what you shoot at them, the building collapses under the onslaught, crushing the Locust and trapping the Brumak at the 'top' of the fallen building.

When you regain consciousness, you're trapped inside the 'bottom' of the fallen building, and a raging inferno surrounds you! Quickly mantle over the beams in the room to get to the (now sideways) elevator. Hit the switch to call it and then quickly mantle inside to take a trip to the 'top' of the building.

When you reach the Brumak, carefully dodge from cover to cover to avoid its furious chaingun barrage. Make your way around the side of the building to get behind the Brumak. Then take out its driver.

Afterward, Marcus has the bright idea of riding the Brumak to the squad's objective...

CHAPTER 5: CLOSURE

Marcus and Dom have hijacked a Brumak and are riding it into the depths of the tunnels. Their destination is the rendezvous point where the Lightmass Bomb is to be planted.

Crush your foes!

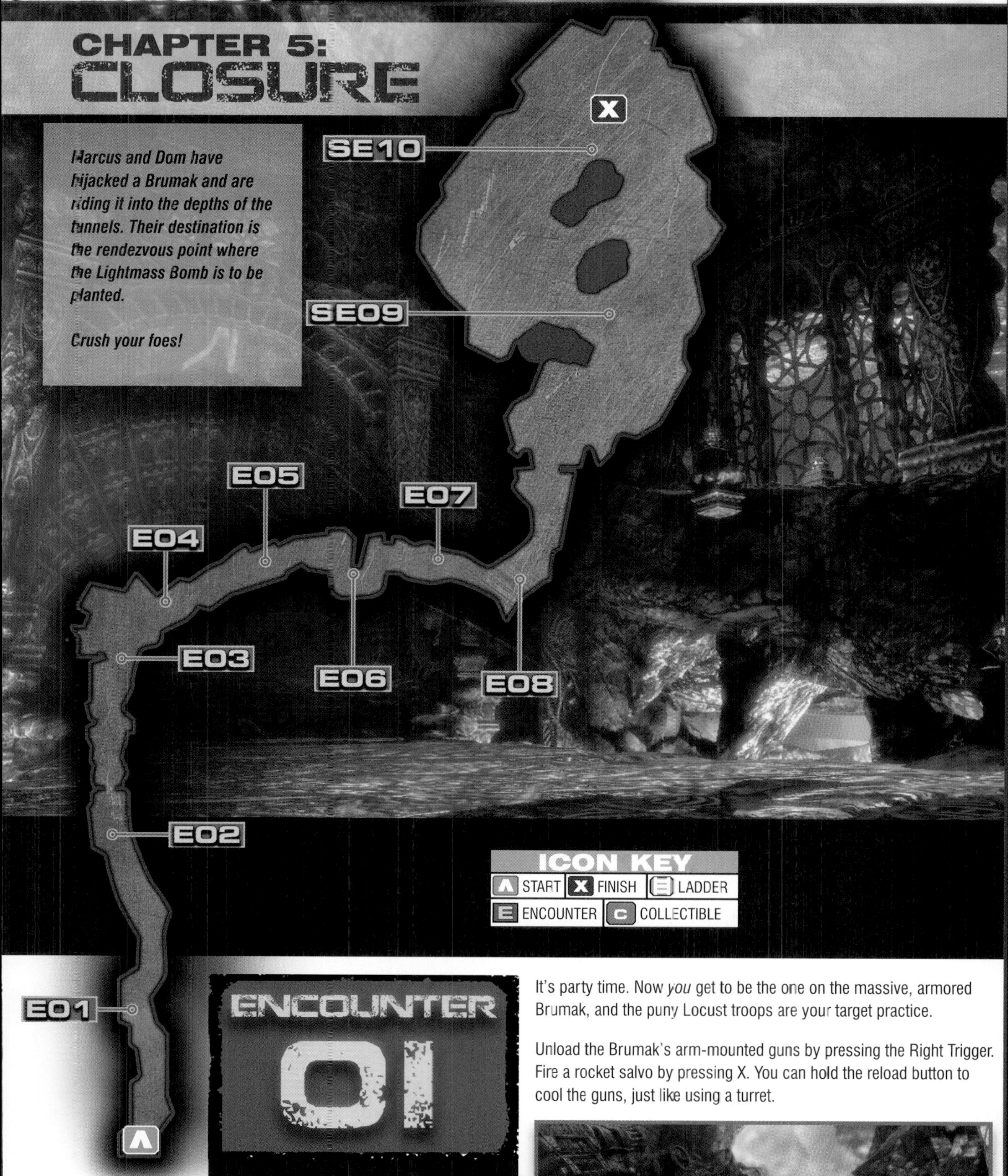

ICON KEY

START	FINISH
LADDER	ENCOUNTER
COLLECTIBLE	

ENCOUNTER 01

ENEMY PRESENCE

DRONES, THERON GUARDS, BOOMERS

It's party time. Now *you* get to be the one on the massive, armored Brumak, and the puny Locust troops are your target practice.

Unload the Brumak's arm-mounted guns by pressing the Right Trigger. Fire a rocket salvo by pressing X. You can hold the reload button to cool the guns, just like using a turret.

Controlling the Brumak is simple; it handles just like a much more cumbersome Gear on the ground.

Unload on the Locust swarm on the ground. Blast the Boomers on the ridge to the left, near where a Corpser bursts out of the wall for a moment.

Continue stomping down the trail. When the first huge doors come into view, several Reavers swoop in and attempt to stop your implacable march. Use rockets to kill them quickly, ideally in pairs, finishing off any stragglers with your Gatling guns.

As you emerge into the cavern beyond the first door, multiple searchlights spot your Brumak and open fire with Troikas. Additionally, a ledge on the chamber's right side has multiple Boomers on it.

Unload on the searchlights and use your rockets to collapse the structures housing the Troikas. Then finish off the Boomers on the right side.

As you march forward, multiple Reavers swoop in and land. If you've cleared out the room sufficiently, you should be able to concentrate on them fully and eliminate them swiftly.

The Corpser that spotted you as you entered the underground bursts forth from the wall here and engages in a brutal melee challenge with your mount. Mash the B Button quickly enough, and your Brumak crushes the Corpser, clearing the path ahead.

A large pack of Locust is on the right ledge here. Take them out with a barrage of rockets and a spray of bullets. Then deal with the Reavers that land on the path in front of you.

Once you eliminate these Locust, bash your way through the huge doors to reach the next chamber.

DEV TIP

A few Nemacyst come flying at you here—watch out for them.

—*ANDREW BAINS*

Heavy enemy resistance greets you as you emerge from the second massive doors. Knock out the buildings the Locust are using on the left of the room. Then fire at the large Locust explosives on the wall to the right, causing the entire wall to collapse.

When you neutralize the two immediate threats, you can turn your attention to the pair of turrets that bracket the path down the cavern's center. Destroy each one in turn before you continue moving.

Take out the left wall by shooting the Locust explosives there. Then down the Grinder firing at you from a spire on the cavern's right side.

Finally, use extreme firepower to punish several Reavers that drop in on the path in front of you.

As you reach the cavern's sharp left turn, a huge Locust Torture Barge comes into view. Multiple Locust onboard fire at you with Troika and Boomshot.

Aim at the Barge's legs that anchor it to the ceiling. If you disable two of them, the entire creature plummets into the Imulsion, quickly eliminating the threat. Alternatively, you can just concentrate your firepower on the Barge's face. It will eventually fall down.

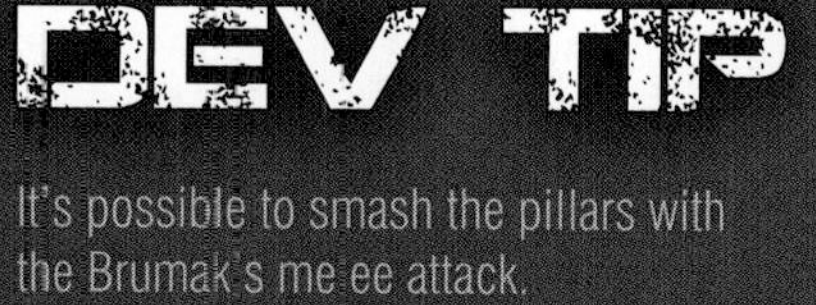

It's possible to smash the pillars with the Brumak's melee attack.

—*ANDREW BAINS*

Beyond one last door, this huge chamber is the ideal location to detonate the Lightmass Bomb.

However, you must first create an opening in the ceiling to allow the Ravens carrying the bomb to get into the chamber.

There are three pillars in the chamber. You must destroy each one to trigger the ceiling's collapse.

You can see the first one almost as soon as you enter the chamber. Destroy it by raking it from top to bottom with Gatling fire and rockets.

As you move farther into the huge cavern, Reavers and a few Seeders assault you with rockets and Nemacyst mortars. You *can* shoot down inbound Nemacyst, which is helpful for limiting the damage you take.

As you move through the room, use the pillar bases for cover (to a greater or lesser degree, depending on the difficulty level). Once you demolish all three pillars, the roof comes crashing down, allowing the Ravens and the rest of Delta Squad to fly down into the cavern.

Continual exposure to the Imulsion that coats the cavern's floor horribly mutates the Brumak that Marcus and Dom rode to get here. The creature transforms into a massive Lambent Brumak. While Cole and Baird manage to pick you up in one Raven, the other Raven drops the Lightmass Bomb as the mutating Brumak smashes it.

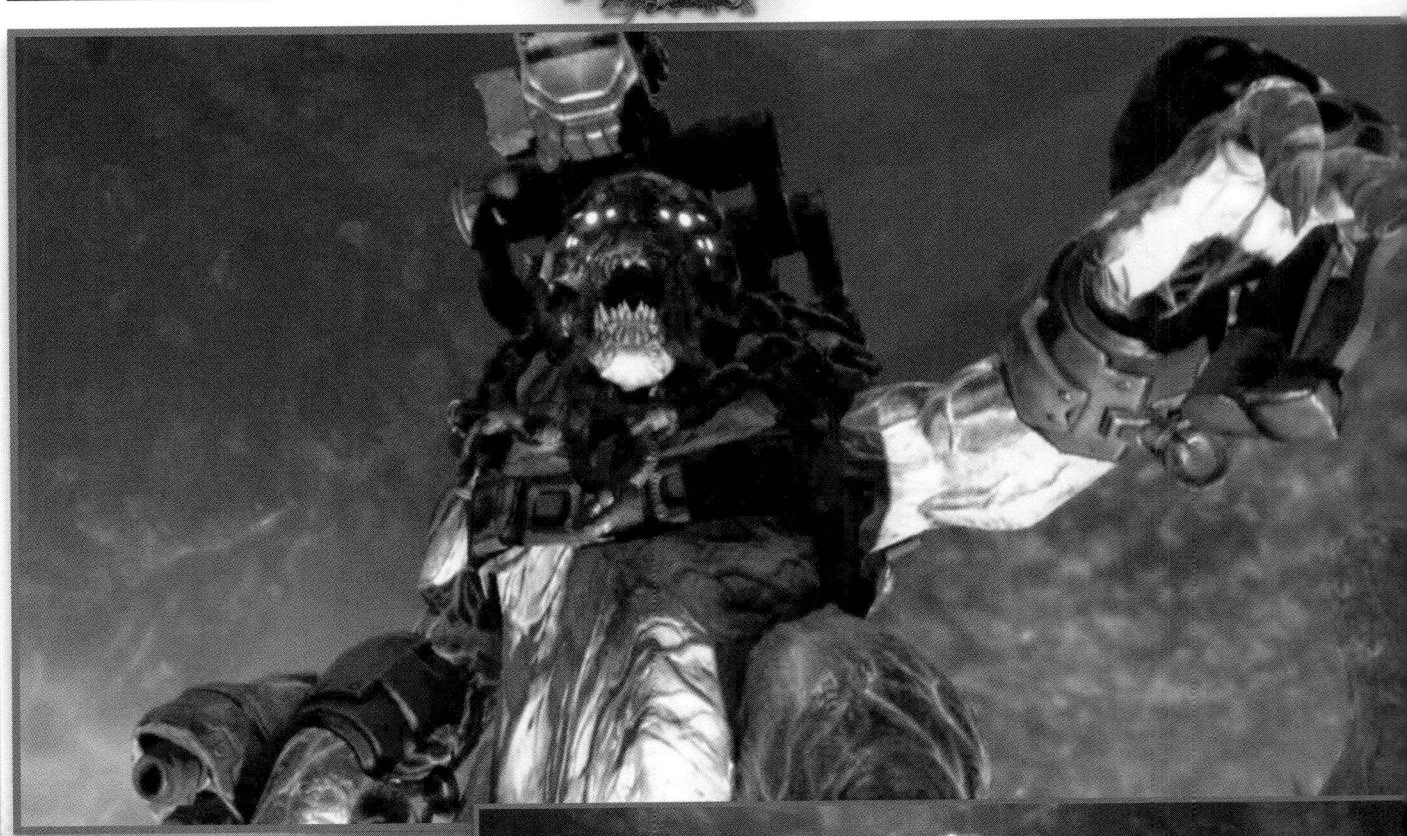

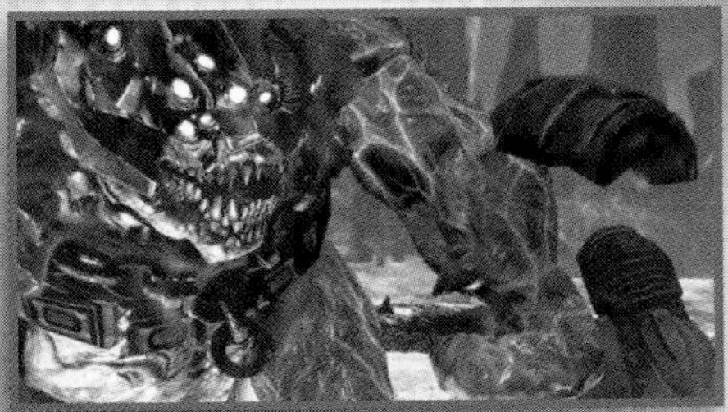

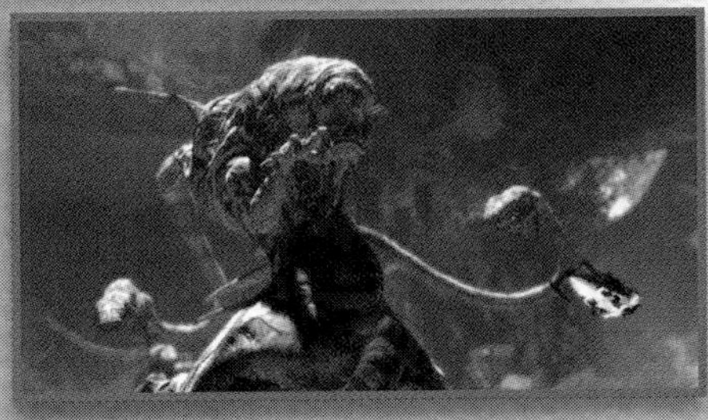

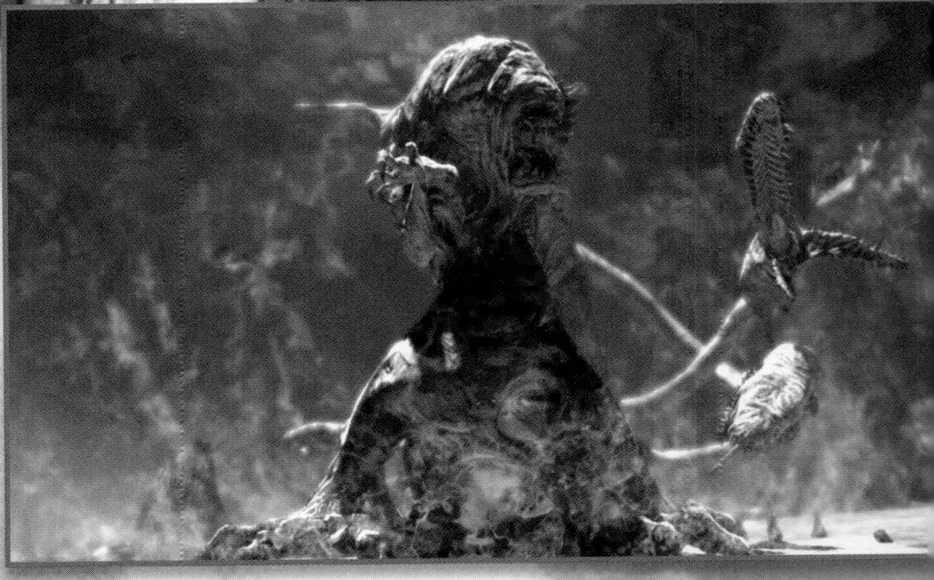

A quick discussion of their options brings to light the thought of using the immense Lambent creature as a makeshift bomb. If it explodes like the Lambent Wretches did, the sheer force of the explosion should suffice to sink Jacinto.

When you regain control of Marcus, target the Hammer of Dawn at the monstrous mutant creature. Blast it with all the fury of the orbital satellite bombardment. Once the creature suffers enough damage, the chain reaction begins, and Delta quickly evacuates the sinkhole.

Sit back and enjoy the ending…and be sure to wait through the credits.

MULTIPLAYER WARFARE

When it comes to playing Gears of War, a lot of fans come for the single-player campaign but stay for the multiplayer action. Gears of War serves up some extremely addictive multiplayer, and Gears of War 2 offers tons more in-your-face multiplayer mayhem. But with so many new weapons, features, and modes added to the game, you might need a little refresher. This chapter discusses all the basics of each mode, the weapon stats, and some high-level strategies to help keep you alive. Following this chapter, we analyze each level in painstaking detail. There you'll find detailed maps showing all the weapon, spawn, and capture locations, along with a wealth of strategy for every mode—especially Horde—for each of the 10 level maps. We even throw in some extra tips for those favorite maps from the original game that were lucky enough to receive a fresh coat of paint. So read on, fellow fraggers, and let us give you the ultimate head start on the competition!

TACTICS

DBNO

One of the new features in *Gears of War 2* is the ability to crawl away from an enemy once you've been downed. Veteran players refer to being "downed but not out" as being "DBNO." By rapidly tapping the A Button, you can now quickly crawl toward your teammates to make it that much easier for them to revive you. Of course, if you equip a Frag Grenade before being downed, you can crawl toward enemies and detonate the grenade when they move in to finish you off. The choice is yours: crawl back to the safety of your friends or be a martyr and take the enemy with you! When you are DBNO (and do not have a grenade equipped), pressing the Right Trigger raises your hand above your head to help your teammates locate you easier. Be careful though; when you raise your hand, you are not able to crawl, and this feature does not prevent enemies from executing you. Also, your character calls out to be revived. It doesn't happen each time you raise your hand, but roughly every other time.

COMBAT

Combat in multiplayer *Gears of War 2* is significantly different than single-player combat. The most obvious difference is that you're up against other living, breathing humans. While the Locust are mighty foes, it's hard to beat the ingenuity of a human opponent. You have to anticipate completely different sets of actions when you play against humans, and you have to be that much more careful how you advance.

Arguably, the most significant change is that cover becomes slightly de-emphasized —though only *slightly*. Because human opponents do not have perfect accuracy, one can move around the battlefield more freely than in the campaign. And let's be honest, most players tend to run, somersault, and try to blast you at close range anyway, but this is definitely less prevalent in *Gears of War 2* due to stopping power. This *does not* mean that you should engage in open combat outside of cover. But it does mean that mobility becomes much more important, both as an offensive and a defensive strategy.

The dynamics of multiplayer combat also change significantly depending on the number of players and the game mode you're playing. Two-player Wing Man is significantly different than five-player Annex, which, in turn is also considerably different from Execution or even Guardian. Players tend to find themselves intentionally or accidentally in one of the following three situations:

- **Lone Wolf:** *Gears of War 2* is very much a team-based game, and you almost always have at least one or two people (or bots) on your team. Nevertheless, there are times when you feel like you're on your own. Any number of factors can create such circumstances, from an inability to communicate with your teammates to a disparity in skill level. If you're forced to fight alone, be prepared to ignore basic team tactics and map-specific strategy and adjust your play style to one that focuses on self-preservation. Use cover and try and funnel enemies toward chokepoints. If you pick up a new weapon, be sure to clear the area immediately. Rely heavily on long-range weaponry, and be sure to set up a defense with proximity mines. Employ hit-and-run tactics and hope that the other team fans out. Thin the enemy herd by preying on foes that leave the safety of the group.

MP WARFARE

Deadly Duo: Whether or not you're playing the Wingman game mode, you sometimes naturally team up with a friend or another player of equal skill and play round after round together as a duo. This can be a particularly fun and effective way to play, particularly if the other people in the match fail to develop any solid partnerships or team tactics. To excel as a duo, you must both make an effort to coordinate attacks, stick together, and to move effectively through the map. Leapfrog one another as you advance, and do your best to lure enemies into your partner's line of fire. Two players that take their roles seriously, bait their enemies, cover one another, and use the landscape to their advantage can be far more effective than a five-player team that fails to communicate and acts as a group of lone wolves.

Team Domination: No matter how skilled the individual players on the opposing team, a well-coordinated team will almost always beats one that fails to communicate effectively. Team tactics can be as simple as telling others which weapon pickup you're rushing toward, or as complex as setting up a crossfire trap and having other players lure enemies into the blender. The keys to successful team-based play change from map to map, but a few simple guidelines almost always apply:

Avoid running off in separate directions.

Call out enemy locations.

Lend a hand to teammates, even if it's just suppression fire.

Use the round's initial moments to agree on strategy and to decide on who's doing what. Make sure nobody travels alone, unless part of the team strategy is sending a lone wolf get the drop on the enemy. Make sure your team operates with a specific goal and isn't just running around hoping to spot an enemy.

TRAINING GROUNDS

Use the Training Grounds option on the main menu to play through five multiplayer lessons against bots. Anya goes over the rules for each of the matches and provides basic instruction about reviving fallen teammates, performing executions, and securing capture points. Training Grounds is a great place for first-timers to cut their teeth with the game. Advanced players might assume that these five tutorials don't offer much to them, but playing through the lessons yields an Achievement so there's always an incentive.

FLOW

Flow is a concept that applies to shooters of all types. It simply refers to where players *can* move through a level, and where they actually *do* move through a level *most of the time*. Knowing a map's flow is a fundamental aspect of fighting effectively on it. Once you learn a map's basic layout, the weapon and capture locations, the spawn points, and so on, you need to know where enemies typically flock. Understanding flow is the difference between reacting to enemy movement (and hoping to survive) and using the enemy's movement to your advantage.

At the basic level, flow is dictated by a combination of spawn location and simple geography. For example, imagine that your team spawns on one end of the map and your opponents can choose one of three possible paths to reach you. If one of those paths is far safer than the others—or if it leads to a highly coveted weapon pickup—then you have insight into the level's basic flow.

You know that enemies can come from only three directions. You also know that one direction is preferable. As a result, you can quickly examine the terrain on your side of the map and figure out where to take cover, where to watch, and where enemies can be flanked.

ORGANIZED PLAY

Flow often holds sway in casual multiplayer matches, and sometimes even in ranked games with fairly skilled players. However, two skilled and organized teams facing off against each other can start to violate the "rules" of flow.

The reason for this is simple: both teams know the map extremely well, often perfectly! As a consequence, they have a very good feel for where the other team is, where their teammates are, what a sound from around the corner signifies, what a weapon pickup means in terms of player position, and so on.

The result of this knowledge is that whole teams may move in what would normally be seen as strange or erratic patterns. You might see a full team rush a single route far more aggressively than would be safe in a casual game with less organized players. You might see a lone player make a flanking attack against a good chunk of the opposing team while the rest of his teammates distract the opponents.

This sort of play is often a guessing game between the two teams, as each tries to outthink, outflank, and overwhelm the opposition. This level of competition doesn't come without dedicating a sizable amount of time to practice matches, but the rewards—bragging rights and personal satisfaction—can be worth the effort.

If this sort of a match sounds appealing to you, look online for some of the *Gears of War 2* leagues and ladders. Very competitive clans and groups tend to seek out these venues for more serious matches than you can normally find playing with just a few friends online.

Knowing a map's flow, you're unlikely to get caught on the wrong side of cover and blindsided by half the enemy team. Similarly, you are much more likely to face your targets as they come into view, preferably from favorable ground. You also have a much better idea of how and where you can approach or flank the enemy advance if you are playing aggressively.

Beyond a map's basic geography, other factors influence the amount of traffic in certain parts of a map. What game mode are you playing? Where are the power weapons located? Where is the current objective? All of these considerations influence flow.

Often, one learns a map's natural flow through sheer repetition—it's not uncommon for people to play dozens of matches in a single night. Ever wonder how it's possible for veteran players to kill you from around a corner with a 'lucky' Frag Grenade mere seconds after the map starts? It isn't really luck at all. They know there's a good chance that a target will enter a certain area within a few moments after a round starts. Throwing a grenade is simply playing the odds that a player will show up to eat the damage. It's really that simple.

HOW WE COVER FLOW

Flow might be something you learn over time through repetition, but that doesn't mean we can't give you a head start. Consult the "Spawn Point Awareness" and "Essential Tactics" sections of each map chapter to gain an early understanding of how battles typically shake out on each of the maps. These two sections, combined with knowledge of high-powered weapon locations, will certainly advance you along the learning curve toward total domination!

WEAPON DATA

Veterans of the original *Gears of War* are in for a few surprises when they jump online with the sequel. There are several distinct changes in relative weapon power, along with the major addition of stopping power. It's now possible to slow down charging enemies by shooting them while they roadie run, regular run, or even dodge roll. The following tables provide the power of each weapon. They also reveal the relative changes in power from *Gears of War* to *Gears of War 2* for those weapons that were in both games.

In the following table:
"+" = Weapon's power has been increased.
"-" = Weapon's power has been reduced.

MP WEAPONRY:
AMMO CAPACITY, DAMAGE AT RANGE, AND FIRING RATES

WEAPON	MAG SIZE	BASE DAMAGE	SHORT RANGE	MEDIUM RANGE	LONG RANGE	FIRING RATE	RELOAD RATE
Boltok Pistol (-)	6	200	270	250	200	60	2.0
Boomshot (+)	1	525	525	525	315	60	2.5
Boomshot Bomblet	-	150	150	150	90	-	-
Gnasher (-)	8	500	450	450	300	8	3.0
Gorgon Pistol	24	55	55	55	33	1200	2.0
Hammerburst	17	80	80	80	48	250	2.0
Lancer (-)	50	38	38	38	23	550	2.5
Longshot	1	350	420	350	350	60	3.0
Mortar (hip-shot)	1	1000	1000	1000	600	60	3.5
Mortar (cluster)	1	800	800	800	480	60	3.5
Mortar Bomblet	-	800	800	800	480	-	-
Mulcher	500	50	50	50	30	1250	6.0
Scorcher	50	700	700	700	420	850	2.5
Snub Pistol (-)	12	55	55	55	33	700	2.0
Torque Bow (+)	1	708	708	708	425	60	3.0
Hammer of Dawn	20 sec.	1500	N/A	N/A	N/A	N/A	3.2

MP WEAPONRY:
MELEE AND HEADSHOT DAMAGE WITH STOPPING POWER

WEAPON	BASE DAMAGE	MELEE DAMAGE	STOPPING POWER	HEADSHOT DAMAGE
Boltok Pistol	200	338 (Avg)	0.50*	200%
Boomshot	525	338 (Avg)	-	-
Gnasher	500	338 (Avg)	0.40	110%
Gorgon Pistol	55	425 (Avg)	0.25*	300%
Hammerburst	80	338 (Avg)	0.35	110%
Lancer	38	Chainsaw	0.25*	150%
Longshot	350	463 (Avg)	0.25*	300%
Mortar	1000	N/A	*(see below)	-
Mulcher	50	N/A	0.25*	-
Scorcher	700	425 (Avg)	0.18	-
Snub Pistol	55	338 (Avg)	0.25*	200%
Torque Bow	708	475 (Avg)	-	110%
Hammer of Dawn	Special	238 (Avg)	-	-

* *The Mortar either blows targets to pieces or concusses them around. For weapons with equal stopping power values, the effect is most noticeable on weapons with a high rate of fire.*

GRENADES

WEAPON	CASUAL DAMAGE	NORMAL DAMAGE	HDCR/INS DAMAGE	AI DAMAGE	RADIUS	MELEE DAMAGE
Ink Grenade	300/sec.	300/sec.	300/sec.	300/sec.	512	120+Ink
Frag Grenade	2000	1400	1000	1000	10 Yards	TAG!
Smoke Grenades	-	-	-	-	512	Concussion

The most notable change in multiplayer weapon stats is that the Gnasher's power has been toned down. You should expect fewer roll-and-blast skirmishes. Additionally, the Boomshot and Torque Bow are more powerful than their predecessors. The Longshot, while still very powerful, is no longer an automatic one-shot-kill with Active Reload. It's also worth noticing that the Gorgon Pistol, while not a very powerful weapon in general terms, is positively lethal when you manage to land a headshot. The extremely fast firing rate, combined with the 300% damage increase for headshots, makes it a very deadly weapon in the right hands.

EXECUTIONS

Gears of War 2 multiplayer gives you more ways than ever to put a blood-soaked exclamation mark on your victory! The Curbstomp and Chainsaw executions were great ways to express your dominance in the original game. Now there are so many butt-kicking executions to perform, you'll find yourself purposely avoiding headshots just for the thrill of performing the perfect in-your-face finishing move to thoroughly embarrass your opponent. After all, that's what this is all about, right?

KICK 'EM WHEN THEY'RE DOWN

Perform all eleven unique Executions to earn the Kick 'em When They're Down Achievement.

1. *Curbstomp*
2. *Neckbreaker (when meatshielding someone)*
3. *Boomshield Spike*
4. *Generic Quick Execution*
5. *Torque Bow Quick Execution*
6. *Shotgun Quick Execution*
7. *Longshot Quick Execution*
8. *Face Punch*
9. *Boltok Pistol Long Execution*
10. *Torque Bow Long Execution*
11. *Longshot Long Execution*

QUICK EXECUTIONS

Quick executions are performed by tapping the B Button as you stand over a downed opponent. They come in handy when you need to execute the opponent quickly, before another foe rushes you.

Face Punch: Perform the Face Punch execution after downing an enemy. Press the Y Button while holding any weapon except for the Torque Bow, Sniper Rifle, or Boltok Pistol.

Longshot: Down an enemy and press the Y Button to swing the Longshot overhead like a club and bash the enemy to death with the rifle's stock.

Gnasher: You can use the Gnasher to perform a jaw-breaking execution on a downed enemy. Press the B Button to flip the Gnasher into the air, grab it by the barrel, and swing it like a golf club at the enemy's head.

Torque Bow Decapitation: Stand by a downed enemy and press the Y Button while holding the Torque Bow to use its blades and your character's boot to decapitate the victim.

Grenades: The downed player is tagged with the particular grenade selected. The normal grenade tagging animation is played.

Frag Grenade: When the grenade's timer expires, the enemy explodes. Nearby enemies suffer damage or explode, depending on their distance. The player that initiates the tag can also be hurt or killed if he does not escape the blast.

Ink Grenade: A DNBO player is not killed instantly when he is tagged with an Ink Grenade. Rather, he suffers damage as if he is standing near it. Of course, he can't get away from the grenade and it inflicts enough damage to kill the downed player within seconds.

Smoke Grenade: This inflicts no damage, but nearby enemies of the tagging player are affected (according to team damage rules, if applicable). The DBNO player doesn't die from the detonation and doesn't suffer any damage.

LONG EXECUTIONS

Chainsaw: Use the Lancer to chainsaw an enemy in half by pressing the B Button. You can do this with a downward slice while facing the enemy or by sawing upward, through the crotch, while standing behind the enemy. This is the only execution that doesn't require downing an enemy.

Curbstomp: Rush up to a downed enemy and press the X Button to crush his head beneath your boot.

Neckbreaker: You can snap an enemy's neck while dragging him around as a meat shield. This happens automatically after prolonged use, or you can press the X Button to do it manually.

Boltok Pistol: Press the Y Button. Down an enemy while carrying the Boltok Pistol and spin the weapon around in the air before cracking it across the fallen foe's skull.

Boomshield Spike: Press the Y Button to slam the Boomshield onto the back of a downed enemy, thus impaling the target with the spikes on the bottom of the shield.

PLAYING WITH OTHERS

The addition of multiplayer gaming makes a great game like *Gears of War 2* that much better, giving you the chance to test your skills against players from around the world—or those sitting next to you. Whether you want to play split-screen with a friend, set up a System Link party, or go online with Xbox Live, this section has you covered. Keep reading for explanations of the gameplay options, what the different modes allow you to do, and for information on setting up playlists and more.

SERVER OPTIONS

TRACKING STATS

If you want your stats tracked, play on either Public or Private Xbox Live. Choosing Local does not save your score to a leaderboard.

PUBLIC XBOX LIVE

Create a party of up to five players, set up a Playlist and enter a match against another team of five based on the team's composite TruSkill rank. You can also filter for mode types that you specify in the Playlist settings. Players vote on which gameplay mode and map to play once a match is set up. This is a marked departure—and improvement—from the way ranked matches were handled in *Gears of War*. Now you can move from match to match as a team and return to the Multiplayer Party Lobby as a unit after each map. Take on other teams comparable to your team's skill and earn up to five different ranking icons. Keep in mind that Public Matches are akin to "Ranked Matches" and you will suffer a penalty for exiting a match prematurely, so man up and finish what you start!

The Playlists group gameplay modes in the following manner (Playlists can change at any time; this is the layout at game release):

- **Players Choice:** Allow the players to vote on any of the modes, not including Horde or Wingman.
- **Elimination:** Warzone, Execution, and Guardian.
- **Territories:** Annex, King of the Hill, and Submission.
- **Horde:** Horde.
- **Wingman:** Wingman.
- **Downloadable Content:** Any gameplay mode, played on maps available for download through Xbox Live. All players must have the downloadable maps.
- **Flashback Players' Choice:** Contains the five remake maps from the original *Gears of War* game.

PRIVATE XBOX LIVE

This mode functions the same way a private, unranked match in the original *Gears of War*, except with added functionality and increased user-friendliness. For those new to *Gears of War,* a Private Match is one you limit to people on your Friends list who you then invite to form the party. It doesn't show up on the Public servers and cannot be joined by anyone you don't invite. Form a group of up to 10 players in the Multiplayer Party Lobby, pick your settings, have a single host make the selections (or put the map up to a vote), and use bots to fill out the teams if you want to.

SYSTEM LINK

Select this option if you have multiple Xbox 360 consoles connected directly to one another for System Link play. This is also the LAN method of playing.You can have up to two players on each console. For full instructions, consult the user's manual included with your copy of the game.

LOCAL

Local has all the same functionality as a Private Xbox Live match, except that you play offline with bots. It's possible to add a second player to the lobby in split-screen, but that person must sign in with his or her profile on the main menu screen. Stats are not saved in Local matches.

GAMEPLAY SETTINGS

- **Total Rounds:** Set the match length to last between 1 and 15 rounds. This is not a "best of" scenario, nor is there a mercy rule. Shutouts are possible. The total number of rounds selected is the number you play, so make sure everyone in the lobby is committed to playing however long it takes—nobody likes a quitter, so leave before the match begins or see it through to the end.
- **Number of Bots:** Use between 0 and 9 bots to fill out the teams with AI-controlled characters. There are no bots on Public Xbox Live matches.

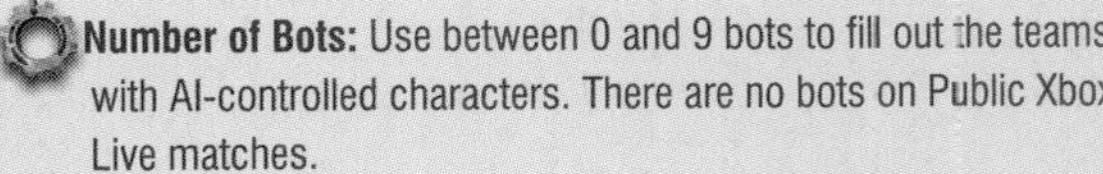

- **Bot Difficulty:** Choose between Casual, Normal, Hardcore, or Insane difficulty settings for the bots in your match. Bot AI settings in Multiplayer affect actual intelligence, accuracy, and so forth—they always play by the same rules as humans regardless of difficulty.

Bleed-Out Time: Choose how long it takes downed players to bleed out (or get back up in Execution or Wingman matches). Choose between 5, 10, 15, 20, 30, and 60 seconds. We recommend a bleed-out time of 10 seconds, but it's strictly your call.

Friendly Fire: Turn this setting on if you want teammatess to be able to damage each other with their weapons. Friendly fire adds a realistic quality to competition that can be fun. However, it can also be abused by people who purposely perform team-kills to grief other players. Turn this setting on with caution.

Map Selection: Either the host can pick the map or the choice is opened up to player vote. The map with the most votes gets played. If there is a tie, a map that didn't receive votes is chosen at random.

Weapon Swapping: The default setting has weapons cycle between an initial and an alternate weapon assigned to each weapon spawn location (some don't alternate). However, you can lock the weapons into a non-cycling mode or even customize the gameplay by swapping the weapons any way you like.

WEAPON SELECTION

One big change from *Gears of War* is that players can now select the weapon with which they start. Also, note that gold versions of the Lancer (only in the Limited Edition of the game) and Hammerburst (accessed from a token given at Midnight Madness events on launch day) are also available.

CHARACTER SELECTION

Players can select from a number of COG and Locust skins for their onscreen character. Use the Multiplayer Settings within the Options screen to customize your preferences, saving you from cycling to it each time you play.

BENJAMIN CARMINE

VICTOR HOFFMAN

MARCUS FENIX

AUGUSTUS "COLE TRAIN" COLE

DAMON BAIRD

DOMINIC SANTIAGO

THERON SENTINEL

CYCLOPS

BEAST RIDER

DRONE

SNIPER

GRENADIER ELITE

GRENADIER

THERON GUARD

UNLOCKABLE CHARACTERS

MULTIPLAYER MODES

WARZONE

To win, eliminate all members of the opposing team. You get one life per round.

The classic team deathmatch mode, Warzone pits two teams of five against each other. Eliminate every player on the opposing team to win a round. The first team to reach the preselected number of round victories wins! Exercise caution and use cover, as bullets can kill you from afar once you're downed. Once you're on the ground, your only hope is to crawl behind cover and have a teammate save you before the enemy finishes you off. The ability to crawl to safety is one of the best new features of the game, so don't give up just because you're downed!

Sticking together to defeat outnumbered enemies is the recipe for success in Warzone (and in Execution). The power weapons, located at strategic hot zones across the map, give you an edge over the enemy. However, use caution when you try to acquire them. Most are placed at equal distances from each opposing spawn point, ensuring that they are hotly contested. Pop Smoke Grenades for cover, and use flanking maneuvers to distract or drive back the enemy long enough to grab the upgraded weapons. These powerful weapons combined with solid team tactics will yield consistent victories for your team.

EXECUTION

To win, eliminate all members of the opposing team via one-shot kills or execution finishing moves. You get one life per round.

Execution puts a twist on basic Warzone combat. The primary theme is still five-on-five team deathmatch, but you *cannot* kill a downed player without performing an execution (barring explosive deaths or headshots with the Longshot). Execution, true to its name, requires combatants to get up close and personal, delivering one of the many brutal executions that the game offers in order to earn a kill. Depending on the bleed-out time for the match, you may be able to get up in time to pay back the opposing player who downed you in the first place. You will automatically die the third time you're down but not out. Some weapons can execute from afar, such as a headshot with the Longshot or a Boomshot gib.

Because players can now crawl to cover in *Gears of War 2*, it's even more critical to be near a downed foe to finish off him or her efficiently. If you can, travel with your teammates nearby, so they can cover you while you go in for the kill. Or, if you want, employ the martyr strategy: equip a Frag Grenade and rush suicide-style at an enemy group. Let them down you, and then detonate the Frag Grenade as they come to finish you off. As in Warzone, the first team to reach the selected number of round victories wins the match.

ANNEX

To win, capture and hold different key locations to collect enough points. Teams get infinite respawns.

Annex is essentially mobile Cap & Hold. At the start of the match, a random weapon on the map is designated the target area. You must secure that area by standing within the animated ring around the weapon. Stay within the ring long enough, and the point becomes controlled by your team. Areas capture faster with more friendly players inside the ring. The team controlling the location gains one point for every second they hold it.

You earn points toward the victory score for as long as your team holds the area. You don't have to stay in the circle to keep control of the ring once your team possesses it. However, if you have more teammates in a ring than enemies, your control cannot be broken. Also, sitting down but not out in a ring counts as being alive inside of it, so you can still hold onto an existing point by crawling or staying inside. Smoke Grenades are vitally important in Annex, both for the cover they provide and for the ability to knock a ring free from enemy control. Because you can win Annex only by controlling the victory points, straight kills and deathmatch tactics are de-emphasized, but only *slightly*. You can expect a brutal brawl for the area to erupt as soon as both teams are focused on it. Unlike Warzone or Execution, Annex has a periodic respawn timer—every 15 seconds, players on both teams who were killed respawn at their initial spawn points. As a consequence, if you manage to clear a point and control it, you can expect a concentrated wave of enemy players to arrive every so often. Use the maps provided in this book and your own experience with map flow to anticipate their arrival. Be ready for them with unfriendly firepower.

To win the war of attrition and begin gaining points, make every possible effort to throw yourself at the capture point while it's being contested. Some players should take up defensive positions outside the capture area to avoid grenades and power weapon attacks that precede a rush from the opposing team. But it's good to keep one player inside to preserve the capture. Annex matches see more frequent changes in capture locations. So, spread teammates out between capture points, especially as the number of remaining capture points at a given location dwindles. This ensures an immediate presence at the next capture location. Consider abandoning a capture location altogether when the remaining points are low. If the other team commits too many players to the point they currently hold, you'll be in a good position to quickly grab the next capture point before they can respond. Of course, if you're already losing and the round is winding down, then you should grab a Frag Grenade and rush the capture point as a martyr. Let the enemies down you, and then pull the pin as they move in for the execution. With any luck, you'll dislodge the capture point long enough to let your team move in for the steal. Another strategy is to set up proximity mines or ambush players along high-traffic areas between capture spots.

KING OF THE HILL

To win, capture and hold one key location per round to collect points. Teams get infinite respawns except when defending a captured location.

King of the Hill is different from Annex in that there is only one capture point for the entire round and it follows execution rules. Also, players securing the point must stay in the ring to score. Leaving the capture point makes it fade back to a neutral, un-captured state, opening it up to enemy capture. While your team holds the objective, you and your comrades do not respawn. Also, unlike Annex, capture breaks are instantaneous, rewarding suicide runs to slow enemy scoring.

Have one teammate stay within the capture area to fulfill the scoring requirement for King of the Hill matches. Those not staying within the capture circle or defending the vicinity should make a run for a power weapon when there's a lapse in pressure from the opposing team. For both Annex and King of the Hill, remember that your opponents spawn on alternating sides of the map. Keep this in mind as you prepare for the continuous waves of attacks that are in store. Smoke Grenades are vitally important in King of the Hill, both for the cover they provide and for the ability to knock a ring free from enemy control.

GUARDIAN

To win, kill the enemy Team Leader and eliminate all members of the opposing team. Teams get infinite respawns while their Team Leader is alive. The enemy Leader must be executed.

Guardian is a *very* team-oriented mode. Each team has a Team Leader that must be protected at all costs. Respawning is enabled in Guardian mode, *but* only while your Team Leader is alive. Once your Leader is killed, respawns for your team are disabled. As long as your Team Leader is standing, your team can still make a comeback, even if all of your other players are taken out. The Team Leader must be executed, while other players do not. A Leader has infinite revives and will respawn automatically after 15 seconds. The HUD displays the location of the enemy Leader; use Taccom to locate your own Leader.

Protecting your Team Leader while simultaneously flushing out the enemy Team Leader is the key to each match. Teams that keep this principal in mind prevail over those that blindly charge into battle as they would in a Warzone or Execution match. Essentially, players can assume one of three roles in a Guardian match: Team Leader, Defender, or Attacker. Divide your teammates evenly between these roles at the start of each round, ensuring that your team has adequate defense and offense.

As Team Leader, your number one priority is to stay alive so your teammates can continue respawning. At the start of each round, immediately move to an easily defensible position, preferably one with a higher elevation from which to view approaching enemies, or one with a chokepoint through which attackers must funnel. An ideal location is near a grenade spawn. Set up proximity mines at entrances to your defensive position and continue replenishing your grenade supply as attackers fall victim to your traps. Have an escape route in mind in case the enemy team breaks through your defenses. At some point, you may have no choice but to fight your way out of a bind. Communicate with teammates to report your status and call for help.

In a typical five-versus-five match, consider leaving two team members behind to defend the Team Leader. These players play the role of guardian, this mode's namesake. Use proximity mines liberally around the defensive position, much like the Team Leader does. Defenders can afford a riskier approach, taking cover closer to the direction from which attackers approach or venturing out to grab a weapon before falling back to a defensive stance. The other two team members fulfill the role of attacker, whose only goal should be to hunt down and kill the enemy Team Leader. If at all possible, avoid unnecessary skirmishes with other enemies until the opposing Leader is eliminated. Grab whatever power weapons you can en route to the opposition's Leader. Try paving your way with grenades to clear out defenders protecting the enemy Leader. Each round can provide a different challenge, so be prepared to adapt your approach accordingly. If you're struggling to get near the opposition's Leader and your own has faced little danger, send three attackers and leave behind one defender. Continue to improvise based on the match's flow. Maintain a balanced team strategy to find success in Guardian matches.

SUBMISSION

To win, shoot and capture the defending Meatflag and carry him to a specified location. Teams get infinite respawns.

Submission replaces the flag with a Meatflag, a roaming computer-controlled player. You must find this target, down him, and then pick him up as a meat shield, carrying him to the goal area to score a point for your team. The Meatflag cycles between three different guys. Of course, this target isn't friendly, and you may find yourself taken out by his shotgun, or even executed should you get taken down in his vicinity! Teamwork is paramount in Submission. Move toward the target as a group, down the target, and then provide covering fire for the player carrying the target to the goal.

Obtain the target and drag him, against his will, into your team's capture location long enough to win the round. You must hold the Meatflag in the ring for a few seconds to score. The Meatflag is extremely deadly up close. The Meatflag is so lethal that he has his own line on the scoreboard. But he can't take you down outside the range of his shotgun blasts. Down him from a safe distance and dash in to claim him while he's out of commission. Do this quickly before the Meatflag gets back up and the opposing team claims him. Sometimes it makes sense to let the other team knock down the Meatflag. You can then fire a high-powered weapon at the enemy team member and take the Meatflag for yourself. Time this well, and the enemy player won't know what hit him! Smoke Grenades are the most effective way to get an opponent to drop the Meatflag. If you drop the Meatflag, you have only a small window to reclaim him. If he resets to a neutral state, then the goal point moves to a new location and your team will lose any ground it made dragging him across the map. Smoke Grenades are great, both for cover and to knock a Meatflag free from enemy control. Always check the delivery point for proximity mines before you walk into it. The Meatflag absorbs most of the damage inflicted on you.

Watch for the Meatflag to get knocked loose from either a teammate or the enemy. It's not uncommon for all players within the Meatflag's close proximity to quickly die by his hands if he regains his feet before someone else claims him. If you manage to take the Meatflag hostage, stick to the simple logic that the shortest distance between two points is a straight line. Take the most direct route to your goal. The Meatflag slows you down immensely, so there's no reason to get cute—that only increases the time it takes to capture him. The only time to stray from this strategy is when your teammates have already started to secure a specific path for you. Also, it's worth the effort to pick up an upgraded pistol if you are going to be carrying the Meatflag. However, players not burdened with the Meatflag can make up ground quite quickly. If you're defending a teammate who is dragging the Meatflag to the capture point, follow the same strategy and clear a lane that is as direct as possible.

WINGMAN

To win, eliminate all opposing teams. The match winner is determined by the number of total kills. You get one life per round. Enemies must be executed.

Wingman is the ultimate in cooperative warfare. You and a buddy are up against four other teams of two. Alternatively, five players can play, each one paired up with one bot. This game mode plays out like a much more intimate variation of Warzone. While most deathmatch tactics and strategies apply, the greatly increased number of hostile targets makes moving from point to point *much* more dangerous. Teamwork is vitally important—moving together and flanking opposing teams is the path to victory in Wingman. Matches follow execution rules, and you get only three down but not outs. DBNO lasts longer in this mode so enemies have more time to finish you off.

Coordinated aggression is the key to success. You face up to four rival teams, as opposed to facing one enemy team in every other competitive, team-based game mode. A player must remember that everyone except his or her sole teammate is an enemy. Just because you're on the Marcus team, it doesn't mean an approaching Cole or Baird is on your side—they're coming to kill you, not to revive you!

Keep the scoring system in mind. Unlike the round-based scoring in other game modes, the winner of a Wingman match is the first team that reaches a designated number of points. This takes place over as many rounds as necessary to reach that total. Your team earns an extra point for surviving the round, a huge advantage to the surviving team. Teams must be aggressive; hanging back and surviving longest is not an effective strategy. Taking an overly defensive approach keeps you from racking up the kills. At the same time, exercise some discretion, because getting knocked out early doesn't increase your score either. Take advantage of the spawns nearest the power weapons to quickly obtain them. Leapfrog with your teammate's movements. Stay close enough to each other to quickly take down the opposition and keep each other alive. Plant grenades behind you as you go, as it is very easy to get flanked.

HORDE

Up to five players cooperate to survive wave after wave of the Locust Horde. You get one life per wave and respawn between waves. High scores are tracked per map.

Horde is a very special new game type in *Gears of War 2*. Unlike the other multiplayer modes, Horde is a *cooperative* multiplayer mode. You and up to four friends face a literal *horde* of Locust. Wave after wave assaults your team, and you must repel and slay all opposition to progress. There are 50 rounds to complete in Horde. Every 10 rounds, the difficulty ratchets up, as the Locust grow harder to fend off. Your whole team's score is broken down after every round, thereby showing you who the heroes are and who needs to go back to basic training. Fortunately, players respawn at the conclusion of each round, provided at least one player manages to defeat the remainder of the wave.

WAVE COMPOSITION

Each wave of Locust you face may be a little different from the last time you played. It's important to understand that the waves aren't comprised of predetermined enemy groups. Rather an allotment of points governs the wave's total makeup. Each enemy that spawns costs a certain number of points to generate, and the wave is complete when all of its allotted points are exhausted. The points tally is displayed onscreen as a small red meter that gradually empties as you kill off more and more Locust. Each of the enemies has a specific cost and is restricted to appearing only in set waves.

FIVE ROUNDS OF 10

There are 50 rounds total in Horde. But, in terms of each wave's behind-the-scenes construction, realize that there are only 10. Instead of thinking of a particular round as "Round 34," we recommend thinking of it in terms of 3-4. Similarly, round 20 could be considered round 1-10 and round 7 expressed as 0-7. Thus, the final round—the vaunted round 50—is really round 4-10. But this is just semantics; what matters is that you will see the same enemies in round 11 as you did in round 1, and likewise for rounds 8 and 28.

- The maximum number of Locust units active at any single moment depends on the number of players. Difficulty application is identical to Single-Player.

- Your score resets if you continue after losing. Spectators can talk to the living an can therefore continue to be useful by pointing out enemy positions.

- The Horde receives increases to health, accuracy, and the amount of damage they inflict at the start of each successive round of ten waves. The following table shows the changes that take place to make the Horde tougher in the later waves—same numbers of enemies, but much, much harder to kill! Enemy health is the same as in single-player mode per each corresponding difficulty setting.

- All weapons respawn 30 seconds after there are fewer weapons of a given type in play (with remaining ammo) than there are pickups for that weapon. In Horde mode, weapons in enemy possession count toward this. For example, if there is one Mulcher pickup in the level, it will not respawn while there are Grinder enemies in play.

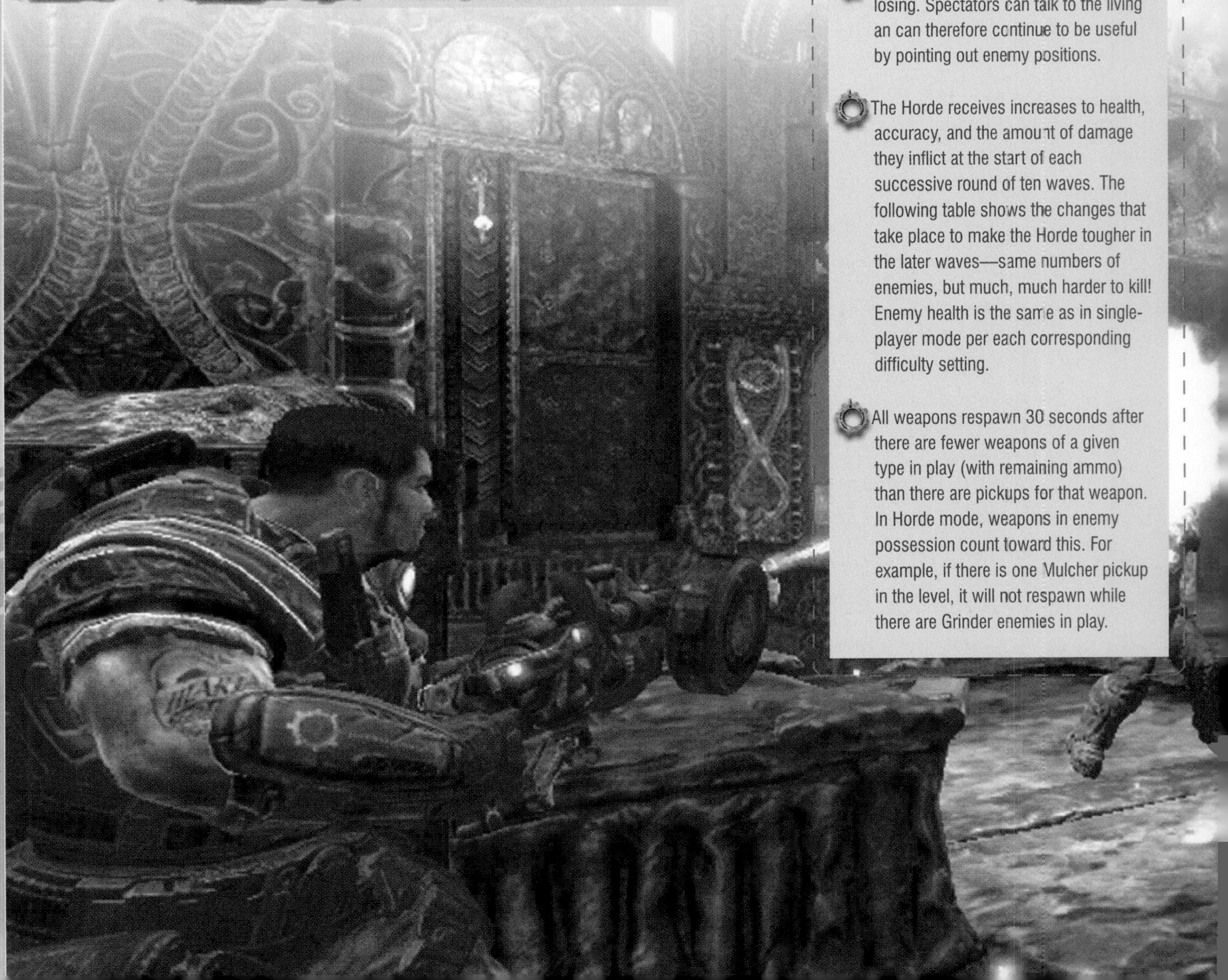

HORDE DIFFICULTY MODIFIERS

STARTING ROUND	HORDE CHANGES
Wave 11	2x Health
Wave 21	2x Health, 2x Accuracy
Wave 31	2x Health, 2x Accuracy, 2x Damage
Wave 41	2.5x Health, 2.5x Accuracy, 2.5x Damage

MAP CHAPTER COVERAGE

The following pages are devoted to each of the ten multiplayer maps that come with the game. These pages contain detailed maps, as well as strategy for each gameplay mode specific to each map. Because some of the content and terminology may be new to you, we thought we'd describe each section that you'll find within a given map's analysis:

MAPS: Each chapter contains a primary map that shows the spawn points, weapon locations, and typical hot zones. Hot zones are areas where the action is often the most intense. Avoid straying into these areas alone or without first reloading your weapon! We also provide mini-maps, which show mode-specific capture and spawn points for objective-based game types and for Wingman. Lastly, we include a detailed strategic map for Horde mode. It shows you where we recommend placing members of a five-person team, where to plant grenades, the path of the Horde (contingent on players occupying the positions marked on our maps), and the locations of ammo crates.

BATTLEFIELD SPECIFICS: Each map has at least one or two features that allow unique interaction with the environment. Whether it's an avalanche crashing down from the mountains, a car that explodes when it's shot, or a sophisticated laser security fence, this section covers it, describes how it impacts gameplay, and for which modes.

SPAWN POINT AWARENESS: The initial weapons rush in multiplayer Gears of War 2 is so integral to success that knowing exactly where you are when you spawn is absolutely vital. You have to know which way to turn to get to the weapons first. This section reveals subtle clues you can use to quickly identify the side of the map on which you've spawned. It also describes which way to turn as you exit the spawn area.

ESSENTIAL TACTICS: As much as we'd like to, we can't ignore the reality that many online matches boil down to people using the same handful of tactics over and over. These tricks and habits vary from map to map but seldom change between game modes. You can expect to see them employed countless times, and for good reason: they work. There are ways to counter some of these tactics, but some of them are worth adopting. After all, if you can't beat 'em you might as well join 'em.

WHERE WAS HE?: It happens to everyone. You're lining up the perfect shot, you think you're totally concealed behind cover, and all of a sudden your character's head disappears and the sound of an exploding watermelon fills your living room. A moment later, you're in the lobby of the dead, shouting the three infamous words for which these tips are named. Consider these our ruthless "when-you-least-expect-it" tips. You won't make many friends, but you're guaranteed to elicit some laughter at another player's expense.

TEAM STRATEGIES: This is the meat and potatoes of our multiplayer coverage. This section contains detailed strategy for each of the multiplayer modes, whether it's Warzone, King of the Hill, or any of the others. We discuss the capture and spawn points where appropriate, how and when to secure the different weapons, and even where to camp your leader for maximum protection in Guardian mode. Strategies vary based on your spawn point as well as the capture location (where applicable), and we made sure to give you the tips for success no matter the situation.

HORDE: This extremely addictive mode adds a cooperative, team-based element to multiplayer that is sure to challenge everyone who puts the disc in the tray. And we mean everyone! Here you'll find a detailed attack plan for dealing with the Locust onslaught. We've assigned roles and responsibilities to each of your team's five players. The accompanying map illustrates each player's position, where he or she should patrol, and where the most Horde units will spawn (contingent on players occupying our recommended positions). Study this section closely before you go online. Take a moment with your team to agree on the roles outlined in this section. Ignore our tips at your own peril!

AVALANCHE

Authors' Favorite Modes: Guardian, Wingman, and Horde.

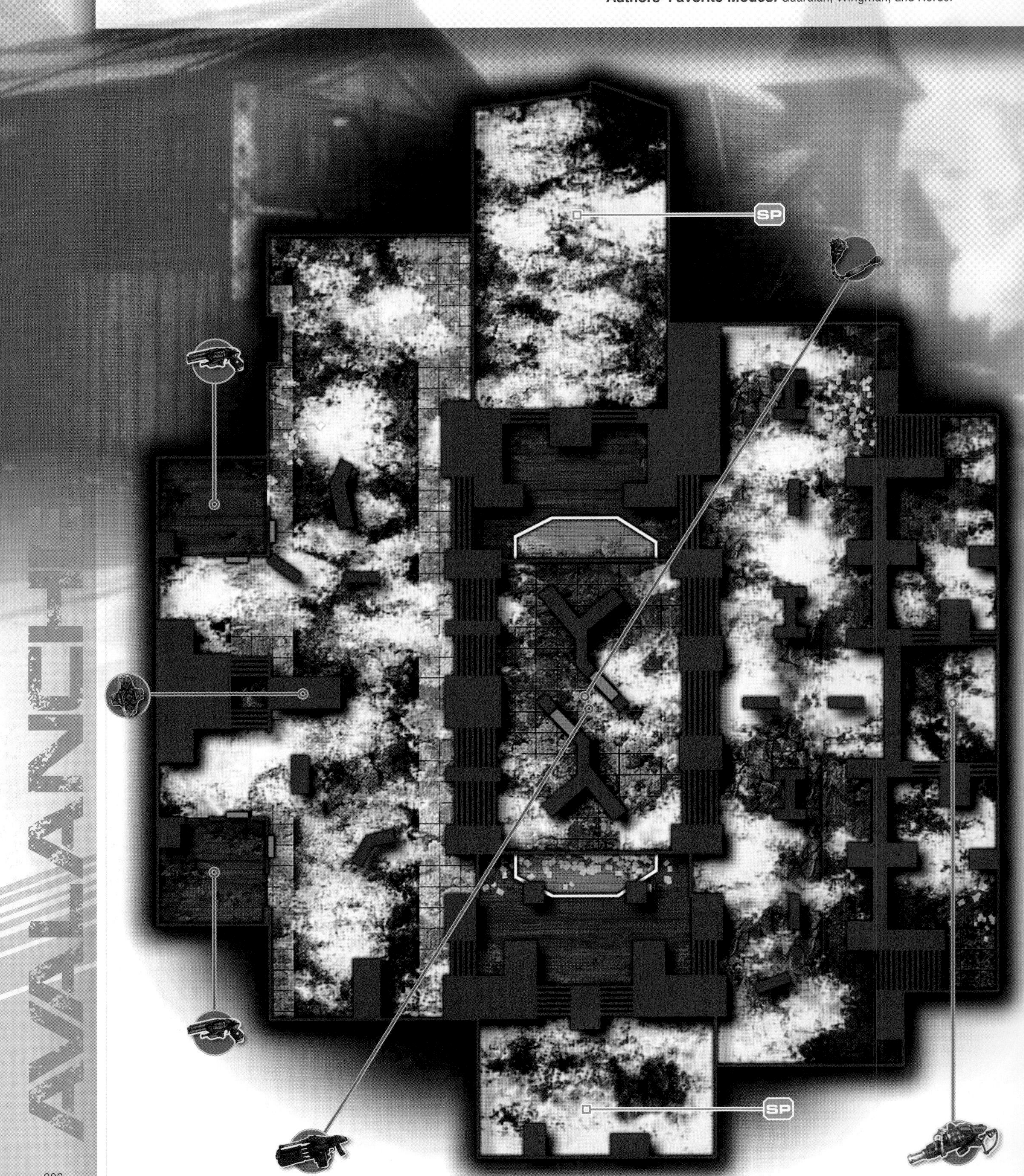

Set high in the mountains during an unrelenting winter, this map forces the COG and Locust teams to battle not only one another, but also the frigid conditions. Staying true to its name, this map features a ground-shaking avalanche that crashes down from the snow-capped peaks to the south of town, carpeting the area in suffocating snow. The inviting lodges and cabins that line the map's perimeter offer a place to escape this white wall of death, and perhaps the gunfire as well. But there can be no fireside repose until the war has been won.

Avalanche is a roughly symmetrical map with a central courtyard, a street to the north with two cabins, and an elevated monuments plaza to the south. There is a good deal of firepower on this map, particularly after the avalanche comes and the Boomshot atop the gazebo is put in play. Teams begin the match from the eastern and western sides and have the same chance of getting the Boomshield, Mulcher, or Frag Grenade inside the gazebo. There are plenty of places to take cover on this map, and some even offer a slightly elevated view of the main hot zones. Nevertheless, the powerful weaponry, the ever-looming avalanche, and the subsequent rush for the Boomshot make good communication and teamwork absolute necessities here.

WEAPON CYCLES

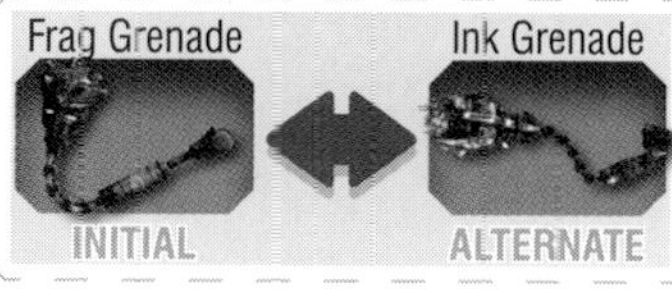

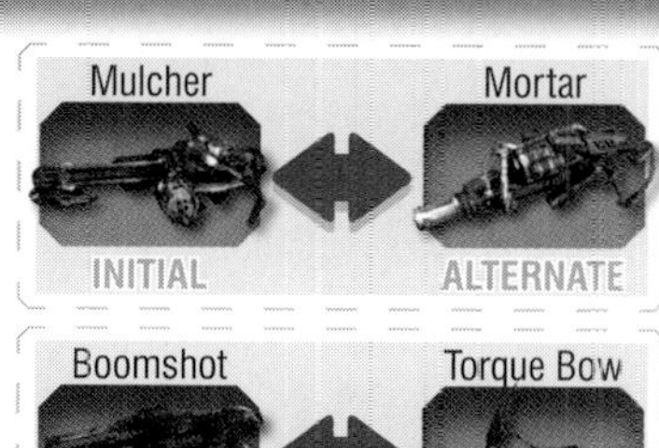

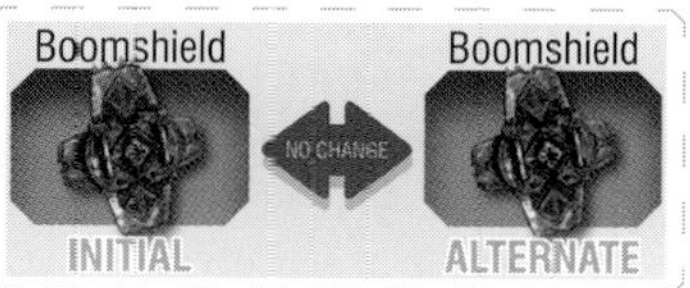

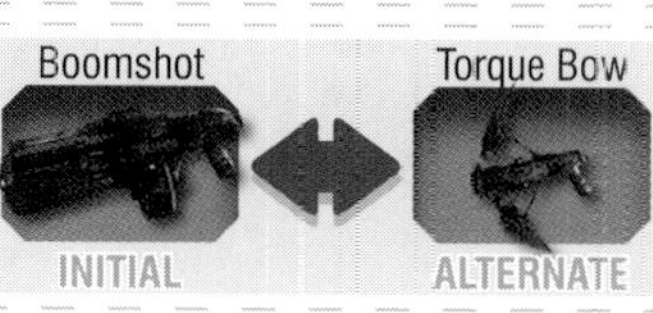

BATTLEFIELD SPECIFICS

AVALANCHE!

The mountains are a hostile place, especially in winter. Those who've never seen nature's icy wrath are about to experience it firsthand. It begins with a rumble and ends with an eerie, mist-shrouded silence ten seconds later. But the deadly moments in between are enough to send the bravest COG running for cover! An avalanche crashes down from the southern mountains between 30 and 90 seconds into the round and kills every player it contacts as it buries the central courtyard in eight feet of snow. Players must flee to the map's extreme edges or get swept up in the slide. However, the courtyard isn't the only deathtrap. The avalanche first hits the upper plaza where the Mulcher is located. Run for the plaza's corners if you're up there when the controller starts to rumble and the ground begins to shake. You must vacate the area with the patches of snow to escape the avalanche.

Keep clear of the courtyard and the area near the Mulcher until the snow settles. Then rush out onto the snow and grab the Boomshot!

The avalanche does more than just dole out immediate death to the players caught in its path. It topples the stone arch, buries the courtyard, and sends vehicles flying through the air like a child's toys. The fallen arch and toppled statues come to a halt atop the settled snow, providing cover for those who venture out when the flakes settle. The thick blanket of snow allows access the Boomshot positioned atop the gazebo in the courtyard.

SPAWN POINT AWARENESS

Regardless of which side of the map you spawn on, your first move is typically toward the Mulcher (south) or toward the Boomshield (north), especially because the Boomshot (or Torquebow) isn't accessible until after the avalanche. Some subtle signs indicate which side of the map you spawn on as you wait for the round to start, but the large stone arch serves as a terrific landmark as well. If you ever get disoriented or aren't sure which side of the map you're on, just look for the large stone arch (pre-avalanche). It's on the courtyard's southern side and is closer to the Mulcher. Move away from it if you're after the Boomshield.

1 EAST SPAWN

The eastern spawn point places the entire team on the ground outside the lodge, on the outside of the map. There aren't any stairs and the two small balconies and greenery serve as instantaneous identifiers of the eastern spawn. This spawn point is also much larger and has more snow on the ground. Head left for the Mulcher or to the right for the Boomshield and Boltok Pistol.

2 WEST SPAWN

The spawn point on the west is a bit smaller than the one on the east. Therefore, it often spawns some members nearer the stairs leading into the house. This spawn point is recognizable by the lone balcony above the two doorways, the presence of the dumpsters, and the slightly larger sets of stairs leading inside. Head to the right for the Mulcher/Mortar, or venture left for the Boomshield and Boltok Pistol.

ESSENTIAL TACTICS

Pistol and Shield: The team that secures the Boomshield and either of the pistol pickups first definitely has a big advantage on this map. Make every effort to lock down the map's northern portion at the match's start. Try to sweep enemies toward the player with the Boomshield so he or she can finish them off with little risk of harm.

Buried Alive: The avalanche slides down from the mountains at the map's southern end, above the Mulcher/Mortar pickup. Although it occurs at a random time between 30 and 90 seconds into the round, anticipate the oncoming avalanche and do what you can to down enemy forces in its path whenever possible, particularly if a full minute passes without an avalanche. Listen for the air raid siren to blare, alerting you to the avalanche. When you hear it, back out of the kill zone, simultaneously doing what you can to down the opposition. The best case scenario is that you down an enemy and one of his teammates foolishly attempts to revive him when the avalanche hits—two for one! You'll be able to mantle over the railing near the side lodges after the snow comes to a halt. You can even run directly up to where the Mortar is without having to use the stairs. There may not be many enemies still standing after the avalanche, but you should expect activity to increase near the center of the map, given the change in flow.

WHERE WAS HE?

There aren't too many places on this map where you can hide and still be part of the action, but the park benches on the street beneath the Mulcher is one such place. Take cover behind the narrow, far end of the benches and surprise enemies as they run from the cabin to the stairs leading up to the Mulcher.

Fragging the Mulcher: Frag Grenades can be especially helpful in dislodging enemies camped near the Mulcher's spawn location. Toss them from the street below the Mulcher, particularly when the avalanche siren begins to wail. Rushing the Mulcher directly is a recipe for disaster. Instead, use the grenades to disrupt the other team. Then split up and charge their spot from both sides to avoid losing too many units.

TEAM STRATEGIES

WARZONE & EXECUTION

The map's power weapon locations—a Mulcher/Mortar flip and a Boomshot/Torque Bow combo—are both affected by the avalanche, which occurs each round. You can obtain the Mulcher/Mortar on the upper terrace right off the bat, but staying in that position is deadly once the snow pours down. The terrace's elevated position is ideal for spotting and firing on enemies. Set up shop in the middle of the terrace until the sirens sound. Then move off to the left or right, outside the snow tracks' permanent boundaries on the ground.

The Torque Bow/Boomshot spawn is atop a gazebo and is inaccessible until the avalanche comes to a rest and the snow clears. Get into position just outside the avalanche's path and rush the position as soon as the snow stops moving. If the opposition also attempts to rush the location, use the stone walls as cover. Another option is to obtain the Boomshield and slowly advance to the weapon's position behind its cover. Once you reach the weapon's position, switch to the weapon that you intend to swap out. Doing so forces you to drop the Boomshield. Quickly swap weapons and then reclaim the shield. The upgraded offensive and defensive power at your disposal will turn the tide of the match.

The map's northern end contains a Boomshield in the back of a pickup truck and two pistol pickups opposite one another. Pairing the Boomshield with either the Boltok or Gorgon Pistol is a lethal combo in this area. This spot is out of the way from the Mortar and Mulcher (assuming whoever claims them doesn't run too far), and it's safe from the avalanche threat. Securing this pair of weapons or helping a teammate do so sets you up nicely to go after either the Torquebow or Boomshot in the wide-open middle of the map.

SUBMISSION

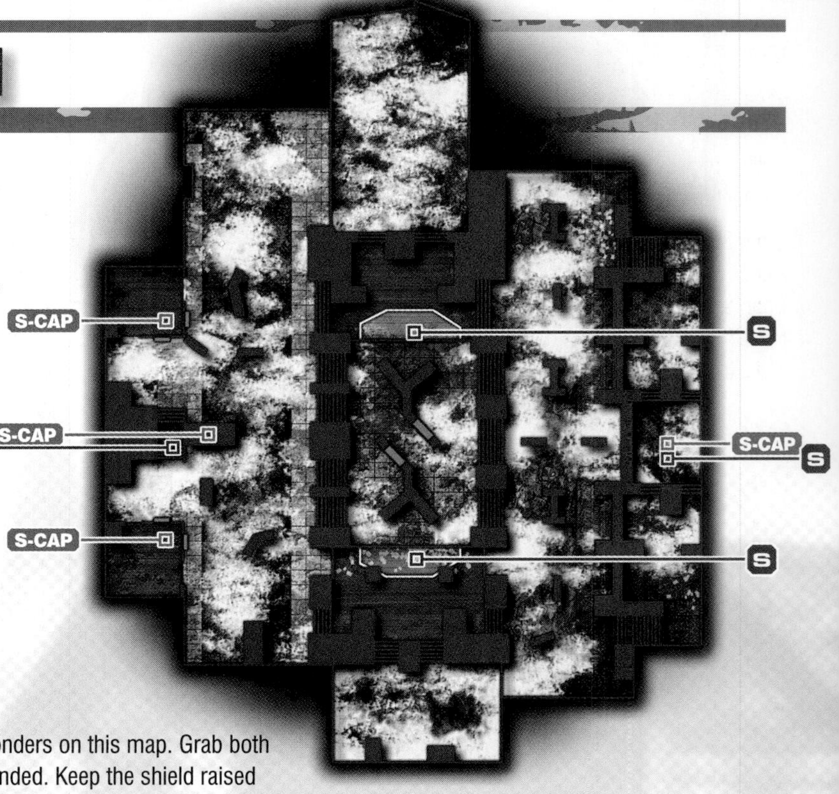

The Stranded can spawn on either end of the map or down in the lower portion. The avalanche does not come into play, so the grenades in the middle are always available, but the Boomshot and Torquebow are out of play. The absence of those weapons places an emphasis on securing the Mulcher/Mortar, especially when the capture point is at that pickup's location. Lay down covering fire from the elevated perch as your teammates drag the Stranded to the goal, confident that there will be no avalanche to leave you out in the cold.

Using the Boomshield and Gorgon Pistol combo can work wonders on this map. Grab both and advance ahead of the teammate who is dragging the Stranded. Keep the shield raised for cover and keep moving. Your progress is slow, but it matches that of your teammate with the Stranded. The combined defensive edge you both gain should keep you moving forward steadily while teammates harass opponents and scout ahead. We highly recommend this tactic!

Use the wooden structures near the two spawn points as you drag the Stranded across the map. These areas provide increased cover and allow teammates to protect you from both directions more easily. Leave proximity grenades on entrances to the rear of your advance to slow the enemy pursuit.

When the capture point is in one of the two pistol locations, plant a proximity grenade in the corner between the two windows. This position is hard to identify by an opponent dragging the Stranded in for a score.

WINGMAN

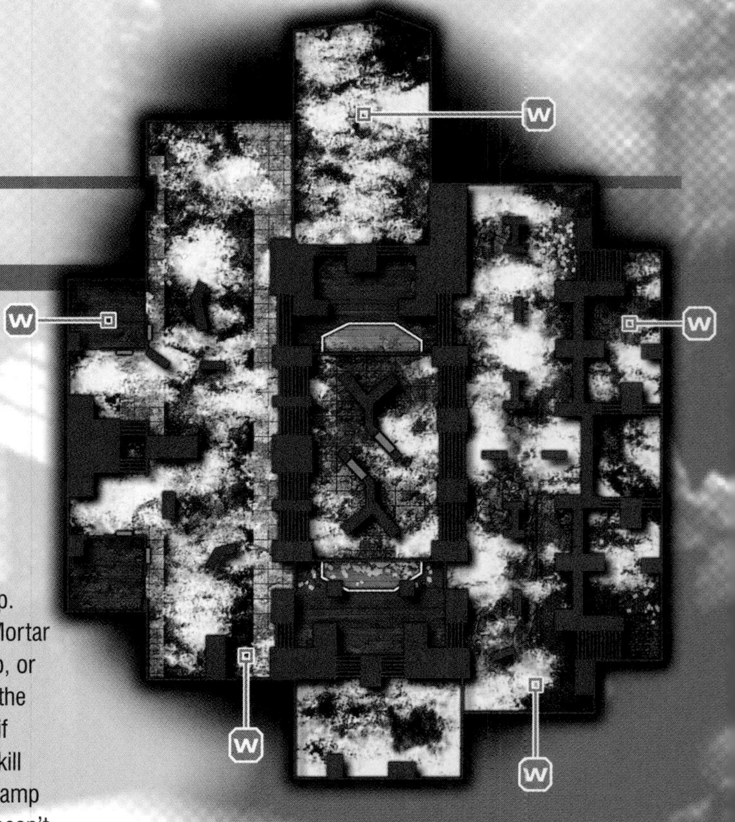

There's always an advantage to gain in Wingman depending on where you and your partner spawn. On Avalanche, the team with the biggest initial advantage is the one that spawns in either of the pistol rooms. Have one teammate grab both the pistol and Boomshield. Then advance on enemies together, downing them from behind the Boomshield's cover. The unencumbered teammate can run in for the execution.

Another good spawn position is nearest the Mulcher/Mortar pick-up. Grab it and fire a few Mortar rounds around the map, or mount the Mulcher on the central railing and see if anyone runs into your kill zone. However, don't camp out too long, because racking up kills is the name of the game—and it doesn't take long before the avalanche crashes down!

GUARDIAN

Unlike most maps, the spawn areas on Avalanche do not present an ideal position for the Team Leader to assume a defensive stance.

Other than the space between the two doorways, there is no cover and no chokepoint of any kind. Advance as a team to the map's northern end and allow the Team Leader to obtain the Boomshield before falling back into one of the pistol rooms. Place proximity grenades on the room's doorways and between the windows. The Boomshield provides the necessary protection, while the upgraded pistols down charging enemies. The overhead cover neutralizes Mortar fire.

Another tactic is to move as a unit to the map's southern end to obtain the sole power weapon available at the match's start (Mortar/Mulcher). Have the Team Leader set up camp in the corner, next to one of the staircases that lead up to the elevated platform. This keeps the Team Leader out of the avalanche's path and allows him or her to participate offensively with the power weapon. Place proximity mines on the stairwell nearest to your position and watch for Frag Grenades getting tossed from below. This setup can even lead to enemy casualties from the avalanche as it floods the area.

Occasionally rush a few players through the map's lower portion in an attempt to storm the enemy leader. Grab the grenades for a chance to apply a Frag Tag or to flush out the enemy leader with an Ink Grenade's toxic cloud. Many teams try to keep their Team Leader in either of the side houses or by the spawn point, so check their first.

ANNEX & KING OF THE HILL

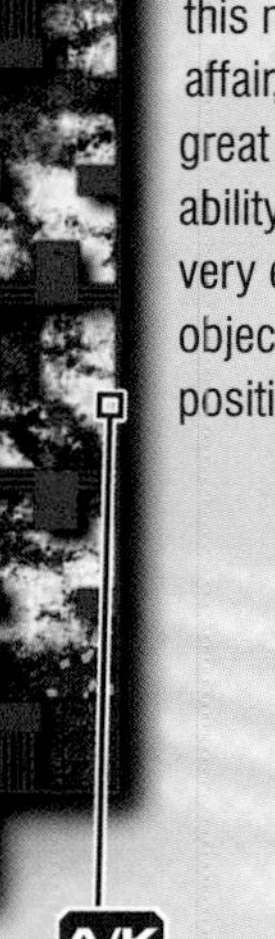

The avalanche does not occur during Annex or King of the Hill matches, so the Mortar/Mulcher are the only long-range power weapons. Unfortunately, the continual need to run from capture point to capture point in Annex matches limits their usefulness. Instead of trying to drag around one of these heavy weapons, focus on obtaining the Boomshield early and hold onto it for its defensive boost as you defend capture points.

Make every effort to be the first team to secure the capture points on this map. The central Frag Grenade location can be a back-and-forth affair, but the Boomshield and Mortar/Mulcher capture points offer great opportunities for extended defense. The elevated position and ability to obtain the Mortar or Mulcher make the map's southern end very easy to hold. At the northern end, the Boomshield, the cover objects in the street, and the two Pistol rooms make breaking that position very difficult.

When you try to break one of these positions, be sure to pick up the Frag or Ink Grenades on the way. Lob them in ahead of your attack. When you attack the Boomshield position, consider grabbing the Mortar to clear the area, as there is very little interior cover here. This is especially important during King of the Hill matches, when at least one enemy player must be inside the capture circle in order to score.

HORDE

AMMO

AMMO

1

2

3

4

5

Although the level's signature cascade of snow doesn't manifest itself during Horde matches, this is still a very tricky area for playing Horde. Teams should congregate on the raised platform near the Mulcher to gain superior elevation. Spread out along this southern area to protect the upper region and trap Horde members in a crossfire on the street below. Instructing one swift player to secure the Boomshield from the map's opposite end during an early round proves very helpful later in the game.

Ammo: There are two ammunition crates on this map: one directly below the Mulcher, and the other on the map's northern end by the Boomshield.

Variables: The avalanche doesn't occur during Horde, so what you see is what you get. The match takes place as-is right from the start, and there is no way to obtain the weapon atop the gazebo in the plaza.

It's important to protect the person manning the Mulcher or Mortar, but do not group the entire team in this area. It's much better to spread out toward the stairs on either side of this upper area. Use the park benches in the plaza below for cover. This puts your team in position to cut down the enemies as they leave the cabins. It even provides a chance to shoot them through the fence on the left spawn point.

Securing the map's southern portion forces the Horde to spawn at the northern end. This provides plenty of opportunity to kill them with the Mortar as they cross the yard. Many other Locust spawn in the two side-areas behind the cabins, where the teams spawn during Warzone matches. Avoid straying into either of the cabins, as you run the risk of getting vastly outnumbered, and you open the opportunity for the Horde to spawn closer to the Mortar position.

KNOW YOUR ROLE

The following tactics correspond to the numbered positions marked on the accompanying map. Follow these tips carefully for maximum survivability. These tips assume a five-person team.

1 The person least skilled at run-and-gun tactics should head to the Mulcher/Mortar position and put it to use from atop the platform. This player's primary responsibility is to eliminate the distant enemies, before they get too close and render the Mortar useless. Avoid drifting too far to the left or right. Whatever you do, stay on the raised platform to maintain your superior elevation. In addition to eliminating distant enemies, this player should serve as a spotter, calling out where the Locust are coming from and where other players may need help.

2 Claim a position on the left stairs, with your back to the mountains. Place grenades at the top of the stairs to serve as a last line of defense against any Locust that get past you. The person on the left staircase has a somewhat harder job than player #3 because many of the spawning Locust shoot through the metal fence behind the cabin. Use the side of the stairs for cover. Focus your attention on the cabin exit and the enemies appearing in the spawn area behind it. Maintain communication with player #4 and help revive one another as necessary.

3 Player #3 must maintain a last line of defense on the fortified area's right side by keeping enemies from scaling the stairs on this side of the map. Plant proximity mines at the top of the stairs to disrupt any enemies that make it past. Focus on assisting player #5 with the enemies exiting the right cabin. Keep your sights on the cabin exit and the courtyard stairs near the center, as this is where a lot of enemies go. Player #3 needn't worry about getting shot by Locust hanging out in the right side spawn point. But this also means he or she can't see how many are about to emerge from within the cabin. Keep your head up and assist player #5 by reviving him as necessary.

4 We recommend that this player get the Boomshield at the match's start and then quickly retreat to the sandbags near the bottom of the left stairs. This player must be skilled with close-range combat. Watch for enemies emerging from the cabin and from the courtyard, as well as those that shoot through the spawn point's iron fence behind the cabin. Gather up dropped weaponry from the slain Locust, and try to make periodic dashes for Frag Grenades. You can place them at the cabin exit and on the corner of the building near the courtyard.

5 Player #5 should take cover at the far end of the benches near the stairs. He or she is in prime position to rack up a number of kills as enemies exit the right cabin. Assist player #3 by keeping the Locust from advancing up the stairs toward player #1's position. Coordinate ammo grabs with player #4. The player in this position can freelance a bit at this end of the map. But stay out of the cabin to avoid giving the Locust a chance to spawn too close to your team's fortified area. Watch the number of remaining Horde to make a dash for grenades and other weaponry—especially a dropped Boomshield—before anyone kills off the final enemy.

BLOOD DRIVE

Authors' Favorite Modes: Execution, Wingman, and Horde.

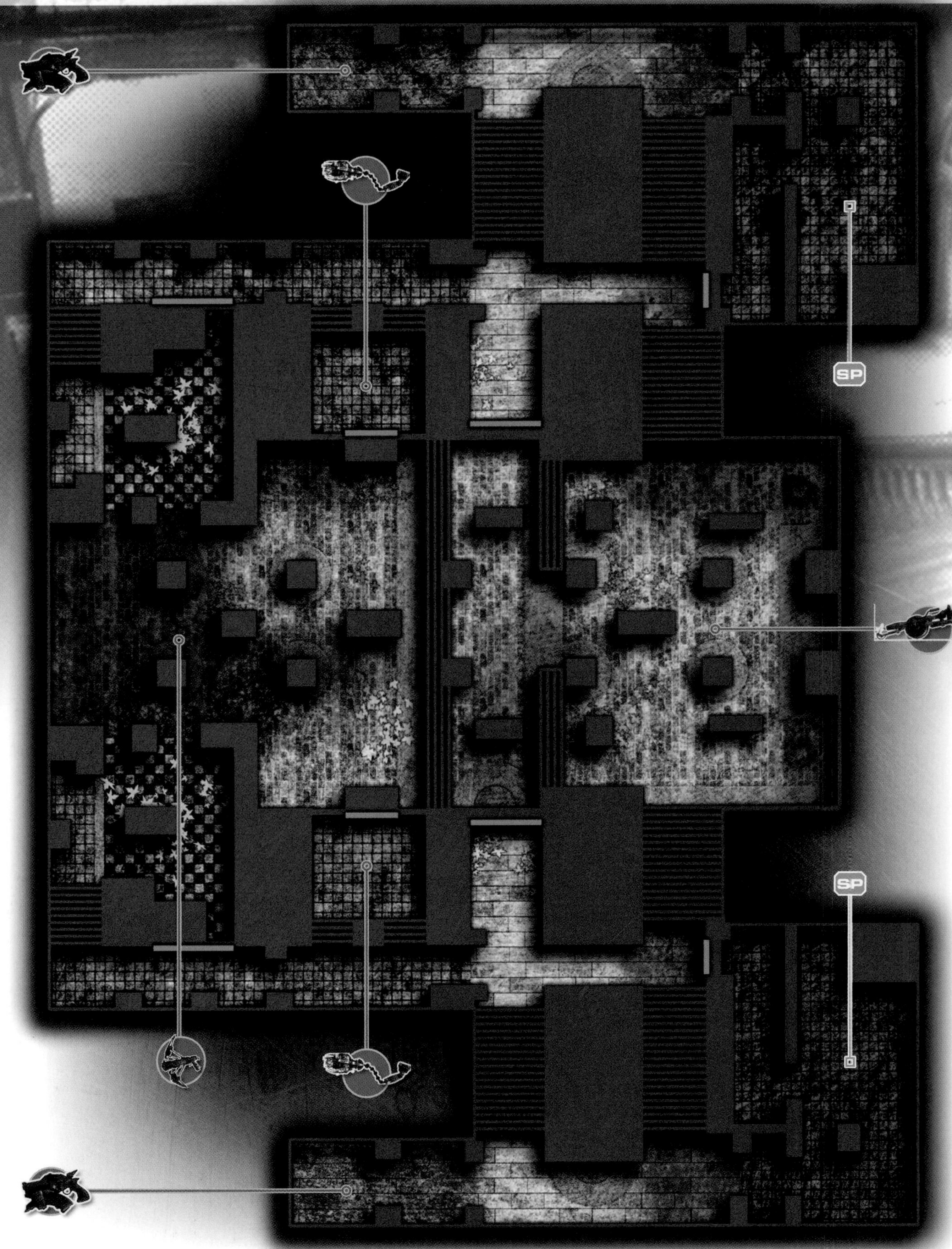

When those in charge of the hospital's blood drive came up with the slogan "Give so they can live," you can bet they wanted their visitors to donate something other than bullets and explosive-tipped arrows. Of course, the hospital has long since been vacated thanks to the Locust's reemergence and the terms giving and living have taken on new meanings in this war-torn era. There aren't any medics here to stitch the unfortunate back together, and the only outpatients are those who put the map's many grenades to use most effectively.

Blood Drive is a symmetrical map not only in its design but also in its weapon distribution. Both teams have the very same access to an advanced pistol, grenade pickups, the Torque Bow (or Longshot, depending on weapon cycle), and Scorcher under the train tracks. Most of the map is on a multi-level set of facing staircases that descend from the spawn points to the street area, but there are interiors as well. Each team can descend through the hospital on their side of the map to slip out unnoticed into the shadows of the bridge supports. Those who command the lone power weapon and the most grenades will typically rule the day!

WEAPON CYCLES

Initial	Alternate
Gorgon Pistol	Boltok Pistol
Ink Grenade	Frag Grenade
Torque Bow	Longshot
Scorcher	Scorcher (No change)

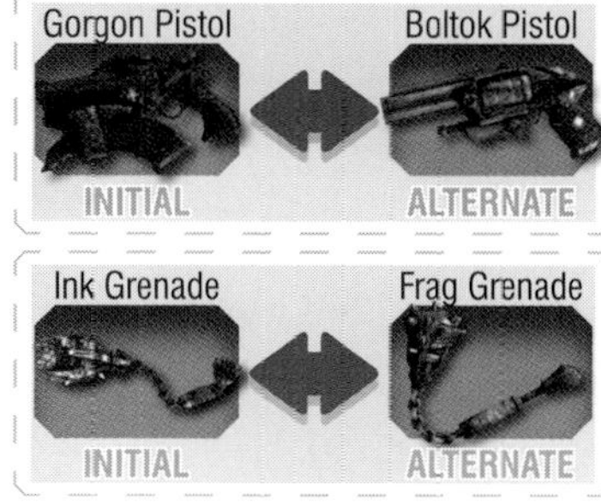

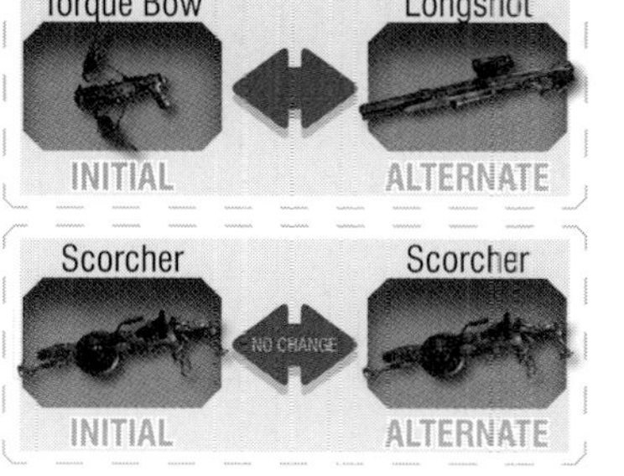

BATTLEFIELD SPECIFICS

FOG

What you see is what you get on Blood Drive. This map doesn't feature any interaction with the environment, nor does it have treacherous weather or locked doors. Instead, the map's main environmental variable is the fog that impedes visibility across the map. It's all but impossible to see the opposition's spawn area atop the stairs from the other side of the map. Snipers who set up on the middle landing can see their counterparts on the landing across the map, but only slightly.

Is it fog or smog? Who knows? Who cares? You can't see the enemies on the upper level, but you can still kill the ones on the middle!

SPAWN POINT AWARENESS

The mad dash to the Torque Bow (or Longshot) makes it essential to exit the spawn room quickly and to know which way to go once you descend the stairs. Thanks to the two doorways in the spawn room, things can be a bit confusing in the opening moments. The first door just leads to a sniper's nest, so ignore it. Instead, run through the doorway with the lamp on the doorjamb and continue the turn to start down the stairs. The Torque Bow is on the side of the street nearest the stairs.

1 EAST SPAWN

If the draping boughs of red leaves are on the left side of the spawn room, then you are on the east side of the map. Head down the hall and out the door to the right. To secure the Torque Bow, sprint straight down the stairs and angle to the right once you're on the street below the tracks.

2 WEST SPAWN

If the branches of red tree leaves are on the right side of the starting point, then you are on the west side of the map. Sprint out the door on the left, continue the turn onto the stairs, and sprint straight down the stairs toward the street below. The Torque Bow is on the left.

ESSENTIAL TACTICS

Rush the Torque Bow: Ready your lone Smoke Grenade and toss it at the bottom of your opponent's stairs as you race toward the Torque Bow at the start of the map. Have one or two of your teammates move to the landing on the middle of your stairs to provide covering fire while you and two others rush for the Torque Bow. A lot of blood will be spilt in this initial flurry of activity, so be ready for it—have the Gnasher ready!

It's Raining Grenades!: With just one non-pistol pickup on this map and two grenade pickups, it's not unusual for combat to involve quite a few proximity mines and lobbed grenades. Gather up the grenades in the hospital entrance on your team's side while teammates rush the grenades under the tracks, opposite the Torque Bow. Position proximity mines on the pillars in the center of the map, then retreat up the stairs as you turn to lob them at your pursuers. As an alternative, you can try to coordinate a simultaneous carpet-bombing of the lower area with each of your team's initial Smoke Grenade. Knock the opposing team members on their backs and rush in for the kill!

I Want to Hold Your Head: Few maps make picking up a downed opponent to use as a shield as critical as it is here. The constant barrage of gunfire and grenade explosions makes it imperative to possess something that partially absorbs these impacts. Using a meat shield forces you to move slowly and employ only a pistol, but this isn't necessarily a limitation thanks to the alternating Gorgon and Boltok Pistol pickups on this map. Turn around every now and then so you can see when your meat shield has been reduced to just a torso and head. You need a meat shield with arms and legs for full protection, so start looking for a new one when your current bullet sponge has been reduced to nubs and stubs.

EPIC SAYS...

Because grenades play such a huge role in the outcome of this match, counter your opponent's hunger for these explosives by immediately planting one back at the grenade spawn point as a proximity mine. This tactic won't win you any friends, but, then again, people who object can always fire a round or two at the grenade pickup before they approach it, just to be safe.

WHERE WAS HE?

Have every member of your team plant his or her initial Smoke Grenade on the upper end of the staircase, and then retreat to your spawn. Swap to your Gnashers and wait for the enemies to come up the stairs and trip the five grenades. Finish them while they're down!

TEAM STRATEGIES

WARZONE & EXECUTION

Deliberation is necessary to stay alive on Blood Drive, particularly when playing Warzone. The alternating Torque Bow and Longshot pickup is the lone power-weapon drop on the map. Use cover to approach the weapon and toss a smoke grenade to cover your approach as you grab it. Immediately retreat up the steps on your team's side of the map, at least to the middle landing, where you can use the weapon from cover. Another great place to use the Torque Bow or Longshot is from within the closet-like room near the spawn point. This area has a small window that looks out onto the map and provides tremendous cover.

Grenades gain value on this map due to the scarcity of power weapons, not to mention the three available grenade pickup locations. Set up as many traps as possible on your side of the map and lure the opposing team into your area, perhaps by securing the Torque Bow and retreating up the steps. Grab grenades on the middle level and plant them near the entrance to the room with the hospital beds. To add an extra layer of protection, use the Ink Grenade under the train tracks opposite the power weapon spawn point. Another deadly tactic, especially in Execution matches, is to instruct your sniper to quickly down as many enemies as possible and then lob an Ink Grenade at them as they crawl. This will likely finish off several of them, but will also damage any of their teammates who come to revive them.

Because most of the action ends up taking place in the street and on the lower halves of each staircase, the interior passage through the hospital lobby is often forgotten. Use it to surprise the enemy! However, in order to pull this off, send at least three of your teammates down the stairs toward the street to trick the enemy into thinking you're making a standard frontal assault. These teammates create a distraction while the other two squad members rush through the hospital rooms and flank the opposition from the middle level of their staircase. Using this strategy too often defeats its purpose, but it can be effective if you employ it sporadically. Not only does this tactic stand to win you the round, but it can also make securing the premium weapon easier in the next round, as the opposing team proceeds with extra caution, wary of another flanking move.

SUBMISSION

There's no way around it: those playing Submission on Blood Drive should prepare themselves for a blood bath. The capture points are the two grenade rooms and the Torque Bow and Scorcher weapon spawns. The Stranded always originates somewhere in the street beneath the dilapidated train tracks. This mode almost always results in a very messy tug-of-war between the two teams, with little opportunity to employ a thorough strategy. Nevertheless, some approaches work better than others. Try out some of the following recommendations the next time you're in an endless struggle to capture the Stranded.

Thanks to the frequent respawns you will experience, you might occasionally exit your team's spawn point mere steps away from their capture point at the pistol location. Plant your Smoke Grenade at a hidden location near that area's entrance. Then run to the second level to grab the Ink Grenade and do the same with it. Using two different types of grenades next to one another might sound redundant, but the effects are priceless. The Smoke Grenade will knock the Stranded free, and the Ink Grenade will likely poison your opponent before he can crawl to safety or retrieve the Stranded. This is an excellent way to "play goalie" on this map and keep the enemy from winning.

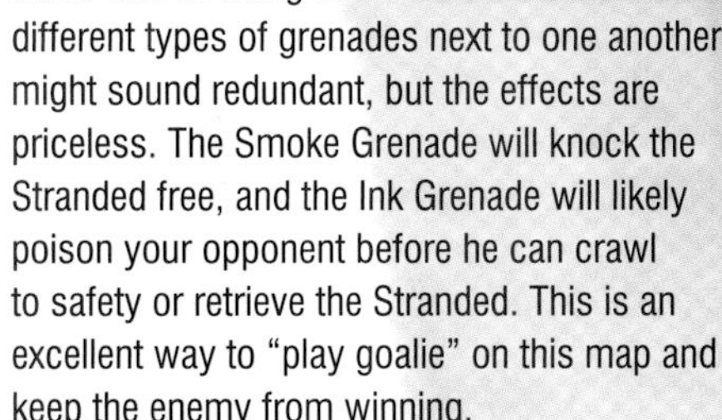

There is almost always strength in numbers (unless a Frag Grenade is rolled at your feet), and it's particularly important to keep your team together and move in unison on Blood Drive. Eliminate at least a couple opponents before you down the Stranded and attempt to move him to the capture location. One team member should acquire the Torque Bow (or Longshot) and provide covering fire from the second-level terrace on your team's side of the map while the other four move the target.

Opponents will be knocked off of the Stranded near you almost constantly. Take advantage of the moment before the Stranded stands back up to grab the downed opponent and use him as a shield. This will protect you from almost certain death at the hands of the newly freed Stranded. And it will give you a chance to knock him back down. Once the Stranded has been knocked down (pistol whip him while you're using a shield), break your hostage's neck and grab the Stranded.

WINGMAN

The scarcity of power weapons and the high level of carnage on this map make it more important than ever to use downed opponents as meat shields for as long as possible. Advance in a back-to-back formation with your teammate, and punish your enemies from behind your mobile cover.

Another practical tack, especially if you spawn under the train tracks, is to grab the Torque Bow (or Longshot) and quickly relocate to the top level on one end of the map. Place proximity grenades on the stairwell for warning and protection, and pick off enemies on the ground level from the window inside the team spawn room. Your teammate can cover you from the second level and continually grab the grenades that spawn there, tossing them into the bedlam on the streets.

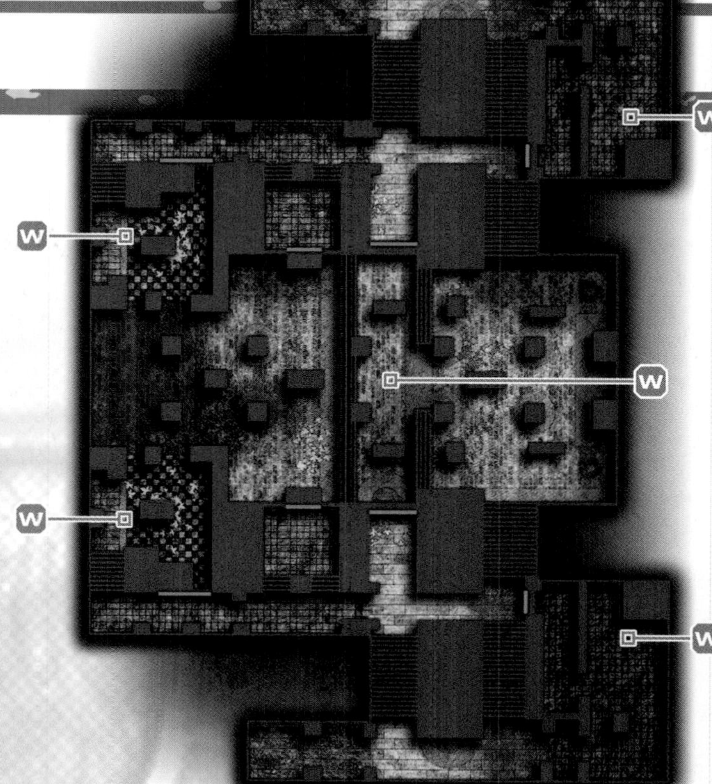

GUARDIAN

The spawn points on this map make for an ideal defensive position from which to defend the team leader, thanks to its position on the map's top level and its lone entrance. While the entire team attacks the opposition's leader, your team leader should grab the Ink Grenade from the second level. He can use it and his initial Smoke Grenade as proximity mines on the entryway to the spawn. Replenish as necessary.

The team leader can contribute yet remain largely out of the fray from the small room with a window off the spawn point. This vantage point overlooks a portion of the street, and one can fire upon the exit from the second floor interior from here. Take care to avoid exposing yourself too much to enemy fire, particularly if the Longshot is in play.

Assuming your enemy will employ similar tactics, mix up your approach by occasionally rushing through the hospital rooms straight to the opposing leader's spawn. This allows your team to slip past any enemies defending near the street, and it keeps them safe from the enemy leader's fire. Send two or three players (leave one for defense) and Roadie Run the entire distance without stopping, if possible. If you can, grab a downed enemy to use as a shield.

ANNEX & KING OF THE HILL

The ample grenade supply spreads throughout the level, particularly near the capture locations. This makes defending a captured point easier than on most maps, especially if friendly fire is off. To counter this, after you respawn, grab grenades from the opposite side of the map and toss them ahead of your attack. Doing so can damage enemy units and harmlessly detonate any proximity mines while you're still out of range. This allows your team to rush in, secure the capture point, and place one or two of your own proximity mines.

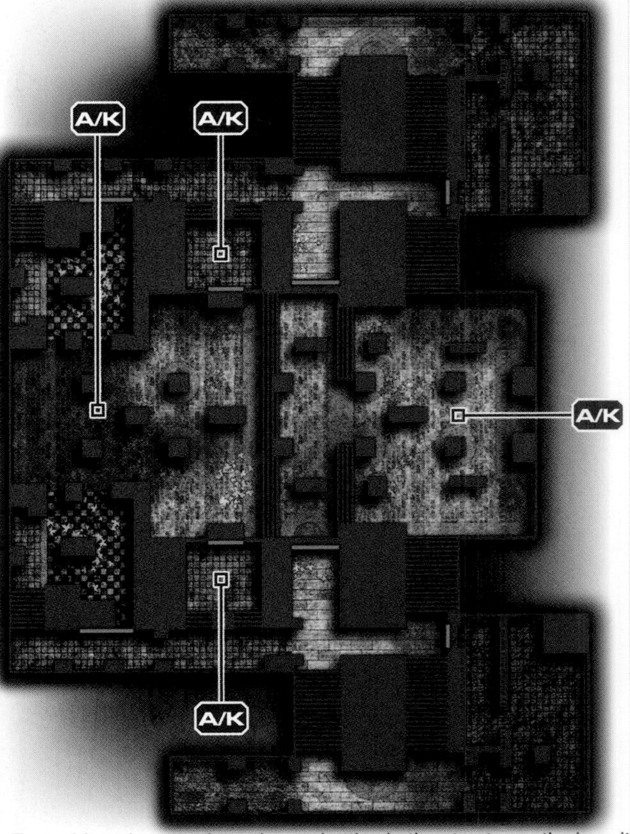

To avoid getting caught up in any battles in the street, use the hospital rooms as a quick way to travel between capture points in Annex matches. All weapon drops are potential capture points with the lone exception being the pistol spawns, so keep players well spaced to begin capping these locations as quickly as possible. Once they're captured, move to the perimeter and instruct your team to fan out to the other capture points, keeping their guns aimed at the active location.

King of the Hill matches take place exclusively on the street and inside the hospital at the grenade locations—neither of the upper pistol rooms is used. One team gets a relative advantage when the capture location is at the grenade area on their side of the map. Break their hold on it by sending two players up the stairs as decoys while the other three rush from within the hospital. Use the hospital gurneys and other apparatus on the elevated floor as cover to clear out the enemy before capturing the point.

HORDE

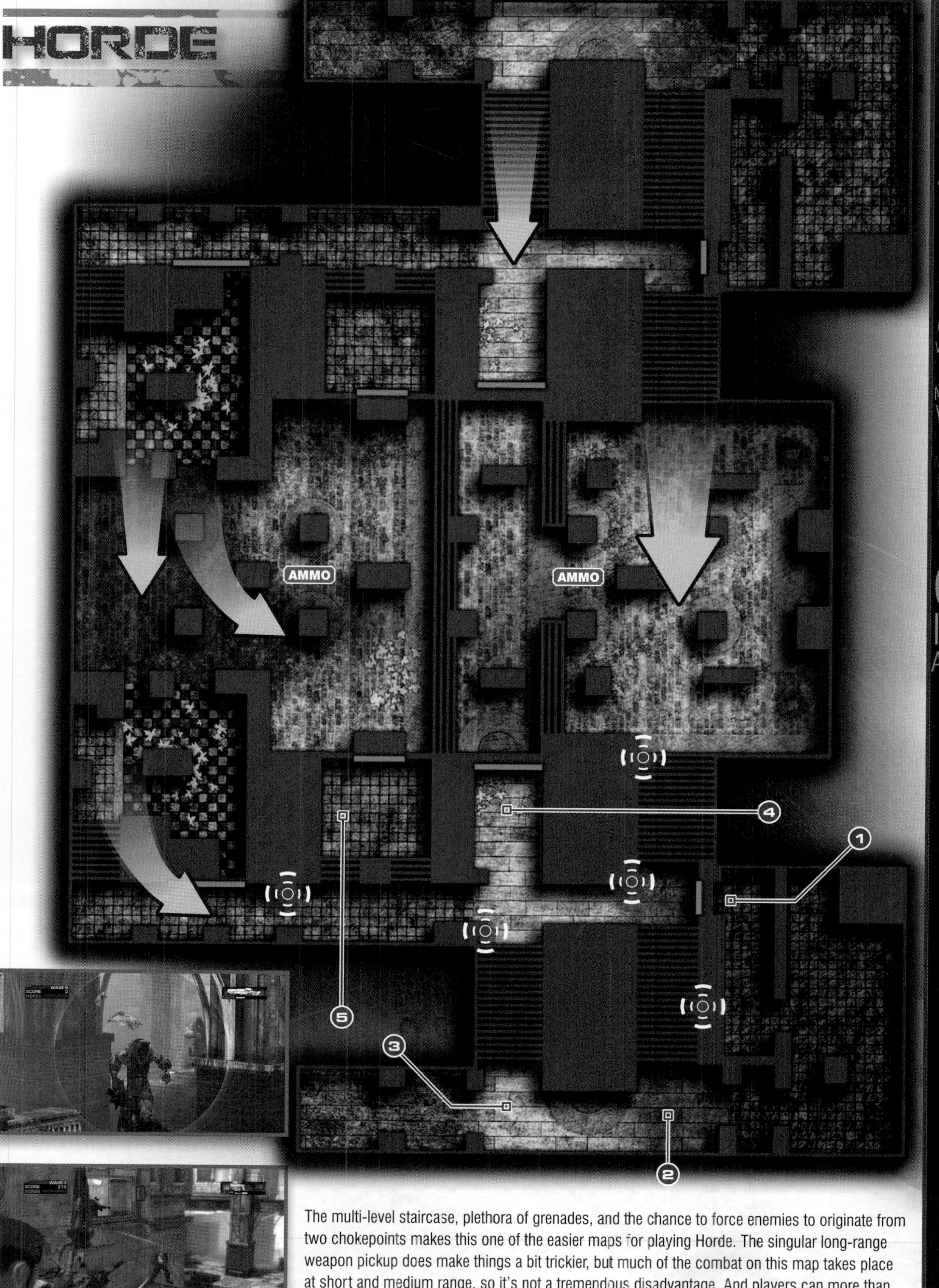

The multi-level staircase, plethora of grenades, and the chance to force enemies to originate from two chokepoints makes this one of the easier maps for playing Horde. The singular long-range weapon pickup does make things a bit trickier, but much of the combat on this map takes place at short and medium range, so it's not a tremendous disadvantage. And players can more than compensate for the lack of a Mortar or Hammer of Dawn (which would be devastating on this map) by deploying numerous proximity mines across the base of the stairs and inside the hospital.

Ammo: Both of the two ammo crates are located under the elevated train tracks in the center of the map. One is near the Ink Grenade pickup while the other is near the Torque Bow.

Variables: The fog makes it difficult to spot enemies at the top of the opposing staircase. But this really isn't that much of a factor, given the quantity of enemies attacking at close range.

Ilt should go without saying that teams must avoid congregating on the street beneath the tracks. Doing so opens them to attacks from enemies spawning on both stairs and inside both hospital rooms. Teams that stay under the train tracks will quickly find themselves outnumbered, surrounded, and taking bullets from every direction. Fortunately, there are alternatives.

A team of three or four could make a pretty valiant stand against the Horde by taking up a defensive position inside the hospital. You'll have access to grenades and will gain a slight height advantage by staying on the upper landing. It's not foolproof, but it's worth trying.

Taking up positions at the top of either staircase forces enemies to spawn from far across the map or down below in the street. Some teams may want to try splitting their forces between the upper level of each opposing staircase, but we recommend keeping all five members close together. Purposely dividing your forces between two spots that each have two approaches may work in the short-term, but not in the later waves. Instead, by entrenching at the top of the stairs and making forays to the street only to replenish ammo and grenades, the team can force the Horde to funnel through the hospital and the stairs near the street. A team of five people committed to the roles described in the following section can easily cover both of these positions.

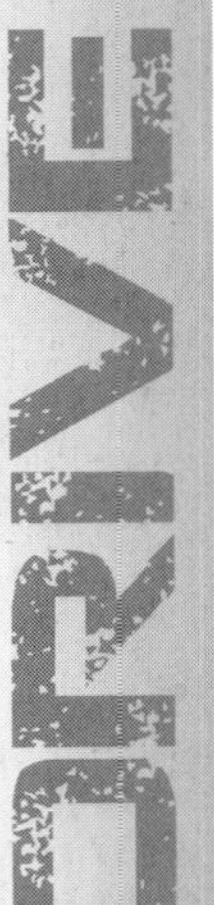

KNOW YOUR ROLE

The following tactics correspond to the numbered positions marked on the accompanying map. Follow these tips carefully for maximum survivability. These tips assume a five-person team.

1 The team's best sniper should rush for the Longshot and retreat to the window near the upper team spawn point. Place the Smoke Grenade at the entrance to the team spawn. Then duck inside the alcove with the window and use the Lancer and Longshot to take out enemies on the street below. This vantage point doesn't provide a complete view of the battlefield, but it does offer a tremendous line of sight into the hospital's hallway. Because this person is likely to be the first to spot Locust approaching from within the hospital interior, he or she should call them out to players 4 and 5 and, when possible, snipe them from afar. Although there is only one approach to this room and the Horde must get past your entire team to eliminate this player, he isn't completely safe. Theron Guards and Boomers will no doubt attempt to take him out. So, using cover, even in this elevated sniper's nest, is critical.

2 The team's best close-range combatant should assume this role and take position outside the team spawn location, atop the stairs. This player's charge is to maintain the proximity mines on the stairs leading down to the street and to cut down as many enemies as possible making their way across the street. This person's role is important because many of the enemies come his or her way. Other players can lend support, but aside from a grenade or two that may be inside the spawn area, this player is the last line of defense. Although all players should try to revive one another, player 2 should not stray to the other half of the staircase to revive players 3, 4, or 5 unless all of them are downed. Vacating this position, even for a few seconds, risks allowing the Horde to advance too far up the stairs.

3 The player in this position is allowed to freelance around the upper half of the stairs and lend a hand wherever the fighting heats up. His primary role should be to revive fallen comrades and to use his Lancer and the nearby pistol pickups (perhaps with a meat shield) to soften up as many enemies as he can. Securing ammo or additional grenades is not this player's responsibility. Instead, he is there to assist wherever he's needed and ensure that the other team members are alive and that the sniper is not under duress.

4 Player 4 has the important frontline job of patrolling the lower half of the staircase, assisting players 2 and 5 with approaching enemies, and making sure that any Locust trying to cross the street is immediately put down. This person also serves as a scout and must call out enemy locations so the other players can respond accordingly. Player 4 can stray down into the street when necessary to plant proximity mines and to collect ammunition, but he shouldn't stay down there too long. Lastly, this player should collect dropped weaponry from the street and lower stairs, delivering them to players 2 and 3. Drop them in favor of more common weapons that might be further up the stairs so the players at the top can use powerful, long-range weapons without running all the way down to the street.

5 In many of our Horde strategies, the fifth player is a luxury, free to roam the map and lend support wherever it's needed. That is not the case here. The fifth player in this formation has the heavy responsibility of continually replacing tripped proximity mines at the street-level hospital entrance and inside the interior hallway. As much as possible, he should try to remain outside the hospital and on the stairs' middle landing, but this player is indeed the primary defense against Horde units making their way through the lobby. Most of the enemies attack from the street, so the burden isn't terribly great, but some attack waves have the capacity to overrun the interior space. Should this happen, player 5 must immediately retreat to the exterior, where players 3 and 4 can assist him. Lastly, it's important that player 5 avoid obstructing the sniper's view of the hospital corridor.

DAY ONE

Authors' Favorite Modes: Warzone, Submission, and Wingman.

DAY ONE

The war with the Locust comes to a crossroads in the urban jungle of Day One. Here teams must fight it out amongst the carnage the Locust infestation has wrought on one of Sera's grandest cities. Burned-out cars, a broken water main, and a massive crater serve as backdrop to the fighting yet to come. This once idyllic intersection, home to an arcade and theater, is now the territory of one of the largest Seeders to ever break the surface.

Teams take the battlefield on the northern and southern ends of this cross-shaped map. Each team has its own respective balcony to ascend to, one with a Longshot the other with a Hammer of Dawn. Those looking to forsake the two perches will find plenty of cover on the streets and inside the arcade on the ground. Pistols can be found on the corners perpendicular to the balconies, and there's a Boomshield inside the arcade. There aren't any grenades to pick up on the map, so each combatant should use his or her initial outlay carefully.

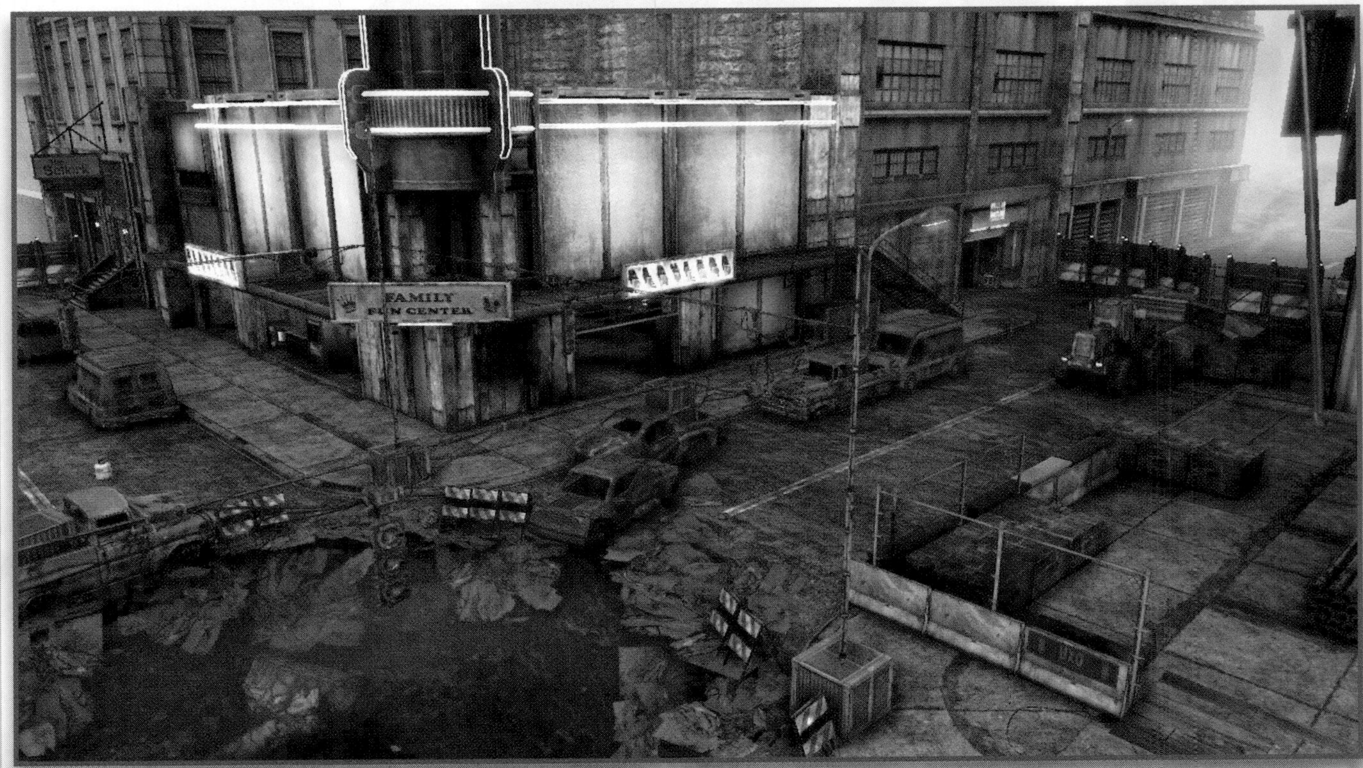

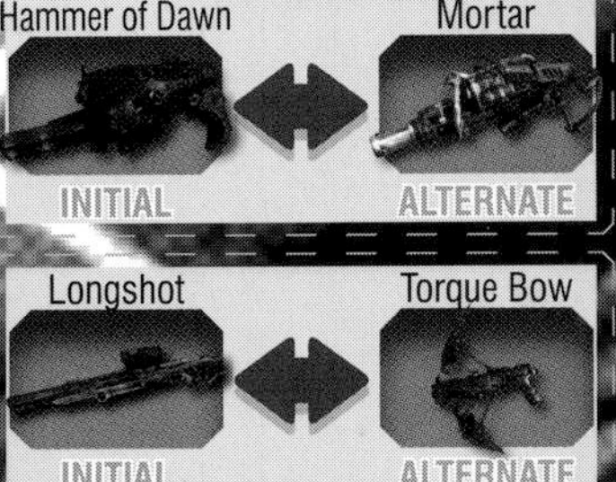

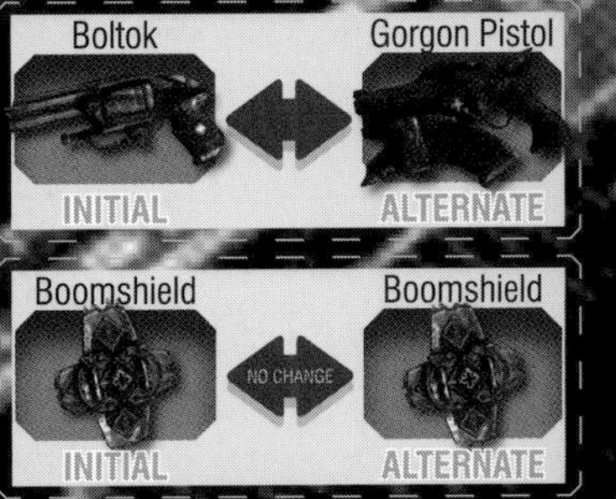

BATTLEFIELD SPECIFICS

SEEDER

The enormous crater in the middle of the map wasn't created from an asteroid collision, as one might be prone to think. No, this crater is actually the home of one of the largest Seeders ever seen. It's completely harmless to players—it doesn't spew any Nemacysts—but this doesn't mean its screeching won't send shivers up COG spines across the map. The Seeder typically emerges from its subterranean hollow only once per match, then vanishes just as suddenly as it arrives. New players will no doubt be distracted by its presence, so take advantage of any turned heads or lapses in concentration you encounter! To avoid potential confusion, the Seeder doesn't appear during Horde matches.

Don't let this massive beast distract you from your target!

EXPLODING CARS

Sure, the cars in the road serve as great cover, but three of them can actually be detonated on command. Each of the three traffic-lined branches of the intersection has a car with external fuel tanks just below the doors—there is a tank on both sides of the car. These tanks are as rusty as the cars themselves, but are cylindrical in shape and easy to distinguish from the rest of the car. Shoot the tank twice to create a small fire inside the car's interior, and then stand back and watch as it erupts moments later! The exploding cars inflict very little damage to the player, but every little bit helps!

Wait for an enemy to take cover behind one of these cars, and then blow it up!

SPAWN POINT AWARENESS

The two spawn points are on the northern and southern ends of the intersecting roads. The massive depression in the center forces teams to either advance to the east or west, toward the two staircases leading up onto the balconies atop the theater and arcade. Depending on the gameplay mode (see below), you'll likely want to make a mad dash for the balcony nearest your spawn point at the start of the map to procure one of the two deadlier weapons. Fortunately for you, it's easy to figure out which one to go for. Unlike some of the other maps, you can rush for your side's nearest weapon pickup without competition from the enemy team. That's because your adversaries have their own weapon to go after, and the distance to your side's weapon limits the chance of them beating you to yours.

1 NORTH SPAWN

Those starting at the northern spawn point will recognize where they are at once by noticing the yellow theater marquis to the left. Perhaps even more instantly recognizable is the water-filled trench and large concrete block in the center of the road. Regardless of which landmark you prefer, the path is the same: sprint toward the neon yellow sign and cut the corner on an angle to reach the stairs leading up to the balcony. That's where the Hammer of Dawn (or Mortar) is located.

2 SOUTH SPAWN

The southern spawn point is easily recognizable thanks to the arcade's neon blue lights on the corner to the left. Those fortunate enough to begin nearest the arcade have the option of grabbing either the Boomshield inside the arcade at ground level or running up the stairs around the corner to procure the Longshot (or Torque Bow).

ESSENTIAL TACTICS

Elevation Devastation: Players from both sides will be drawn to the two opposing balconies on the facades of the theater and arcade. These positions offer a grand view of the battlefield, and they are the spawn locations for the map's most powerful weaponry. Each team begins the round closer to one of these balconies than the other, so the initial rush will see little contention. Try to disrupt your opponents by sending three of your squad mates to their balcony at the start of the fight. They won't be expecting it, and you just may get their primary weapon in addition to your own!

Light My Fire: Just because there aren't any grenade pickups on this map doesn't mean there isn't plenty of fiery goodness to unleash upon your foes. Each round features three explosive cars that you can detonate with a couple of shots from any weapon. Use these to your advantage by targeting those nearest your enemy, particularly when they're taking cover near one of the cars.

Jojo Vs Jimmy: All is not lost if you fail to secure either of the advanced weapons on the balconies. Just head inside the arcade under the blue neon lights and take up position behind the counter. Use the Boomshield to block enemy fire from the side door and place your grenade on the foosball table. The interior of the arcade offers full protection from the Mortar and Hammer of Dawn, and you'll force your enemy to draw in close. The arcade cabinets funnel them directly toward you for easy pickings!

WHERE WAS HE?

You get only one grenade on this map, so you might as well make it count. Plant it on the back of the divider wall near the Longshot. A lot of players will immediately grab the weapon and hop over the wall into cover—what a surprise they'll get!

TEAM STRATEGIES

WARZONE & EXECUTION

It's important to begin each round with a sprint forward and to the left, regardless of your spawn location. Climb the ramp to the elite weapon nearest you. The higher ground provides a good vantage point when you attack enemies on the ground, but you can also use these elite weapons to attack players on the opposite balcony. Focus your attacks on that location first. Once that threat is removed, you're free to attack forces on the ground. Coordinate with teammates to accompany you up to the balcony to watch your back and to serve as a spotter. If you're going for the theater balcony where the Hammer of Dawn (or Mortar) is located, your best bet is to stick close to the marquis on the corner's apex. If you're racing for the Longshot (or Torque Bow) atop the arcade, be sure to mantle over the divider near the weapon to gain full 360-degree cover.

With no objectives to worry about other than eliminating the opposition, you're free to target the exploding cars in the area. This is especially true if you down a player near one of these makeshift bombs and see a teammate coming to revive him. Shoot in anticipation of the downed enemy's teammate because it takes roughly two seconds for the tank to explode. The car's explosion won't necessarily kill the player, but it might be a big enough diversion to give you the upper hand. This technique can help you accumulate multiple kills quickly.

Not everyone can be the first to sprint up the stairs to the balconies. If you prefer to remain grounded or you simply get outpaced on the initial rush for weaponry, consider heading to the arcade to get the Boomshield. Combine this powerful melee-neutralizing shield with the pistol pickup in the building on your right as you head out of the spawn. The combination of arcade cabinets and the Boomshield provides a high degree of cover. You may not like the idea of camping, but this is a great place to dig in and force opponents to get up close and personal, thus giving you an advantage.

SUBMISSION

The Stranded member spawns down either of the two short side streets to the east and west, where the teams do not spawn, near the center. Regardless which side he spawns on, he's equidistant from both teams and usually near one of the cars that can be detonated. The capture location to which you must bring the Stranded can be as close as the Boomshield or pistol locations, or as far away as the balcony atop the arcade.

Working around the Seeder hole's perimeter in the middle of the map forces you to skirt the edges, leaving you open to attacks from ahead and behind. Have two teammates advance ahead as an escort, one with the Boomshield, while the other two guard the rear.

Send team members to one or both of the special weapon locations to provide covering fire while moving the Stranded. The path to the goal usually leads from one side of the street, around the intersection, and over to an opposite corner. The ability to pick off enemies with the advanced weaponry—especially the Hammer of Dawn—while advancing the Stranded is key. The player on the balcony should use his or her initial Smoke Grenade on the stairs to cover his or her back. Even this might not be enough, so pay attention to flanking maneuvers as you follow the action below. We recommend this tactic only for a full team of five players, as leaving just one or two players to advance the Stranded without proper aerial cover is not effective.

WINGMAN

Acquiring the elite weapons isn't always necessary in Wingman because enemies must be executed, but the weaponry on this map's balconies is capable of one-hit kills. There is only one way to access the Longshot and Hammer of Dawn combinations up on the balconies, so move to those locations together and have one teammate take the weapon while the other covers the stairwell. On their way up to the balcony, both players should set their Smoke Grenades on the stairs—spaced adequately apart—to serve as an alarm.

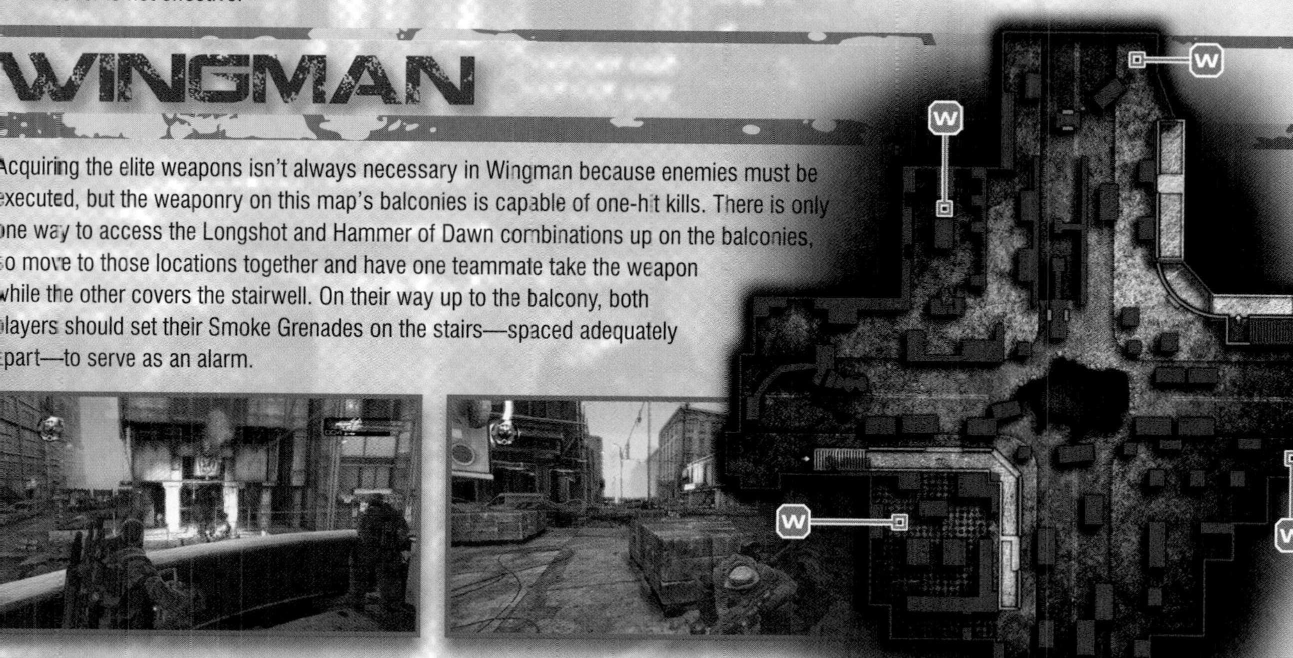

While using cover is always critical to success, it's arguably even more important on Day One. Using the many cover objects—cars, arcade games, barricades, etc.—to flank opponents gives you an offensive advantage, and it keeps you hidden from those on the balconies. Exploit these features in Wingman by instructing one teammate to stay in cover and blindfire with the Lancer or Hammerburst. Meanwhile, the other teammate flanks the pinned down or distracted opponent and attacks. A great place to employ this defensive approach is inside the arcade, where the counter and the Boomshield offer substantial cover.

EPIC SAYS...

Hang back and see which way the other teams go on this map. You'll have a better chance of staying alive and picking off distracted foes by circling the perimeter in the direction opposite the one everyone else takes.

GUARDIAN

The Boomshield provides a decided advantage in Guardian, and you should consider your team lucky when you spawn nearest the arcade. Have the team leader grab the Boomshield and stay behind the counter in that building with at least one teammate for protection. This gives the leader additional armor and keeps him safe from Mortar or Hammer of Dawn attacks. Be sure to use your Smoke Grenade as a proximity mine, as the arcade cabinets provide more than enough cover for attackers to get in close.

Another approach worth considering is to use the Hammer of Dawn or Mortar. When you spawn on the side of the map nearest the theater, have the team leader climb to the balcony where the Hammer of Dawn spawns. Send at least one teammate along to protect the stairwell area. The team leader can use the weapons here from cover. This is important because a skilled sniper can eliminate him with a single shot from the opposing balcony.

ANNEX & KING OF THE HILL

All of the capture points are on the ground level: the two pistol locations and the Boomshield spawn. Because the Smoke Grenades that players start with are the only grenades available, all teammates should use them as proximity mines around the capture point's perimeter once you control it. The Boomshield can be very helpful for defending the capture point because the Hammer of Dawn and the Mortar cannot reach the interior capture locations. Take the Boomshield with you as you run between the different capture points.

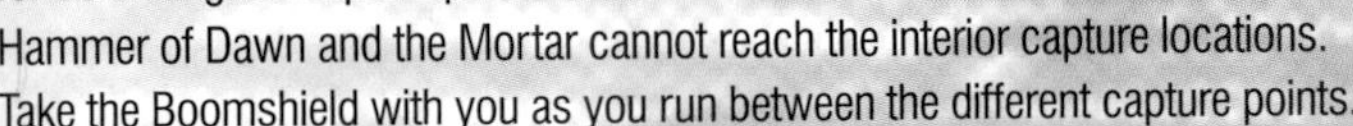

One can reach each of the capture locations fairly quickly, so camping out between them isn't as crucial here as it would be on larger maps. Nevertheless, you should always be aware of the time remaining for each capture location and start moving out before time expires. There's no telling which Annex location will be targeted next, so move to the center of the map to avoid confusion regarding which location the icon points toward.

The capture locations provide a great deal of cover from which to down opponents rushing the area. As you try to overtake enemy-controlled capture points in King of the Hill, throw a Smoke Grenade in first to take down anyone in the circle—at least one enemy has to be there for the opposing team to gain points. Then rush in for the score. The Boomshield location can be very well defended, so being the first team to secure it is vital in King of the Hill. If you're unable to do so, fall back and regroup with the Longshot or Torque Bow, and then make a concerted push to retake it with your whole team working in unison.

On this map, the special weapons have very different applications in the territorial game modes. Both the Longshot and the Torque Bow can take out opponents inside the capture points. The Hammer of Dawn and Mortar cannot reach enemies within the capture locations due to overhead cover. These weapons can only destroy or slow down opponents as they transition from one capture point to another. Using them in this way isn't as critical as artfully wielding a Gnasher or Lancer. So, send the teammate least skilled in run-and-gun warfare up to the theater balcony to lend this additional layer of support.

HORDE

This is a challenging map on which to play Horde, but the two balconies give players an elevation advantage. They also force the Locust to funnel through a single approach (one per balcony). This map offers a lot of places to set up a defense, such as inside the arcade or at the end of a longer street. But these positions don't offer the sweeping views of the battlefield, and they require longer runs to the heavy firepower.

Ammo: The two ammo crates on this map are near the central crate, on the east and west side-streets. Their position facilitates running down the stairs and quickly securing additional ammo before the next wave arrives.

Variables: The explosive cars can be detonated only once per match, so save them for the later waves when their impact will be greatest! As we previously mentioned, the Seeder that appears in other game modes doesn't show up in Horde mode.

Employing a crossfire-based strategy centered on using the balconies controls the flow of enemies from multiple spawn points. It also diverts the attention of the Locust. Many of the Locust spawn at the northern and southern ends of the street, while a lesser number originate from the building with the UXO banners. Regardless of where they spawn, they instantly split between pursuing teammates at the arcade and those on the balcony by the theater.

It's important to keep your head down even when you're on a balcony, as the Theron Guards and Boomers can arc their weapon fire over the protective railing for an instant kill, particularly during the latter waves. Similarly, the team should be in constant communication to alert one another where enemies are appearing, how close they are, as well as which ones they're targeting. Ammo can be scarce for those manning the Mortar and Torque Bow, so it's important that these two people don't waste shots by targeting the same enemy. Lastly, many of the larger enemies wield a Boomshot, Boomshield, or Mulcher. Prioritize these enemies (and any others you see), divvying them up throughout your squad. Even the lowly Wretch eventually proves hard to kill with standard weaponry.

EPIC SAYS...

Have a player get the Boomshield and head onto the arcade balcony. He should position himself right where the railing meets the solid outer wall, with his back to the player who is sniping. The Boomshield, cover from the two walls, and the fact that there is only one way up onto the balcony makes this position almost impenetrable. Instruct a second teammate to stand behind him and shoot over his shoulder at the enemies coming up the stairs. Together, this creates a nearly unbreakable defense and offers excellent protection for the sniper.

KNOW YOUR ROLE

The following tactics correspond to the numbered positions marked on the accompanying map. Follow these tips carefully for maximum survivability. These tips assume a five-person team.

1 Each of the roles discussed here is critical to your team's success, but having a highly skilled sniper is vital. Let the person most experienced with the Longshot and Torque Bow move to the arcade balcony and set up shop near the center of the roof. Ammo isn't abundant, so don't waste it on lesser foes or those in a dead sprint toward your other squad mates. Instead, focus on enemies far in the distance and those that are difficult to bring down without a precise headshot or two. Strafe back and forth between the corner of the building and the divider near the weapon spawn, and drop your two standard weapons in favor of the Torque Bow and Longshot.

2 This player's primary role is to serve as bodyguard for the sniper. Stick between the sniper and the stairs leading down to the street, and fire on anything that moves no matter how small it may be. This player should also call out enemy locations when possible and assist teammate #3 in defending the western side-street. Help bring down enemies from the balcony, and descend to the street only when you need to get additional ammo or revive player #3.

3 This person has to be a skilled close-range combatant. This player's role is to serve as the frontline defense against the Horde ambush and to accumulate weapons and ammo from the deceased. Stick to the western side-street's far end, and retreat up the stairs to the balcony only when necessary. This player should be able to accumulate extra grenades from fallen Locust members. Use them on the cars and on the wall adjacent the stairs leading up to the balcony to better protect the two players stationed there.

4 The addition of a fourth player gives the team the luxury of a comrade on the theater balcony. This person can use the Hammer of Dawn (or Mortar) to annihilate the Locust as they appear at the street's north and south ends. Place a Smoke Grenade on the stairs to guard the balcony's approach. Focus on groups of large enemies and avoid using this location's elite weaponry on singular enemies.

5 A fifth player really turns the tables in your team's favor by giving the Hammer of Dawn and Mortar operator much needed protection on the balcony. The fifth teammate should take up position on the stairs leading up to the theater balcony. This position allows him to protect the player on the balcony and spot enemies as they approach from down the street. Collect the weapons of the deceased littering the street and retreat to the balcony where they can be put to better use.

HAIL

Authors' Favorite Modes: Execution, King of the Hill, and Horde.

There's a storm brewing amidst the cloudy skies above Hail, and the forecast isn't for the faint of heart. Just as the action begins to heat up in the streets of this asymmetrical map, the skies open and unleash a torrent of chilling rain. And, as if the hampered visibility isn't bad enough, the rain is often followed by a skull-piercing burst of razorhail. We're not talking pea-size pellets either! The razorhail that is this map's namesake comes down in lethal shards, forcing friends and foes alike to seek shelter from the storm. Close-quarters carnage typically ensues... The weather cycle follows this pattern: clear, rain, hail, rain, and then repeat from the beginning.

The two spawn points are on opposite sides of the map, safely under the roofs of buildings near the rubble piles. The three train cars strewn across the curving street provide respite from the incoming storms. The center car also provides a Torque Bow to the first player to reach it. A massive awning partially covers the central promenade up the steps from the street, but several areas are exposed to the elements, particularly near the Boomshot and Longshot. The map contains a wealth of advanced long-range weaponry and Ink and Frag Grenades, but don't overlook the importance of having a powerful sidearm at the ready. The circling hailstorms consistently force players indoors, where they're often just a pistol whip away from their enemies.

BATTLEFIELD SPECIFICS

WEATHER

It doesn't take long on this map before the weather's far-reaching effects are felt. The conditions periodically shift from calm overcast skies to rain, then to razorhail. The rain sometimes shifts back to sunny skies, but a lightning crack signals an instantaneous shift to razorhail, which can last for up to twenty seconds. The razorhail starts out slowly and then ramps up to a deluge of extremely sharp crystals that can down and kill a player's character in ten seconds. Taking cover isn't an option—it's a necessity! Whether you're in the streets and need to duck into a train car or up the steps and take cover under the canopies, you must get under a roof as soon as possible. The razorhail routinely kills players who stray too far from cover or who underestimate how long until it ends. You'll be pleased to know that the razorhail doesn't fall on Submission, King of the Hill, and Horde mode.

Be sure to get under cover from the razorhail, else you risk catching a deadly case of brain-freeze!

SPAWN POINT AWARENESS

Both teams begin the match indoors, but on opposite sides and with very different options. The team that begins at the northern spawn has an advantage in that they are much closer to the Longshot location—it's on the level above them. They're also two steps closer to the Torque Bow than the opposition. The flipside to this is that the team spawning on the map's southern side can quickly reach the Boomshot and fall back to the safety of the covered bridge on the map's southeastern corner. Both teams have access to a Gorgon Pistol and Ink or Frag Grenades.

1 NORTH SPAWN

The northern spawn point is easily identifiable thanks to the low ceiling and dark interior. The team starting at this point should immediately send three players out into the street on the right to race toward the Torque Bow in the center train car. Send two other players through the warehouse to procure the Ink Grenades on their way up the stairs to the Longshot. Take up cover and prepare for the opposition's rush toward the Boomshot.

2 SOUTH SPAWN

The team starting at the map's southern end begins inside an ornate hallway with a large staircase leading down to the street directly in front of the spawn. Heading to the right leads players up a curving staircase to a covered bridge that provides an excellent vantage point and easy access to the Boomshot. Those starting at this end of the map have a slight disadvantage when it comes to securing the Torque Bow in the center train car. But the proximity to the Boomshot and the ability to hole up inside the covered bridge makes up for this shortcoming.

ESSENTIAL TACTICS

A Train to Catch: Most matches begin with an initial rush for the Torque Bow (or Longshot) located in the central train car. The team starting on the map's northern end has a slight advantage and should be able to secure this weapon most of the time, provided the other team doesn't take a more aggressive tack. Instead of simply hoping to beat the other team in a footrace, the team starting at the end near the covered bridge should run toward the train car and lob a Smoke Grenade into it, hoping to knock out those who get there first. Jump through the window to collect the prize.

Defend the Bridge: The covered bridge at the map's southern end provides an excellent view of the battlefield and forces enemies to approach from two narrow staircases. A team that camps this bridge and sets up a proximity mine defense has a decided advantage over the opposition. With their backs to the edge of the map and their flanks armed with explosives, these players can keep their heads down and pick off the opposition with ease. Although this position doesn't offer an unobstructed view of the entire map, nobody can approach unseen.

WHERE WAS HE?

One especially ruthless way to eliminate enemies, particularly in an Execution match, is to down them during the start of a hailstorm. You won't get credit for the kill—the razorhail will—but you'll win the match.

Beware the Ice: The falling razorhail adds a uniquely dangerous element to playing on this map, and it should always be on your mind. It's important to scope out overhead cover, and it doesn't hurt to count how long the razorhail falls to try to cheat the race for the next weapon drop. The hailstorm doesn't always last twenty seconds, and it does taper off toward the end, but you can run out into the razorhail once you've counted to eleven. You'll suffer some damage but the razorhail will stop falling before it kills you. Of course, you still have to watch for enemy fire. But if everyone else is focused on the fight taking place under cover, you should be able to sneak away and land a special weapon for your efforts.

TEAM STRATEGIES

WARZONE & EXECUTION

The fear of being downed during a hailstorm should be on all players' minds during the initial rush for the advanced weaponry. This is particularly true for those set on duking it out for the Torque Bow in the train car. The Torque Bow and Boomshot are heavily contested, given that the team spawning to the north has a clear advantage in securing the Longshot. Use Smoke Grenades and increased numbers to your advantage, and try to down enemy players just as the lightning strikes and the razorhail begins.

When you're going for the Longshot, have one teammate immediately sprint for that weapon. Then move into position to cover the other two primary weapon areas. This is especially helpful if opponents get stuck either inside one of the train cars in the street or are waiting for the razorhail to stop so they can grab the Boomshot. Keep in mind that the Longshot area is not covered, so take up a position near the main stairwell. This area is under the protection of the canvas awning and has a good view of both elite weapon spawns.

One tactic worth employing as the match winds down is to grab the Longshot (or Torque Bow) from the train car and stealthily relocate to either of the two other train cars. Camp this location by keeping your head down and waiting in the shadows. Pan the camera around to view the approach to the central car. This allows you to monitor any activity on the street or near the main staircase leading up to the circular plaza.

Perhaps the single best tactic is to acquire the Longshot and/or Torque Bow and set up a defensive stronghold in the covered bridge at the map's southern end. This provides an elevated vantage point of most of the map, including the two elite weapon spawns. And it's covered from razorhail exposure. Grenades spawn at one end; plant them at both ends as a warning and protection system. This is an excellent sniping location and not a bad place to make a last stand if you're outnumbered.

EPIC SAYS...

There are ways to be very sneaky when dealing with the Booomshot, both from a defensive approach and when on offense. For starters, teams spawning in the warehouse should go up the stairs and take cover behind the wooden crates on the pavilion's left side. This is the perfect place to attack the opposing team as they go for the Boomshot. On offense, take the Boomshot over to the south side of the circular pavilion. Find cover near the short wall near the large container. This vantage point gives you a clean shot at the combatants holing up in two of the three train cars below.

SUBMISSION

You can find the Stranded at one of two locations: in the central plaza near the Boomshot weapon drop or outside the northernmost train car in the street. The capture points rotate between the three advanced weapon locations. Many of the capture locations require trips outdoors but the rain and razorhail don't fall, so there's no concern of the weather forcing the Stranded's release.

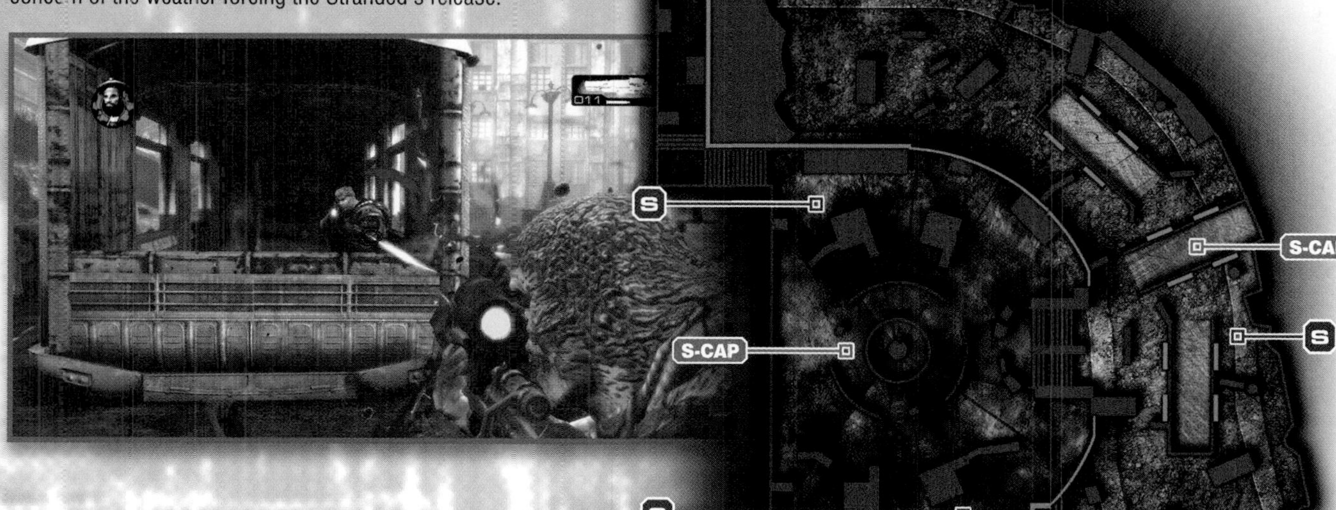

Because the Stranded's spawn and capture locations are so close to one another, brute force is often essential for success. Grab the Boomshot or Mulcher if they're handy. But first and foremost, keep the pressure on the other team by instructing teammates to provide plenty of suppression fire with their Lancers and Hammerbursts.

Several factors make grenades particularly effective on this map; these include the close proximity of players, as well as movement slowed by dragging the Stranded to the capture point. Grab the Frag or Ink Grenades on your way out of your spawn point. Lob them into a crowd of enemies to score multiple kills and to knock loose the Stranded. Similarly, protect yourself from other teams using the same tactic by taking their downed bodies as meat shields. Use the extra layer of protection to help escort your Stranded-carrying team member to the capture point.

This map's most explosive weapons are located in the capture points. Run ahead to the capture point to grab a Torque Bow or Boomshot as the opposing team approaches with the Stranded. This is an especially useful tactic if you're outnumbered at the moment. While charging at the opposing team with guns blazing only gets you killed, using the Torque Bow or Boomshot from afar can go a long way toward slowing their progress and freeing the Stranded. Even if you can't take out all of them, playing goalie can buy your teammates time to arrive on the scene.

WINGMAN

One lucky team spawns inside one of the train cars on the street, just a few steps away from the Torque Bow (or Longshot) in the central train car. The team fortunate enough to start here should instantly grab the weapon and fall back into their starting point. This maintains cover from the razorhail and allows team members to pick off enemies on the main stairwell or in the street.

The other two elite weapon pickups are subject to razorhail. Move quickly with your teammate to obtain these weapons. Then fall back to a covered position either under the canvas awning or on the covered bridge atop the stairs at the south. Don't get trapped in the alley near the map's northern end or within the innermost ring of circular walls in the central plaza; both of these areas are exposed to the elements.

Those who don't secure an elite weapon aren't out of luck. Move to the street and use the Lancer or Hammerburst, combined with a few grenades, to down enemies as the rain gives way to razorhail. Duck for cover while they struggle to crawl to safety, away from the razorhail's debilitating deluge. Having two Lancers focused on one enemy brings him down twice as fast and earns you an easy remote kill—the razorhail ensures that the opponent doesn't get up!

Although it's important to rack up a number of kills in Wingman, this map allows you to fall back to a defensive position and pick off enemies from afar, especially with either the Torque Bow or Longshot. Move to the southern bridge and use the Ink Grenade that spawns on one end as a warning and defense system. Use your initial Smoke Grenade to trip up enemies approaching from the curved stairwell. Use the long-range weapons to take out enemies engaged in other skirmishes. Then stand back-to-back and cut down any final foes trying to approach through the opposing chokepoints.

GUARDIAN

The team leader shouldn't stray too far from the spawn areas thanks to the lengthy sightlines, abundant long-range weaponry, and hailstorms that make moving across this map particularly dangerous. As much as possible, avoid travelling outside the spawn point. The southern spawn area contains a room with two entrances and a pillar for taking cover; this is as close to a chokepoint as the map presents. Grab the Ink or Frag Grenades from the southern bridge, and plant proximity mines on the outer sides of the two entrances. Then sit tight and hope your advance units can keep you safe.

The northern spawn, on the other hand, does not contain a clear chokepoint. Grab the Frag Grenades near the stairwell leading from the spawn area to the central plaza. Use them as proximity mines where approaching enemies cannot see them. Possibilities include the outer wall at the bottom of the stairwell and the large metal crate in the direction of the spawn. Take cover behind the wooden boxes opposite the staircase and ready your Lancer of Gnasher.

There are different tactics for taking down the enemy leader, depending on where your team spawns and whether your target is roaming the level or hiding. From the southern spawn, grab the Longshot or Torque Bow and head to the southern bridge to scan the map for the leader and to eliminate inbound enemies trying to hunt for your leader. This should keep the other team on edge long enough while your teammates rush forward to pursue the leader. Starting from the northern spawn, acquire the Boomshot (or Mulcher) and fall back to the defensive position between the spawn area and the central plaza. The wooden boxes here provide an ideal place to mount the Mulcher and fire on the stairwell from the central plaza or attackers heading toward your spawn area.

ANNEX & KING OF THE HILL

On Hail, the capture points for Annex and King of the Hill are the three elite weapon pickup locations. The periodic hailstorm appears during Annex matches but not during King of the Hill games. During Annex matches, stay within the vicinity of the large central plaza, especially near the main stairwell. This gives you nearly immediate access to all three capture locations.

The capture point above the northern spawn is almost always captured by the team starting nearest it, at least initially. This is arguably the easiest location to defend, especially in King of the Hill, when razorhail doesn't force players to vacate the ample cover in this area. Those approaching from the southern spawn should take an extra few seconds to grab grenades and power weapons along the way, as they'll need them to break the enemies' hold on that location.

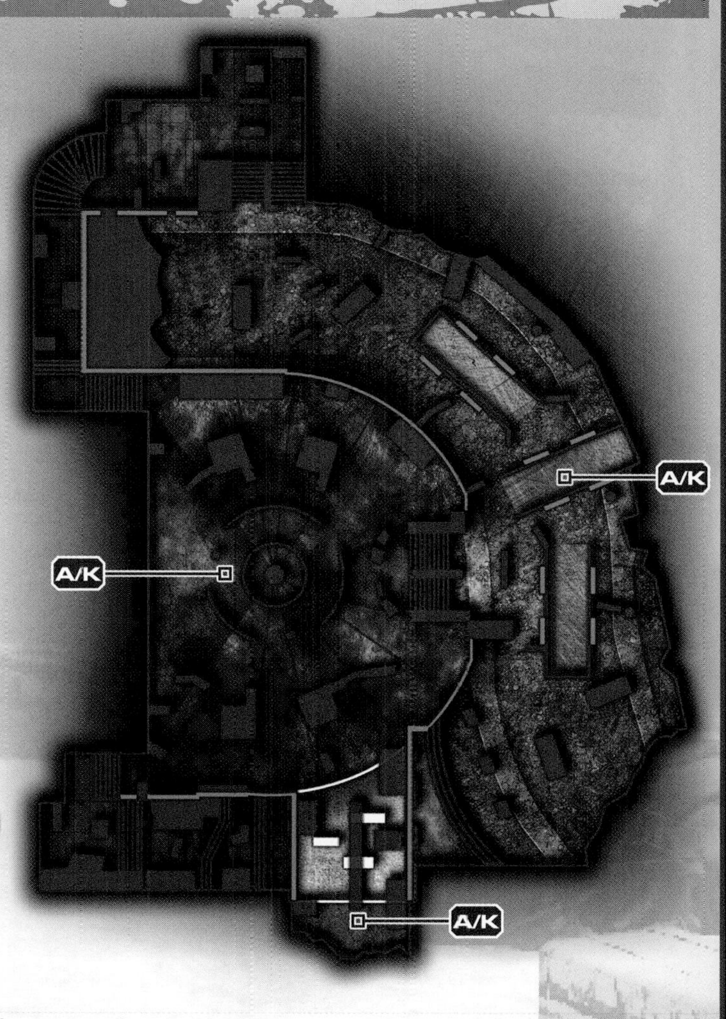

When you try to hold the train car location, set up proximity mines near the car's entrance. For Annex, have one teammate take cover in the shadows of the car's rear. For King of the Hill, have someone crouch in the circle. Other team members should split up and commandeer the two adjacent trolley cars, preferably two in each. This offers plenty of cover (in case of a hailstorm) and gives a grand view of the approach from either direction.

The capture point located in the plaza's center is the most difficult of the three to capture and defend due to its central location and relatively little cover in the capture circle. This is exacerbated in Annex matches when the periodic razorhail deluge plays a factor. In Annex, once the location is captured, immediately fall back behind one of the walls that box in the area. Try to keep the enemy outside the splash area of the razorhail. For King of the Hill matches, plant proximity grenades at various points in the stone circles around the central pillar. Have teammates take cover behind these two low walls. Use the Boomshot or Mulcher against approaching enemies. Set up a teammate with the Longshot on the covered bridge to pick off opponents as they approach from the street.

Ammo: The two ammo crates on this map are on opposite ends of the street. One ammo crate is directly below the covered bridge at the map's southern end. The other is far to the north, near the massive pile of rubble.

Variables: The razorhail doesn't fall in this mode, so there's no chance of lucking into a mass enemy extinction. On the bright side, you can make those mad dashes for weapons and ammo without worrying about getting caught out in the rain.

This is a great map on which to play Horde. Teams can position numerous Frag and Ink Grenades near the stairs and scan much of the map from a single vantage point. Enemies spawn from numerous locations and march southward down the street toward the covered bridge. Teams should definitely take up position there. This spot eliminates any chance of the enemy spawning behind the team. It also offers tremendous access to ammo, the Boomshot, additional grenades, and, to a lesser extent, the Longshot or Torque Bow. Plus, you can't beat the sightlines!

The following strategy forces the Locust into a parade of sitting ducks...albeit very large ducks carrying massive weapons. By taking position at the end of the street, the COG team forces the Locust to march down the road and across the pavilion, toward the two staircases leading up to the bridge. Many of the Locust lumber straight toward their target, while others try long-range weapons or sprinting from cover to cover. The elevation of the bridge, windows, and stairs gives the COG units a perfect window on the fight, making it easy to spot numerous enemies and cherry-pick those posing the most immediate threat.

KNOW YOUR ROLE

The following tactics correspond to the numbered positions marked on the accompanying map. Follow these tips carefully for maximum survivability. These tips assume a five-person team.

1 The central figure in this formation should take up position in the center of the covered bridge, armed with the Longshot and Torque Bow. It can be difficult to acquire both during the opening waves on the harder difficulty settings. However, if this person and one other teammate sprint for the two pickups during the first wave, they should be able to keep each other alive. From this point on, use the weapon spawn on the street to replenish ammo for the alternating Torque Bow and Longshot as they appear. This player's primary responsibility is to take out as many Drones, Grenadiers, and Kantuses from the greatest possible distance. Always aim for the head to conserve ammo, and wait for the enemy to stand up from behind cover. It's all about thinning their numbers while conserving ammunition.

2 A player skilled with using the Boomshot and adept at placing proximity mines should be to the point man's right. Use the Ink Grenade that spawns on the covered bridge to set up a perimeter defense on the steps leading down to the circular plaza. Then continuously rush for the Boomshot and Mulcher that spawn in the plaza's center. The approach from the street should be well-covered by other teammates, so this player should focus his undivided attention (and firepower) on the enemies making their way under the canvas awnings toward the team's right flank. Move about when you wield the Boomshot, but descend to the bottom of the stairs and steady the Mulcher on the cover there when you do your Locust-grinding.

3 The third member is every bit as vital to the team's success as the first two. This person must use grenades to set up proximity mines at the top of the stairs leading down to the street from the southern team spawn location. Use the Lancer and weapons collected from fallen Locust to set up in the window near the curved staircase inside the building. From there, lend support to player #1. Help eliminate the enemies making their way down the street or taking cover near the train cars. Coordinate with players #1 and #4 concerning ammo and weapon pickups. Additionally, this player must communicate well with the team's designated sniper to avoid targeting the same enemies and thus wasting ammo.

4 The fourth player offers the team a frontline defense on the street. He or she should focus on softening up the larger enemies to make killing them easier for the perched gunmen. This player should stick close to the stairs leading into the building in the street's southeast corner. However, he or she should also have the freedom to freelance on the street and even make a run for the Longshot (or Torque Bow) near the team's northern spawn.

5 The player occupying this role has the same freedoms and responsibilities as player #4, but on the other side of the bridge. Stick close to the stairs leading up to the bridge from the circular plaza to avoid straying too far from a reviving pick-me-up. But feel free to roam around to get a better angle on enemies. Collect fallen weaponry and grenades and set up further perimeter defenses, particularly on the steps coming up from the street and near the warehouse entry. Finally, assist player #2 in obliterating enemies trying to cross the plaza.

JACINTO

Authors' Favorite Modes: Annex, Guardian, and Horde.

The match begins and immediately two low-altitude helicopters shatter the silence. Perhaps they're lending support to another squad at a different location. Your team is alone, left to fend off the attackers on your own. The choppers are barely out of sight before the bullets start to fly and the sounds of chainsaws replace the signature whirlybird noises. It won't be long before the marble-lined walls and floors of this palatial courtyard are stained red by the horrors of combat. The most beautiful estate in all of Sera is about to be turned into just another battlefield.

In terms of architecture, navigation, and size, Jacinto is without doubt the most complex multiplayer map. Its grand size, winding passages, and one-way mantles make it the toughest to learn for first-timers, but it's an exciting challenge for veteran players. The beauty of Jacinto lies not in the flowers and stunning steeples and towers, but in the weapon placement. Every major weapon location is exposed to at least one of the others. The Torque Bow position is one of the most exposed pieces of real estate in the entire game, yet it also offers a clean shot at those attempting to secure the Hammer of Dawn and Mortar. Similarly, players opting for the latter two weapons can quickly take out enemy units moving in for the former. Each side of the map also has its own grenade tower that provides an excellent place to hide a leader in Guardian. They also serve as a critical sniper perches in other modes. Don't let this complex map intimidate you: practice it, study it, and embrace it.

WEAPON CYCLES

Longshot / Torque Bow

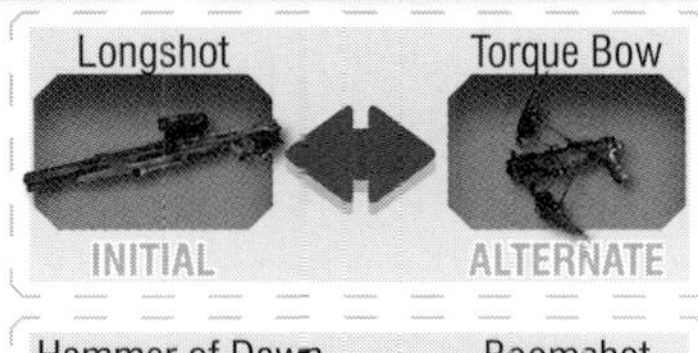

INITIAL / ALTERNATE

Boltok Pistol / Gorgon Pistol

INITIAL / ALTERNATE

Mortar / Mortar

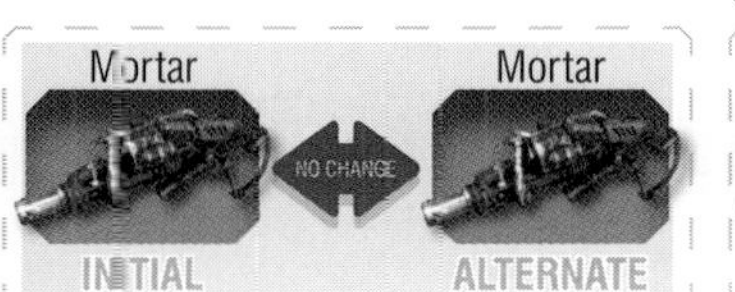

INITIAL / ALTERNATE

Hammer of Dawn / Boomshot

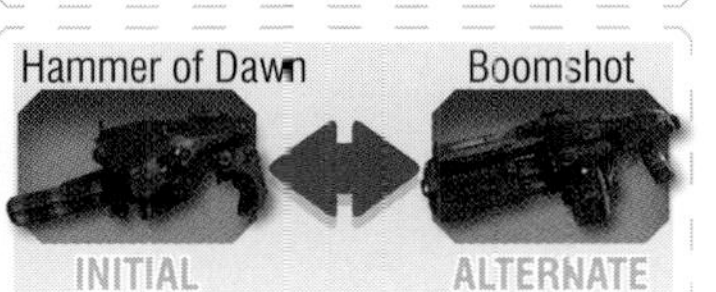

INITIAL / ALTERNATE

Ink Grenade / Frag Grenade

INITIAL / ALTERNATE

BATTLEFIELD SPECIFICS

ONE-WAY MANTLES

Jacinto is the lone multiplayer map with pieces of cover that can be mantled over in only one direction. Four short walls can be mantled from the eastern or western sides of the map toward the center. They're just ordinary walls on one side, but the other side features a small flowerbed and a short, spiked fence. Players can't take cover against this side of the wall, nor can they mantle over it. This feature limits players' advances toward the upper rooms with the grenade pickups. It also controls the flow of people to and from the area near the helicopter.

Those metal spikes aren't tall, but they're sharp enough to keep you from taking cover or mantling over them!

SPAWN POINT AWARENESS

The angled approaches from the map's southeastern and southwestern corners make knowing which side of the map you're on much easier. The approaches from both spawn points lead to stairs that ascend toward the central hot zone, where much of the fighting on this map occurs. Additional identifiers can help you gain an even quicker fix of your location on the map. Read on for clues:

1 EAST SPAWN

You're on the eastern side of the map when you see the trees on the left side of the spawn point. This is your cue to sprint ahead and turn hard to the left to go after the Longshot or descend the stairs toward the Mortar. Those seeking the Hammer of Dawn should run straight and angle to the right.

2 WEST SPAWN

If the trees are on your right at the start of the round, then you're at the western spawn point. Sprint up the steps and turn hard to the right to go toward the Longshot, or continue turning to the right to descend the steps to the one-way mantle near the Mortar. Head left instead for the Hammer of Dawn.

ESSENTIAL TACTICS

Murderer's Row: It's not by coincidence that the Mortar, Torque Bow, and Boomshot weapon pickups are aligned in a row. It's possible to fire on the Torque Bow/Longshot location from either of the other two major weapon pickup spots, and vice-versa. You have to be very careful when you go after an upgraded weapon on this map. A skilled sniper can race to the Longshot, turn, and quickly snipe an opposing player as he or she picks up the Mortar or Boomshot.

WHERE WAS HE?

Grab the Torque Bow or Longshot as quickly as you can, and then retreat to your spawn point. Watch for the enemy to make a move for the Mortar, and snipe him as soon as he picks it up. He won't see you in that area, and people trying to use these massive weapons make easy targets.

Hammer the Mortar: Every now and then you face off against a team that always sends one or two people for the Mortar as soon as the match begins. Have a couple of your teammates tie up the rest of the enemy team near the Longshot location while you race around to get the Hammer of Dawn or Boomshot. Partially descend the stairs to the Mortar on the enemy's side of the map—where they're less likely to expect you—and open fire!

Fall Back and Defend: The one-way mantles make this one of the only maps were a defensive stance affords you the opportunity to escape. Use the grenades to set up a line of defense near the statue and stairs closest to your spawn point. Then climb the stairs to where the Ink Grenades are. Stay under the roof's cover for protection from the Hammer of Dawn and Mortar, and tempt the enemy to rush you. The proximity mines alert you to their presence and knock them down. Finish them off if you can, or flee over the one-way mantle if you can't hold them off. Turn and fire as they hurdle the mantle in pursuit.

TEAM STRATEGIES

WARZONE & EXECUTION

With seven weapon drop locations, Jacinto features more than enough firepower to go around. The perfect symmetry of this mostly open-air level makes obtaining these weapons a dangerous undertaking. Both teams arrive at the party at the same time. Have teammates provide suppressing fire while you rush the exposed power weapons along the map's dividing line.

You can find a Mortar at the map's far southern end, near the helicopter. Use Smoke Grenades to cover your approach, and take cover behind the metal crates between the weapon and the helicopter. You can also use Smoke Grenades as proximity mines to protect you while you fire the Mortar. Have teammates call out enemy positions on the main level near the Longshot/Torque Bow pickup. Rain terror on them with the Mortar from below. The Mortar is also an important way to provide cover for teammates obtaining the weapon from the highly-exposed pickup there.

The Longshot/Torque Bow drop might be the hardest weapon pickup in any *Gears of War* game to date. There no nearby cover and it's positioned atop a small ramp accessible from either side. This map's long sightlines make either weapon a great asset, but you mustn't rush it without care. Use Smoke Grenades and suppressing fire from the walls nearest its location to cover a teammate attempting to grab the weapon. Consider downing one or two enemy players before making a dash for the drop. Immediately fall back to fire from the friendly side of the map.

Grabbing either the Hammer of Dawn or Boomshot requires a lengthy dash through the upper area and down to the map's northern end. The position provides some cover but puts you in a dead end if the opposition quickly closes in on you. Teammates can provide covering fire from the small, enclosed area opposite the Longshot/Torque Bow location overlooking the pickup.

SUBMISSION

This is a complex map on which to play any of the goal-based games. Attempt this only after you learn the map. The Mortar position near the helicopter is often the capture point, but you must remember to take the central approach and not the sides. Typically, you approach that area from one of the sides when you try to get to the Mortar. But that's not possible with the Stranded in tow. Don't cost yourself valuable seconds going the wrong way!

Because the Mortar location is visible from the two spawn points, consider sniping or using the Torque Bow from afar to break up an opponent's capture attempt. This can give your teammates a chance to secure the Stranded without engaging in direct combat. Continue using this elevated perch to provide covering fire for your team.

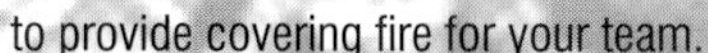

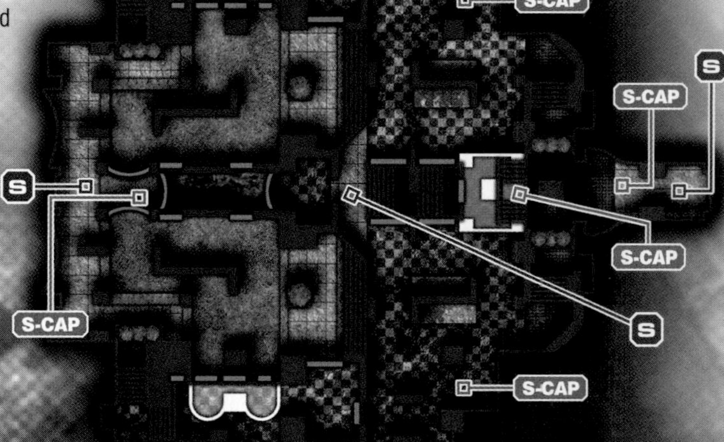

Exploit the power weapons on this map, even if they're not located at an active capture position. Don't underestimate the benefit of downing or killing multiple enemies in one shot with the Hammer of Dawn or Boomshot.

The Stranded often spawns near the capture point to which he's meant to be brought, more so than on other maps. Keep this in mind and make an early effort each round to claim him first, just in case.

WINGMAN

Playing Wingman on such a large, complex map requires a delicate approach. The central area near the Longshot/Torque Bow pickup crawls with enemies and is a hard place to survive. Avoid rushing into the main confrontation area at the start of each round. Instead, linger near the perimeter and rush in to cherry-pick kills as other combatants down one other. Once the Longshot/Torque Bow area is clear, have one teammate run in to grab the weapon. The team that spawns nearest the Hammer of Dawn pickup is in an excellent position to rack up the kills by unleashing the powerful blast on unsuspecting combatants across the map.

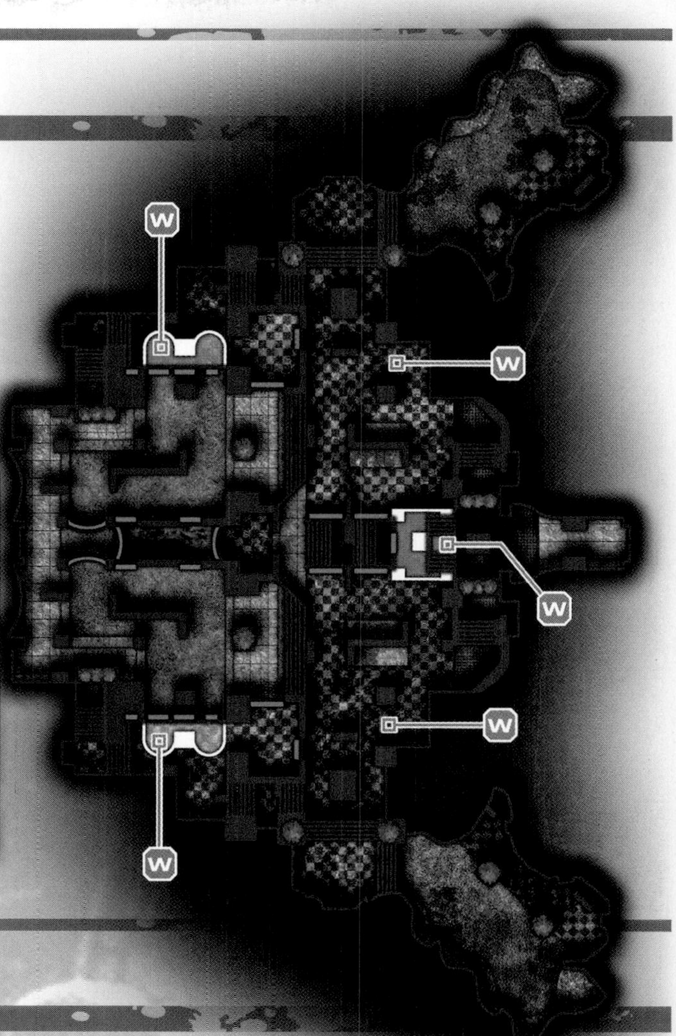

GUARDIAN

This map offers no foolproof camping areas in which to protect the Team Leader. Nevertheless, some areas are better than others. The clear favorite is the area between the grenade spawn and the Hammer of Dawn/Torque Bow drop. The grenade room offers overhead cover from Mortar fire and a steady supply of proximity grenades to plant on objects leading to your camping area. Drop back to the corner so you can see the Hammer of Dawn/Boomshot drop. Take comfort knowing that the wall between that location and yours is a one-way mantle and can be crossed only from your side. This forces enemies to approach your position from the grenade drop and funnels them through an adequate chokepoint. Cover that area with your Lancer and replenish the proximity mines as necessary. Retreat toward the Hammer of Dawn/Boomshot location if necessary.

There is a really good chance that the enemy Team Leader and his defenses are focused on the area near the Torque Bow, where you should send most of your team as a distraction. Have one or two players take the long way around the map's northern end—behind the Boomshot location, under the overhang beneath the enemy Team Leader's hiding place, and then up the stairs. This is the best way to advance on the Team Leader without getting caught up in the main firefights.

To break the preceding defense, consider rushing three of your players up to the grenade area while one teammate waits near the low wall between that area and the Hammer of Dawn/Boomshot drop. The idea is to flush out or kill the enemy leader in one fell swoop. Communication is key, as your Team Leader must be aware of his precarious position and be poised to retreat if necessary.

ANNEX & KING OF THE HILL

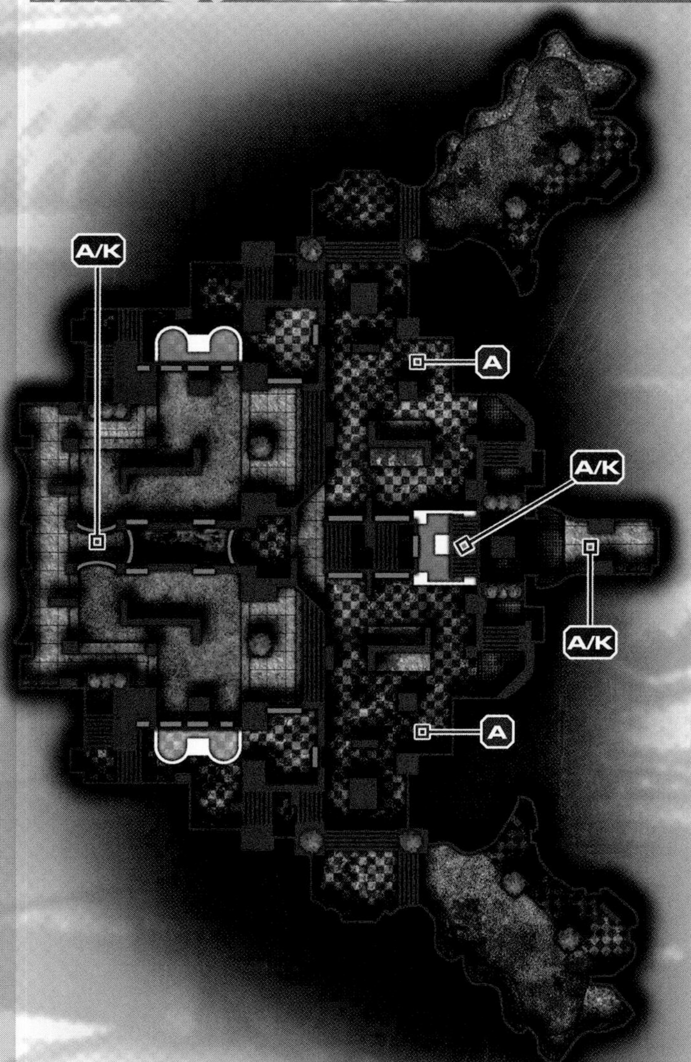

This map's large number of capture points makes it imperative that your team be familiar with the various ways to get around, specifically the stairs and one-way mantles. You can monitor several of the weapon locations from a concealed location, perhaps allowing you to clear an area of enemies before your team advances to secure the point.

For example, when you try to capture the pistol location, take control of the grenade pickup overlooking it. This is the perfect place to stand and lob grenades at would-be position-breakers. Use the re-spawning grenades as proximity mines to protect against flankers.

Make every effort to get to the Mortar capture point before the enemy. Grab the Mortar and take cover behind the low walls near the helicopter. Continually fire rounds at the shortest distance possible to canvas the capture point and its approach. This suppresses the enemy long enough to capture the point and to extend your defenses.

The Boomshot and Hammer of Dawn allow you to flank the Longshot capture point and get in attacks from visual cover. The Longshot/Torque Bow capture point is one of the most difficult to secure in the entire game. Keep throwing bodies at the enemy, and rely on the Boomshot and Mortar to weaken their grip on the capture point if they get to it first. This is an excellent time to load up on meat shields too, as there is no other cover at this capture point.

Whether you're defending or attempting to break the Boomshot/Hammer of Dawn position, grab the Longshot or Torque Bow and occupy the room between that pickup spot and the Boomshot capture point. This room provides a perfect view of the Boomshot/Hammer of Dawn spot, albeit without cover. This puts you in an excellent position to move to the next capture point in Annex matches.

HORDE

The abundance of high-powered weaponry, one-way mantles, and the map's massive size make playing Horde on Jacinto one of the most enjoyable and challenging experiences in *Gears of War 2*. There are a number of exciting strategies to employ on this map, including roving hunting parties. But we recommend sticking together and using the one-way mantle near the Ink Grenades and Hammer of Dawn to your advantage. Stay safely behind the one-way mantle to force the Horde to loop around and come up the stairs... that is, if they can make it.

Ammo: The two ammo crates are along the area's center spine, near the Torque Bow pickup and back near the Boomshot pickup.

Variables: The one-way mantles give you a very handy advantage. They force enemies to loop around and approach from a singular direction. And they allow you to escape if necessary!

By climbing the stairs near the spawn point to the room with the Ink Grenades, you can set up near the stairs and the statue to protect any teammates up top. Others can make a quick dash for the power weapons and retreat to this area to prepare for the onslaught. The upper walkway offers excellent sightlines, and the one-way mantle eliminates any risk of getting surrounded. Spreading out a bit down toward the main battle area keeps teammates from getting in each another's way. It also allows you to distract some Locust long enough for teammates to attack with the Hammer of Dawn or Longshot.

One of this spot's main benefits is that it forces the Locust to cross the main area's wide-open expanse. This prevents them from spawning behind you. Look for opportunities to dash out for the Longshot/Torque Bow and Boomshot/Hammer of Dawn. If you get the chance to claim them, quickly retreat to the safety of the stairs. Use the statues and blocks for cover. Focus your firepower on enemies nearest the hallway leading to the stairs—don't let any slip past. Your entire team should make a point of placing as many proximity mines as possible in the area leading to the stairs.

KNOW YOUR ROLE

The following tactics correspond to the numbered positions marked on the accompanying map. Follow these tips carefully for maximum survivability. These tips assume a five-person team.

1 This player's primary role is to use the Ink and Frag Grenades in the upper room to maintain a set of proximity mines on the stairs. One person can have only two active proximity mines at once, so enlist player #2 to plant extras. When you can't place more proximity mines, stand near the windows and use your standard weaponry to soften up the approaching Horde. Call out enemy locations to the others and rain down grenades on those who get close.

2 This role is not for the faint of heart! Player #2's job is to help maintain the network of proximity mines at the base of the stairs. He or she must also finish off any enemy that makes it past the front-line defense. Exploit every piece of ammo and dropped weaponry you can get your hands on, but don't venture far from your post. Use the statue at the base of the stairs for cover and lend fire support wherever necessary. Player #2 should be skilled with the Gnasher and, once it's dropped, the Boomshield and Boltok Pistol.

3 The person filling this role enjoys a relatively stress-free bit of freelancing, provided he or she sticks to the upper walkway area near player #1 and helps eliminate enemies near the Hammer of Dawn pickup. Near the end of a wave, hurdle the one-way mantle to get a fresh Hammer of Dawn or Boomshot. Then sprint back around the front and up the stairs to return to your station. This player doesn't face direct danger as much as his or her teammates. But he or she can score a lot of kills by using the high-powered weaponry from an elevated position. In case the team gets overrun, it's player #3's responsibility to flee the area to be the sole survivor that carries the team to the next round.

4 Player #4's role is similar to that of player #2. But this person works further "upstream," toward the enemy spawns. Use the cover between the statue at the base of the stairs and map's center area to place proximity mines and to distract Locust advances. This is a tricky job, so this person has to be very skilled and not too stubborn to retreat when necessary. Player #4 should keep an eye on the Hammer of Dawn pickup to cut down foes coming from that direction before they get too close.

5 Player #5 parallels player #4's role. However, this person should focus more on the Torque Bow pickup. This is where most of the action comes from, so it's important to avoid straying too far from the stairs and one-way chokepoint on which the team relies. Stay on the move, advancing and retreating as necessary, and coordinate attacks with players #4 and #2 when you can. Although it can prove too risky, try letting the final Horde unit survive long enough to retrieve the Mortar before you start the next wave.

PAVILION

Authors' Favorite Modes: Annex, Execution, and Horde.

PAVILION

The solemn quiet of the Pavilion's hallowed halls lies in stark contrast to the maelstrom about to erupt outside. The crisp autumn air filled with fluttering leaves is quickly pierced by machinegun fire and the shrill sounds of incoming mortar rockets. The wide-open spaces, lengthy sightlines, and lack of aerial cover combine to make Pavilion an area that puts the most powerful COG weapons to the test. You'll find no Torque Bows or Longshots here; this is a place where the bog boys come to wield even bigger weaponry! Mulchers and Mortars rule the battlefield. Those who fail to secure either of these mighty machines are forced to battle it out for the Boomshield located on the map's southern end.

The map is perfectly symmetrical, both in terms of geometry and weapon placement. Neither team is ever closer to a weapon or valued piece of cover than the other. Teams must coordinate a plan of attack in the first few anxious moments, as it's imperative that they either concede the Mulcher and retreat to the map's upper portion or dedicate their forces to securing the Mulcher and the sandbagged security that area brings.

WEAPON CYCLES

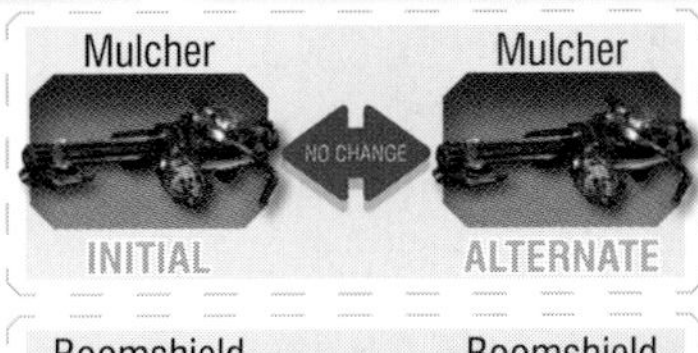

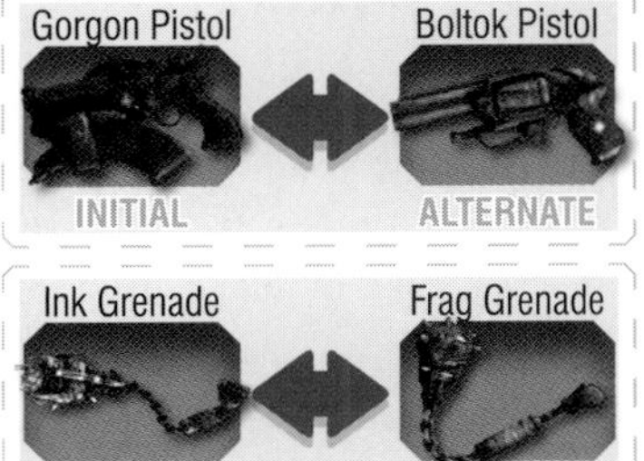

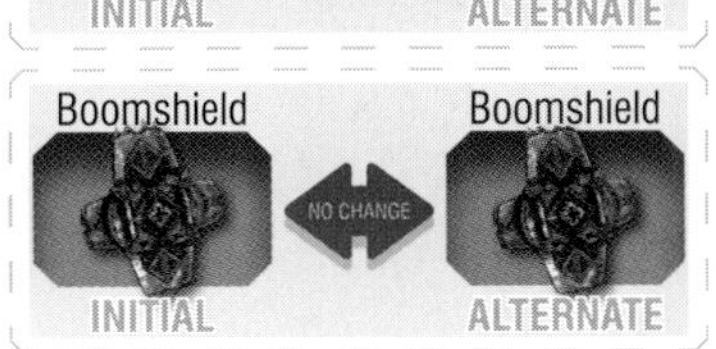

BATTLEFIELD SPECIFICS

UPPER HALL ACCESS

The doors in the upper hallways, near the two primary spawn points, remain sealed during all 5-on-5 gameplay modes. This forces players from both teams to sprint down the corridor and out into the courtyard opposite one another. However, the upper hallway doors are open in Wingman and Horde. This seemingly trivial detail carries with it critical implications. In Wingman, the open doors accommodate the additional three spawn points without crowding. However, in Horde, the open doors make forcing the Locust through a singular chokepoint impossible.

There's nowhere to hide when these massive doors are open!

MORTAR GATES

The Mortar is located inside a small, locked alcove on the map's lower portion, behind the main cupola. One can access this weapon of mass dismemberment from either side, but only one of the gates can be opened per weapon respawn. Players must rush to the gate on their side and press the button on the wall near the gate. The other side cannot be opened until the weapon respawns. Both of these gates are open at the start of the round in Submission, Annex, King of the Hill, and Horde.

Sprint to the lower area and shoot through the gate to down the enemy picking up the Mortar!

SPAWN POINT AWARENESS

The two primary spawn points are located inside lengthy hallways on the map's east and west sides. Players from both sides are funneled down their respective ramps and out opposing doors, into the crisp air of an autumn afternoon. But there is no time to hesitate. Those planning to challenge for the Mulcher, Mortar, or Boomshield must immediately identify where they are on the map and sprint in the proper direction without delay. Look to the massive doors adjacent the spawn point to quickly pinpoint your location on the map. Because some players spawn a little ahead of the doors, the shack near the grenades up ahead is another indicator of your side of the map—the shack will be on the side of the map that you occupy.

1 WEST SPAWN

The massive doors will be on the right. Sprint down the hallway and out the door on the right. Angle left to proceed to the Mulcher or Mortar, or make a hard right turn and head up the grassy slope toward the Boomshield.

2 EAST SPAWN

If the giant doors are to the left of the spawn point, then you know you are on the map's east side. Sprint down the stairs inside the hallway to the exit on the left. Then branch off to the right for the Mortar or Mulcher, or make a hard left turn to ascend the slope toward the Boomshield.

ESSENTIAL TACTICS

The Gates of Mortar: Because only one of the two gates near the Mortar can ever be opened per weapon respawn, it's in your best interest to rush to the Mortar and open the gate on your side even if you have no intention of using the Mortar. Doing so makes it impossible for opponents to reach the Mortar without first making their way clear across the map, which means passing the cupola.

Secure the Mulcher: Both teams make a mad dash for the Mulcher, located in the cupola outside the two hallway exits. Your team must either fully commit to getting this weapon or decide up front to attempt a different tack. The sandbags and nearby cover make flushing the opposition out of this stronghold very difficult. If you're playing with teams of five, send three team members on offense to repel the opposing team's rushers. Your other two can then work together to claim the Mulcher and revive each other should one get cut down.

The Boomshield Crawl: A stubborn, patient player who holes up inside the cupola with the Mulcher can be very difficult to dislodge. If you lack the numbers and the pest refuses to be drawn out from under cover, then your best bet is to make a dash for the Boomshield and slowly inch your way toward him while you use it for protection. Slam the shield into the ground to deploy it as cover. Then crouch down behind it—this offers better protection than walking with the shield. Wait for the Mulcher to overheat or wind down, and then carefully throw a grenade into the cupola. Rush the cupola with the Gnasher or Gorgon Pistol to finish off the rascal while he's down.

EPIC SAYS...

Never leave the spawn area without first grabbing the grenades near the shack. They are key to winning the initial fight for the Mulcher. Toss one at the cupola as you reach the bench to send the opposition scurrying.

WHERE WAS HE?

Plant a grenade on the wall inside the Mortar location. The Mortar is an irresistible piece of bait that will undoubtedly lure some unsuspecting sucker right to your trap.

TEAM STRATEGIES

WARZONE & EXECUTION

Warzone and Execution on Pavilion are nearly identical experiences, with Execution offering a little more opportunity for risk, as players can revive themselves and get back into the action. The map configuration is the same on both modes. Teams spawn inside the halls on either end of the symmetrical map and emerge to face the cupola containing the Mulcher. This immediately induces a battle for what is probably the map's most important strategic position. The Mulcher is a brutally punishing weapon that lives up to its name, so obtaining it should be a priority. Additionally, the physical layout surrounding the Mulcher's location is ideal for using the weapon. One can use the sandbags lining the cupola's perimeter to mount the gun and cover the exits of both halls and the alleys leading down from the map's upper portion. The cupola's ceiling offers some cover from Mortar fire, though a well placed volley from the map's lower portion can be dropped close enough to kill anyone taking cover inside the cupola. The biggest risk in using the Mulcher from this position is the possibility of getting flanked or attacked from the rear. To prevent this, one teammate can act as a spotter, staying in cover near the player wielding the Mulcher, watching his or her back and identifying targets.

Another valued weapon on this map is the Mortar. The Mortar can deal explosive death to multiple targets simultaneously on this largely open map. Obtaining the Mortar involves manipulating the gated room in which it is stored. The room is closed on both sides and can be opened only by pressing the X Button near the green light on either side. Once one gate is opened, the other remains shut for the round's duration, or until the Mortar has been expended. The metal gate can be fired through, so beware of opposing players setting an ambush when you pick up the Mortar. This is especially true in Warzone, when your opponent doesn't need to perform an execution. When you secure the Mortar, tell your teammates and give them your position so they can call out targets. You'll be able to hang back on the map's lower northern portion and provide the equivalent of aerial support.

If you're unable to obtain either the Mulcher or Mortar, turn your attention to the Boomshield and a more defensive tactic. Combine the shield with either the Gorgon or Boltok Pistol to deal damage as you withstand enemy fire with the shield. The Boomshield won't provide cover from Mortar fire, but one can use it to displace an enemy in the Mulcher location. Grab Frag or Ink Grenades and approach the Mulcher behind the shield's cover. A well-placed grenade can either kill or flush out an opponent camped out in the Mulcher cupola.

SUBMISSION

The Stranded objective begins the match at either the grassy area near the Mulcher, near the Boomshield, or at either of the two rooms containing the Gorgon Pistol. The goal locations vary amongst the weapon drops, excluding the grenade locations. If the Stranded is near the Mulcher, take control of him and fall back toward your spawn hallway to benefit from the cover of teammates. Then work your way toward the goal. Have teammates cover your retreat with the Mulcher to pin down the enemy as you slowly drag your hostage to the capture point. When the Stranded is in one of the pistol locations, use the grassy slopes that run parallel to your starting hallway to move your prisoner. Have teammates cover your rear and scout ahead to cover your advance. The Mulcher again provides great covering fire, as its location can guard most of the terrain that must be traversed in order the move the Stranded to the capture location.

Some well-placed rounds in the captor's kneecap can go a long way toward freeing the hostage from your opposition's grip, but the Mortar makes it even easier! Stand back and carpet the battlefield with the Mortar to down the Stranded and annihilate the other team. Have your comrades rush in and lay claim to the prize.

WINGMAN

There are as many viable strategies for Wingman as there are spawn points. For starters, if you're fortunate enough to spawn near the Mulcher, have one teammate pick it up and other cover the rear and flank. Use your Smoke Grenades as proximity mines to cover the cupola's rear entrance while the teammate serves as a spotter. The Mulcher will likely scatter the other couplets, so send the non-Mulching half of your team to get the Mortar. This is admittedly a risky move, but a team that can secure both the Mulcher and Mortar will be very tough to beat.

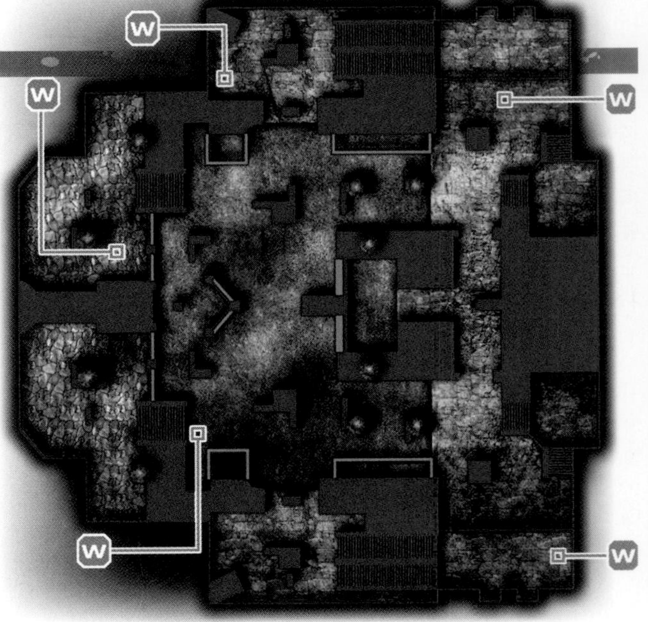

Consider making a mad dash for the Boomshield if you spawn outside the upper hallway access. Stay extremely close together and allow the shield-wielder to lead the way while the other player backpedals behind. This tactic requires a more defensive approach, but if the shield carrier downs an opponent, have the follower quickly move in for the execution. Camping in the Boomshield area provides a great chokepoint but beware of Mortar fire. Keep your ears open and your heads down!

One lucky Wingman duo spawns directly near the Mortar. Move together to obtain this powerful weapon and set up behind cover at the bottom of the stairs. Instruct the teammate without the Mortar to go to the top of the stairs to spot targets and intercept rushers. Use proximity grenades near the Mortar pickup to slow down flankers and to alert you to their presence.

Lastly, the two pistol locations provide great protection and the opportunity to camp out and pick off unsuspecting passersby. Use your standard-issue weapons to cover the two entrances and set up proximity mines on the stairs. Attack with Gnashers when enemies enter your kill zone. Use the deep interior corner and rear stairwell to set up a crossfire situation. If possible, send one member of your team to get the Boomshield to increase your available cover.

GUARDIAN

Guardian on Pavilion plays much like Warzone and Execution with the additional emphasis on protecting the team leader. As team leader, use the hallway where you spawn as your defensive position. Grab the Ink Grenades and set them up as proximity mines near the entryway. You can then take cover behind the column next to the grenades or behind the metal boxes and cover the lone entryway. Continue to pick up more grenades as the others are tripped—repeat this process.

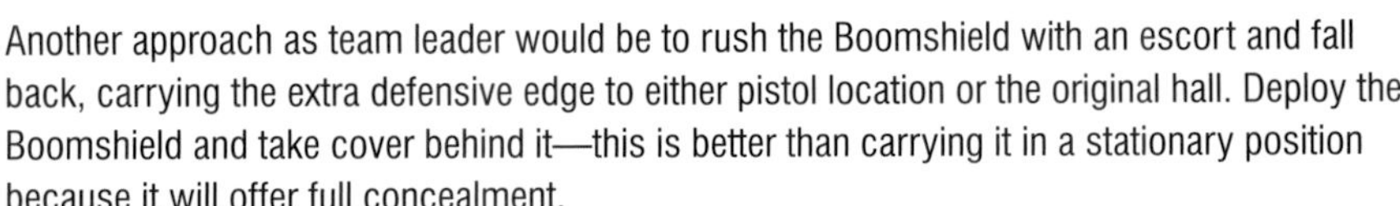

Another approach as team leader would be to rush the Boomshield with an escort and fall back, carrying the extra defensive edge to either pistol location or the original hall. Deploy the Boomshield and take cover behind it—this is better than carrying it in a stationary position because it will offer full concealment.

When you go after the opposing team's leader, focus on obtaining the Mulcher. Then use it to fire into the opponent's hallway. Have your teammates rush the entry to take out the leader, assuming he or she is in there. Teams that take care to hide their leaders often protect them near the spawn point, in the tunnel near the Boomshield, or in either of the rooms with the pistols. Exploit your Warzone skills to flush them out!

ANNEX & KING OF THE HILL

From a defensive perspective, each of this map's capture locations has its strengths and weaknesses. The two pistol locations are perhaps the easiest to defend. They have cover from Mortar fire, multiple corners inside from which to ambush enemies and take cover, and a side stairwell area in which to drop back and lure in the enemy for a close-range kill. Placing proximity grenades on the interior walls, unseen by attackers, can also wreak havoc on the opposing team.

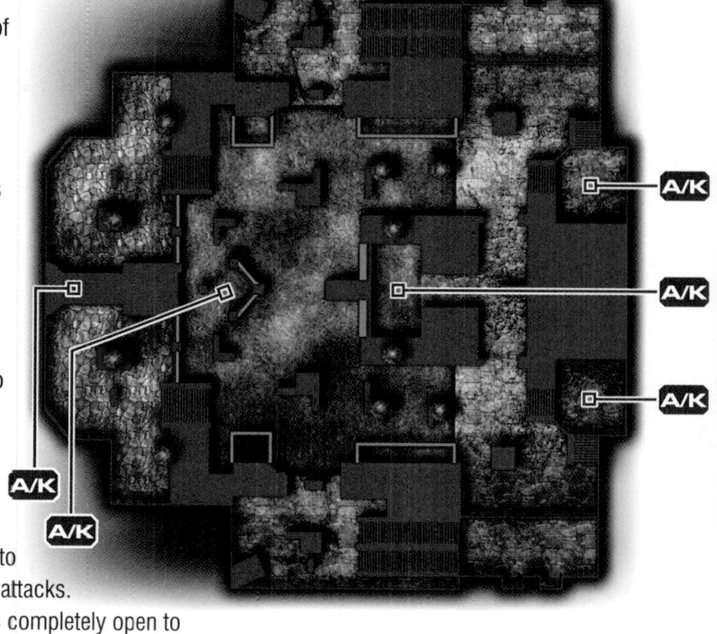

The Boomshield capture point has one way in, along with a handy shield to help fend off frontal attacks. However, the area is completely open to Mortar fire, so keep your ears open when you defend that spot. Dive into the tunnel and away from the capture point temporarily to avoid any potential splash damage. The Mulcher and Mortar capture points are both susceptible to crossfire, especially the Mortar position, which provides minimal cover. Have your team push through to cover both sides of the location before you make the capture, or you may get taken out before you gain control of the location. Instruct your team to shoot anything that moves near either staircase!

EPIC SAYS...

The Boomshield capture point can be tough to dislodge from the enemy team, especially because they can run into the tunnel to escape Mortar attacks. Surprise your enemy by lobbing an Ink or Frag Grenade up into the capture point from the main courtyard below. You're all but guaranteed to catch them by surprise, especially if you have one or two teammates keeping them busy from the other side.

One tactic that works particularly well on this map in Annex matches is to set up defensive positions between capture points to gain an advantage in capturing subsequent locations. Watch the point timer tick down and prepare for the next location. One way to do this, especially while holding one of the pistol capture locations, is to grab the Boomshield and set up a roadblock between the two pistol rooms. This positions you near three of the potential capture points and enables you to run interference on any enemies trying to cut through that area.

The stairwells leading down to the Mortar capture point provide ambush points and cover on either side at the bottom. Implanting a stronghold in this spot also has the advantage of putting you in a position to quickly transition to the Mulcher should the next capture point move to that area.

Utilizing these transitional areas is not as crucial in King of the Hill because the capture point remains stationary throughout the entire round. Leave one team member to stay inside the capture point and spread out to cover enemy advances and obtain weapons. Setting up a Mulcher on one of the approaches to a pistol location creates an almost impenetrable defense. Focus on branching out incrementally to slow the enemy advance. When you defend the Boomshield location, have two players cover both sides of the alley near the tunnel. The other two should set up opposite those locations, near the closed hallway doors, to cover the grassy slopes heading up to that area.

The Mulcher and Mortar locations are open to attacks from multiple directions, but they provide some rather potent firepower to help offset this drawback. Use the Mulcher generously from in its position to keep the enemy at bay. Use the cover at the base of both stairwells to defend the Mortar position against attacks from above. Try to keep Frag or Ink Grenades handy—equip the grenade so you can detonate it after getting picked off if you're the last man standing and the enemy is closing in.

HORDE

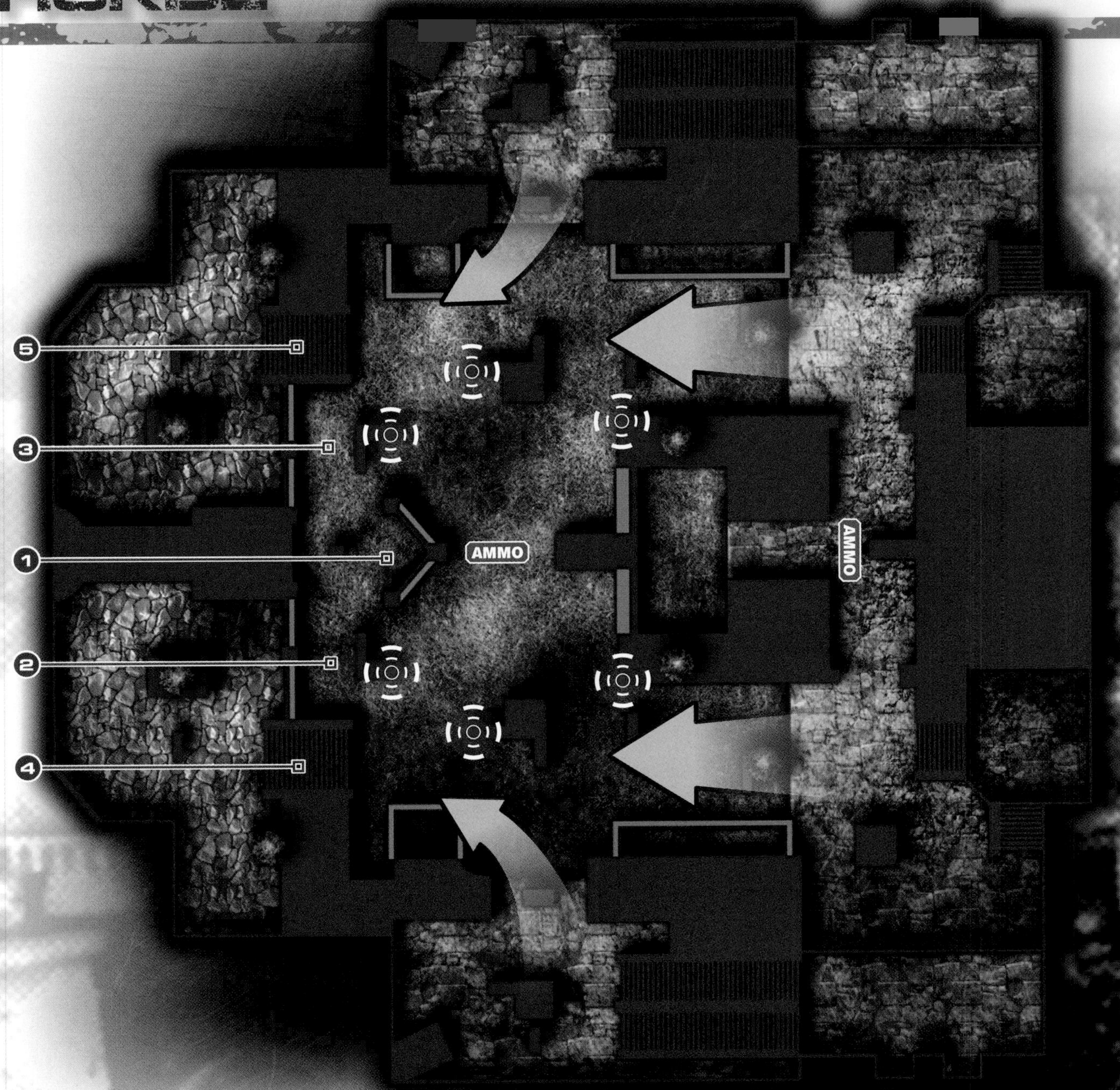

AMMO

AMMO

1

2

3

4

5

This is one of our favorite maps for playing Horde because it allows you to set up a perfect military alignment, forcing the Locust to attack from few locations. Locust primarily originate from the hallway exits (both upper and lower), from near the Mortar, and also by the two pistol locations. Positioning the entire team on either end of the map forces them to attack from afar. However, using the area by the Mulcher gives your team the most powerful weaponry and it offers the best sightlines. Just keep in mind that this plan requires a full team. Those playing with three or fewer players should take up position near the Boomshield instead.

Ammo: There are two ammo crates on the map, one near the Boomshield and the other in front of the cupola.

Variables: The upper doors leaving from the hallway are open in this mode. Similarly, both of the gates near the Mortar are also open.

Many of the enemies make their way out of the hallways or down the grassy slope and take cover behind the planter and by the park bench. Some even mantle over this cover in a dead sprint, attempting to rush your location. Planting grenades on this bit of unused cover to serve as proximity mines catches more than a few unsuspecting Locust off guard.

Those members of the Horde that don't use the planters or benches will likely try to get in between the sandbags and wall, attempting to slip out of the Mulcher's range. Keep an eye out for enemies slipping into this blind spot and eliminate them as soon as possible. Having to relinquish the Mulcher in order to drop an enemy behind the cupola allows the other foes to advance rapidly, making ultimate survival that much more difficult.

KNOW YOUR ROLE

The following tactics correspond to the numbered positions marked on the accompanying map. Follow these tips carefully for maximum survivability. These tips assume a five-person team.

1 The point man playing Horde on Pavilion secures the Mulcher within the cupola. Everything else must revolve around keeping this person safe. The sandbags provide the perfect platform to steady the massive weapon. Swiveling the weapon makes it possible to cut down enemies exiting either hallway, as well as those coming down the grass slopes. This position is vulnerable to attacks from behind. Remain stationary inside the cupola and do not exit this position unless absolutely necessary.

2 The second player should take a position to the point man's flank, behind the row of sandbags to the west. This player's role is to use the Lancer or Hammerburst to cut down enemies exiting from the hallway doors. He or she also serves as the last line of defense against enemies that make it up the stairs from below. Dash into the hallway between rounds to collect grenades. Use them as proximity mines on the planter and park benches in front of the hallway exits. Be sure to grab the ammo crate as well. Limited strafing is necessary to get better angles on enemies, to lend support to the other players, and to revive fallen comrades.

3 The third player's role is similar to that of the second, but it covers the map's eastern side. Take cover behind the sandbags to the point man's left. Use the Lancer to help eliminate enemies making their way down the grassy slope on the east. Call out enemy locations to serve as a spotter for the Mulcher operator, and place grenades on the planter and park bench during the brief intermissions. Limited strafing is necessary to get better angles on enemies, to lend support to the other players, and to revive fallen comrades.

4 A fourth player creates a decided advantage by bringing the Mortar into play. It also eliminates the chance of Locust Horde spawning on at least one side of the lower northern patio. Stay near the stairs in the northwest corner and assist the second player with enemies that advance too closely. Use the Mortar to fire from the base of the stairs in the direction that player #2 specifies. This player should also help revive any players on the upper courtyard so the others can focus on fighting.

5 Having a fifth player in the map's lower northeastern corner all but eliminates the chance of ever having an enemy spawn near the Mortar. Advance and retreat from the stairs to the Mortar location to assist where necessary, whether you use standard-issue machineguns or the Mortar. This player should also be responsible for reviving players #1 and #3.

RIVER

Authors' Favorite Modes: Execution, Submission, and King of the Hill.

RIVER

The tranquil river running through this alpine village will run red with the blood of many as you fight it out on this narrow, symmetrical map. A lone bridge spans the river in the map's center, serving as a border between the enemy factions. A Boomshot below the bridge and a Mortar on top tempt foes into converging on this area, and close-range combat often results. Meanwhile, a two-story cabin on each side of the river provides an unrivaled sniper's perch. Will the snipers cancel each other out or will one reign supreme?

River is a lengthy, but compact map that lends itself to several different play styles. Those who prefer close-range combat will get their fill, but the multiple long-range weapons and extensive sight lines allow others to hang back and pick off enemies from afar. Both sides of the map are mirror images of one another, and they contain the same weapons pickups. The only way to reach the other side is by taking a chance in crossing the bridge or by splashing through the river below it. River is one of the game's most scenic maps. However, the many hiding places, the likelihood of sniper fire, and the jumbled piles of wreckage make this a scary map to traverse without backup.

WEAPON CYCLES

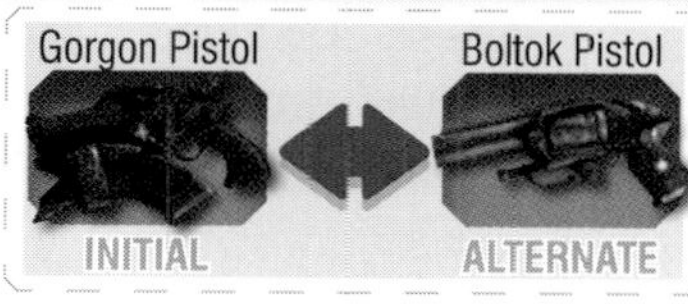

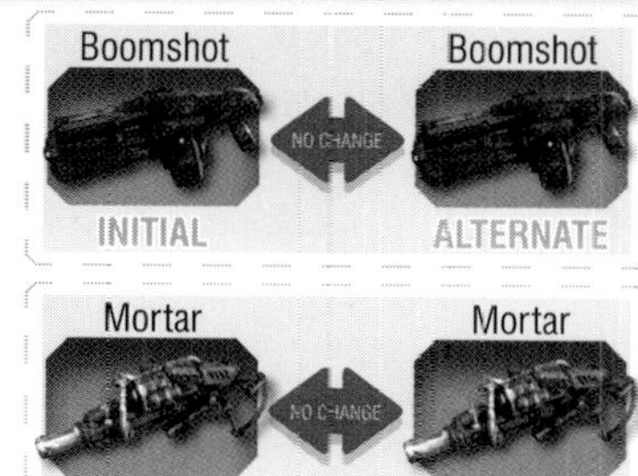

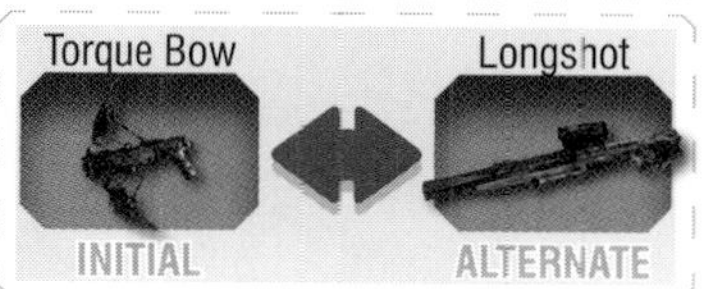

BATTLEFIELD SPECIFICS

EXPLODING VEHICLES

A number of bombed-out vehicles are scattered on the bridge and a pair of COG trucks near each of the barns. You can detonate these vehicles, possibly to create a convenient diversion or to startle (or lure) enemies out of cover. To explode these abandoned wrecks, simply fire at their engine blocks. Note that the vans at the ends of the bridge do not explode.

The vehicles don't pop on the first bullet or two, so bear this in mind when you're trying to time the explosion.

SPAWN POINT AWARENESS

This perfectly symmetrical map plays the same from both sides. The weapon pickups are identical and in the exact same locations respective to the spawn points. One of the few differences you may or may not notice is the direction the water flows. And that has no bearing on gameplay.

1 UPSTREAM SPAWN

The map's western edge contains the upstream spawn point. Those wondering which side they're on can quickly tell by the leafless tree straight ahead. Also, the river is close by on the left.

2 DOWNSTREAM SPAWN

The river takes a jog away from the downstream spawn point on the map's eastern edge. Other than the river not being immediately visible to the player's left, the tall, flowering trees are a useful clue as to which side of the map you occupy. But again, the map plays the same from both sides, and knowing whether you're upstream or downstream has no impact on what you need to do.

ESSENTIAL TACTICS

Sniper Duel: The fastest and best sniper on your team should immediately race to the barn, run up the steps to the second floor, and claim the Longshot or Torque Bow. Know that someone on the other team is likely doing the exact same thing, so shoulder the weapon, train your sights on the barn across the river, and open fire. Eliminating the other team's sniper the second he or she gets the weapon makes it safer for your team to secure the Mortar or to simply rush the other team's side of the river and lay waste to them.

Long-Range Killer: The barn's elevated perch is hard to beat in terms of sniper positions, but everyone will expect you to be there. Another idea is to take the Longshot and retreat back through the river in the direction of your spawn point. Hide alongside the riverbank, way off in the distance, as far from the bridge as possible. From there, pick off any enemies that enter the river. You can shoot them before they even know you're there.

Hang Back and Wait: Gather up the grenades in the cabin on the right and advance toward the bridge. Plant proximity mines on each of the vehicles and inside the barn. Enter the barn's ground level. The barn's roof protects you from Mortar blasts and the enemies will be forced to chase after your team. When the grenade blasts knock them off their feet, you'll have time to counter.

WHERE WAS HE?

At the start of most matches, you can count on a foe rushing to grab the Longshot or Torque Bow in the barn on the enemy side of the river. Show him the error of his predictable ways by running into the river and quickly lobbing a Smoke Grenade up into the barn where the weapon pickup is.

TEAM STRATEGIES

WARZONE & EXECUTION

Each round is likely to start with an initial dash to the barn in the distance. This brings you to the Longshot/Torque Bow drop, located on the structure's second floor. There is an identical location on the opposite side of the map, so be wary of the opposing team grabbing the same weapon at roughly the same moment and opening fire on you. This corner perch and the window near it provide an excellent sniping spot. To cover your flank, use proximity mines on the pillars near the stairs that lead to the second floor.

Each round, the central bridge that connects the map's two sides contains a Mortar. The Mortar is within equal reach of both teams, thus making this weapon drop a highly contested location. Smoke Grenades, suppression fire and superior numbers all come in handy when you try to capture this weapon. Should you get the Mortar, fire one shot immediately into the opposite barn to scare off a possible sniper there. Then fall back to your side of the map before you fire any shells. The Mortar can be very useful for flushing out or killing enemies on the barn's upper floor, where the roof is mostly open.

EPIC SAYS...

If you notice the enemy team rushing toward the Boomshot, you just might be able to take their sniper spot and attack their blind side. Hurry across the bridge and up into their barn to take the Longshot/Torque Bow. Open fire on them as they presumably come out of the river on your side of the map. Put one or two partners in your team's sniper position and take them in a crossfire!

The Mortar isn't the only explosive weapon on the map. Each round, the Boomshot is in the river, directly beneath the bridge. The bridge supports provide cover from which one can fire and hide. This drop's somewhat isolated location can often lead to one-on-one standoffs, not unlike the rush for the Torque Bow on the Canals map. Wait for your enemy to make the first move and down him in the water before you finish him off and claim the Boomshot as a prize. Move up the ramp on your enemies' side of the river and flank them. At this point in the round, most of the enemy team is often in or near the barns and not expecting someone to advance from the area of the spawn.

SUBMISSION

One can initially find the Stranded on or below the central bridge, as well as near either of the two barns. The capture points are the two pistol locations. Because the spawn and capture locations are sometimes very close to one another, you have to be aggressive in claiming the Stranded at the start of the match for a quick win. Doing so can also help avoid a speedy loss.

There are several options for moving the Stranded from one side of the map to the other. You can go over the central bridge or under it, through the river. Going through the river can be a longer trip, but it can be an easier path if the enemy has the bridge covered. Have a teammate scout ahead to obtain the Boomshot and clear the way.

Grab the Mortar and move to the side of the map opposite your team's capture point. Fire a continuous volley at the area surrounding the capture point as your team moves in. Your fire will keep the enemy suppressed and score some kills as they attempt to block your impending score. One can use the Longshot and Torque Bow in a similar fashion, but the Mortar's blanketing fire is preferable in a game mode that requires brute force and persistence.

WINGMAN

As with other maps, your team's spawn point location can give you an advantage right off the bat if you know how to exploit your good fortune. When you spawn near one of the barns, quickly acquire the Longshot or Torque Bow. Begin firing on the enemy teams spread across the map. Move quickly to secure the upper barn vantage point, as most players are still out in the open and present easy targets.

Each round, one team spawns in the river near the Boomshot. When your team spawns there, quickly acquire the weapon and move together up to one side of the river. Take cover behind the low wall opposite the ramp out of the river. Acquire the grenades if they're available. From here, you should have no problem blasting distant enemies and picking off downed opponents. Try to coordinate your attacks. Have the teammate with the grenades lob them at a group of foes to down them, and then finish them off with the Boomshot.

Resist the urge to go for the Mortar when you play Wingman. You're way too susceptible to fire from teams in the two barns. Remember that there are four enemy teams, not just one, so both barns are likely hostile territory! Instead, try to hang back and cherry-pick enemies engaged in other fights.

GUARDIAN

The small cabin near the spawn point presents one potential camping spot for the Team Leader. The steady supply of grenades helps to fortify the position. However, with two entrances, the location is not ideal. At least one teammate should hang back with the leader for extra protection. Be prepared to run for the barn at a second's notice.

The barn provides a more defensible position than the cabin, but teams should alternate between the two positions to keep the enemy guessing. Grab the Frag or Ink Grenades on your way there. If a teammate has already taken them, grab the Smoke Grenade that he or she dropped. Set proximity mines on either side of the barn's sole entrance and watch over the entry from the sandbag cover on the first floor. The Longshot/Torque Bow upstairs can bolster your team's offense, but be very cautious, as a sniper is likely waiting to line you up from the opposing barn.

Rush three players through the river for the Boomshot. When you're attempting to assassinate the other Team Leader, continue straight to the enemy's side of the map. Try the barn first, as this is the most likely place for the Team Leader to camp. Then move to the cabin, checking behind the two vehicles where the pistols spawn.

ANNEX & KING OF THE HILL

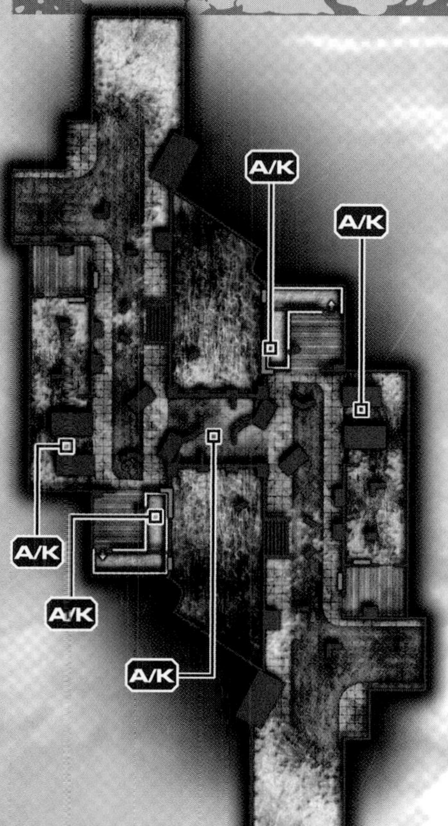

The weapon locations are capture points for Annex matches, and the Longshot/Torque Bow is an ideal position from which to cover or attack the other locations with long-range attacks. This also positions you to quickly capture one of the hardest locations to break. Swap out the Gnasher for the power weapon, and keep your Lancer (or Hammerburst) to supplement your upgraded weapon.

When you hold the Boomshot location in King of the Hill matches, have one teammate stay in the circle to maintain scoring. Have all other teammates take cover behind the bridge's support columns. The player in the middle should keep moving back and forth, keeping the bridge's legs between him and incoming fire.

The pistol locations can be hard to break thanks to the cover provided by the two trucks surrounding them. Use Mortar fire to blanket the location while teammates rush in to capture the point. When you defend the pistol locations, use the Grenades in the nearby cabins to place plenty of proximity mines around the point.

The highly visible Mortar location can be difficult to defend in King of the Hill matches. Use the sandbags as cover when you're in the circle, and have your teammates fall back to the end of the bridge to provide suppressing fire. The Longshot/Torque Bow drop is an ideal position from which to snipe. Try taking both to defend from both directions. Use proximity mines to cover your rear while you provide cover for your teammate out on the bridge scoring the points.

RIVER

River is a difficult map on which to play Horde, thanks to the power weapons and superior elevation in the area's center. These factors make it very hard to isolate the Horde spawn points, mandating that you defend two lines of approach. Fortunately, there is so much offensive firepower and so much cover that it's not as bad as it could be. In other words, the barn gives you a chance.

Ammo: The two ammo crates are on the bridge, one near the barn on the east side and one on the west side. It's a little risky to go after the crate on the bridge's opposite side, but it's not impossible.

Variables: Beware the explosive vehicles parked outside the barn, as they can explode from enemy fire just as easily as from your team's guns.

The two-story barn is an excellent source of cover. Use it as your team's home base when you play Horde. Its location and construction provide adequate cover and plenty of good sightlines. And you can use it to lure enemies through a chokepoint in a last-ditch effort. Hopefully, you won't have to let Horde members get this close, but placing proximity mines on the doorway just might save your team in a tough fight.

Using the barn as a home base allows two members to snipe from the upper level: one from the balcony and another out the front door. Meanwhile, the other three can bring the fight to the Horde on the street outside. Having a pair of teammates provide covering fire allows the others to gather up dropped enemies, the Mortar, and even the Boomshot. The team members outside the barn should return to the area near the vehicles and sandbags as soon as possible. Avoid splitting up unless you're making a quick run for a weapon or ammo.

KNOW YOUR ROLE

The following tactics correspond to the numbered positions marked on the accompanying map. Follow these tips carefully for maximum survivability. These tips assume a five-person team.

1 The best sniper on your team should take the second-floor walkway inside the barn. This person should use the cover from the wall to the right of the pickup. Focus on eliminating Horde units in the opposing barn, those crossing the bridge and any Locust in the river. It's a tough job, but it carries little risk of getting eliminated, provided this player stays behind cover. Alternate weapon pickups with player #2, who also uses the Torque Bow and Longshot in this location.

2 Player #2 watches player #1's back and hangs out on the middle landing inside the barn to snipe enemies outside. When necessary, this player also takes down enemies out on the bridge. Take turns collecting the weapon pickup with player #1 and lend support from inside the barn whenever possible. Climb to the upper level to snipe with player #1 or to lend support to the ground by sniping distant foes marching down the street. This person is a bit of a freelancer, but he or she shouldn't leave the barn.

3 The team member most skilled at using the Mortar should take this role. It's important for this player to maintain a pair of proximity mines near the barn entrance. He or she should be able to fight at close range. This person also has to get the Mortar and quickly retreat without getting downed. Take the Mortar back to the sandbags in front of the barn and open fire wherever the other players say the enemies are congregated. The Horde often come from your spawn point and across the bridge. Get a feel for the distances required to hit certain spots, and wait for the Horde to get within your preferred targeting range.

4 Player #4 should take the crucial position between the ramp leading up from the river and the bridge. The enemies come from down the street, across the bridge, and up from the river. It's up to player #4 (with help from player #5) to cut them down before they get too close. If the others do their jobs well, there shouldn't be too many units coming from across the street. But it's difficult to track the Horde as they go under the bridge. Try planting a proximity mine on the wall near the path that leads into the water. Make occasional forays down into the water to collect dropped weapons and, more importantly, the Boomshot. Just be careful not to fire it at enemies near COG units.

5 The wall running between the parked vehicles and the small cabin serves as a great piece of cover for the freelancing player #5. This team member's primary job is to soften enemies for the others and lend fire support when possible. But this person must also make frequent trips into the cabin to replenish his or her grenade stash. It's up to player #5 to replace detonated proximity mines outside the barn.

RUINS

Authors' Favorite Modes: Annex, Warzone, and Wingman.

*The COG units take the fight to the Locust's home as they clash in the confusing arena known as Ruins. This map offers a significant change of pace from the maps to which **Gears of War** fans are accustomed. The Ruins map has several narrow corridors, a complex multi-level design, and an architectural style that can make navigation tricky. Ruins is an old-school deathmatch-style map the likes of which hasn't been seen in **Gears of War** before!*

This is not the place for solo exploration. Teams should split into groups of two and three or even stick together as a larger unit to avoid being outnumbered during the surprise face-to-face encounters that are so common here. Several valuable long-range weapons occupy this map. You'll also find the precious Boomshield, which is possibly more valuable on this map than any other. Follow the lower path from the starting point to get the Boomshield while the other teams go for the Scorcher or Torque Bow. A team controlling the Boomshield can march as a unit and pick off enemies that struggle to flank the shield's massive presence in this tight area.

WEAPON CYCLES

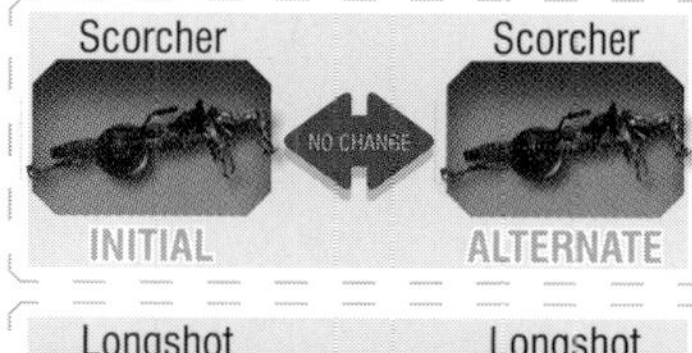

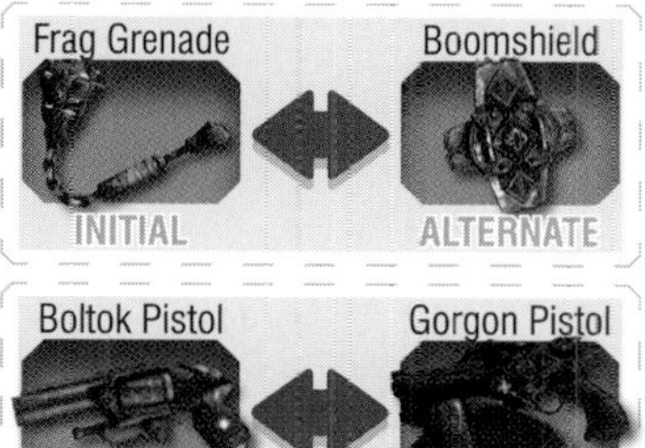

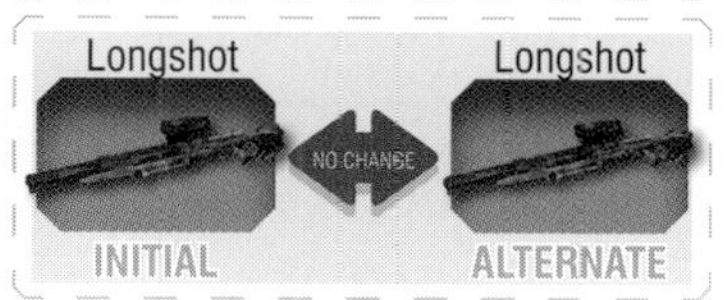

BATTLEFIELD SPECIFICS

RISING COVER

At first glance, this map's central area doesn't have much in the way of cover. But as players draw close to the edge, motion-sensing walls rise from the floor to provide cover. These rising walls feature pink lights, making them visible as you approach. Players can anticipate the walls rising up and slip into cover against them, even when they're still down—they rise up in time for the player's character to slam against them. Once they're triggered, the walls stay up for the remainder of the round. They retract into the floor before the subsequent round begins.

You can SWAT Turn from one rising wall to the next, even if the wall isn't extended yet.

IMULSION PLUNGE

Those who have ever worried about being knocked off a platform will have to overcome their fears if they hope to secure the Scorcher on this map. The central bridge over the Imulsion pool and the platforms on the sides near the Sniper Rifle and Torque Bow are places on this map where a Smoke Grenade blast can indeed knock a player off the platform. Falling off the bridge into the Imulsion causes instant death. Now, before you swear off ever going for the Scorcher, keep in mind that four walls rise up to provide some cover. Furthermore, you can get knocked off the bridge only if you're near the edge.

Watch out for Smoke Grenades near the Scorcher—the blast can knock you off the bridge into the Imulsion below.

SPAWN POINT AWARENESS

Never was there a map with such complete symmetry as Ruins. The only difference between the two halves on the entire map is that one side has the Torque Bow and the other has the Longshot. Unfortunately, the level's architecture provides no obvious indication of which side of the map you're on when you spawn. One extremely subtle clue can tell you which side you're on: the glimmer of moonlight on the wall's gold trim. Regardless which side you spawn on, your three options are the same: You can run up the stairs on the left and go for the Scorcher on the bridge, you can descend the lower steps just beyond the bridge to go for the Frag Grenades or Boomshield, or you can go straight ahead toward the pistol or around the corner for the long-range weapon on your side. There's no way to tell which weapon (Torque Bow or Longshot) is on your side, but since they alternate between rounds it doesn't really matter.

1 SOUTH SPAWN

The spawn on the map's southern side looks exactly like the one on the northern side except that the moonlight reflects off the spawn room's right side. This is your tell, albeit a subtle one, that your team spawned nearer the Torque Bow.

2 NORTH SPAWN

The northern spawn point is identical to the southern one except that it lacks the moon's shimmering glow on the gold embossing. Those who appear in this slightly darker corner of the map will know that they are closer to the Longshot than the other team.

ESSENTIAL TACTICS

Form a Patrol Party: Stick together, grab the Boomshield and/or Frag Grenades, and go hunting for the enemies. Most teams can't stick together no matter how hard they try. A group of five teammates circling the lower ring and gradually making their way up to the main level will no doubt encounter isolated opponents and quickly tilt the balance in their favor. Just watch out for Frag Grenades!

Cross-Map Dash: Most people will run up to the bridge only to get the Scorcher, even if they plan on crossing over to the other side. However, the pickup alert notifies everyone to their presence. Split up your team and have two members cross the bridge *without* picking up the Scorcher to avoid alerting the enemy to their presence. This allows them to attack their adversaries from behind while your other teammates distract them up front. As powerful as the Scorcher is, sometimes it's best to leave it alone and therefore keep your location secret.

WHERE WAS HE?

Have your Smoke Grenade ready and rush toward the Scorcher pickup on the bridge above the Imulsion. Take cover behind the pop-up wall and gently toss the Smoke Grenade at an enemy unit appraoching from the other side—someone almost always goes for the Scorcher. A Smoke Grenade on this narrow doesn't just knock down your target; it can actually knock a player straight into the Imulsion!

Hold the Bridge: There is just enough pop-up cover on the bridge that hosts Scorcher for a team to use the elevated spot to pick off enemies. Rush the bridge with three members of your team and have the other two secure the Longshot/Torque Bow before they rejoin the party atop the bridge. Spread out so that everyone is behind cover and away from the bridge's edge. Use the superior elevation to rip the enemy team apart as they circle the area in plain view.

TEAM STRATEGIES

WARZONE & EXECUTION

This map's highlight is the Scorcher atop the level's highest accessible platform. Race up the steps from the spawn area and take cover behind the walls that pop up before you reach the flamethrower. The weapon is the same distance from both teams, so don't rush in blindly to claim it. Advance toward the Scorcher only when the immediate area is secure or you know no enemies have come for it. Continue across the bridge to flank the enemy.

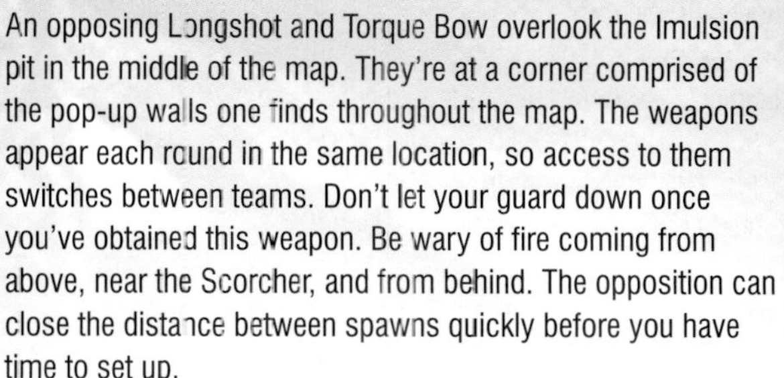

An opposing Longshot and Torque Bow overlook the Imulsion pit in the middle of the map. They're at a corner comprised of the pop-up walls one finds throughout the map. The weapons appear each round in the same location, so access to them switches between teams. Don't let your guard down once you've obtained this weapon. Be wary of fire coming from above, near the Scorcher, and from behind. The opposition can close the distance between spawns quickly before you have time to set up.

A Boomshield paired with either the Boltok or Gorgon Pistol is a valuable combo on this arena-style map. The disorienting corridors lead to many close encounters; the Boomshield's defensive edge paired with the pistol's increased stopping power proves invaluable. This is especially true when you consider that the Boomshield can absorb all direct fire from the Scorcher!

SUBMISSION

The Stranded sometimes spawns on the platform with the Scorcher and sometimes in the small alcoves opposite the Longshot and Torque Bow drops. The capture points are the three power weapon spawns. The capture points are sometimes next to the Stranded's spawn location. You can't afford to go running off in search of better weaponry—head to the Stranded's location immediately!

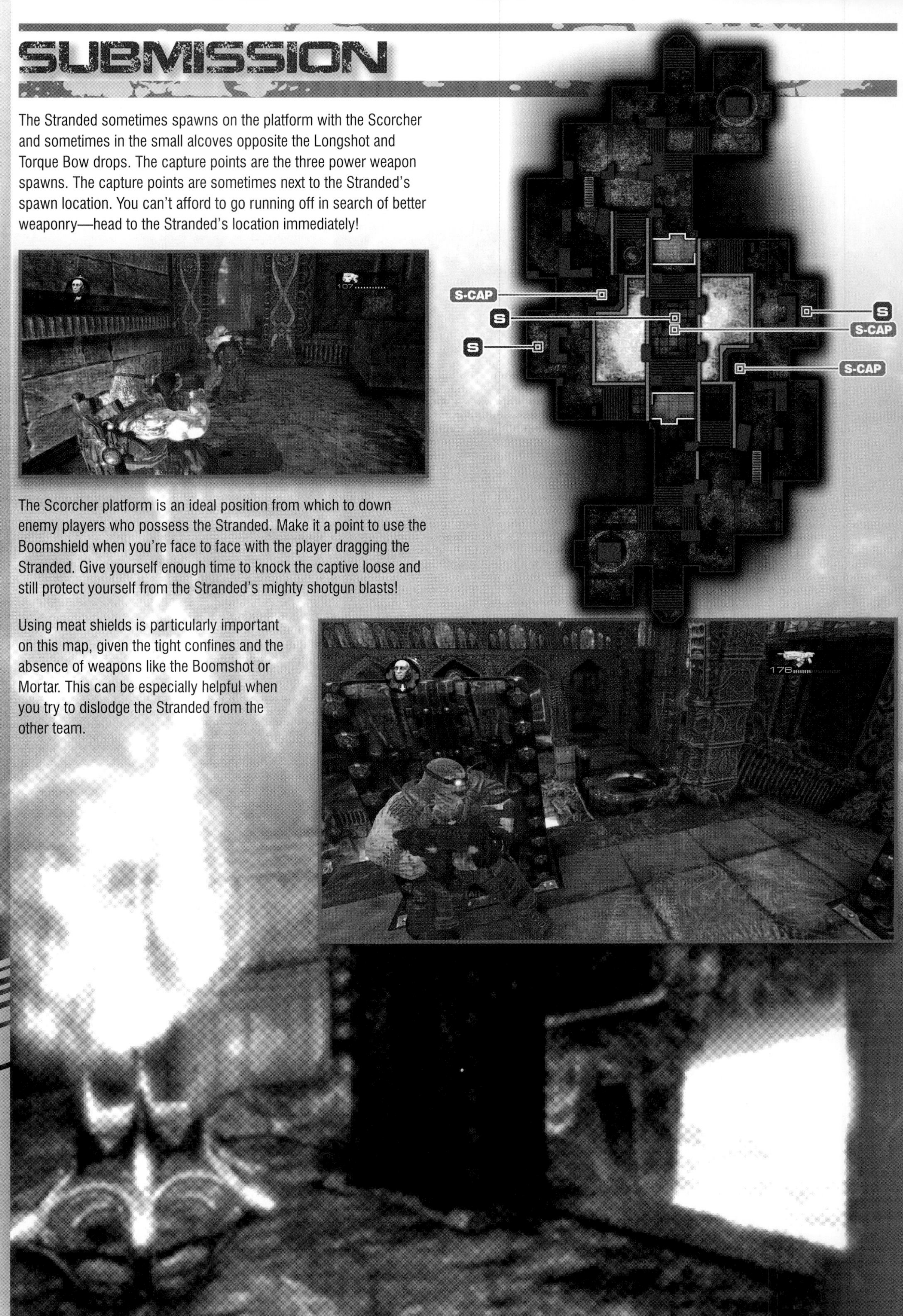

The Scorcher platform is an ideal position from which to down enemy players who possess the Stranded. Make it a point to use the Boomshield when you're face to face with the player dragging the Stranded. Give yourself enough time to knock the captive loose and still protect yourself from the Stranded's mighty shotgun blasts!

Using meat shields is particularly important on this map, given the tight confines and the absence of weapons like the Boomshot or Mortar. This can be especially helpful when you try to dislodge the Stranded from the other team.

WINGMAN

Each round, one lucky team begins near the Boomshield pickup. When it's your team's turn, have one teammate use its cover to down enemies while another teammate waits in tow, ready to run in for the execution. Pair the Boomshield with a pistol upgrade, which is available around the corner from both the Longshot and Torque Bow.

When you spawn near the Longshot or Torque Bow, take the weapon and move to the Scorcher platform to gain a commanding view over the map's central area. One teammate can defend against opponents rushing up the stairs while the one with the long-range weapon picks off distracted enemies elsewhere on the map.

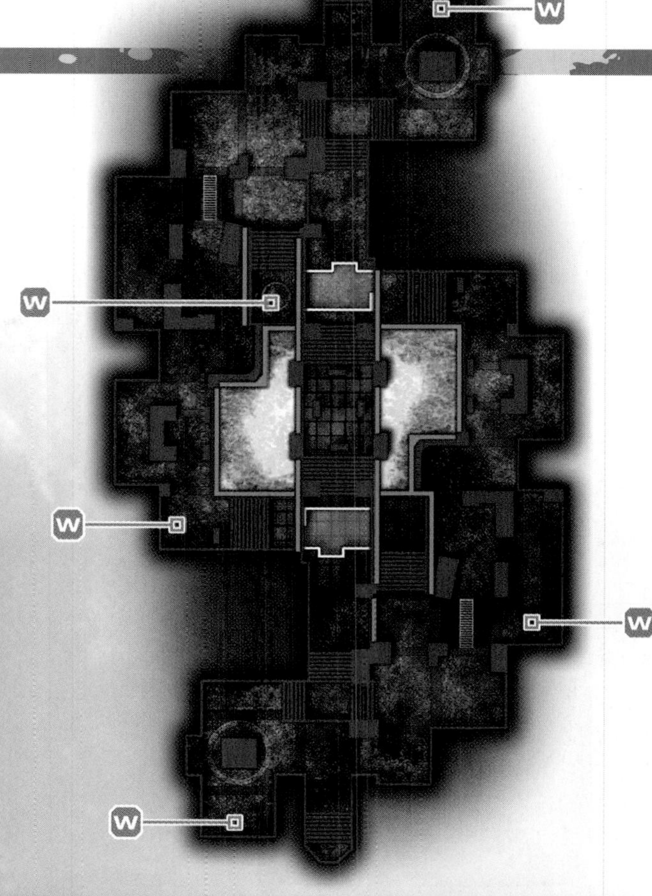

EPIC SAYS...

The team that spawns near the Frag Grenades can anticipate an enemy team rushing toward the nearby Torque Bow. Quickly grab a Frag Grenade and bounce it off the wall at the top of the steps so it ricochets straight toward the Torque Bow. You won't necessarily knock anyone into the Imulsion, but you just might down a pair of enemies. Rush up and finish them off, if they're still alive.

The disorienting corridors throughout this map can make players lose their bearings and run aimlessly in circles. To pad your kill total, exploit players' navigational difficulties by planting proximity mines on the most heavily trafficked intersections. Place them on the ends of walls coming up from the downstairs and by the Scorcher bridge to catch enemies by surprise.

GUARDIAN

If the leader stays in the spawn area, enemies will spawn on top of him and take him out. At least two teammates should protect this person at all times. You might even decide to roam the map as a group of three. The quickness with which the two teams can converge and the absolute lack of chokepoints make defending your Team Leader very difficult. Have someone collect the Boomshield and pass it to the Team Leader. Collect the Frag Grenades for use as proximity mines. This is one map where the best defense is a good offense. Keep the Team Leader as safe as possible by rushing the opposing team and taking out their Team Leader as quickly as possible.

ANNEX & KING OF THE HILL

The three capture locations on Ruins are the Scorcher, Longshot and Torque Bow weapon pickups. The Scorcher location has a clear view of both of the other capture points. Consider leaving one team member in that spot to lay down covering fire and harass the opposition when they attempt to capture either of the other points.

Remember to always take the lower path when you run between capture points. This offers some cover and allows you to grab the Frag Grenades or Boomshield, both of which come in hancy on this map. The Frag Grenades can be invaluable for clearing out the enclosed Longshot and Torque Bow capture areas. The Boomshield can help hold a position, particularly against Scorcher fire.

HORDE

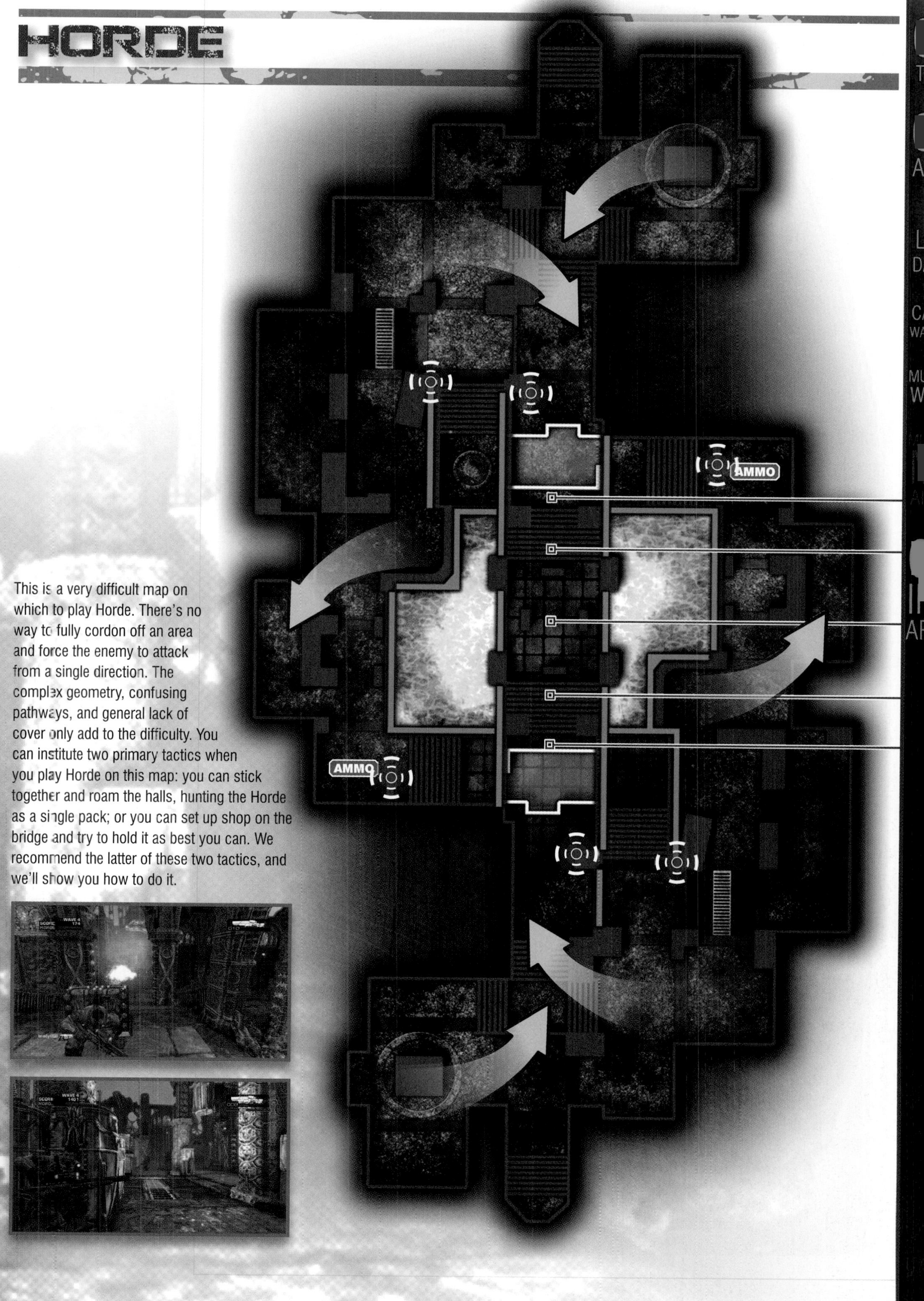

This is a very difficult map on which to play Horde. There's no way to fully cordon off an area and force the enemy to attack from a single direction. The complex geometry, confusing pathways, and general lack of cover only add to the difficulty. You can institute two primary tactics when you play Horde on this map: you can stick together and roam the halls, hunting the Horde as a single pack; or you can set up shop on the bridge and try to hold it as best you can. We recommend the latter of these two tactics, and we'll show you how to do it.

Ammo: There are two ammo crates on this map, between the main team spawn points and where the Torque Bow and Longshot are located.

Variables: The pop-up cover stays up permanently once it's triggered, so it won't be an issue. Guard against the possibility of getting knocked off the bridge into the Imulsion. Watch for incoming grenades and Boomshot blasts!

The team should split up across the bridge, taking cover behind the pop-up walls and using the sides of the stairs for extra protection. Enemy fire comes from all directions, but the Horde can get up close from only two sides. Split your team to have two on each side of the bridge and a fifth player up top, serving as a spotter. The Locust fire at those on the bridge from the perimeter, so you must shoot fast and stay in cover, particularly when the Theron Guards start to appear! This is a very difficult map for Horde mode, but it can be very rewarding as well. Just be sure to target Kantuses as soon as they emerge, else their Ink Grenades will render the bridge useless and force the team to split up and run.

KNOW YOUR ROLE

The following tactics correspond to the numbered positions marked on the accompanying map. Follow these tips carefully for maximum survivability. These tips assume a five-person team.

1 The first player to the bridge should proceed to the top, take the Scorcher, and lend support where needed. This person primarily serves as the spotter, calling out enemies where he sees them and alternating between the Scorcher and Lancer to lend a hand where it's appropriate. Use the bridge's height to soften up distant foes, enabling the others to kill them that much faster.

2 **3** These players should stick close to the stairs, but make an occasional run for the Longshot and Torque Bow. When you seek long-range kills with these power weapons, take a position atop the steps on either side of the bridge. When you're out of ammo, descend the stairs and lend the front-line defenses some extra firepower. These players should avoid crossing the bridge to avoid accidentally leaving one side unprotected. This also limits any confusion atop the bridge with player #1.

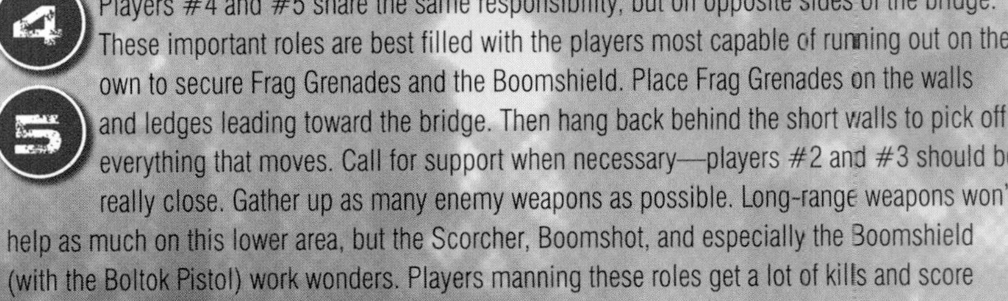

4 **5** Players #4 and #5 share the same responsibility, but on opposite sides of the bridge. These important roles are best filled with the players most capable of running out on their own to secure Frag Grenades and the Boomshield. Place Frag Grenades on the walls and ledges leading toward the bridge. Then hang back behind the short walls to pick off everything that moves. Call for support when necessary—players #2 and #3 should be really close. Gather up as many enemy weapons as possible. Long-range weapons won't help as much on this lower area, but the Scorcher, Boomshot, and especially the Boomshield (with the Boltok Pistol) work wonders. Players manning these roles get a lot of kills and score plenty of points, but the risk of getting overrun is high.

SECURITY

Authors' Favorite Modes: Execution, Annex, and Horde.

SECURITY

Few maps force players to get as up close to one another as this map does. Set in a prison block, Security has little more than a short interior hallway, an open courtyard, and a raised platform sealed off with a laser-based security system. As teams exit their respective spawn points, they are immediately within each other's firing range. Some players run into the bunker for cover or to deactivate the security system. There's little opportunity to plot an attack route or set up a defense on this map. No, teams have to react quickly and come out swinging or risk elimination.

Security is a symmetrical map. Both teams have an equal chance at securing the Mortar, the Scorcher, and the Gorgon Pistol located along the map's center line. The security fences limit access to the Mortar and Scorcher, but a coordinated rush to the deactivation button and the weapons can net either of them fairly quickly. Some players may hang back and wait for the other team to deactivate the fences. The interior corridor near the Scorcher is the only spot on the map completely safe from Mortar fire, so watch where you run.

WEAPON CYCLES

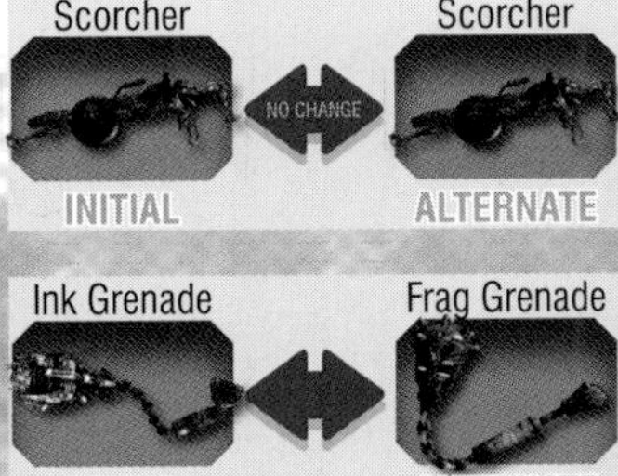

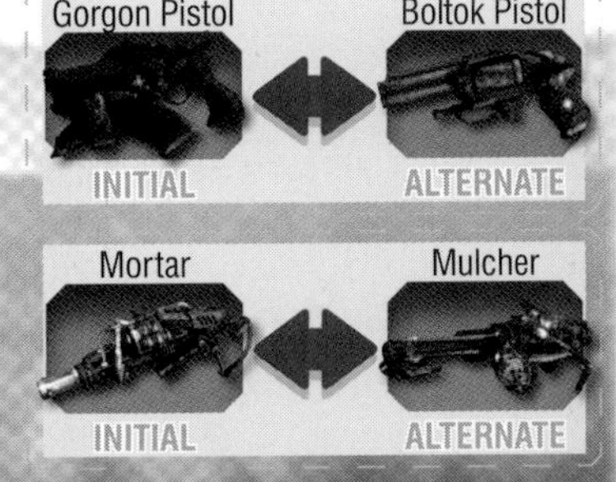

BATTLEFIELD SPECIFICS

LASER FENCES

Regardless of the game mode, all the action on this map revolves in one way or another around the laser security fences. Don't take these fences lightly—they eviscerate anything that touches them. Players should keep a healthy distance. The map contains two control buttons that deactivate the security fences for thirty seconds. One button is on the terrace overlooking the main street. The other is inside the large, cordoned-off area up the stairs, near the sandbag fort with the Mortar. Press the button on the terrace to disable the lasers and make a run for the Mortar or the Scorcher (located inside). A warning that the lasers are about to reactivate sounds five seconds before the lasers come back online, so consider your movements carefully.

Be extra careful near the pink neon glow of the security lasers!

SPAWN POINT AWARENESS

Security is a perfectly symmetrical map with all of the weapon pickups equal distance from both teams at the start of the round. Both teams have the same chance of securing an upgraded weapon or lowering the laser fences. There are even arrows near the spawn points directing players which way to go.

1 WEST SPAWN

Those starting at the western spawn point will know which way to go thanks to the arrows pointing to the right on the shack outside the spawn point. Make a U-turn to the right to climb the stairs toward the security control button and the Scorcher, or stay on the street to fight it out in the center.

2 EAST SPAWN

The eastern spawn looks virtually identical to the western one, but the arrows on the nearby shed point to the left. If the arrows aren't enough of a clue for you, the shed's roof on this side of the map is open toward the spawn point. If you can see the trees sprouting from the open roof, then you know you're on the eastern side of the map.

ESSENTIAL TACTICS

Poison the Mortar: There's a pretty good chance that the opposition will make a dash to get the Mortar. Quickly run to the Ink Grenade on your side of the map, and take cover in the alley leading toward the Mortar. Wait one or two seconds after the security fence is deactivated, and lob an Ink Grenade at the sandbags protecting the Mortar. If you time it right, you'll trap the enemy in the toxic cloud just as he or she picks up the Mortar. Open fire to finish off your hapless victim and then claim the Mortar for yourself once the cloud disperses.

Put the Map on Lockdown: Send your entire team toward the deactivation button and secure the corridor and terrace area. This gives you a commanding view of the whole courtyard. This strategy also makes it impossible for the enemy to get the Scorcher or Mortar. They'll have no choice but to throw their entire force at you from within the bunker. Plant a few proximity mines in the corridor and pick them off as they funnel toward you through the narrow passage.

WHERE WAS HE?

This is a risky move, but pulling it off yields some funny results! If you find yourself alone against one or two enemies, try to deactivate the security fence and hide in the small alcove with the Scorcher. Don't pick it up. Instead, just hide there in anticipation of an unsuspecting enemy wandering into the range of your Gnasher.

Grenade Traps: You can create a lot of commotion by planting your Frag and Ink Grenades near the Mortar and Scorcher pickups and then retreating to a hiding spot. You may even want to further entice foes into taking the bait by deactivating the security system for them. Wait for an enemy to trigger the grenade, then pop out and finish him off!

TEAM STRATEGIES

WARZONE & EXECUTION

Security is a compact map defined by the laser security fences that regulate access to certain areas. There are two distinct regions accessible only by disarming the security system. Players deactivate the system by using two green buttons, but only one of them is accessible at the start of the match. Run out into the street and quickly turn back into the bunker on the inside. Follow the path to the small terrace, where you'll find the security button. Once the system is deactivated, it stays offline for thirty seconds before it rearms, at which time it can be turned off again. The map's two power weapons are located behind the security system's protective laser beams, so coordinated movements to manipulate the system are key. The Scorcher is in the interior portion, between the two spawn points. A Mortar/Mulcher pickup is in the large area on the map's southern end.

Once the security system is disabled, the Scorcher is the quicker weapon to obtain. However, exercise caution, as both it and the Mortar/Mulcher drop are equidistant from the two spawn points. The button to disarm the security system is around the corner from the Scorcher, on the terrace overlooking the map's central portion. Note that this is the only button that's accessible when the round begins. There's another one near the Mortar/Mulcher, but it can be used only after someone accesses that area. When you have the Scorcher, stick to the map's interior portion, between the two spawn points. Exploit the cover provided by the two alcoves around the corner from the Scorcher's location. Ambushing the enemy up close neutralizes the Scorcher's range deficit relative to the assault rifles.

Controlling the area around the Mortar/Mulcher is essential. No other weapon on the map matches the Mortar's long-range, destructive power. The laser gates often serve as a barricade to opponents who would otherwise rush the position. This lets the player wielding the Mortar concentrate on making accurate shots without fear of getting flanked. One option is to send all teammates to the Mortar/Mulcher drop and concede the Scorcher to the other team. For a more balanced approach, send two teammates to turn off the security system and obtain the Scorcher while the other three team members control the Mortar/Mulcher area.

SUBMISSION

Playing Submission on Security is a messy affair. The Stranded spawns at two locations in the street, either near the Boltok/Gorgon Pistol pickup or on the terrace next to the deactivation button overlooking the street. All weapon locations are potential capture points and the security gates are active. As you can imagine, this complicates matters. Some teammates must deactivate the security gates while others transport the Stranded. Taking opponents as meat shields is vital if you hope to stay alive long enough to help your teammates bring the Stranded where he needs to go.

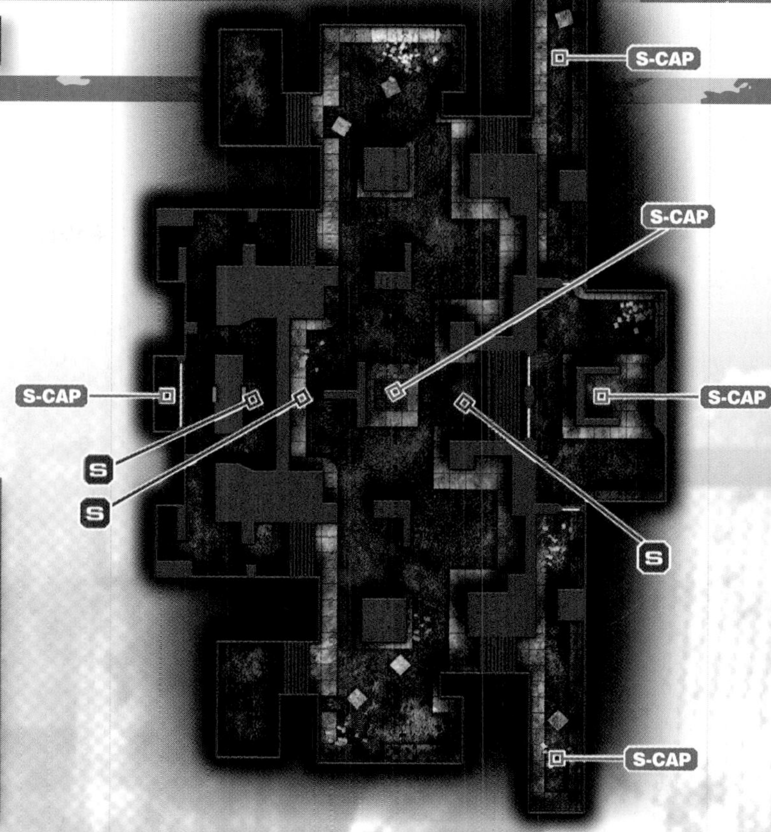

The Scorcher capture point presents specific difficulties. When you're defending or trying to drag the Stranded to the Scorcher location, your best bet is to have someone race ahead, acquire the weapon, and stay in cover near the deactivation button. Prepare to power down the defense system as your team draws near for a score. Or use the Scorcher to defend the button from the other team when they attempt to score.

WINGMAN

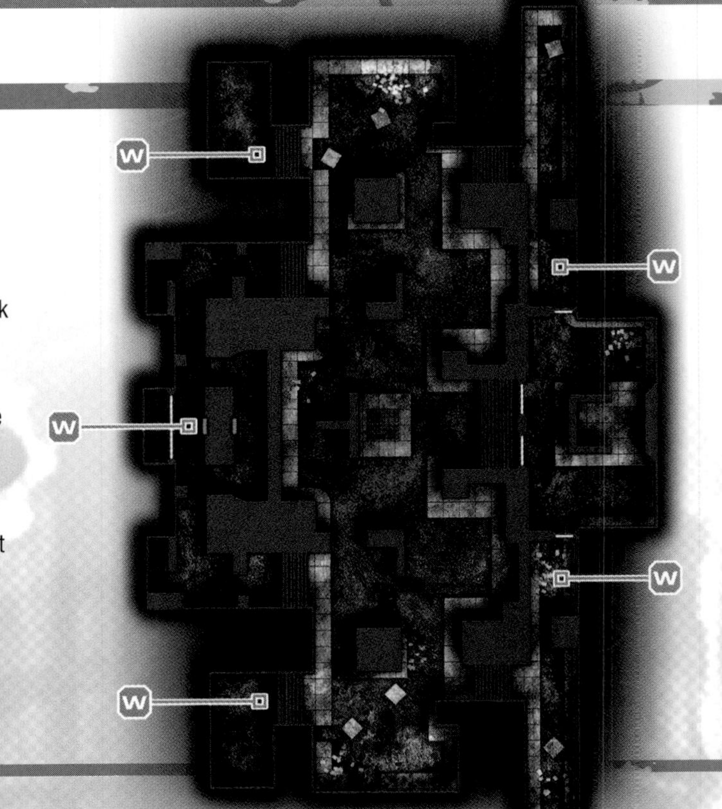

When you spawn near the Scorcher, quickly acquire the weapon and move together to down opponents. The teammate without the Scorcher should take an enemy as a meat shield and lead the way around the map looking for victims. Replace the meat shield with newly-downed opponents, and combine this protection with either the Boltok or Gorgon pistol for added firepower.

The Mortar/Mulcher combo can deliver kills in bunches but it hampers your mobility. If you use it, one teammate can fire Mortar shots around the street area while the other covers him from opponents rushing in under the barrage. Once you use up your Mortar shots, grab the Frag/Ink Grenades at the end of the nearby alley. Hurl them into skirmishes throughout the map. Both of these tactics rely on exploiting distracted foes and are less successful when there are only a few remaining enemies.

GUARDIAN

The alleys where the Frag and Ink Grenades are located can serve as chokepoints in which to set up a defense for your Team Leader. Use the Frag Grenades as proximity mines on the stairwell's two sides leading up to the alley that contains the grenades. Use the Ink Grenades near the stairs, and pair it with your discarded Smoke Grenade to knock down and poison charging enemies. Listen for incoming Mortar fire and watch for foes moving in with the Mulcher from that weapon's drop area.

Controlling the Mortar/Mulcher area can be very effective for protecting the Team Leader and constantly harassing the enemy team. Covering three entryways is less than ideal, but the laser gates will likely be active part of the time. This allows a few players to control access to the area. Have the Team Leader fire Mortar or Mulcher rounds while two teammates cover the entrances. The other two teammates can go on assault missions to kill the enemy leader. Controlling this position ensures that all team members can operate without fear of Mortar fire.

ANNEX & KING OF THE HILL

The laser gates maintain their functionality during Annex matches. When the Scorcher location is the capture point and you control it, fall back to cover the deactivation button. Keeping the enemy from pushing the button also prevents them from capturing that location. With this in mind, move out to the next capture point earlier than usual, knowing that it will take your opponents longer to capture that spot if they even try.

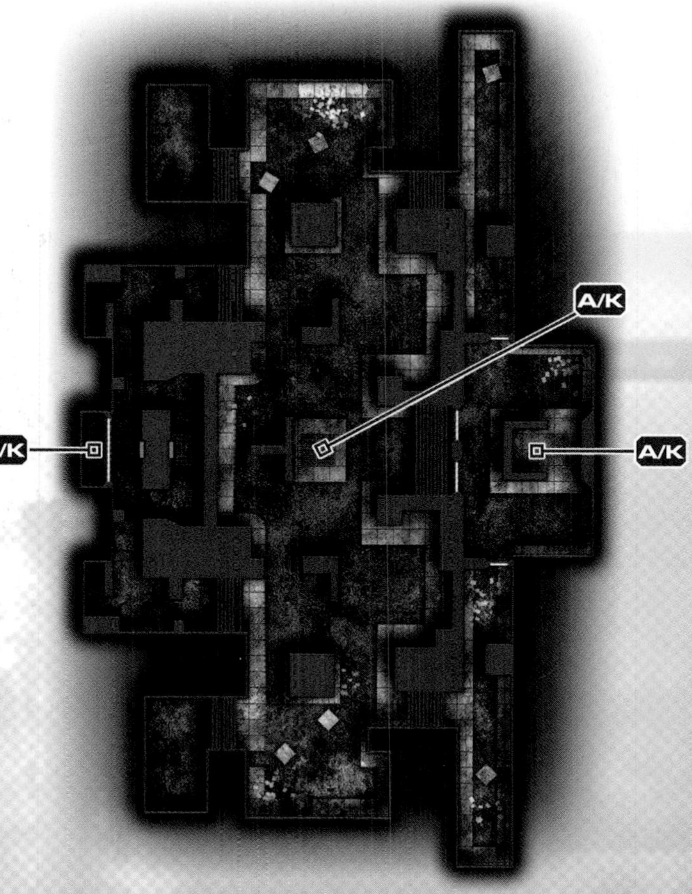

When the pistol location is the capture point in King of the Hill, divide your forces to fully use the resources that the map provides. Have one teammate rush the deactivation button to allow another teammate to quickly acquire the Mortar. The other three team members can then focus on capturing the point. Leave one team member in the circle to earn points while the other two hang back in support, ready to revive or take his place in the capture area. The teammate who deactivates the laser gates is in an ideal position to provide covering fire from the terrace overlooking the street.

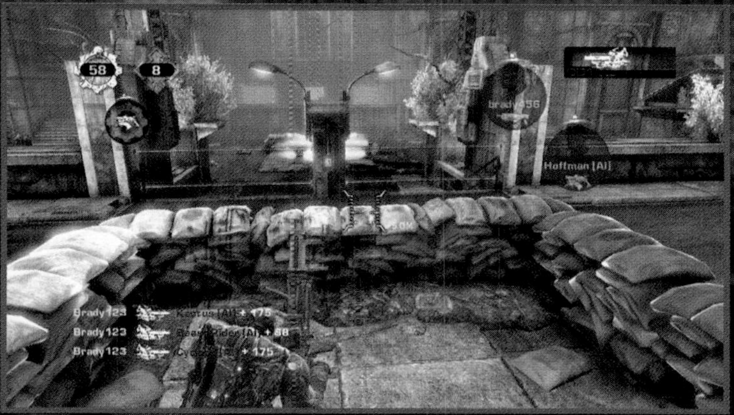

HORDE

As was the case with Ruins, playing Horde on a map of this size can be challenging. But in our opinion, this is one of the best maps for it thanks to the complexity that the security fences provide. They help keep the bad guys out, but they can also trap you in if you're not careful! Taking a defensive position inside the fenced-off area near the Mortar/Mulcher spawn gives you an excellent vantage point. It's a relatively easy place to defend, provided you have four teammates. But don't expect to spend the entire match here. The Kantuses will do everything they can to poison the entire area with Ink Grenades. You may have to split up frequently and regroup elsewhere on the map.

Ammo: The two ammo crates are located in the central courtyard, not far from the Gorgon Pistol location. They aren't very difficult to get, no matter where your team camps out.

Variables: Don't take unnecessary risks with the security fences. They stay down for only 30 seconds, and you should avoid lowering them in the middle of a wave. Instead, lower them at the end of a wave to collect ammo and dropped weapons. Train the Mulcher on the terrace's deactivation button to hopefully keep the enemy from lowering the fences.

A five-player team can be very successful by quickly deactivating the security fence and running to the sandbags where the Mortar is. Make sure someone grabs the Scorcher en route. The Mortar and Mulcher give your team an excellent advantage. The sweeping view of the courtyard and narrow approaches from the side alleys allow you to corral enemies into predictable locations. The security fences give you plenty of protection for most of each wave, but you must remember to avoid getting too close to them.

The Kantuses often try to hang back and poison the entire inner area with Ink Grenades. They must be your priority targets. Nevertheless, should they swamp the area with Ink Grenades, just drop the big weapon, hit the button to lower the fence, and run together to the bunker. Hold off the enemies inside the inner corridor. Remember to plant proximity mines as you go. Wait for the action to calm down before you return to the area with the Mortar. Make sure your team sticks together as you relocate to the other spot, else you run the risk of getting picked off one at a time.

KNOW YOUR ROLE

The following tactics correspond to the numbered positions marked on the accompanying map. Follow these tips carefully for maximum survivability. These tips assume a five-person team.

1 The player most skilled with the Mortar and Mulcher should rush to grab whichever one appears and put it to immediate use. Stay behind the sandbags and use the Mortar to canvas the courtyard whenever Locust groups are on the move. Use the Mulcher to rip apart enemies on the distant terrace, preventing them from deactivating the security fence. Theron Guards and other Locust equipped with long-range weapons often set up outside the bunker. Use the Mulcher to cut them down.

2 **3** Players #2 and #3 are primarily responsible for covering the side alleys, one per side. They must make occasional forays outside the fence to pick up and plant Frag Grenades on the walls leading down the alley. It's best to do this after the start of a wave to avoid getting cleaned up with the rest of the dropped weapons. These players must also stay behind adequate cover, perhaps even behind the sandbags if necessary, to avoid getting shot. The Locust don't focus entirely on the alleys, but they approach from this side often enough to warrant dedicated team members. Use whatever weapons you have to keep them from getting too close to the fence. They can't walk through the fence, but you have to hold them back to limit the number of teammates they can target.

4 This player must strike a balance between lending additional front-end support without getting in player #1's way when he's using the Mulcher. Take cover at the top of the stairs, inside the security zone. Help pick off enemies that get too close to hit with Mortar fire, or those outside the Mulcher's firing angle. Take every opportunity to secure higher-powered weapons dropped by the Locust. The Scorcher comes in handy, but the Torque Bow and Boomshot are even more useful from this position. Player #4 must also use whatever grenades he or she can acquire to maintain a pair of proximity mines at the base of the steps.

5 The area inside the security zone can get claustrophobic with five people running around. It's best to have player #5 hang back at the area's rear and simply lend support where it's needed. Listen and watch closely to see where most of the Locust come from, and lend additional firepower where it's needed. Avoid picking up high-powered weapons because the other players have a greater need for them. Instead, this player should make his primary goal to revive fallen teammates and to simply lend occasional fire support. Serve as a spotter, shoot the Locust, and keep your teammates alive. This player doesn't score the most points, but he or she fills a vital role nonetheless.

STASIS

Authors' Favorite Modes: Execution, Submission, and Horde.

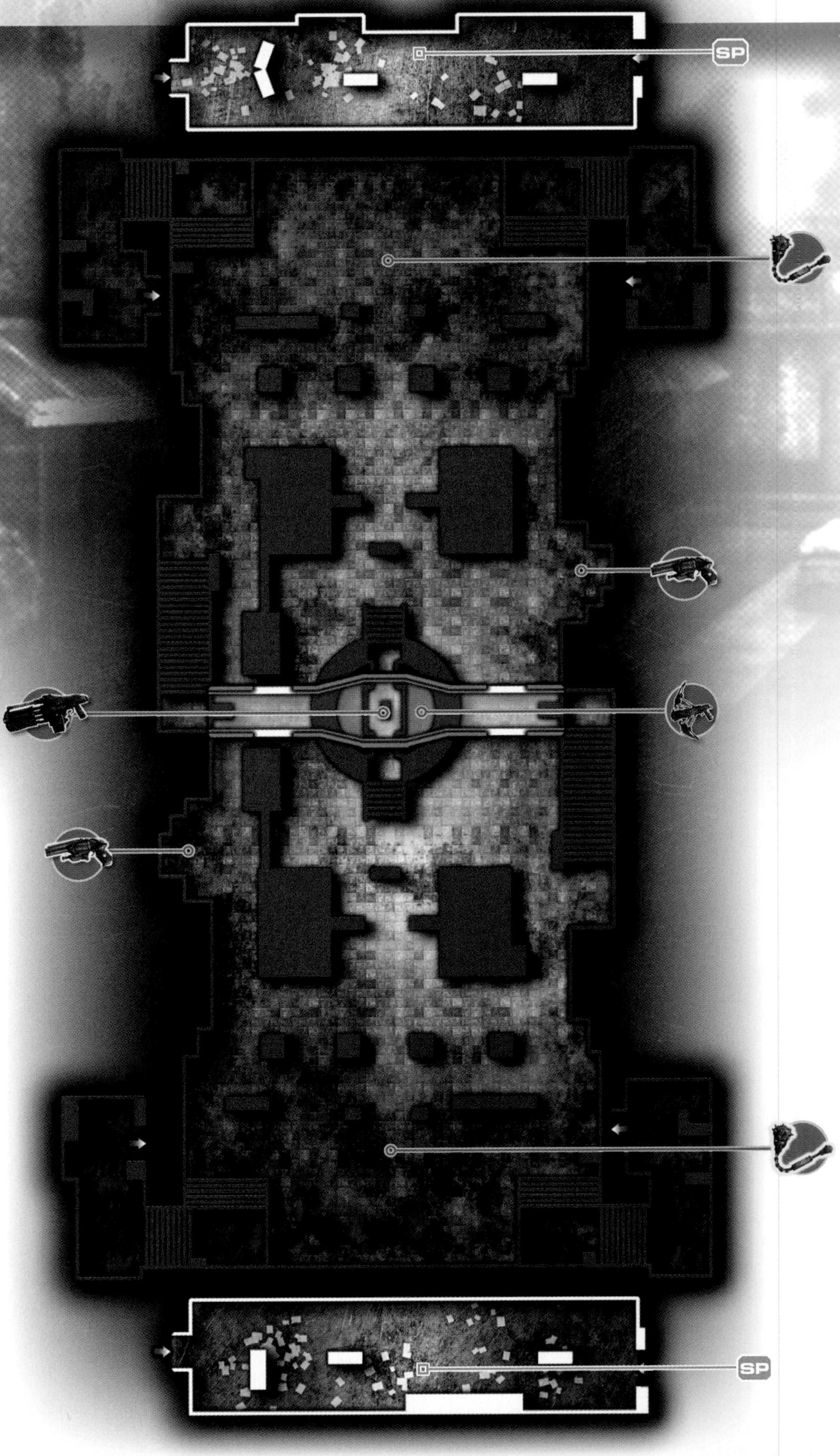

SP

SP

An empty warehouse, a catwalk, and row after row of stasis tanks stands between you and the opposition. One team begins in an elevated office, the other on the rainy street outside. Both teams have equal access to a number of high-powered weapons, but they must navigate the pipes, walls, and columns in order to reach them. Fences offer small pieces of cover, and the grated catwalk surface is equally porous. Adding further intrigue to the question of what is and what isn't bulletproof, the glass windows near both spawn points are destructible.

Much of the action on this map takes place down on the warehouse floor, amongst the pipes and stasis tanks. But that doesn't mean those who prefer to go high can't participate. Players who hang out near the spawn points or who dash for the catwalk in the warehouse's center can target enemies throughout much of the level. The symmetrical map looks quite different depending on the spawn point where you begin. However, the shapes of the areas and distances to the weapon pickups are all the same. Also, the stairs up to the catwalk are on the right side of the map, no matter which spawn point you use. Descend the stairs on the left (as viewed with your back toward the windows) and then head straight up the stairs on the right to reach the catwalk. Once you're there, take cover quickly! Otherwise you'll be a sitting duck.

WEAPON CYCLES

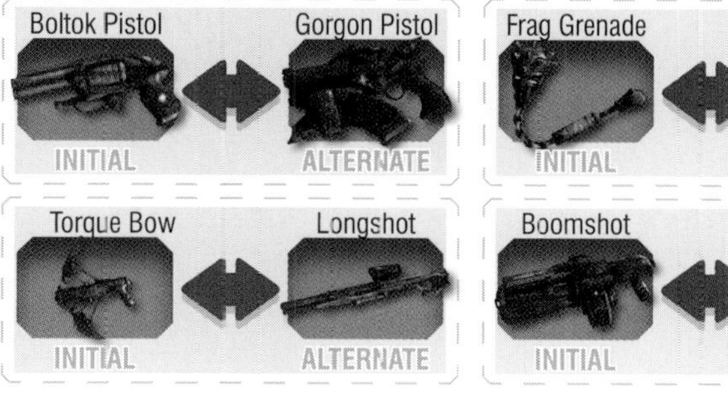

Initial	Alternate
Boltok Pistol	Gorgon Pistol
Frag Grenade	Ink Grenade
Torque Bow	Longshot
Boomshot	Mulcher

BATTLEFIELD SPECIFICS

BREAKABLE WINDOWS

The two spawn points place the teams upstairs and out of the main warehouse area. Both locations have a number of large windows that provide a view of the action inside. These windows are very thick and they haven't been cleaned in years. You can see through them, but not well. Take a moment to blast through a window before you try to aim at the distracted players below. This is particularly important if you want to use the Torque Bow, as the arrows you fire will otherwise stick in the window. Any gun can shoot through the glass, but the Gnasher is by far the best tool for the job, thanks to its wide spread. The other weapons just leave individual bullet holes and don't really cause the glass to shatter.

Use the Gnasher to shoot through large chunks of the window at once to get a better shot.

SPAWN POINT AWARENESS

This is a unique map in that the two spawn points are incredibly easy to differentiate. Appearances aside, they are identical in terms of navigation and strategy. Regardless of whether you start outside in the rain or upstairs in the office, the two staircases leading down to the factory floor are the same. The stairs going up to the catwalk are in the same place, and the other weapons are evenly distributed as well. The only measurable difference between the two sides has to do with which side of the central pillar the Torque Bow is on, and that is a trivial detail.

1 NORTH SPAWN

The team spawning inside the office is on the northern side of the map. Descend either staircase to the warehouse and either go to the right to get the Boomshot, straight for the Torque Bow, or venture left for the Boltok Pistol.

2 SOUTH SPAWN

The southern spawn location is outside in the rain, in an area that is nearly identical to the northern spawn in terms of shape and cover opportunities. But it looks completely different. The team spawning here has the same tactical and navigational options as the other, thanks to the map's two halves being near mirror images of one another.

STASIS

ESSENTIAL TACTICS

Too Sexy By Far: Rush down the right-hand set of stairs at the start of the round to get to the catwalk first. Securing the Boomshot or Mulcher on the catwalk can very quickly turn the match in your team's favor. This is particularly advantageous in Execution matches. Even if the enemies on the ground manage to down you, they can't finish you off before you regain your feet. Stand up, do your little turn, and let your wrath rain down on them.

WHERE WAS HE?

It's not an easy move to pull off, but try to snag the Longshot and quickly run to the opposition's spawn point. They'll anticipate someone trying to snipe from the opposite set of windows, but few will expect a sniper to aim at them from their own spawn location!

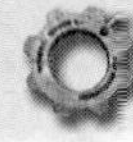

Torque Bow as Bait: Few can resist the draw of the Torque Bow/Longshot at the start of the match, especially if it appears to be uncontested. Quickly advance down the side of the map, past the stairs to the catwalk, and wait for the enemy to move onto the center platform to get the weapon. Toss a Smoke Grenade and swarm him as soon as he bends down to pick it up. Players are extremely vulnerable when they pick up a weapon. Sometimes the excitement of getting to it first can be distracting. Instruct one player to hang back and contribute some extra firepower from the upper windows.

Hang Back and Wait: It doesn't make sense to continually rush down the stairs to the warehouse when you face a team that is much stronger than yours. Instead, have everyone plant their initial Smoke Grenades on the stairs and behind tables and ledges near the spawn point. Wait for the enemy to approach. The force of the Smoke Grenade detonations knocks them off their feet, allowing you to finish off at least one or two of them. This might not win you the match, but it gets you some points and levels the playing field.

TEAM STRATEGIES

WARZONE & EXECUTION

This warehouse's central area holds the four power weapons, one on the ground level and one on a catwalk directly above. The Torque Bow and Longshot alternate on the ground level, while the Boomshot and Mulcher alternate up above. Obtaining these weapons is dangerous, as neither presents ideal cover. The lower weapon at least has a pillar. Enemies can quickly flank the position. Though assault rifle bullets can penetrate the chain-link fence surrounding this spot, Torque Bow arrows cannot. This places you at a temporary disadvantage when you go after the weapon. Focus your early effort on controlling the upper level for its improved vantage point. You can easily fire the Boomshot down on enemies. The Mulcher is somewhat harder to wield from this position due to its inherent maneuverability limitations. Firing from the hip yields easier aiming at the cost of accuracy. Consider dropping back to ground level before you open fire with the Mulcher.

When you approach the lower power weapon position, grab the Frag/Ink Grenades located just before the pipe archway as you enter the central area. Lob your Smoke Grenade to the other side of the map, then do the same with the grenade pickups. The combination of smoke, concussive blast, and either explosions or poison makes obtaining the power weapon and falling back significantly less risky.

The spawn areas can be used as sniping spots when you obtain the Longshot. Grab grenades on your way back to the spawn to protect yourself from flanking maneuvers. Use the Gnasher to shoot a wide opening in the window, and then switch to the Longshot for sniping duty. However, bear in mind that teams swap spawn sides throughout the match, so you'll likely have enemies spawn behind you if you camp.

SUBMISSION

Controlling the Boomshot/Mulcher position is crucial either when you move the Stranded or when you try to break up the enemy's scoring chances. The catwalk location has a clear view of the scoring areas. A quick dash to the stairs provides a shot at the area beneath this weapon pickup. The destructive power of the weapons atop the catwalk wreaks havoc with the other team and breaks the Stranded free almost instantly.

A similar approach works with the Longshot/Torque Bow combo. Acquire the weapon and take to the catwalk or stairwell leading up to it to increase your firing field. With two elevated teammates picking off the enemy, the other three team members can quickly collect the Stranded and move him to the capture point. Use downed enemy players as meat shields to help you stay on your feet and outlast the opposition. This is vital if they focus their efforts on the ground and ignore your elevated teammates.

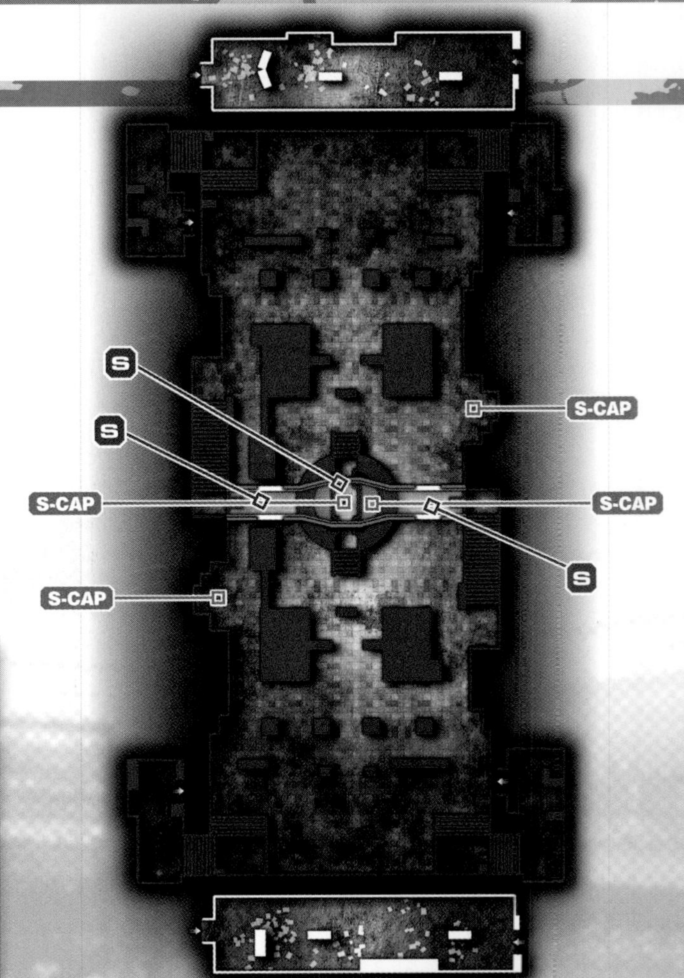

The Stranded often spawns in one of two ground-floor locations in the map's central area. It's then just a short distance to one of the pistol locations. Be aggressive at the beginning of each round to keep the opposing team from pulling a fast one on you.

WINGMAN

Work as a team to acquire the Boomshot or Mulcher if at all possible. Both weapons can deliver long-range kills and save you the risk of rushing in close for an execution. Whenever you down a player, wait a few extra seconds to see if a teammate rushes in revive him, or if someone from another team tries to steal a kill. The Boomshot destroys multiple targets in close proximity, and the Mulcher can also take out multiple targets in short order.

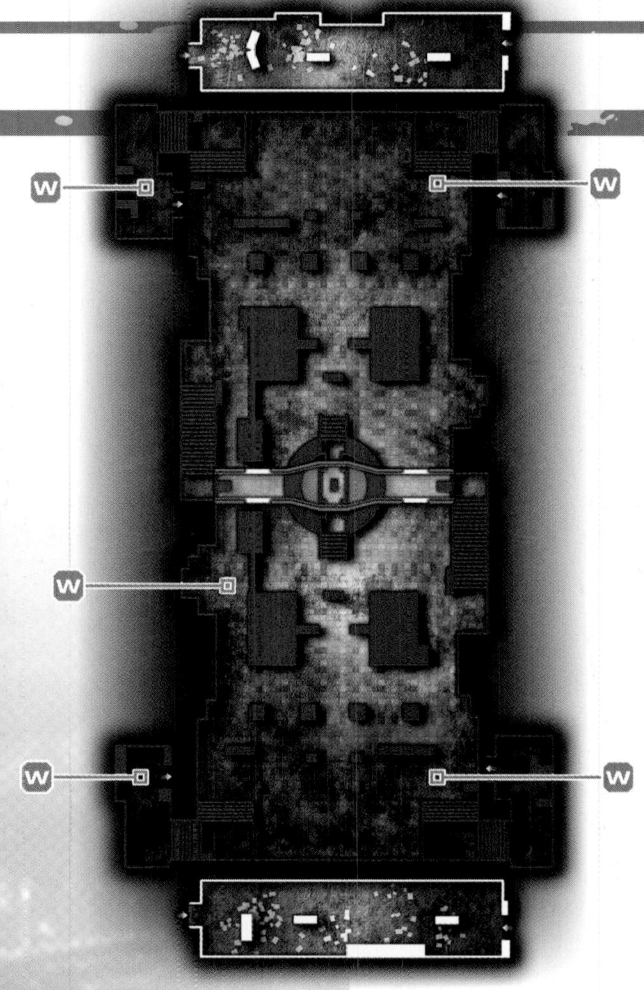

The Longshot/Torque Bow weapons require greater precisions and lack the destructive power of the Boomshot/Mulcher. But they're still worth acquiring if the risk isn't too great. Consider going after these weapons later in the round, when there's less chance of getting downed as you collect them. Before then, use the trusted Lancer or Hammerburst to down remote opponents before you move in for the execution.

As always, use the mobile cover that meat shields provide. Moving in back-to-back formation with each teammate carrying a meat shields keeps you on your feet and the enemy off theirs. Toss in upgraded pistols to really make this approach work for you.

GUARDIAN

The spawn areas are not good places to camp. Teams swap spawn sides throughout the match, so if you hang back long enough the enemy team will spawn on top of you.

With the two Team Leaders hanging back, usually with partners, seize this opportunity to snag the power weapons in the middle. Use them to assassinate the opposing leader. When the Boomshot is available, grab it as quickly as possible and rush the opponent's spawn. Conversely, one team member can make the slow journey back to your spawn point with the Mulcher to bolster your defense.

ANNEX & KING OF THE HILL

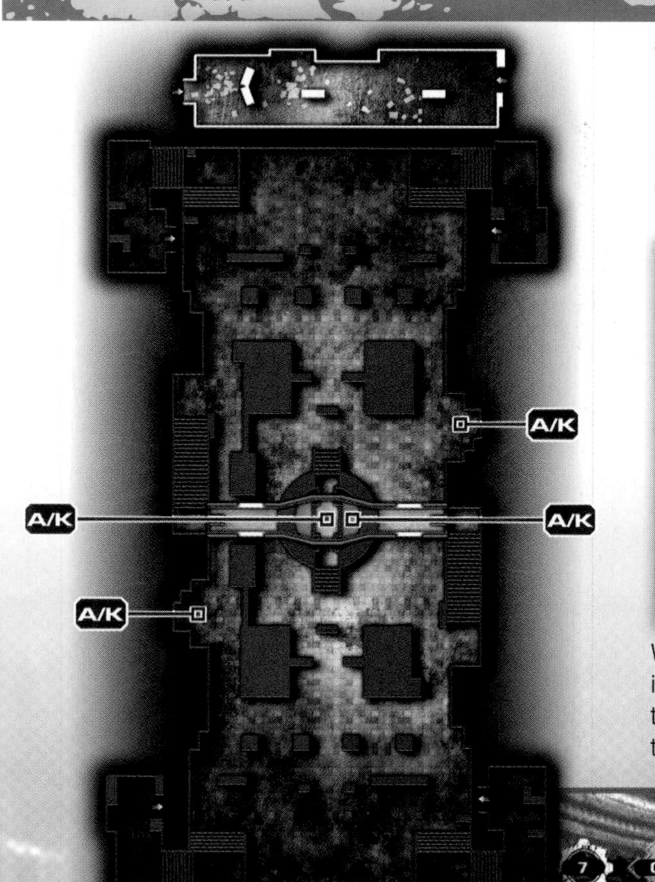

The capture points on Stasis are the two power weapon locations, as well as the two pistol drops. Each trip out of the spawn takes you close to the Frag/Ink Grenade pickup, so stop to grab the power grenades or a discarded Smoke Grenade on each pass. These are invaluable for breaking the opposition's hold on a position, so don't overlook them.

When the Boomshot/Mulcher position is the capture location, do everything in your power to capture this position first. It's a difficult spot to overtake, thanks to the location's limited access. The firepower you gain from either of these weapons goes a long way toward keeping your enemy at bay.

When you hold the Torque Bow/Longshot position, have a teammate stay in the circle for King of the Hill matches. Others should take positions on the ground, around the chain-link fence's perimeter, to harass enemy attempts to break your hold. Drop everyone back in Annex. The point contains little cover; having your team spread along the central area's perimeter allows you to reach the next capture point in minimal time.

HORDE

Stasis is a fun but challenging map on which to play Horde. The upper spawn areas and catwalk over the map's center provide two very different opportunities to mount a defensive and limit the Horde's approach. We recommend a hybrid plan that secures the upper spawn area but also puts plenty of forces on the ground. These players, near the stairs, cut down enemies before they get too close. The catwalk offers weaponry and a tremendous view of the action. The flipside is that it offers very little cover and leaves the team heavily exposed to fire from below.

Ammo: The two ammo crates are on the map's lower level, between the grenade pickups on either side of the pillar.

Variables: Use the glass in the upper balcony to your advantage by shooting out only a small segment of the window. This way, you can snipe through the glass and preserve some protection from enemy fire.

Although you should maintain at least one team member in the spawn area to prevent the Locust spawning behind you, most of the action takes place on the main floor inside the warehouse. Place two pairs of teammates near the bottom of each staircase so they can work as partners. Their goal is to cut down the Locust before they get too close. Work together to hold the upstairs at all costs so that the team always has a place to which it can fall back.

The Locust primarily spawn on the lower level, at the map's far end. Many also appear at the other elevated spawn room. They have a lengthy, rather complex trip across the warehouse before they can even think about charging the upper stronghold. Your forward teams should frequently use the grenades that spawn nearby. They should take turns claiming the weapons at the Boomshot and Torque Bow pickups. Should things go sour and the Locust overrun your defense system, simply run up the steps to the spawn area. Regroup, wait for the Locust to come up the stairs, and finish off the wave as it rounds the corner. Leave the last foe alive long enough to refortify your position, and try again in the next wave.

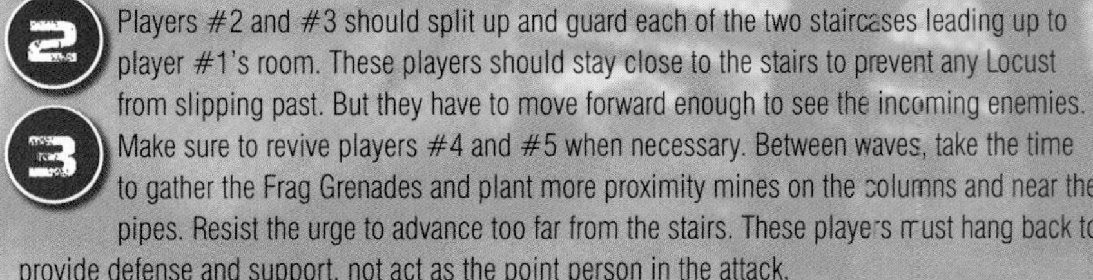

KNOW YOUR ROLE

The following tactics correspond to the numbered positions marked on the accompanying map. Follow these tips carefully for maximum survivability. These tips assume a five-person team.

1 The team's best sniper should quickly grab either the Torque Bow or Longshot from the center and retreat to the upstairs spawn area. Place some proximity mines on the upper area's desks and cabinets just in case. Then begin sniping the Locust down below. Shoot a small hole in the window with the Gnasher. Then use one of the long-range weapons to kill off the larger, slower-moving Locust. To avoid wasting ammo, leave the weaker Locust for your ground troops.

2 **3** Players #2 and #3 should split up and guard each of the two staircases leading up to player #1's room. These players should stay close to the stairs to prevent any Locust from slipping past. But they have to move forward enough to see the incoming enemies. Make sure to revive players #4 and #5 when necessary. Between waves, take the time to gather the Frag Grenades and plant more proximity mines on the columns and near the pipes. Resist the urge to advance too far from the stairs. These players must hang back to provide defense and support, not act as the point person in the attack.

4 **5** The pair filling these roles must be comfortable in the thick of the battle and possess the discipline to resist venturing too far from the rest of the team. Players #4 and #5 split between the two sides of the map, one near each of the staircases. Use the columns and stasis tanks for cover. The responsibility is simple: eliminate as many Locust as possible by any means necessary. Make the occasional foray up to the catwalk to get the Boomshot or Mulcher, but return quickly. Most of the Locust approach from the two side alleys, past the pistol pickups. Thus, it's essential to stay near players #2 and #4 and focus on the sides of the map. Player #1 can take out many of the Locust coming across the center, so resist the urge to drift toward the middle. It's best to err on the side of safety and stay close to the stairs leading up to the spawn area.

DOWNLOADABLE CONTENT

Every new copy of the Gears of War 2 game includes a code that you can use to download updated versions of five favorite maps from the first game. These bonus maps are available through Xbox Live, and they're compatible with each and every Gears of War 2 multiplayer game type. The weapons placements have changed, and each of the maps has been given a very different look. But the geography of the levels is the same as their original counterparts.

As noted in the *Multiplayer Warfare* chapter, gold versions of the Lancer (only in the Limited Edition of the game) and Hammerburst (accessed from a token given at Midnight Madness events on launch day) are also available.

CANALS

WHAT'S NEW?

 The water is now ice.

 The initial placement of the Torque Bow is now a Boomshot, but it alternates with the Torque Bow.

 The Boltok Pistol weapon drop now has a Gorgon Pistol at that location, but it alternates with the Boltok.

BASIC STRATEGY

The addition of a fifth player on each team makes the initial rush for the Boomshot beneath the central bridge a much harder fight. Take at least two teammates with you when you make the rush for the Boomshot, while the other two teammates secure your team's Longshot. Don't risk getting into a sniper duel with the enemy on the far side of the map. Instead, crouch down and make your way to the side of the bridge. Enemies are almost guaranteed to advance from pillar to pillar along the sides of the map. Plant your Smoke Grenades to serve as a warning system on one side, and focus your fire on the other. Coordinate at the start of the round which side the Boomshot squad should move to once they secure it.

SURVIVING THE HORDE

This is a really fun map for Horde, and it actually plays similarly to Ruins, given the need to dig in on a bridge. The team should take advantage of the first wave's low-level enemies to secure all of the weapons on the map, including both Longshots and the Frag Grenades. Regroup on the center bridge where the Frag Grenades spawn, and set up your defense there. Have one sniper cover the map's north side while the other snipes to the south. Instruct one player to watch the eastern staircase while another monitors the western one. The fifth player should freelance back and forth, lending fire support where necessary. This player should also use the respawning Frag Grenades to lay a series of proximity mines on the pillars and stone blocks away from the stairs leading onto the bridge. Note that teammates may need to assist in this effort, as each player can have only two mines planted at any given time. Once a player places a third mine, the first one explodes.

Should the team have to flee the scene and relocate, either of the other bridges will suffice. Just try to get back to the center bridge as soon as possible. Taking a position on either of the end bridges does not preclude Locust from spawning behind you near the team spawn. Being on the center bridge puts you furthest from the Locust spawn points and provides the most time for you to react.

WEAPON CYCLES

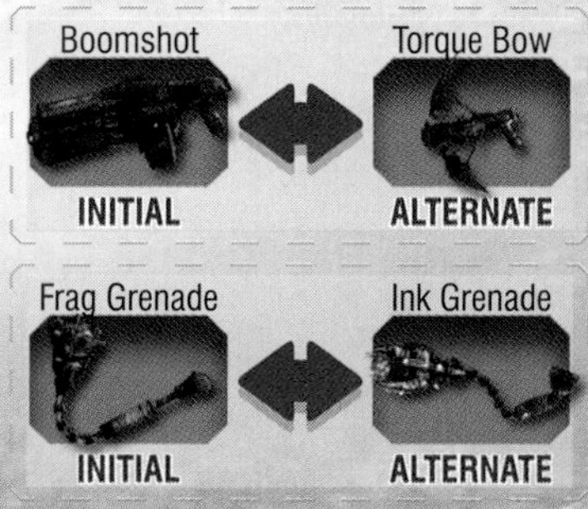

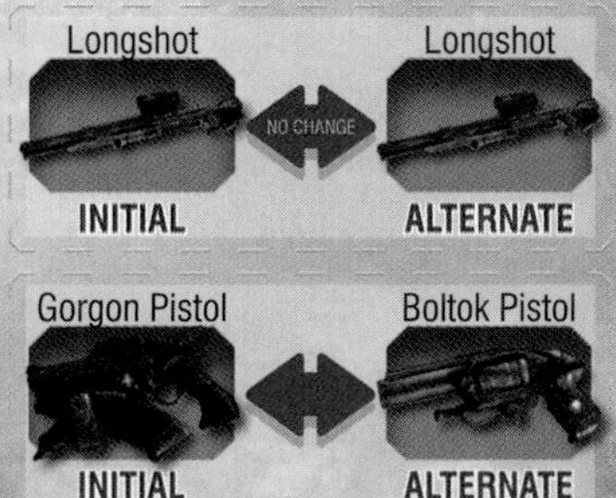

GRIDLOCK

WHAT'S NEW?

 The famed city square is now covered in grass and weeds, and everything is starting to crumble with age.

 The Hammerbursts in the corner towers are now Gorgon Pistols, and they alternate with the Boltok Pistol.

 The much sought-after Longshot is now initially a Torque Bow, but it alternates with the Longshot.

The Frag Grenades in the street have been replaced with Ink Grenades, and they alternate with the Boomshield.

BASIC STRATEGY

If there was ever a map that saw nearly every player consistently using the same tactics, it's Gridlock. Adding a fifth player to each team is not likely to change it. The initial rush for the Torque Bow/Longshot and Boomshot still takes place. But now, teams can send some support with the person trying to secure the Boomshot. What *does* stand to shake things up a bit is the inclusion of the Boomshield. The weapon pickup in the center of the street is a Boomshield on even-numbered rounds. The Boltok Pistol respawns as a Gorgon Pistol, the perfect compliment for the Boomshield! Now you're ready to pick off any remaining enemies.

SURVIVING THE HORDE

Teams will feel right at home playing Horde on Gridlock, as so many players naturally gravitate to the central tower where the Torque Bow/Longshot is located. This is an ideal place to set up a defense against the Horde, especially after other players secure the Boomshot and/or the Boltok Pistols and Gorgon Pistols from the side towers. Place as many as two players with long-range weapons along the front edge. They can crouch behind the wall to take out the Horde as they spawn in the central road straight ahead. Instruct two additional players to split up and monitor each of the staircases. The fifth player can lend support where it's needed and replace spent proximity mines at the base of the stairs.

WEAPON CYCLES

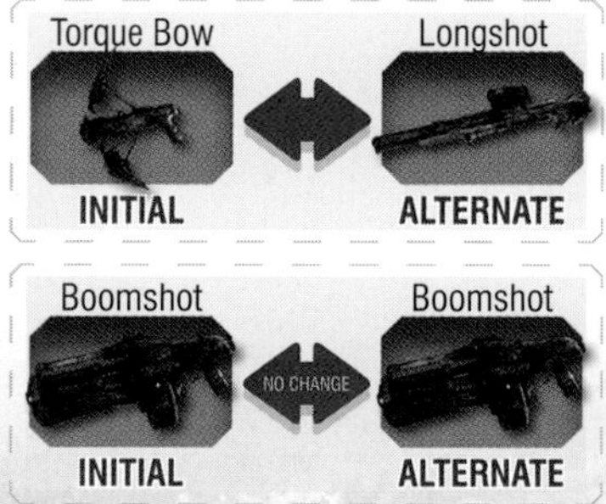

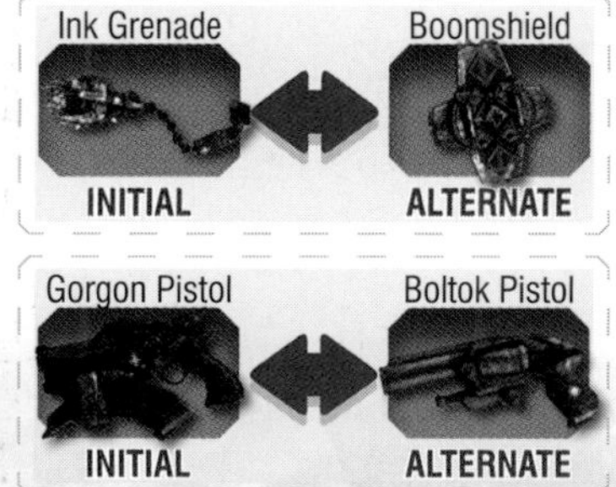

MANSION

WHAT'S NEW?

 The dark and stormy night of the previous Mansion map has been replaced with a beaming ray of sunshine.

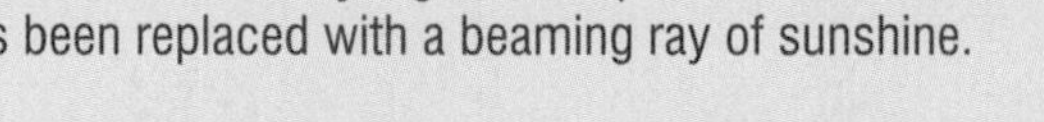

The Frag Grenade on the porch has been replaced with an Ink Grenade that alternates with a Frag Grenade.

 The Longshot on the balcony inside the house has been replaced with a Torque Bow, but it alternates with the Longshot.

 The Hammerbursts have been replaced with Gorgon Pistols that alternate with the Boltok Pistol.

BASIC STRATEGY

The changes to this map's weaponry are very subtle, particularly since the Boomshot has been left as-is. Teams typically split up to secure the long-range weapon on the balcony inside the house and the Boomshot in the gardens. Having a fifth player certainly makes this easier. Consider sending three players to the garden and two up to the balcony to get the Torque Bow/Longshot. Expect the opposition to either rush through the house's front door or enter via the upstairs hallway opposite the one you used. If you have the time, rush to their side of the house and place proximity mines inside the doorway. Opponents won't see them, and they certainly won't expect them! Hang back and finish them off as they enter.

SURVIVING THE HORDE

Gather the Boomshot and Ink Grenades outside and move into the mansion. The upstairs balcony inside is the best place to mount your defensive stand, as enemies cannot sneak up behind you. However, enemies can still utilize four narrow approaches. One person, preferably the one with the Boomshot or Torque Bow, should watch the front door and serve as a spotter. The other four should split up into pairs. Each pair has to cover an upstairs entrance from their respective side of the map. They also have to hold back any enemies that come up the stairs from the ground floor. It's not easy because the enemies seem to come from everywhere. Keeping proximity mines on the three doorways certainly helps to limit the Locust advance.

WEAPON CYCLES

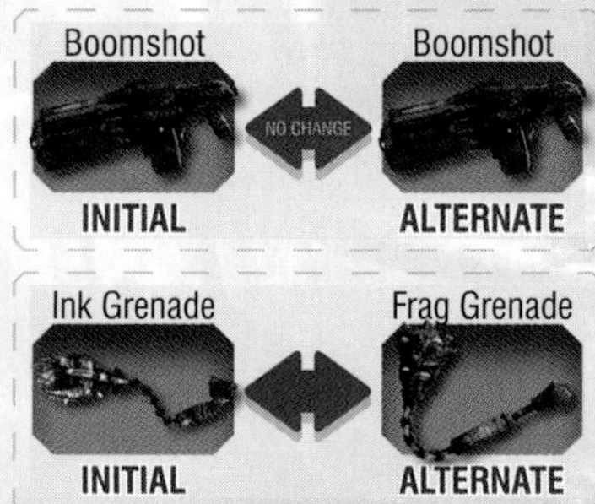

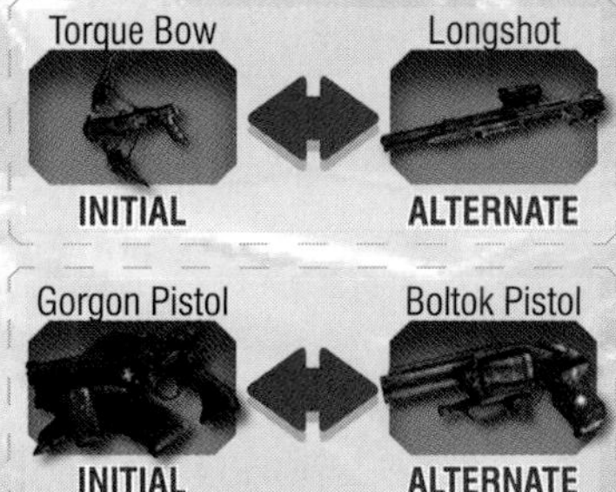

SUBWAY

WHAT'S NEW?

 The Torque Bow location now has a Mulcher, but it alternates with the Torque Bow.

 The Longshot location now has a Torque Bow, but it alternates with the Longshot.

The Boomshot has been replaced with a Scorcher.

 The Frag Grenade location now has an Ink Grenade, but it alternates with the Frag Grenade.

 You can detonate the cars scattered around the level with gunfire, and you no doubt notice plenty of falling ash from nearby fires.

BASIC STRATEGY

The boost in team size certainly helps to split the action between the inside and the outside, as teams will be more willing to divide their forces at the start of the match. The team that starts inside the subway station should immediately secure the Mulcher and Scorcher, and then relocate to the base of the stairs near their spawn point. Watch for enemies coming down from outside. Look for an opportunity to use the Mulcher on anyone in the center of the terminal. If possible, sneak through the subway car, pick up the Ink Grenade, and toss it up at the balcony above to potentially poison the enemy with the Torque Bow. The team starting on the outside should instruct players to dash to the Torque Bow position and try to snag an instant kill on anyone trying to pick up the two powerful weapons inside. The remaining action will likely take place on or around the large central staircase, so approach that area carefully.

SURVIVING THE HORDE

This is an extremely difficult map on which to play Horde, thanks to the arena's scale, the subway interior's complexity, and the multiple approaches. The best place to mount your defense is up the stairs from the interior spawn point. This allows you to get the Mulcher and some grenades and claim a position with only two approaches. Watch for Locust coming up the stairs from the inside, where the teams sometimes spawn. Also, watch for them coming around the corner from the front of the subway building. Use the cars and other pieces of cover to plant your proximity mines. Have three teammates, including the one with the Mulcher, mow down the Locust that attack from the outside. Have your other two teammates take cover at the top of the stairs, eliminating Locust that try to sneak up the stairs behind you.

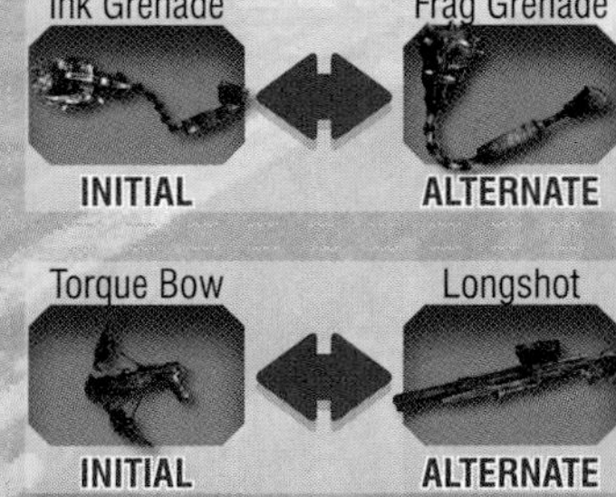

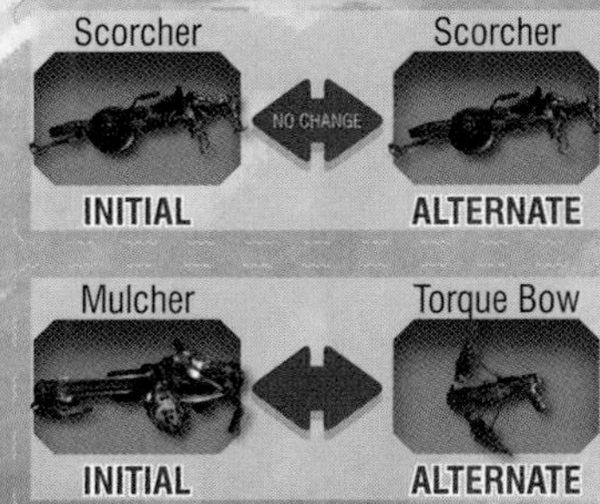

SUBWAY

TYRO STATION

WHAT'S NEW?

The Boltok Pistol is replaced with the Gorgon Pistol, but it alternates with the Boltok.

The Torque Bow is replaced with the Longshot, but it alternates with the Torque Bow.

The Frag Grenades under the tracks have been replaced with Ink Grenades, but they rotate with Frag Grenades.

BASIC STRATEGY

Tyro Station plays very much the way it did in the earlier version, only now you can count on even more carnage and mayhem during the initial clash under the tracks. Teams consistently rush at least three members down the stairs to the underground area while the other two go up top to secure the Longshot/ Torque Bow. Those willing to risk getting run over by the train can snag the Hammer of Dawn, which is seldom contested. Set up behind the containers with the Hammer of Dawn, using it on the enemies near the Longshot across the tracks. With any luck, your squad can distract them long enough for you to rain the lasers down on them. Another approach is to skip the weapon pickups on the exterior, sending extra units down the stairs between the tracks, the objective being to surprise opponents already engaged in combat with your troops down below.

SURVIVING THE HORDE

This is another very difficult map for playing Horde. The train is not in play during Horde matches, but the exterior's wide-open approaches still make it a very difficult place to mount a defense. Unfortunately, the underground area is far too compact to recommend it. Instead, we suggest you gather the weapons on the upper train platforms and claim a position near one of the team spawn points. This allows you to use the Hammer of Dawn and the long-range weapons without interference. It also limits the Locust to two approaches. Have two people watch the stairs leading up from the underground. The other three should focus on the lengthy ramp leading down from the tracks.

WEAPON CYCLES

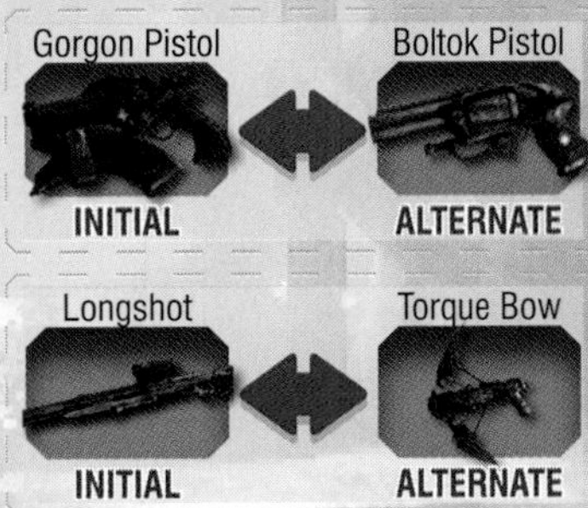

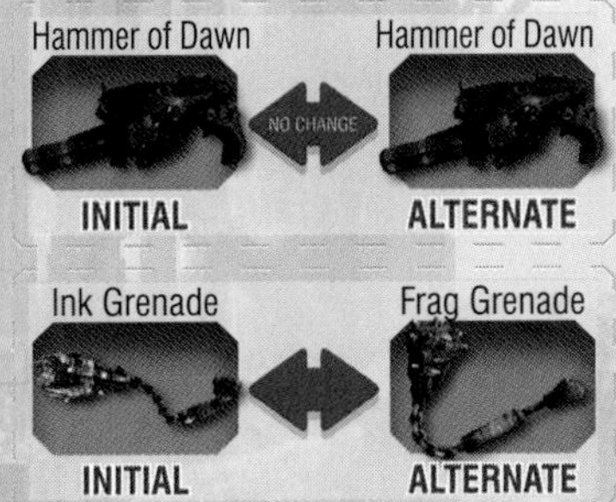

COG INTEL ARCHIVE

WAR JOURNAL

The War Journal is a new feature in *Gears of War 2*. It allows you to quickly check your advancement in all facets of the game.

You can see how far along you are toward a particular multiplayer Achievement, or see a list of mementos gathered during the campaign.

COLLECTIBLE CHECKLIST

The following list will help you quickly determine which War Journal collectibles you've located, as well as those you still need to find. If you need more assistance, just flip to the appropriate Act and Chapter in this guide's campaign walkthrough. All of the collectibles have images, more detailed location descriptions, and their exact positions are marked on the map for the corresponding Chapter.

ACT I

Chapter 1

	COLLECTIBLE	LOCATION
01	Eagle Newspaper	On the ground in the first alley as you begin training.
02	Ambulance Driver's Log	After you go down the ladder at the end of the training, turn right and walk into the small room at the end of the alley.

Chapter 2

	COLLECTIBLE	LOCATION
03	Doctor's Journal	After the fuel tank ambush, go up the left hallway and into a room on the left side.
04	Jacinto MedicalCenter File	Center of the office area, between two desks.
05	Cog Letterhead	Outside the cafeteria in the left hallway; check a left side room.
06	COG Proclamation	When you enter the hospital lobby, stay upstairs and check the ground on the right side balcony.
07	COG Tags	Just outside the hospital; check behind the pillar to your right.

Chapter 3

	COLLECTIBLE	LOCATION
08	Grindlift Spec Sheet	On the Rig, just to the left of the ladder on the wall.
09	Ammo Requisition Form	After you hop off the Rig to fight the Locust; check near the bushes to the left before you approach the cover.

Chapter 4

COLLECTIBLE	LOCATION
None	Collectible #8 can still be picked up here if you didn't grab it in Chapter 3, but collectible #9 must be grabbed at the end of Chapter 3.

Chapter 5

#	COLLECTIBLE	LOCATION
10	Jacinto Sentinel Newspaper	On the second floor of the building you enter at the start of the level.
11	Memorial Inscription	On the wall of the memorial, just after the second Ticker ambush, before you head up to the fuel station.
12	Landown Delivery Driver's Note	Inside the fuel station, at the back.
13	COG Tags	Inside the dark tunnel, in a small room on the left side, just before you pass the cars blocking the tunnel.

Chapter 6

COLLECTIBLE	LOCATION
None	

ACT 2

Chapter 1

COLLECTIBLE	LOCATION
None	

Chapter 2

#	COLLECTIBLE	LOCATION
14	Grindlift's Pilot Journal	Cut through the vines by the second rockworm, on the ground by a Grindlift.
15	Kantus Scroll	After the Troika ambush and Reaver fight atop the rock spire; check the ground at the back of the area.

Chapter 3

#	COLLECTIBLE	LOCATION
16	Locust Emblem	Just after the first battle with the Kantus; check the ground on the right when you go through the gate.

Chapter 4

#	COLLECTIBLE	LOCATION
17	Ilima City Help Wanted Ad	After the first battle, head up the slight slope to the right to find it on the ground near a Gorgon Pistol.
18	COG Tags	After Cole rejoins the squad, check in the back of the ruined building on the ground.

Chapter 5

#	COLLECTIBLE	LOCATION
19	Ilima City Journal	Just after Baird rejoins the squad, check down a rock spur on the right side of the cave.

Chapter 6

#	COLLECTIBLE	LOCATION
20	Car Gold Magazine	On the ground to your left as the level begins.
21	COG Tags	After you speak with Carmine, check on the ground near the left wall, just before you go up a sloped ramp. Look carefully, they're grimy!

ACT 3

Chapter 1

COLLECTIBLE	LOCATION
None	

Chapter 2

	COLLECTIBLE	LOCATION
22	New Hope Computer Printout	Just inside a small office to the right of the hall as you begin this chapter.
23	New Hope Interoffice Memo	After you enable the first turret, check a door on the right side of the hall, then kick open a door and check the ground in the small office.
24	New Hope Medical File	Inside a room with turrets on the roof; check inside the room behind the switch that deactivates the turrets.

Chapter 3

	COLLECTIBLE	LOCATION
25	New Hope Journal	After you exit the facility, check the building to your right.
26	Captivity Marks	Before you board the final train, face the back of the train yard and run into the small building there. Examine the wall inside to find the marks.

Chapter 4

COLLECTIBLE	LOCATION
None	

Chapter 5

	COLLECTIBLE	LOCATION
27	Stranded's Journal	Up the stairs in the center of the ruins, just after the first Gunboat appearance.

Chapter 6

COLLECTIBLE	LOCATION
None	

ACT 4

Chapter 1

	COLLECTIBLE	LOCATION
28	Locust Terminal	At the end of the chapter, examine the Locust Terminal that is not the one you examine to finish the chapter.

Chapter 2

	COLLECTIBLE	LOCATION
29	Locust Prisoner's Journal	After the second Locust Terminal, head left and check the back of the cave to find it on the ground.

Chapter 3

	COLLECTIBLE	LOCATION
30	Locust Jailer Document	At the start of the level, go down the stairs to the right. Turn right into the hall, and check on the ground at the end of the hall.
31	Human Finger Necklace	When you enter the room where the doors start to close, Roadie Run quickly through the room, through the second closing door on your right.

Chapter 4

	COLLECTIBLE	LOCATION
32	Locust Calendar	After you go up the stairs at the start of the chapter, check the back of the platform for this oddly-shaped object.
33	Locust Defensive Plans	After you extend the bridge, cross it and go left down the hall; it's on the ground by an ammo pack.

Chapter 5

#	COLLECTIBLE	LOCATION
34	Locust Invasion Map	Past the lift that comes up on the side of the palace; check an alcove to the right.
35	Trinity of Worms	After the path split, go up the stairs where the Grinder was located and check the ground by the ammo pack.

Chapter 6

#	COLLECTIBLE	LOCATION
36	Locust Tablets	On the ground between pillars at the back of the room as you begin the chapter.

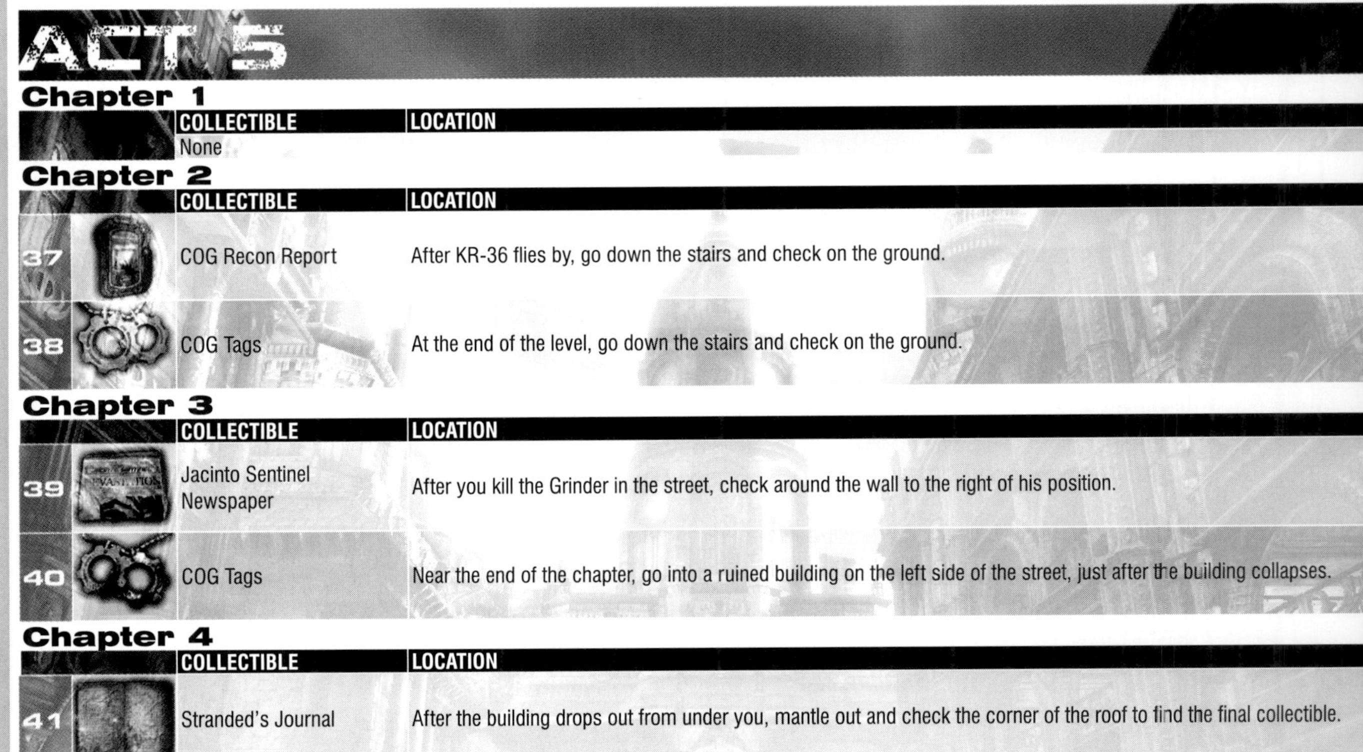

ACT 5

Chapter 1

COLLECTIBLE	LOCATION
None	

Chapter 2

#	COLLECTIBLE	LOCATION
37	COG Recon Report	After KR-36 flies by, go down the stairs and check on the ground.
38	COG Tags	At the end of the level, go down the stairs and check on the ground.

Chapter 3

#	COLLECTIBLE	LOCATION
39	Jacinto Sentinel Newspaper	After you kill the Grinder in the street, check around the wall to the right of his position.
40	COG Tags	Near the end of the chapter, go into a ruined building on the left side of the street, just after the building collapses.

Chapter 4

#	COLLECTIBLE	LOCATION
41	Stranded's Journal	After the building drops out from under you, mantle out and check the corner of the roof to find the final collectible.

Chapter 5

COLLECTIBLE	LOCATION
None	

ACHIEVEMENTS

Gears of War 2 Achievements are split between the campaign and multiplayer. Most multiplayer Achievements don't have any special trick for earning them, other than practicing and playing a lot! Many campaign achievements are based on completing certain goals in the story.

ACHIEVEMENT	GAMER POINTS	NOTES
Green as Grass	10	Train the rook (any difficulty)
It's a Trap!	10	Story Progression in Act 1 Chapter 2
Escort Service	10	Story Progression in Act 1 Chapter 4
Girl About Town	10	Story Progression in Act 1 Chapter 6
That Sinking Feeling	10	Story Progression in Act 2 Chapter 4
Freebaird!	10	Story Progression in Act 2 Chapter 5

ACHIEVEMENT	GAMER POINTS	NOTES
Heart Broken	10	Story Progression in Act 2 Chapter 6
Longitude and Attitude	10	Story Progression in Act 3 Chapter 3
Tanks for the Memories	10	Story Progression in Act 3 Chapter 4
Water Sports	10	Story Progression in Act 3 Chapter 6
There's a Time for Us	10	Story Progression in Act 4 Chapter 2
Better Wrapped in Beacon	10	Story Progression in Act 4 Chapter 3

ACHIEVEMENT	GAMER POINTS	NOTES
Have Fun Storming the Castle	10	Story Progression in Act 4 Chapter 6
Horsey	10	Story Progression in Act 5 Chapter 1
You Are The Support Son	10	Story Progression in Act 5 Chapter 2
Brumak Rodeo	10	Story Progression in Act 5 Chapter 4
Does This Look Infected to You?	10	Story Progression in Act 5 Chapter 5
Tourist of Duty	25	Complete all campaign Acts on Casual Difficulty
Guerilla Tactician	50	Complete all campaign Acts on Normal Difficulty
Artist of War	75	Complete all campaign Acts on Hardcore Difficulty
Suicide Missionary	150	Complete all campaign Acts on Insane Difficulty
Collector	5	Recover 5 Collectibles (any difficulty)
Pack Rat	15	Recover 20 Collectibles (any difficulty)
Completionist	30	Recover all 41 Collectibles (any difficulty)
One Night Stand	10	Complete 1 chapter in Co-op on any difficulty (Marcus or Dom)
Open Relationship	30	Complete 10 chapters in Co-op on any difficulty (Marcus or Dom)
Friends with Benefits	50	Complete all Acts in Co-op on any difficulty (Marcus or Dom)—Unlocks Gamerpic
Crossed Swords	10	Win 10 chainsaw duels (any mode)
Pound of Flesh	10	Use a meat shield to save your life 5 times (any mode)
Organ Grinder	10	Kill 30 enemies with a Mulcher mounted on cover (any mode)

ACHIEVEMENT	GAMER POINTS	NOTES
Shock and Awe	10	Kill 30 enemies with the Heavy Mortar (any mode)
Said the Spider to the Fly	10	Kill 10 enemies with a planted Frag Grenade (any mode)
Crowd Control	10	Melee 10 enemies down with the Boomshield equipped (any mode)
Smells Like Victory	10	Kill 30 enemies with the Scorcher flamethrower (any mode)
Once More, With Feeling	10	Perform 30 Perfect Active Reloads (any mode)
Takes a Licking	10	Melee 30 Tickers (any mode)
Variety is the Spice of Death	30	Kill an enemy with every weapon in the game (any mode)
Kick 'em When They're Down	30	Perform all 11 unique executions
Seriously 2.0	50	Kill 100,000 enemies (any mode)
Photojournalist	10	Upload a spectator photo
Standing Here, Beside Myself	10	Win 3 matches of Wingman (Public)
Beat the Meatflag	10	Capture 10 Meatflags in Submission (Public)
It's Good to be the King	10	Win 10 rounds of Guardian as the leader (Public)
You Go Ahead, I'll Be Fine	10	Win 3 matches of King of the Hill (Public)
Back to Basic	10	Successfully complete the 5 lessons of multiplayer Training Grounds
A Parting Gift	20	Kill 10 enemies with a grenade while down but not out (any mode)
Party like it's 1999	30	Play 1999 rounds of multiplayer (any mode)
Around the World, Again	30	Win a multiplayer match on each of the 10 shipped maps (any mode)
Dirty, Dirty Horde	20	Survive the first 10 waves of Horde (any difficulty, any map)
Hoard the Horde	30	Survive all 50 waves of Horde (any difficulty, any map)

GEARS VETERANS

You are to be rewarded for your service. Players who have completed specific Achievements in the original *Gears of War* immediately gain certain special perks in *Gears of War 2*. Check the following list for details.

GEAR VETERAN REWARDS

GEARS OF WAR ACHIEVEMENT	GEARS OF WAR 2 REWARD
Completed Chapter 1	Unlock Carmine in multiplayer
Found 10 COG Tags	Unlock Minh Young Kim in multiplayer
Killed Raam	Unlock Raam in multiplayer

Written by Phillip Marcus, Doug Walsh, and Jim Morey
Map Illustrations by Rich Hunsinger (www.generatorstudios.com)

DK/BradyGames, a division of Penguin Group (USA) Inc.
800 East 96th Street, 3rd Floor
Indianapolis, IN 46240

ISBN: 978-0-7440-0964-4

Printing Code: The rightmost double-digit number is the year of the book's printing; the rightmost single-digit number is the number of the book's printing. For example, 08-1 shows that the first printing of the book occurred in 2008.

11 10 09 08 4 3 2 1

Printed in the USA.

SPOILER WARNING!

The attached foldout reveals pieces of the *Gears of War 2* story! To avoid spoiling the plot, play through the game before you read this foldout!

BRADYGAMES STAFF

Publisher
David Waybright

Editor-In-Chief
H. Leigh Davis

Licensing Director
Mike Degler

Marketing Director
Debby Neubauer

International Translations
Brian Saliba

CREDITS

Title Manager
Tim Fitzpatrick

Screenshot Editor
Michael Owen

Book Designer
Doug Wilkins

Production Designer
Tracy Wehmeyer

ACKNOWLEDGMENTS

BradyGAMES most sincerely thanks everyone at Epic for their unwavering support during an incredibly busy time. On behalf of gamers everywhere, thank you for another truly superb *Gears of War* saga. To Michael V. Capps, Rod Fergusson, Cliff Bleszinski, Chris Mielke, and Chris Perna: thank you for making this guide possible, for your generous hospitality, and for your tireless work on our behalf. A thousand thanks to the entire team for contributing your time and your hints to improve this guide, including (in alphabetical order): Prince Arrington, Andrew B[illegible], Adam Bellefeuil, Jim Brown, Phil Cole, Dave Ewing, Stuart Fitzsimmons, Jerry Gilland, Steven Haines, John Liberto, Warren Marshall, John Mauney, Robert McLaughlin, Dave Nash, Matt Oelfke, Mikey Spano, David Spalinski, Ken Spencer, and Jonathan Taylor.

Phillip Marcus: The creation of the *Gears 2* guide has been a large and unusually challenging project. I must tip my hat to Tim Fitzpatrick, for organizing the crazy mess of creators responsible for bringing you this book, including myself, Doug Walsh, Rich Hunsinger, and Jim Morey. I also want to thank Chris Mielke at Epic, who had to deal with an unending stream of requests on the smallest details about *Gears 2*; his patience and forbearance are greatly appreciated.

Gears 2 is a big game, and it is filled with a lot of really cool stuff. Whether you prefer the campaign or multiplayer, I hope this guide helps you enjoy it more in some small way.

Doug Walsh: As the author of the original strategy guide for *Gears of War* and a huge fan of the game, I'm very pleased to have been a part of writing this book. I owe tremendous thanks to Tim Fitzpatrick and Leigh Davis of BradyGAMES for juggling the schedule for me so that I would have time to be a part of another *Gears* project. As is the nature of multiplayer gaming, I couldn't have done it alone. I need to thank not only my multiplayer partner, Jim Morey, but also the rest of his "Gears with Peers" crew who helped keep us sharp. Our weekly matches are something I look forward all week. Jim was invaluable in helping formulate a lot of the strategies we came up with, and the book would have suffered without his help. The book also benefitted from the cooperation of the men and women at Epic Games. Huge thanks to Chris Mielke for his excellent hospitality and asset-gathering skills and also to Bastiaan Frank for providing so much insight into the individual maps. Lastly, I'd just like to give one big congratulations to everyone at Epic for truly making a bigger, badder, and more you-know-what sequel to an already great game.

Rich Hunsinger: I would like to thank BradyGAMES, Leigh, and Tim for their help on this project, as well as the opportunity to work on it. Thanks to Chris and all of my new friends at Epic. Many thanks to Doug, Jim, and Phil for the help and company. And most of all, thanks to my beautiful wife Kate for holding down the fort while I was drowning in *Gears 2* blood and graphite. I love you, baby girl.